FAX: Digital Facsimile Technology and Applications, Second Edition

For a complete listing of the *Artech House Telecommunications Library*,
turn to the back of this book . . .

FAX: Digital Facsimile Technology and Applications, Second Edition

Dennis Bodson
Kenneth R. McConnell
Richard Schaphorst

Artech House
Boston • London

Library of Congress Cataloging-in-Publication Data

McConnell,Kenneth R.
   FAX: Digital Facsimile Technology and Applications/ Kenneth R. McConnell, Dennis Bodson, Richard Schaphorst. –2nd. ed.
      p.   cm.
   Includes bibliographical references and index.
   ISBN 0-89006-495-4
   1. Facsimile transmission.   I. Bodson, Dennis.   II. Schaphorst, Richard
III. Title.
   TK6710.M33 1992   91-30309
   621.382'35-dc20   CIP

© 1992 ARTECH HOUSE, INC.
685 CANTON STREET
NORWOOD, MA 02062

International Standard Book Number: 0-89006-495-5
Library of Congress Catalog Card Number: 91-32594

10   9   8   7   6   5

Dedication

*To our wives
Patricia, Priscilla, and Rita*

Contents

Preface

How on earth did anyone transact business in the dark ages BF (Before Fax)? Before fax, a statement that you worked in the field of facsimile brought a blank stare. Most people thought facsimile must be related in some way to box tops that could be sent in for a prize.

In the two years since the first edition of this book, fax has become ever more commonplace. "Fax it to me" is heard everywhere, and has even moved into casual social banter. Cartoons and comic strips frequently focus on fax. Fax users are surprised when they find a company without one. Instead of waiting an unknown time for mail delivery, often five to eight days, confirmed delivery is seconds per page, and the delivery cost is often less than a postage stamp. Exact copies of documents, such as orders for merchandise, shipping statements, invoices, architectural drawings, contract agreements, are valued for their accuracy.

The phenomenal growth in numbers of new fax units following the 1980 adoption of CCITT international standards for digital facsimile has continued. The numbers, as of this writing, are more than 20 million worldwide. Plain paper recording has come to medium-price fax machines, and new features are being added into the low-end models. Even small businesses are considered out of step with the times if they do not have a fax machine.

Facsimile in North America is called "fax"; in some countries it's referred to as "telefax." Fax converts a page (printed, written, or photographic) into electrical signals, rapidly sends them anywhere in the world over a telephone line, and records them as a copy. Today fax is recognized as the primary communication tool for printed or written material just as the telephone is for voice.

When the business day in New York begins, it is almost the end of the day in European cities, and in Tokyo it is already too late for business. For Los Angeles, one must wait three hours and for Honolulu, five hours. Working between New York and Tokyo, questions faxed to Tokyo at the end of the work day have the answers generated during the New York night and then waiting in the New York fax machine the next morning. Fax is ideal for worldwide communication because there is no need for anyone to be there when the fax message arrives.

All of the authors have worked in fax engineering and management for many years, one for fifty years. This book tells where it has been, where it is now, and where it might go at the start of the next fifty years.

Note that some of the material in this book covers standards work that does not have final approval and could have changes at the last minute. The actual standards involved should be checked before proceeding with work based on them. While the authors have exercised reasonable care with the accuracy of the material presented in this book, they are not responsible for consequences of errors of any kind.

Acknowledgments

Alan Pugh, vice-chair of CCITT Study Group VIII, merits particular recognition and thanks for providing the latest information and his views of CCITT activities in fax, the European fax standards, and European market changes in preparation for the European Community. Particular recognition and thanks also go to Steve Urban, chair of EIA/TIA TR-29, Facsimile Equipment and Systems, for providing information on the U.S. activities for preparation of CCITT and U.S. fax standards. Thanks go to Chuck Jacobson and Bob Krallinger, chairs of the EIA Technical Committee on Facsimile for information about activities that occurred at the time the Group 3 fax standards were being formulated. They are also recognized for many direct contributions to the Group 3 fax standards. Steve Perschau and Neil Randall assisted greatly in preparation and review of material on Group 4 fax and image coding.

The authors also wish to thank the following for their helpful information and advice: Bill von Alven, Ajay Batheja, John Bingham, Philip Bogosian, Paul Brobst, George Constantinou, Austin G. Cooley, Lester M. Davis, Joseph Decuir, Bruce DeGrasse, David Duehren, Michel Didier, Roger Free, Eugene H. Gavenman, George A. Giddings, Glenn Griffith, Ralph Grant, Herb Israel, Granger Kelley, Ken Kretchmer, Gary Lucas, Tim McCullough, Lloyd McIntyre, John F. Munch, Jr., Toby Nixon, Bob Robinson, Matthew Shuchman, Steven Rogers, Dave Shaler, John R. Shonnard, Herman R. Silbiger, George M. Stamps, Neil Starkey, Hiroshi Tanaka, Cees F. M. Tellings, Bob Trachy, Virginius N. Vaughan, Bill Webb, Don Weber, Pierre-Andre Wenger, Jim Wilcox, Yasuhiro Yamazaki, Charles Zeigler, and Dr. Mohamed Zennaki.

Chapter 1
Introduction

Although fax was first patented in 1843, fax machines did not come into widespread use until the 1970s. In 1980 when the International Telegraph and Telephone Consultative Committee (CCITT) adopted the Group 3 digital fax standard, the picture changed—fax machine manufacturers began building units to the worldwide standard, businesses found them so useful that demand drove production into high gear, and by the mid-1980s the boom was in full swing.

This book gives the latest information on fax—technical details of the fax standards and new standards in process, standards organizations, what's inside the fax machine, scanners, printers, image compression, fax machine architecture, protocols, modems, communication channels for fax, computers with fax capabilities, fax test charts. This information is intended for engineers, designers, imaging specialists, consultants, and computer programmers. Also included is information for company executives, communication planners, distributors, dealers, retailers, and users of fax—what fax does, how it works, where to use fax, who should have fax machines, fax communication services, marketing of fax, what to look for when buying, how to get the most out of a fax machine, etc.

We also cover the nearly 150 years of fax existence from its early beginnings with the telegraph, to the steps that led to the highly successful Group 3 fax of today, to what can be expected in the future. A comprehensive glossary of fax terminology is also provided that decodes the fax buzzwords in understandable language.

Some sections of this book are written in nontechnical language to assist the beginner considering the purchase of a fax machine or wanting to improve methods of using fax. Other sections are written in technical or semitechnical language for those who want to learn more about design details of Group 3 and Group 4 digital fax machines and systems.

The focus of the book is on the 20 million Group 3 fax machines (and computer equivalents) used by almost all businesses today to send copies of documents anywhere in the world at regular telephone rates and to send them at speeds almost as fast as making copies on an office copier.

The special fax machine designs required for applications such as transmission of news photos, weather maps, newspaper printing masters, and photos from satellites or fingerprints are not within the scope of this book. Although these important applications exist, the number of these specialized fax machines is small (less than 0.3%) compared to the number in office use.

1.1 WHAT FAX DOES

The following description of what goes on inside the fax machine will help the reader to understand the later chapters. Those who are familiar with fax may want to skip the next section or two.

The fax machine is somewhat like an office copier, or rather, two office copiers electrically connected by a telephone line. Compare calling on a telephone with sending a printed page to a distant point. The speaker's voice is changed by a microphone within the telephone into electrical signals sent over the telephone line to the listener's telephone where the signals are changed back to sound by its earphone. For fax, the imaging portion of the "office copier" produces tone signals representing the page being sent. These tone signals pass over the telephone line connection the same way as the voice signals do for speech. At the receiving end, these signals are changed back into an image and printed by the other half of the "office copier." Basically, fax machines are remote office copiers.

1.2 HOW FACSIMILE WORKS

The sending portion of the fax machine must read (called "scan") the page being sent and produce electrical signals that represent it. This task can be compared to that of a person who might take two to four minutes to read a page aloud. The reader starts at the top left side and the entire height of the characters in a line of type is viewed as the eye scans across the page.

For sending by fax, the reading is done electronically, also starting at the top left corner of a page. Fax may read two or more pages a minute, much faster than most people do. Fax does not recognize the printed letters but reads the small black dots that form each character. Imagine the page being sent as printed on very fine graph paper with 200 squares per inch. Fax starts reading a line of type by reading only the row of squares across the tops of the printed characters. Each square is either a black or white dot. Starting at the left end of this row, the black dots plus all of the white dots are read in sequence (1728 dots in all). The process then repeats for the next row just below. It takes 10 to 20 additional rows (scanning lines) down the page to fully read one line of text. A whole page takes 2200 scanning lines (at fine resolution).

At the fax receiver, the imaginary squares corresponding to those squares covered by black markings at the fax transmitter are filled in with black dots. After all of the scanning lines have been read and sent to the fax receiver, all of the printed black dots are in the squares that match those at the transmitter. The black dots printed on the recording page form the characters and lines of the page sent. Thus a fax transmission is converted into a fax copy. The distance between the fax machine sending the page and the fax machine printing the page can be as far as can be reached by telephone.

A light-sensitive electronic device [e.g., a charge-coupled device (CCD) silicon chip] converts the page image into electrical signals, with a strong pulse for each white dot and a weak pulse for each black dot. This electronic image signal is processed into digital format, compressed for faster transmission, and then coded by a modem to send even faster. The modem has a tone-type signal that will go through the regular dial-up telephone system in a manner similar to voice. The receiving portion of the called fax machine answers the call, decodes the received signal, and prints a copy of the original page.

The analog tone signals that Group 3 fax sends over a telephone line are generated by a very efficient, high-speed synchronous digital modem. The receiving modem continually synchronizes on the symbols of the received signal. This results in decoding and storing in the fax receiver line memory, the position of black dots for a line across the page scanned at the transmitter. Each square across the page has its own writing element coupled to the corresponding memory element so that each black dot is in the correct position. The time that each dot is printed is sometime later than the time it was scanned.

Placing the black dots in the proper squares was much more difficult before digital fax machines were developed. Analog fax machines (Group 2 and earlier) had a single scanning spot at the fax transmitter and a single recording spot at the fax receiver. Once the transmitter started sending a page, the receiver spot had to track the scanning spot by starting at exactly the same time and running at exactly the same speed. Because the fax receiver had no way of locking in for synchronism on the received fax signal, each fax machine required a very high precision clock (frequency standard).

1.3 FAX IN THE WORKPLACE

This ability to send exact copies to any other location so easily, rapidly, and at a reasonable cost has made fax equipment a necessary part of most businesses, small as well as large. Many diverse groups or individuals have found the faxing capability to be indispensable—hospitals, law offices, real estate firms, architectural designers, lobbying groups, political organizations, marinas, delicatessens. Recently some supermarkets have started to take orders by fax, a modern evolution of phoning in a grocery order.

Sending pages by Group 3 fax is far simpler than sending messages by computer, PC-fax, or telex. Fax copies may be made anywhere in the world by placing the pages to be sent into the fax machine hopper and pressing a button. The receiving fax machine is usually unattended. Some fax machines even allow a person who wants to send documents to place the pages in the hopper while the fax machine is receiving some other document. The pages feed through rapidly and are stored in fax memory for later transmission to the selected fax recipient. Meanwhile, the original pages may be returned to the file cabinet. The lowest cost fax machines may require more manual effort. The regular voice telephone network is used to connect the sending and receiving fax. All operations may be automatic including dialing, sending the pages, and disconnecting (hanging up) after all pages are received at the distant location. The facsimile machine first dials the distant fax machine listed for a single button pressed (a telephone is not used). The receiving fax machine answers the call, and then the fax machines send short messages back and forth (handshake) to select the highest speed possible before sending the pages (without any action being required by an operator at either the sending or receiving end). Fax copies can be made anywhere another fax machine is plugged into a telephone jack. No conversion of signals is needed to cross international borders.

Fax machines are not the only way of sending and receiving fax messages. Computer text (ASCII) files and image files can be sent directly from a personal computer (PC) to any Group 3 facsimile. A PC-fax board plugged into a slot in a PC allows it to send or receive from Group 3 facsimile equipment. Letters and other documents need not be printed before sending directly from the PC as fax signals. The received fax copy is then sharper than if it had been printed out and then sent from a fax machine. This is because the spots read in the scanning operation do not exactly match the edges of text or graphics, causing ragged edges in the fax copy.

Understanding the pros and cons of different setups will determine the kind of equipment to install. Whether a machine connected to its own telephone line, sharing a line, or a PC-fax board installed in the computer would be better in any given situation must be considered. Cost, of course, is another factor. The lowest priced Group 3 machines are now being quoted at only 3% of the prices of the earliest Group 3 machines in 1980.

1.4 LEGAL AND ILLEGAL FAX USES

With so many fax copies of original documents being generated in various business transactions these days, questions about the legality of these copies are being raised. Some courts have ruled in favor of their legality, thus encouraging expanded use by professionals. Some judges have decided that all papers that can be served on an attorney can now be served by fax. Ominous official levy notices from the IRS may arrive on the desks of employers, banks, and others much sooner when sent by fax rather than by mail.

There is a downside to facsimile usage. Unsavory businesses are attracted by the ease and relative security of making illegal deals by fax. No one sees or hears the other party and it is difficult to be sure the deal is with the company represented by the fax copies. Connecticut has counteracted this problem with a statute that authorizes specific government agencies to intercept fax messages from any make or model of fax machine regardless of any proprietary transmission methods. Each intercepted message identifies both the caller's and receiver's fax numbers, fax machine make and model, length of transmission time, and date. Such information could be of value in the courtroom.

Chapter 2
Standards Activities in Fax

The authors are convinced that without good international standards, all business use of fax, including Group 3, would still be struggling for acceptance in the business community—possibly less than 1% of the current number of fax machines in use would be a more likely usage number. Most of the credit for creating good international standards goes to the International Telegraph and Telephone Consultative Committee (CCITT) and its supporting organizations of technical experts. The CCITT is part of the International Telecommunication Union (ITU), a specialized agency of the United Nations, formed by a treaty between the participating countries.

The other standards groups listed below, plus others not listed, play a role in fax standards. Each has its work program, but delineation of work between the organizations is difficult. Fortunately, liaison and cooperation between the various groups have been very good, thereby reducing the overlap to a reasonable minimum. "The importance of standards for the telecommunications industry cannot be underestimated. Without standards, chaos would result" [1] (see Figure 2.1).

2.1 CCITT

The CCITT studies needs for new types of telecommunication equipment and services and then develops recommendations that act as standards for international communication. Membership is open to users, service providers, manufacturers, national standards organizations, and government agencies. The EIA/TIA TR-29 Facsimile Committee generates input from the United States.

Quoting excerpts from CCITT Blue Book Recommendation A.21:

. . . the United Nations recognizes the International Telecommunication Union as the specialized agency responsible for taking such action as may be appropriate. . . .

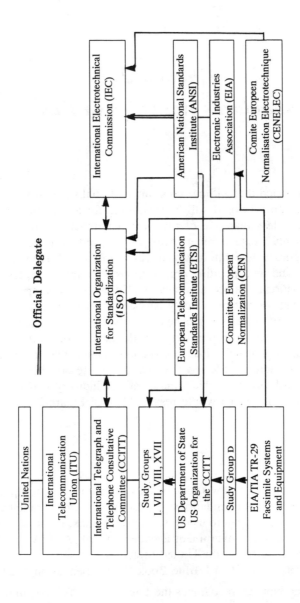

Figure 2.1 Groups working on fax standards.

The CCITT will

. . . promote the development of technical facilities and their most efficient operation with a view to improving the efficiency of telecommunication services, increasing their usefulness and making them, as far as possible, generally available to the public.

It is the responsibility of the CCITT alone to make the decisions regarding the operational, technical (including factors needed to ensure international interworking), and tariff principles of the CCITT-defined telematic services.

Standardization, if required, of hardware and software implementation of terminals, such as printing systems, paper feed, character type fonts, paper characteristics, etc., are outside the scope of CCITT.

. . . in the study of terminals for new CCITT-defined telematic services (e.g., for Teletex, Telefax, Datafax, Bureaufax, Videotex services), ISO in particular is invited to give advice to CCITT based on their work on data systems and data communications. . . .

The CCITT works in four-year plenary periods, but accelerated procedures now allow the ballots for approval of new recommendations to go out within weeks of completion by the cognizant study group instead of waiting until the end of the four-year study period. Publication of the recommendation should be shortly after approval. Formerly, CCITT published the new and revised recommendations only once every four years, taking up to a year in publication. The ninth period ended in December 1988 and the results were published in the so-called Blue Book in 1989. The following CCITT study groups (SG) are involved in the facsimile standards recommendations.

2.1.1 SG I: Operations and Quality of Service

Study Group I is responsible for the definition of (determines what types of services are needed) and operational aspects of telegraph and telematic services such as facsimile, teletex, and videotex. It is responsible for the F series recommendations. Those recommendations affecting fax are F.160-F.353, F.600, F.601, F.710-F.730 Telematic, Data Transmission, and Teleconferencing Services.

2.1.2 SG VII: Data Communication Networks

This study group is responsible for the X series of recommendations on digital data communication networks and services. Those recommendations affecting fax are:

X.1–X.32 Services and Facilities, Interfaces

X.40–X.181 Transmission, Signaling and Switching

X.200–X.219 Open Systems Interconnection (OSI)—model and notation

X.220–X.290 Open Systems Interconnection (OSI)—protocol specifications

X.400–X.420 Message Handling Systems

2.1.3 SG VIII: Terminal Equipment and Protocols for Telematic Services

The chair of Study Group VIII is W. Staudinger (Germany). Vice-chairs are B. Marti (France), A. Pugh (England), V. Sivakov (USSR), V. Macchioni (Italy), and Y. Yamazaki (Japan).

Recommendations (standards) for Groups 1, 2, 3, and 4 facsimile were completed by 1984 (see Table 2.1). Groups 1 and 2 fax have been obsolete for more than five years. Some Group 2 fax may still be in service, but its copy quality is poor, it takes much longer to send documents, and it is more expensive to operate than Group 3 fax. Groups 1 and 2 standards are given in Appendix 1.

Group 3 fax performance has advanced greatly since 1980 when the initial standard was adopted. Further enhancements are being specified as standard options and its performance is undergoing major improvements in resolution, speed, and digital interfaces. Group 3 fax accounts for about 99.7% of the fax machines in use. These standards are given in Chapter 3.

Group 4 fax standards are also undergoing change. So far, Group 4 fax has very limited application. It was designed to operate over digital networks and it will be many years before ISDN provides worldwide access to anywhere near the number of subscriber locations as the PSTN does today. Group 4 fax standards are given in Chapter 4.

2.1.4 SG VIII: Questions

The following list is intended to direct the activity of Study Group VIII, for the Xth Plenary Period (1989 through 1992). The items with asterisks affect facsimile. The other questions show that fax is involved in most of the activity of Study Group VIII.

*1. Revision of recommendations (standards)
*2. Definitions
*3. Study of telephone-type circuit-dependent problems in facsimile transmission
*4. Group 4 facsimile apparatus
*5. Choice of modulation techniques to be used with telematic services connected to the PSTN
*6. Terminal characteristics for mixed mode and processible mode
*7. Digital phototelegraphy equipment

Table 2.1
CCITT Facsimile Recommendations

Group	Recommendation	
1	T.2	Standardization of Group 1 Facsimile Apparatus for Document Transmission
2	T.3	Standardization of Group 2 Facsimile Apparatus for Document Transmission
3	T.4	Standardization of Group 3 Facsimile Apparatus for Document Transmission
2, 3	T.30	Procedures for Document Facsimile Transmission in the General Switched Telephone Network
4	T.6	Facsimile Coding Schemes and Coding Control Functions for Group 4 Facsimile Apparatus
4	T.60	Terminal Equipment for Use in the Teletex Service
4	T.61	Character Repertoire and Coded Character Sets for the International Teletex Service
4	T.62	Control Procedures for the Teletex and Group 4 Facsimile Service
4	T.62bis	Control Procedures for Teletex and Group 4 Facsimile Service Based on Recommendations X.215/X.225
4	T.70	Network-Independent Basic Transport Service for the Telematic Services
4	T.501	A Document Application Profile MM for the Interchange of Formatted Mixed Mode Documents
4	T.502	Document Application Profile PM1 for the Interchange of Processable Form Documents
4	T.503	A Document Application Profile for Interchange of Group 4 Facsimile Documents
4	T.521	Communication Application Profile BT0 for Document Bulk Transfer Based on the Session Service (according to the rules defined in Recommendation T.62bis)
4	T.522	Communication Application Profile BT1 for Document Bulk Transfer
4	T.561	Terminal Characteristics for Mixed Mode of Operation MM
4	T.562	Terminal Characteristics for Teletex Processable Mode of Operation PM.1
4	T.563	Terminal Characteristics for Group 4 Facsimile Apparatus
4	T.400	Introduction to Document Architecture, Transfer and Manipulation
	Open Document Architecture (ODA) and Interchange Format:	
4	T.411	Introduction and General Principles
4	T.412	Document Structures
4	T.414	Document Profile
4	T.415	Open Document Interchange Format (ODIF)
4	T.416	Character Content Architectures
4	T.417	Raster Graphics Content Architectures
	Document Transfer and Manipulation (DTAM) Services and Protocol:	
4	T.431	Introduction and General Principles
4	T.432	Service Definition
4	T.433	Protocol Specification
4	T.441	Document Transfer and Manipulation (DTAM)—Operational Structure

8. Coding of alphanumeric characters and associated control functions for telematic services
*9. Protocols for interactive audiovisual services
*10. Terminal characteristics and standardized options for the teletex terminals
11. Conversion
*12. Telematic interworking
13. Development of conformance procedures to ensure the international compatibility of teletex
14. Syntax aspects of interactive videotex
15. Protocol aspects of interactive videotex
*16. Common components for image communications
*17. Terminal characteristics and protocols for telematic services on ISDN
*18. Group 3 facsimile apparatus
*19. Operational structure of application profiles
*20. Imaging conversion rules interworking between different facsimile apparatus groups
*21. Development of session control procedures for telematic services
*22. Network-independent basic transport protocol for telematic application
*23. Equipment characteristics and protocols for audiographic conferencing
*24. Communication application profiles
*25. Enhancement of the application rules to physical, data link, and network layer protocols for telematic applications
*26. Document application profiles for teletex, Group 4 fax, and message handling services
*27. Document architecture, transfer, and manipulation.

2.1.5 SG XVII: Data Communication over the Telephone Network

When the modem was being selected for Group 3 fax, the group of modem technical experts was known as Special A. They became part of Study Group XVII in the 1970s. Of special interest to fax is the V.$_{fast}$ modem for even faster speeds than the V.17 modem that is now a standard option for Group 3 fax. Single-carrier modem design currently has more activity than multicarrier. A probe scheme for quickly determining the highest possible channel speed does training in both directions at once.

Now there is pressure within the CCITT to combine the modem technical experts group into Study Group VIII, the same group that has the fax technical experts. To some members, the move is logical, because telematic services probably use more modems than any other group, whereas others think the small modem group will get lost in the unrelated activities of SG VIII.

2.2 OTHER STANDARDS GROUPS AND STANDARDS

2.2.1 British Facsimile Consultative Committee (BFICC)

The BFICC does not issue national standards on facsimile; however, the BFICC has been very helpful in CCITT leadership, member participation in the CCITT study groups, and contributions to the CCITT. Many of their ideas become CCITT standards. A good example is the error-correcting mode (ECM) that was developed and tested by the BFICC. Other countries then had to be convinced that this valuable option was needed.

2.2.2 Communications Industry Association of Japan (CIAJ)

The Japanese fax equipment manufacturers belong to this association. The CIAJ has also been very helpful in CCITT leadership and member participation in the CCITT study groups. The CIAJ compatibility testing of early Group 3 fax machines from different manufacturers solved most of the initial Group 3 problems.

2.2.3 EIA/TIA TR-29 Facsimile Systems and Equipment

The Electronic Industries Association (EIA) is a trade association of equipment manufacturers in the electronic industries. The Telecommunication Industries Association (TIA) is the part of the EIA that handles telecommunication matters. TR-29, Facsimile Equipment and Systems, was formed in the early 1960s and adopted the first U.S. fax standard in 1966. At that time, much of the manufacture of fax machines was in the United States, but no standards existed. In 1975, TR-29 became the U.S. fax technical group for CCITT.

Official U.S. representation in the CCITT is through the Department of State, which heads the U.S. National Committee. Voting in the CCITT is limited to national governments (those that can assume international treaty obligations). Study Group D represents the United States for CCITT Study Group VIII. Technical papers generated by TR-29 are presented to Study Group D for an agreed-on U.S. position at meetings held at the State Department just before scheduled CCITT meetings. They become "U.S. contributions." TR-29 members may attend the international CCITT fax meetings as U.S. delegates. TR-29 also prepares and publishes EIA/TIA standards that are also submitted to ANSI for consideration as U.S. national standards on facsimile.

TR-29 has been at the forefront of generating standards for Group 3 and Group 4 fax. It has produced the U.S. national standards for these groups and published the original standards before the published CCITT standards were available. To avoid conflicting national standards, the international standards organizations are attempting to do the primary standards writing, but this was not a problem when the following EIA standards were issued before the corresponding CCITT standards:

EIA-465 Group 3 Apparatus for Transmission (CCITT T.4)

EIA-466 Procedures for Document Facsimile Transmission (CCITT T.30)

EIA-578 and EIA-592 Asynchronous Facsimile DCE Control (Do not yet have CCITT equivalents.)

2.2.4 U.S. Department of Defense (DOD)

Military Standard MIL-STD-188-161C—Interoperability and Performance Standard for Digital Facsimile Equipment covers digital facsimile equipment used for tactical and long-haul communication. The new issue, makes optional certain previously mandatory requirements for DOD-wide users. Multiple modes of operation are provided, including compatibility with fax equipment operating under the North Atlantic Treaty Organization (NATO) Standardization Agreement (STANAG) 5000 and Group 3 fax compatibility. (See Section 3.8.8 in Chapter 3.)

This standard, which is mandatory for DOD (Department of Defense) covers performance standards for both military tactical fax equipment and long-haul secure fax. Classified documents are sent with digital signal output from the fax machine. The interface is bit-by-bit asynchronous with an external clock, and mandatory data rates of 2.4, 4.8, and 9.6 kb/s. When used for processing classified information, the interface to an encryption module prevents classified traffic from passing to the outside world through an unsecured path. The fax equipment must meet classified requirements called Tempest when provided for secure operations. A Type I mode is used for black and white information including screened photographs or Type II mode for gray-scale documents with continuous tone such as photographs. Group 3 mode if available, may be used for sending documents.

Type I fax operates with specifications similar to Group 3 fax, except that it operates on digital networks or with an external modem. MH is used for compressed mode. An alternative forward error-correcting mode using BCH (Bose Chandhuri Hocquenghem) encoding may be used for operating over communication channels with higher error rates (1 in 100 or worse). A bit-interleaving buffer improves the error-correcting performance, especially for transmission bit errors clustered in bursts. Uncompressed mode is available for sending fax through channels with even higher error rates.

Type II facsimile equipment provides for the transmission and reception of gray-scale information using true shades of gray for each pixel as well as black and white information. Up to 16 shades of gray-scale information can be sent using bit plane encoding. Each pixel of the fax recording is set to one of 16 gray-scale shades,

Figure 2.2 Secure fax thermal gray-scale recording. (Courtesy of Cryptek, Inc.)

giving much higher quality recording than available with Group 3 fax (see Figure 2.2). Alternatively, 8 or 4 gray-scale shades may be used to shorten the transmission time.

Tactical fax equipment must meet severe environmental requirements. This was tested successfully in the Gulf War in 1991. Tactical digital facsimile (TDF) equipment handled transmission of classified surveillance photos and messages for headquarters operating units, tactical fighter wings, U.S. embassies, the Marine Corps, and the Strategic Air Command. When the equipment was returned to the manufacturer at the end of the war, it was loaded with sand, but still working. Nontactical secure fax equipment also had a similar role in this war for operations that did not need the full MIL-SPEC designs.

2.2.5 National Communications System (NCS)

The NCS was established on August 21, 1963, by a Presidential Memorandum (titled "Establishment of the National Communications System") to the heads of all Federal Government departments and agencies. On April 3, 1984, President Reagan signed Executive Order 12472 (E.O. 12472) entitled "National Security and Emergency Preparedness Telecommunications." This E.O. was "to provide for the consolidation of assignment and responsibility for improved execution of national security and emergency preparedness (NS/EP) telecommunications functions." This Executive Order supersedes the August 21, 1963 Presidential Memorandum.

The NCS is a confederation of Federal departments and agencies and their telecommunications assets assisting the President, the National Security Council, the Director of the Office of Science and Technology, and the Office of Management and Budget in:

- the exercise of their wartime and non-wartime emergency functions, and their planning oversight responsibilities;
- coordination of the planning for and provision of NS/EP communications for the Federal Government under all circumstances, including crisis or emergency.

The principal assets of the NCS include telecommunications networks of the following departments and agencies: Departments of Agriculture, Commerce, Defense, Energy, Health and Human Services, Interior, Justice, State, Transportation (including networks of the Federal Aviation Administration and the U.S. Coast Guard), Treasury, and Veterans Affairs; the Federal Emergency Management Agency; the National Aeronautics and Space Administration; the General Services Administration (GSA); the Central Intelligence Agency and the National Security Agency; National Telecommunications and Information Administration. There are also four participating agencies: the Nuclear Regulatory Commission, the U.S. Postal Service, the Federal Communications Commission, and the Federal Reserve System.

Executive Order 12472 assigns the responsibility for the Federal Telecommunications Standards Program (FTSP) to the Manager, NCS. The FTSP was initiated in 1972 to provide for the development and coordination of Federal telecommunications standards to ensure the interoperability and proper computer communications interfacing for the NCS. The FTSP emphasis is on the development of standards to facilitate interoperability of the NCS member networks. Specifically, the FTSP assigns the NCS the task of developing Federal standards which either contribute to the interoperability of functionally similar Federal telecommunications networks or to achieving a compatible, efficient, and economical interface between such networks and their attached computer terminals. In the area of facsimile, the NCS has published the following Federal Standards:

1028 Interoperability and Security Requirements for Use of the Data Encryption Standard with CCITT Group 3 Facsimile Equipment

1062 Group 3 Facsimile Apparatus for Document Transmission

1063 Procedures for Document Facsimile Transmission in the General Switched Telephone Network

1064 General Aspects of Group 4 Facsimile Apparatus

1065 Facsimile Coding Schemes and Coding Control Functions for Group 4 Facsimile Apparatus

In the development of the facsimile standards, NCS has conducted many studies to help determine which optional methods are best to incorporate in the CCITT recommendations. An example of such activities is NCS Technical Information Bulletin 90-2, The Enhancement of Group 4 Facsimile to Include Color Imagery.

2.2.6 International Standards Organization (ISO)

The ISO is a nongovernmental, voluntary international organization that prepares standards for industry and trade. However, most of the ISO member bodies are governmental standards organizations. ISO is a member of the CCITT. About 400 international organizations liaison with the ISO (including CCITT). ISO covers a very wide range of subject matter unrelated to fax, including agriculture. Items related to fax include paper size standards and information processing systems (includes telecommunications). Although telecommunications was planned as work for the ITU/CCITT/CCIR, technology integration is causing a blurring of technologies. For example,the ISO developed the seven-layer Open Systems Interconnection (OSI) model for computer communication. The CCITT now has its own identical, but separate, standards. Stand-alone fax machines are now special-purpose computers. Fax capability is also integrated into general-purpose PCs. The OSI model is important to fax now and will be more so in the future. The ISO/IEC/CCITT WG8 image compression color coding compression working group JPEG (Joint Photographic

Experts Group) and JBIG (Joint Bi-Level Experts Group XL2.8) work is expected to apply to color fax systems. The color fax machines now appearing in Japan have been designed to take advantage of this work.

2.2.7 American National Standards Institute (ANSI)

ANSI, the U.S. member organization for ISO, evolved from the American Standards Association (ASA). ANSI does not prepare standards, but coordinates standards preparation and assigns ANSI numbers to standards prepared according to their regulations. These then become national standards. The EIA/TIA TR-29 standards are submitted to ANSI for consideration as national standards.

2.2.8 International Electrotechnical Commission (IEC)

The IEC, established in 1906, originated from decisions reached at an 1890 electrical exposition and conference attended by Lord Kelvin and Charles Steinmetz, plus other scientists from many countries. National committees were formed in each participating country by scientists from that country. The American Institute of Electrical Engineers (AIEE, now the IEEE) played an important role in the IEC foundation and initially functioned as the U.S. national committee. The more than 40 national committees still function today and are involved in an intricate network of standards activities.

2.2.9 CEN CENET (CENELEC)

The European Community (EC) represents a very large market and many specifications have already been adopted. Many of these are ahead of their time. There is a possibility that some standards generated ahead of time will not fit the natural technological development. In this case, the standards either inhibit progress or soon become obsolete without ever gaining acceptance by industry. Group 4 fax went through this type of scenario.

2.2.10 European Telecommunications Standards Institute (ETSI)

ETSI members come from the 12 EC countries, 6 EFTA countries, and Cyprus, Malta, and Turkey. They represent manufacturers, administrators, users, and research bodies. ETSI funnels information to the CCITT study groups.

REFERENCE

[1]   Cohen, E.J., and William B. Wilkens. "The IEEE Role in Telecommunication Standards," *IEEE Communication Magazine* Volume 23, No. 1, January 1985, p. 31.

Chapter 3
Group 3 Facsimile

3.1 THE GROUP 3 STANDARD

The standards for Group 3 fax are Recommendations T.4 and T.30 in the CCITT Blue Book, including revisions completed in December 1988. Recently, accelerated procedures allow the ballots for approval of new recommendations to go out within weeks instead of waiting until the end of the four-year study period. Circulars are issued making the new recommendations official soon after the results of the ballots are positive. The V.17 14.4 kb/s modem and modified modified read (MMR) compression with error-correction mode (ECM) have been approved in this manner. Earlier revisions of T.4 and T.30 were the addition of an optional ECM for transmission and for two smaller page versions of Group 3 fax. They increased the usefulness of the Group 3 standard without compromising compatibility with Group 3 units made to the original T.4 1980 Yellow Book recommendations. The specifications for Group 3 fax are given in Table 3.1.

3.2 THE GROUP 3 SUCCESS STORY

The success of Group 3 digital facsimile resulted from international cooperation in generating an excellent standard written to fill a well-identified need. Fortunately, facsimile engineers worldwide, who had developed the Group 2 analog standard, again cooperated in formulating the CCITT Group 3 digital facsimile standard adopted in 1980. The V.29 modem was initially intended to be used on 4-wire leased telephone channels when conditioned for high-speed data transmission. Bell System literature said their regular telephone lines (PSTN) could not be used at rates higher than 4.8 kb/s. Nevertheless, digital facsimile units successfully used V.29 with half-duplex on the PSTN at 9.6 kb/s and V.29 was incorporated as an option in the Group 3 facsimile standard. One of the most important items in the Group 3 standard is its flexibility, allowing individual manufacturers to add their own innovative features without giving up basic compatibility with standard Group 3 units. Important features are listed below

Table 3.1

CCITT Group 3 Facsimile Specifications

Item	Standard	Options		Small Copy (A5 & A6)			
Scan width							
in	8.46	10	11.9	4.2	5.9	5.9	4.2
mm	215	255	303	107	151	151	107
Pels/line	1728	2048	2432	864	1216	1728	1728
H /in	203			203	203	290	406
/mm	8			8	8	11.4	16
V /in	97.8	196		196/392	138/176	138/176	196/392
/mm	3.85	7.7		7.7/15.4	5.44/10.9	5.44/10.9	7.7/15.4
Ms/line	20	0, 5, 10, 40					
Coding	Modified Huffman	Modified Read, Modified-Modified Read					
Modem							
Fax signal	V.27ter	V.29		V.17			
Bits/s	2400/4800	9600/7200		14400, 1200, 9600, 7200			
Handshake	V.21 (Ch 2)	V.27ter					
Bits/s	300	2400					
Error Correction	None	Error Correction Mode					

Acceptably High Resolution: The standard resolution of 203 lines/in. horizontally and 98 lines/in. vertically provides quite readable copy quality for most text and the fine vertical resolution of 196 lines/in. improves readability of smaller text. Both resolutions are a substantial improvement over Groups 1 and 2 fax machines, which produced readable but fuzzy copy. The standard resolution is adequate for readability of text, letterheads, business letters, and memos. For printed material from brochures, books, magazines, and newspapers, fine resolution should be used. Twice as many pixels must be sent, but the time to send is not doubled. With MR or MMR compression, the efficiency is much better for longer runs. Fortunately, almost all Group 3 fax machines have the higher resolution option.

Pages Per Minute Speed: Group 3 fax machines send two to seven text pages per minute, after 15 s for the first-page initial handshake. The second and following pages of the same fax document do not require this handshake. The sending time per page depends on the number of black markings and fineness of detail. Memory storage and 14.4 kb/s modems are used to send at the highest speeds. Group 1 units took about 6.5 min for every page if they had automatic operation. A number of these units were manually operated and required an additional 1 to 7 min per page of operator time. Pages often needed to be resent because of operator error. Verification of readable copy received and incidental voice conversation added to the inefficiency. Many Group 2 units were automatic and the time of about 3.5 min per page was twice as fast as Group 1.

User-Friendly Operation: Group 3 units are very easy to operate and in many cases are simpler to use than an office copier. Reception of fax documents requires no operator attention. The Group 3 unit is left turned on with low standby power and automatically answers an incoming ring. After automatic reception of the fax document, it hangs up, releasing the fax line until the next call is received. Received fax pages are stacked in a tray. For sending, most Group 3 units have automatic feed of multipage documents. After placing a telephone call to the receiving fax number, the SEND button is pressed when the answer tone is heard, starting the transmission program. The facsimile units handshake to determine the highest speed possible on this particular phone call, and then transmission starts. Nothing more need be done. The operator need not be concerned about the protocols, settings used, or modem compatibility. Operation is far simpler than sending messages by computer or teletex. Many people still shy away from keyboards. Pressing only one button is possible in some auto-dial fax machines, making it unnecessary to dial the receiving fax number or to wait for an answer tone. A directory of fax numbers is stored in the fax machine memory.

Universal Compatibility: Group 3 fax compatibility is similar to telephone compatibility. Although the units are made by different manufacturers and may have different features, all of them can work properly with each other. Any language used for text and any image will be copied in a manner similar to an office copier. It doesn't matter whether the receiving fax machine makes a laser copy, uses thermal recording, or some other method.

Use of Regular Telephone Lines (PSTN): The PSTN is available almost anywhere in the world and a new Group 3 fax machine can be installed with instant availability to 20 million other Group 3 fax machines merely by plugging it into a telephone jack. Group 3 fax on the PSTN has no customs delay or censorship when sending documents to foreign countries, in contrast to mail or couriers. If the PSTN is not used, a private voice or digital channel is needed. These networks have very limited coverage. Connection of fax lines is far more difficult and also more expensive.

Step-Down Modems: These modems automatically test the performance characteristics of the telephone connection and select the highest speed available. Built-in automatic equalization minimizes telephone line distortions making higher speeds available.

Automatic Electronic Handshake: Group 3 units have many different features that must be matched between the transmitter and receiver. The electronic handshake takes care of this automatically and selects the fastest transmission possible between the two units.

3.3 GROUP 3 ARCHITECTURE

To understand the architecture of a Group 3 fax machine, the system is described in basic blocks for the transmitting and receiving functions (see Figure 3.1). For more detail, Figure 3.2 is a block diagram of a typical Group 3 fax machine.

A typical fax transmitter has a CCD *scanner* that works something like a camcorder. The image of the page being sent is focused on a CCD chip that has 1728 photosensors in a single line. The CCD reads brightness of spots in a very narrow line, 0.01 in. (0.254 mm) high, across the width of the page being sent. This generates a pulse for each photosensor, 1728 pulses per line. The pulse amplitude represents image brightness at that point. After each line is completed, the image steps to the next line. (See Chapter 6 for more details.) The *A/D converter* block changes the signal from analog to digital. What were pixels become 1-bit pels. (See definitions of these terms in the Glossary.) A two-line memory stores each pel for two adjacent scanning lines. Modified Huffman (MH), modified read (MR), or modified modified read (MMR) coding then compresses the bit pattern information into a small fraction of the number of bits required before coding. This is called *source encoding* or *redundancy reduction*. (See Section 3.4 for details on Group 3 coding.)

A buffer memory stores the output of the MH/MR/MMR coder for use by the modem. The coder block generates code words containing the picture information in a compressed format that needs only 1/5th to 1/20th as many bits. In the *modem* block this compressed digital signal is further coded and converted into an analog signal that can be sent over the telephone line. When operating at 14.4 kb/s, the modem takes 6 bits at a time and represents them as one of 128 different *pulse amplitude modulation* (PAM) states for transmission as an analog signal. The telephone line has only 2400 baud (changes per second) to convey 14.4 kb/s. The modem coding thus achieves a further 6:1 compression of the signal sent. An FCC, CSA, or other PTT-approved built-in line connection unit (LCU) provides a standard miniature jack RJ-11 or other standard connector for direct connection to regular

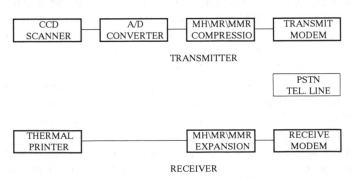

Figure 3.1 Group 3 block diagram.

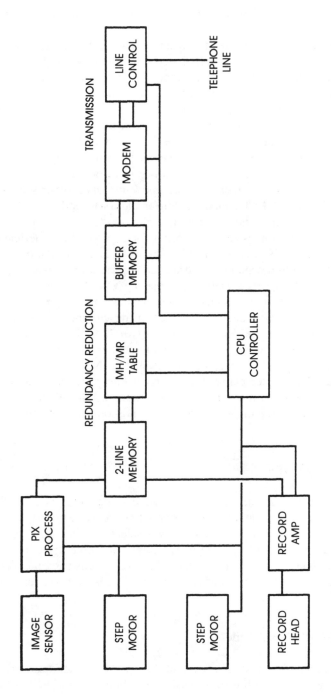

Figure 3.2 Group 3 apparatus block diagram.

telephone lines (PSTN). Another built-in jack allows use of a telephone for dialing or voice communication.

The receiver modem decodes the received analog fax signal, regenerating the digital signal sent by the fax transmitter. The MH/MR/MMR block then expands this fax data to black-white pel information for printing. The thermal printer has wires spaced at 203/in. touching the temperature-sensitive recording paper. Heat is generated in a small high-resistance spot on each wire when high current for black marking is passed through it. To mark a black spot, the wire heats from nonmarking temperature (white) to marking temperature (black) and back to white in a few milliseconds. The *thermal printer* converts the bit stream into a copy of the original page. Almost all Group 3 fax machines either send or receive at one time (half-duplex). Some circuitry and mechanical components serve either sending or receiving functions. The same LCU, modem, buffer memory, coder, and line memories are used for the receiving function in half-duplex mode.

Two slightly different sizes are normal for a page: the American letter size, 8.5 × 11 in. (216 × 279 mm) or the ISO size A4, 210 × 297 mm (8.27 × 11.69 in.). Most Group 3 fax machines are furnished for the normal page size. The same basic fax machine design is used for both paper sizes. For most Group 3 fax machines, the paper length is of secondary consequence since paper in roll form is used for recording. For laser-printing fax machines using cut sheets, the length can be a problem, because printing of one European A4 or U.S. legal paper fax may take two 11-in. pages. Fax machines that can scan the wider B4 paper [255 mm (10 in.)] and A3 paper [303 mm (11.9 in.)] are also available. Not all of these fax machines record on a matching wider paper, but the recording page size may be reduced in both directions to print on the normal 8.5-in. paper width. When a wider scan fax machine sends normal 8.5-in.-wide pages, it sends only the normal width scan of 1728 pels.

3.4 GROUP 3 CODING

When the Group 3 digital fax specifications were being developed, coding for elimination of redundant information (e.g., large white areas) in the page was needed to reduce the sending time. Huffman coding was selected as the starting point. It was a single-line run-length coding, relatively simple to implement, and royalty-free. Huffman coding had the disadvantage that 1728 code words for white runs plus 1728 more for black runs would be needed to cover all possible run lengths across the page.

3.4.1 Modified Huffman Code

CCITT Recommendation T.4 specifies that Group 3 fax machines must incorporate modified Huffman run-length coding of scanning lines. In a scanning line, the start of a white pel is likely to be followed by a long string of white pels before a black pel is reached. In typed text, the white strings, called *runs*, may continue across the whole page.

A scan line is made up of a series of variable-length code words representing horizontal run lengths of all white pels alternating with all black pels. A total of 1728 pels represents a scanning line 215 mm long. The longer run lengths in multiples of 64 pels are in the "terminating code" table, and short run lengths of 0 to 63 are in the "make-up code" table. Only 92 binary codes are then needed for any run length of 0 to 1728 pels by sending the make-up code followed by the terminating code. Black runs have a different probability of occurrence, and have 92 different codes.

For highest coding efficiency, the shortest code words were assigned to the run lengths occurring most often. This is an application of the coding principle first used in 1844 by Morse to send telegraph signals efficiently. To determine which code words should be shortest, the CCITT scanned eight test pages with different languages and content (see Chapter 10). The code words were determined after each black and white run length and the number of times it occurred were tabulated.

Instead of sending a white line across the page as 1728 bits, MH sends a 9-bit code word (the pattern of 1s and 0s) listed in the MH two-table set of code words

Table 3.2
Modified Huffman Terminating Codes

White run length	Code word	Black run length	Code word
0	00110101	0	0000110111
1	000111	1	010
2	0111	2	11
3	1000	3	10
4	1011	4	011
5	1100	5	0011
6	1110	6	0010
7	1111	7	00011
8	10011	8	000101
9	10100	9	000100
10	00111	10	0000100
11	01000	11	0000101
12	001000	12	0000111
13	000011	13	00000100
14	110100	14	00000111
15	110101	15	000011000
16	101010	16	0000010111
17	101011	17	0000011000
18	0100111	18	0000001000
19	0001100	19	00001100111

Table 3.2 (cont'd)

White run length	Code word	Black run length	Code word
20	0001000	20	00001101000
21	0010111	21	00001101100
22	0000011	22	00000110111
23	0000100	23	00000101000
24	0101000	24	00000010111
25	0101011	25	00000011000
26	0010011	26	000011001010
27	0100100	27	000011001011
28	0011000	28	000011001100
29	00000010	29	000011001101
30	00000011	30	000001101000
31	00011010	31	000001101001
32	00011011	32	000001101010
33	00010010	33	000001101011
34	00010011	34	000011010010
35	00010100	35	000011010011
36	00010101	36	000011010100
37	00010110	37	000011010101
38	00010111	38	000011010110
39	00101000	39	000011010111
40	00101001	40	000001101100
41	00101010	41	000001101101
42	00101011	42	000011011010
43	00101100	43	000011011011
44	00101101	44	000001010100
45	00000100	45	000001010101
46	00000101	46	000001010110
47	00001010	47	000001010111
48	00001011	48	000001100100
49	01010010	49	000001100101
50	01010011	50	000001010010
51	01010100	51	000001010011
52	01010101	52	000000100100
53	00100100	53	000000110111
54	00100101	54	000000111000
55	01011000	55	000000100111
56	01011001	56	000000101000
57	01011010	57	000001011000
58	01011011	58	000001011001
59	01001010	59	000000101011
60	01001011	60	000000101100
61	00110010	61	000001011010
62	00110011	62	000001100110
63	00110100	63	000001100111

(see Tables 3.2 and 3.3). Because a 9-bit pattern (010011011) is listed for a 1728-pel white run length in Figure 3.5, this line is compressed by a ratio of 1728/9 = 192. On the other hand, the code word for a 2-pel white run is 4 bits, taking twice as long to send as uncompressed. This is because both of the 2-bit code words available were used for the more frequent black runs of 2 pels and 3 pels.

As an example of how MH coding works, Figure 3.3 shows part of a scanning line with black and white runs and the code words for these runs. The five run lengths shown are 2W + 5B + 5W + 2B + 585W = 599 pels. The code word bit lengths are 4 + 4 + 4 + 2 + (3 + 7) = 29. The white run of 585 pels takes only 15 bits for a compression of 39.

Table 3.3
Modified Huffman make-up codes

White run lengths	Code word	Black run lengths	Code word
64	11011	64	0000001111
128	10010	128	000011001000
192	010111	192	000011001001
256	0110111	256	000001011011
320	00110110	320	000000110011
384	00110111	384	000000110100
448	01100100	448	000000110101
512	01100101	512	0000001101100
576	01101000	576	0000001101101
640	01100111	640	0000001001010
704	011001100	704	0000001001011
768	011001101	768	0000001001100
832	011010010	832	0000001001101
896	011010011	896	0000001110010
960	011010100	960	0000001110011
1024	011010101	1024	0000001110100
1088	011010110	1088	0000001110101
1152	011010111	1152	0000001110110
1216	011011000	1216	0000001110111
1280	011011001	1280	0000001010010
1344	011011010	1344	0000001010011
1408	011011011	1408	0000001010100
1472	010011000	1472	0000001010101
1536	010011001	1536	0000001011010
1600	010011010	1600	0000001011011
1664	011000	1664	0000001100100
1728	010011011	1728	0000001100101
EOL	000000000001	EOL	000000000001

Table 3.3 (cont'd)

Run length (black and white)	Make-up codes
1792	00000001000
1856	00000001100
1920	00000001101
1984	000000010010
2048	000000010011
2112	000000010100
2176	000000010101
2240	000000010110
2304	000000010111
2368	000000011100
2432	000000011101
2496	000000011110
2560	000000011111

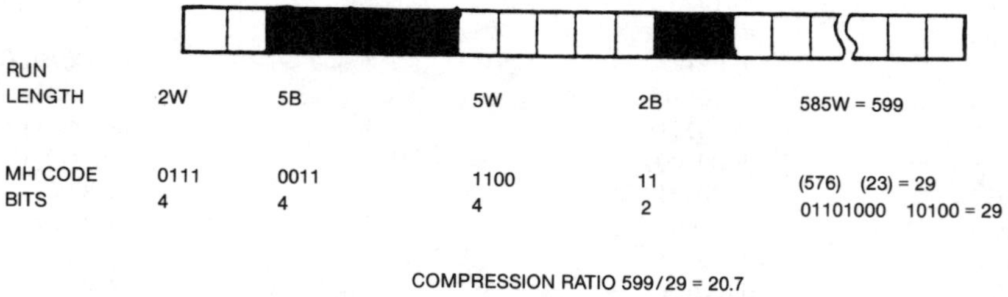

RUN LENGTH	2W	5B	5W	2B	585W = 599
MH CODE	0111	0011	1100	11	(576) (23) = 29
BITS	4	4	4	2	01101000 10100 = 29

COMPRESSION RATIO 599/29 = 20.7

Figure 3.3 Modified Huffman coding example.

At the end of each coded scanning line, an end-of-line (EOL) code (000000000001) is sent. EOL is used as a line synchronization code, allowing the fax receiver to get back in step if a transmission error has occurred in the previous line. To detect an error in the received signal, the receiving fax machine checks the total number of bits in the decoded runs for one line. If the total number is not 1728, one or more errors have occurred. For wider copy fax machines, the total number of bits per line is 2048 or 2432.

If the next bit after EOL is 1, one-dimensional (MH) coding will be used for the following line. If the next bit after EOL is 0, two-dimensional (MR) coding will be used for the following line.

3.4.2 Modified Read and Modified Modified Read Codes

Most information on a page being sent has a high degree of vertical correlation. Modified read (MR) is a relative adressing code, which uses this vertical correlation to achieve a higher compression than modified Huffman coding. The CCITT facsimile recommendations do not refer to the names *modified read* and *modified modified read,* but these names are universally recognized and will be used in this book.

Actual sending time depends on the modem speed, how fast the fax receiver can accept the incoming fax signal, and the number of coded bits per line. The number of coded bits is determined by the amount of black and white information and the coding scheme used. MR coding requires fewer bits than MH coding, and MMR coding requires fewer bits than MR coding.

With two adjacent scanning lines on a page, black pel runs of the second line often start directly under a black pel run in the first line. MR/MMR vertical mode coding uses only 1 bit to indicate this condition. In those areas of the page where there is little vertical correlation, either pass mode or horizontal mode may be used. For coding the differences between the two lines, line memory in the fax machines stores each pel of two scanning or printing lines. The first scanning line in memory is called the *reference line*. It has already been coded, but the location of each black pel of this line is still in memory as a reference for the next scanned line called the *coding line* (see Figure 3.4).

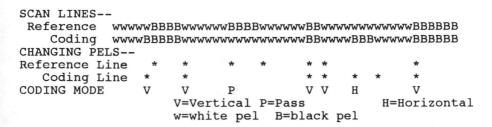

Figure 3.4 Modified read coding modes.

Look at the reference line (RL) and coding line (CL) from left to right along the pair of lines until a pel on either line changes its color (from white to black or from black to white). This is called a *changing pel* (CP). If a pair of CPs on adjacent lines match or are within 3 pels, vertical mode coding is selected (see Figure 3.5).

If the CP pairs are not within ±3 pels, the coding switches to one of two other modes. The pass mode code (0001) is used to skip past two CPs on the RL if the CL continues with the same color to beneath the second RL CP or farther. Vertical coding is again used for the next pair of CPs if they are within the ±3-pel vertical range.

Coded Pel	Left	....		Right	....	
Position	-3	-2	-1	0	+1	+2	+3
Code	0000010	000010	010	1	001	000011	0000011

Figure 3.5 Vertical coding of modified read.

If the next two CPs are only on the CL, the horizontal mode code (001) is used, followed by MH coding of the next two runs. The vertical mode is used again when possible.

When the received fax signal is distorted by a noise pulse (lightning, switching transient, or other cause), errors are made in the pattern of black and white dots in the received copy. To prevent this incorrect pattern from propagating down the page, a MH coded line is sent periodically. At normal resolution this is done every second line (K = 2), and at fine resolution, every fourth line (K = 4). This is referred to as the *K factor*. MMR uses no modified Huffman coded lines (K = ∞) (see Figure 3.6).

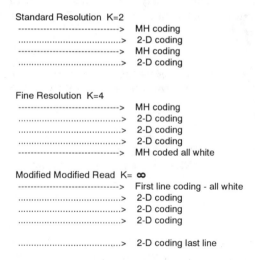

Figure 3.6 K factor for Group 3 fax.

The fastest rate that scanning lines can be sent to a receiving fax machine is determined by the *minimum scan line time* (MSLT), the time taken by the receiving fax machine to print a scan line. The original standard MSLT is 20 ms, but it can range from 0 to 40 ms/line depending on the fax equipment design. The fax transmitter obtains this information from the receiver during handshake and never sends faster, but may send slower. More bits may be required to send part of a page with any of the compression schemes above than by using no compression. If this is the case, the uncompressed mode can be automatically selected for the fax lines involved. The MMR code, described in CCITT Recommendation T.6 for Group 4 fax, was recently added for optional use with Group 3 fax in conjunction with the ECM. The basic coding scheme for MMR is, in principle, the same as MR coding, but the K factor is equal to infinity, the MSLT is zero, and the EOL code is not used. An error-free signal is needed for it to work.

The modem speed is set during the handshake. If a coded line at the transmitter is ready before the fax receiver is ready, the sending must be delayed by adding fill bits, a string of 0s, which are thrown away at the receiver. Fill bits are not needed if the fax receiver has full-page memory (0 ms/line). At 20 ms/line with fine resolution, an 11-in. page would take 44 s (plus the handshake) no matter how fast the modem rate. For this reason, faxes using V.29 and V.17 modems should have multiple-page memory for receiving.

3.5 DIGITAL SYNCHRONIZATION

Before the digital techniques for fax were developed, fax information was sent in real time as an analog signal. The idea of processing the signal by clocking, quantizing, and storing the digital information then seemed like science fiction. Scanning and recording systems were mechanical and it was difficult to mark a straight line down a received page without noticeable jitter (a sawtooth effect in the recording). A single photosensor was common in the scanner and a single writing point in the recorder. Systems that used two or four scanning or recording spots complicated the design by requiring exact alignment between these spots in addition to the real-time drive problems. Mechanically keeping the scanning and recording spots in exact step with the clock was not possible. There was also a drift between the clocks at the transmitter and receiver units. Manual adjustment of the frequency kept the skew within acceptable limits. Digital modems were not available for sending the signals and for furnishing a locked-in sampling clock at the receiver. Practical techniques had not been developed for digital storage of the pixel information of one or two scanning lines.

Digital techniques greatly improved fax machine performance when mechanical movement of a spot was no longer needed for scanning or printing. When the fax receiver modem clock became synchronized with the fax transmitter clock, precise frequency standards were no longer needed. Mechanical movement of the scanning spot was replaced by a stationary CCD chip with reading across the scanning line in exact step with the clock at the fax transmitter. Even the laser printer recording spot that is swept across the page by a rotating mirror is locked into the clock. In the thermal printer, a combination of stationary wires replaced rapidly moving mechanical spots. Each recorded spot now became written in the exact desired spot on the page.

Synchronous operation of the modem used for Group 3 fax signals requires sending signals continuously even if no data are available to send. Because the receiving modem synchronizes on the received signal, it remains locked into the sending modem even during the very short idle periods that may occur. With Group 3 digital fax, there is no moving spot that needs to be accurately timed. Each square across the page has its own writing wire. The received-fax-signal information for which wires should print dots for the next line is decoded and stored before being printed. The printing time is slightly delayed from the time when the line is scanned. The receive modem clock locks into the received data symbol stream rate even if the received carrier frequency is shifted a few hertz by the telephone circuit. When the fax video data are decoded and clocked out for the printer, it is in perfect registration on the recording paper.

3.6 FAX MODEMS

At the fax transmitter, a fax modem (from *mo*dulation/*dem*odulation device) accepts digital picture information, codes it into a complex format, modulates it to form an analog signal, and delivers it to the telephone line. At the fax receiver, the modem decodes the analog signal and converts it back to a duplicate of the digital picture signal fed to the modem at the transmitter. CCITT Recommendation T.4 specifies modulation and demodulation schemes, with the necessary portions of the CCITT modem built into the Group 3 fax machines. A full modem requires an EIA-232 interface, but there is none between the Group 3 fax digital signal and its internal modems. (For this type of interface, see Section 3.11, Asynchronous Facsimile DCE Control Standards).

The mandatory modem requirements for Group 3 fax are CCITT Recommendation $V.27_{ter}$ for sending fax message data at 4.8 and 2.4 kb/s, and V.21, channel 2 (return channel), for 300 b/s handshake signaling used primarily before and after each page. Due to its slow speed, the 300 b/s rate does not require telephone line equalization. The receiving modem for the fax signal, however, has an automatic equalizer to compensate for the telephone line problems of amplitude distortion and envelope-delay distortion. This improves the accuracy of the delivered digital fax signal, resulting in a greatly reduced error rate (see Table 3.4).

Optional modems are V.29 for sending the fax message faster at 9.6 and 7.2 kb/s and V.17 for sending the fax message even faster at 14.4 and 12.0 kb/s and with improved performance over V.29.[1] When operating in V.29 mode at 9.6 kb/

---

[1]Formerly, only a few machines had 14.4 kb/s modems, in the NSF mode. Initially, there was much skepticism that typical phone lines could support such high bit rates, but it was soon shown that a high percentage of fax message can be sent at that speed.

Table 3.4
Group 3 Modems

Bits per Second	Baud Rate	Bits per Sample	Type	Carrier Frequency	Bandwidth in Hertz
14400	2400	6	V.17	1800	550–3050
12000	2400	5	V.17	1800	550–3050
9600	2400	4	V.29	1700	450–2950
7200	2400	3	V.29	1700	450–2950
4800	1600	3	V.27$_{ter}$	1800	950–2650
2400	1200	2	V.27$_{ter}$	1800	1150–2450

s, the digital fax data stream is scrambled, divided into 4-bit segments, and sent at 2400 symbols per second. The modem output signal state changes 2400 times per second (baud rate of 2400) and has 16 different analog signal states, representing every possible arrangement of the 0s or 1s of the 4-bit segments at its input. Each of the 16 states represents a different combination of amplitude and phase (see Figure 3.7).

Phase-jitter and noise cause the received signal state to move about from its assigned amplitude-phase position. When these distortions are severe, the signal state may be in the wrong amplitude-phase position when sampled and be mistaken for an adjacent signal state, causing bit errors. One sample error may have up to 6 bit errors.

Group 3 fax modems automatically test the transmission characteristics of the telephone connection. Before sending data, the modem sends a training signal of fixed format that is known to the receiver. The highest rate available in both fax machines is tried first. If this speed would give too many errors, the next lower speed is tried by the transmitter. If this fails, the modem rate again steps down to the next lower speed. For fax machines that have V.29 modems the rates tried are 9.6, then 7.2, switching to V.27$_{ter}$ for 4.8 and 2.4 kb/s. Fax machines with a top rate of 4.8 kb/s will start the handshake at that speed. This system assures transmission at the highest rate consistent with the quality of the phone line connection. When V.29 operates at 7.2 kb/s, it samples 3-bit segments of digital fax signal. This gives eight analog signal states on the telephone line for the same 2400-baud rate with the same telephone line bandwidth as for 9.6 kb/s. At 7.2 kb/s, the modem receiver circuitry makes a signal state decision on only 8 states instead of 16, and a larger phase/amplitude error is tolerated, lowering the error rate on some telephone channels.

A new higher speed modem specifically for fax use on the PSTN was recently approved by CCITT Study Group XVII as V.17. It is a half-duplex 14.4 kb/s trellis coded modem (TCM) with fall-back speeds of 12, 9.6, and 7.2 kb/s, also using TCM. TCM is a very powerful forward error-correcting algorithm that provides a

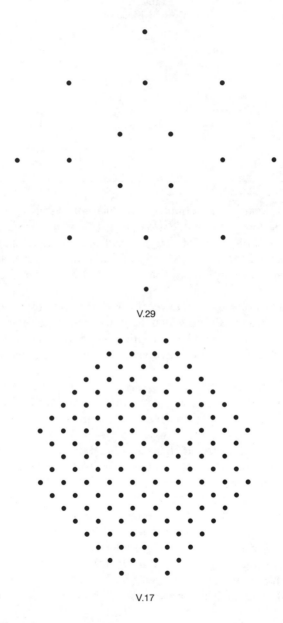

V.29

V.17

Figure 3.7 V.29 and V.17 modem constellations.

signal-to-noise ratio improvement of 3 to 4 dB. Fax transmissions that operate successfully at 9.6 kb/s with the existing 9.6 kb/s V.29 modem can operate 50% faster (14.4 kb/s) with the new V.17 modem. TCM also allows fax machines to operate at 9.6 kb/s on lines that would previously fall back to 4.8 kb/s, and at 7.2 kb/s on lines that would previously fall back to 2.4 kb/s. When operating in V.17 mode at 14.4 kb/s, the modem samples the scrambled digital fax data stream in groups of 6 data bits plus one redundant bit. The extra bit is for forward error correction using trellis coding. The output analog signal has a modulation rate of 2400 symbols per second, the same as the V.29 modem. The bandwidth for both V.29 and V.17 is the same, but the carrier frequency of V.17 is 100 Hz higher than V.29 (with a bandwidth of 600 to 3000 Hz). The analog signal output to the PSTN has a 128-point signal structure (see Figure 3.7).

A reduction in handshake time results from use of a short train of 143 ms at all times except for the initial training when a 1.4-s training signal is used. The V.29 modem uses a long training signal each time it is used in handshaking before starting to send new information. The new fax machines that use V.17 still have V.29, V.27$_{ter}$, and V.21, channel 2, to maintain compatibility with the existing Group 3 fax machines.

At least one modem manufacturer now offers a single-device V.33 modem that includes V.17, V.29, V.27$_{ter}$, and V.21, channel 2. These existing earlier modems are easily incorporated with V.17 into a single modem design. The increased cost of a faster fax machine can be quickly recaptured through reduced phone bills. Also, because V.17 is so similar to V.33, it is relatively easy to add these additional features to V.33 modems. This should result in the addition of fax capability to many products that utilize the V.33 modem.

Performance of some voice channels has been reduced in order to squeeze in more channels. ADPCM channels now use 32 or 40 kb/s rather than 64 kb/s as originally set up for voice in the T-1 PCM telephone plant. The V.17 can be sent through one ADPCM link at 9.6 kb/s, and two ADPCM links at 7.2 kb/s. A major advantage of the V.17 modem is that its TCM signal will pass through the 32 kb/s digitized voice channels that will not pass V.29 signals.

Since international circuits now carry a heavy load of fax traffic (especially at night), equipment that detects a fax call has been added. The V.29 or V.27$_{ter}$ fax signal is then demodulated before reaching the international portion and sent on a 32 or 40 kb/s channel taking 9.6 kb/s or less, saving bandwidth. At the other end of the channel, the fax signal is restored to normal for the analog PSTN channels. V.17 will be included soon.

Extensive fax transmission tests (1824 calls) checking performance of V.17 and other Group 3 fax modems on international fax calls were performed in early 1991. Both cable and satellite circuits, digital as well as analog, were used in 11 countries on four continents. The Group 3 fax ECM and the newly adopted (for Group 3) MMR compression method were used. The following is from a report on these tests [1]:

CONCLUSIONS It is concluded that both V.17 and V.29 modems are fully accommodated by the digital circuit technologies (40 kb/s and 32 kb/s enhanced ADPCM, Fiber Digital Satellite and DCMS) implemented in today's international circuits. A 28% improvement in total call duration and an improvement in call completion percentage from 87% to 94% are realized when V.17 is used, versus V.29 over digital circuits. The study also shows that both V.17 and V.29 modems perform at reduced efficiency over analog international circuits (cable or FM satellite) containing TASI or companders. The V.17 modem, however, still maintains a significant performance advantage over V.29 when transmitting over these analog circuits. . . . A major portion of the circuits in service today are digital and the proportion of analog circuits is expected to reach a level of insignificance by the mid-1990s. . . . These tests show the current state-of-the-art digital network and facsimile technologies have greatly improved the quality of facsimile transmissions.

3.7 PROTOCOL

Protocol is a set of rules that governs communication—in international diplomacy, in physical communication such as mail, or in electronic communication such as telephone, data, or facsimile. To illustrate, envision the U.S. Postal Service protocol for sending a letter. After preparing the letter, the pages to be sent must be put in an envelope of a size that is within certain limits. The address has a line for the recipient's name, another line for the street address, and a line for the city, state, and zip code. Further requirements are proper postage and depositing the letter in proscribed locations. The postal system checks that the mailing protocol has been followed, sorts for the proper destination area, transports the letter, and then delivers it. The steps within the postal system need not be understood by the sender, but it must be understood by those within the system and the proper protocol must be followed for the letter to be delivered. A mismatch in the postal system protocol can result in no delivery.

In a similar manner, Group 3 facsimile protocol is the set of rules that governs communication between a fax transmitter and receiver. The document to be sent, with certain size limits, is placed in the hopper of a fax machine. Pressing a button will call the fax number of the receiving fax machine and start the electronic protocol often called *handshaking*. The two fax machines have an electronic chat back and forth to make sure the connection is good enough and that the transmitter selects only those options that the receiver can handle properly. Rarely is there a mismatch, but if one were to occur, the call would be terminated without sending any of the message. Again, the sender need not know the details of the electronic portion of the facsimile protocol, but the protocol must be rigidly adhered to for proper delivery of the facsimile message. The format used for selecting options and for formatting the fax data signal sent from the transmitter must meet an exacting set of rules.

3.7.1 Signaling for Calling Party Sends

CCITT Recommendation T.30 (Blue Book), specifies the procedures for document facsimile transmission using the PSTN. Making a facsimile call and sending a document is divided into five time phases as shown below:

Phase A—Call Setup: The calling fax dials the telephone number of the other fax machine. The ring signal and the CNG calling tone are received at the called fax machine. The CNG tone beeps indicate the call is from a fax machine instead of a voice call. The called fax machine answers the ring signal by going off-hook, and wakes up the rest of the fax machine. The fax machine can be designed to have the ac power off until the ring signal arrives. Some faxes answer an incoming call immediately, so the ring may not be heard. After a 1-s delay, the called fax sends its called station identification (CSI), a 3-s 2100-Hz tone, back to the calling fax machine.

Phase B—Premessage Procedure: The called fax machine sends its digital identification signal (DIS) at 300 b/s identifying its capabilities, including optional features. Upon hearing this distinctive signal, the caller presses the SEND button to connect the fax machine to the telephone line. An automatic calling fax machine does this unattended. The calling fax automatically sends a digital command signal (DCS), locking the called unit into the capabilities selected. The calling fax sends a high-speed training signal for the data modem. The called fax sends a confirmation to receive (CFR) signal to confirm that the receiving modem is trained (adjusted for low-error operation) and that the fax machine is ready to receive.

Phase C—Message Transmission: The calling fax sends a training signal and then picture signals for the entire page being sent.

Phase D—Postmessage Procedure: The calling fax sends a return to control (RTC) command, switching the fax modem back to 300 b/s, then an end of procedure (EOP) signal. The called fax sends message confirmation (MCF) indicating the page was received successfully.

Phase E—Call Release: The calling fax sends a disconnect (DCN) signal and both fax machines disconnect from the telephone line.

After answering the ring, the called fax machine waits 1 s, sends a 3-s 2100-Hz CED tone followed by 75-ms silence, and then a short burst of 300 b/s DIS code that tells the calling fax machine what standard and optional features are available.

If the call is made manually, the caller presses the SEND button when the CED tone starts to connect the calling fax machine to the telephone line. The calling fax machine then decodes the next burst of DIS it receives, identifying the capabilities of the called fax machine (see Figures 3.8 and 3.9). DIS and other handshake signals are repeated at 3 s intervals if no response is detected.

If the call in Figure 3.8 is made from an automatic dialer, the calling unit starts sending a CNG tone after dialing. CNG is a 0.5-s 1100-Hz beep, sent every 3 s.

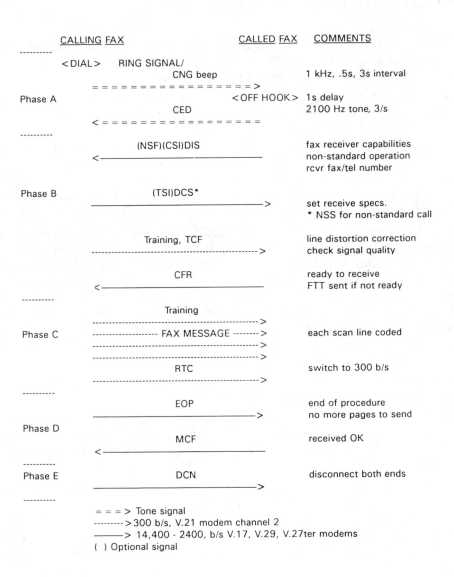

Figure 3.8 Group 3 fax sends one page.

1. Some Group 3 fax machines use EOM incorrectly. If EOM is sent instead of MPS, the next page starts from Phase B, not C. More time is then needed to retrain. If EOM is sent instead of EOP, the fax machine will remain on line for 35 seconds and indicate an error.

Figure 3.9 Group 3 fax sends two pages.

Newer fax machines also send CNG on manual calls. If the call is answered as a voice call, the CNG tone indicates that a machine instead of a person is calling. CNG is used by some fax/voice automatic switching units to connect an incoming call to the fax machine instead of to a telephone. See Table 3.5 for handshake abbreviations.

Optional features, such as subscriber identification, polling, and NSF private options, have been added.

Table 3.5
Group 3 Handshake Abbreviations

Abbre-viation	Function	Signal Format
CED	Called station identification	2100 Hz
CFR	Confirmation to receive	X010 0001 [1850 or 1650 Hz for 3 s]
CRP	Command repeat	X101 1000
CIG	Calling subscriber identification	1000 0010
CNG	Calling tone	1100 Hz on 0.5, off 3 s
CSI	Called subscriber identification	0000 0010
CTC	Continue to correct	X100 1000
CTR	Response to continue to correct	X010 0011
DCN	Disconnect	X101 1111
DCS	Digital command signal	X100 0001
DIS	Digital identification signal	0000 0001
DTC	Digital transmit command	1000 0001
EOL	End-of-line	000000000001 (11 zeros)
EOM	End of message	X111 0001 [1100 Hz]
EOP	End of procedure	X111 0100
EOR	End of retransmission	X111 0011
ERR	Response to end of retransmission	X011 1000
FCD	Facsimile coded data	0110 0000
FCF	Facsimile control field	-
FIF	Facsimile information field	-
FTT	Failure to train	X010 0010
GC	Group command	G1 1300 Hz for 1.5–10.0 s
		G2 2100 Hz for 1.5–10.0 s
GI	Group identification	G1/G2 1650/1850 Hz on 0.5, off 3 s
HDLC	High level data link control	-
LCS	Line conditioning signals	1100 Hz
MCF	Message confirmation	X011 0001 [1650 or 1850 Hz]
MPS	Multipage signal	X111 0010
NSC	Nonstandard facilities command	1000 0100
NSF	Nonstandard facilities	0000 0100
NSS	Nonstandard setup	X100 0100

Table 3.5 (cont'd)

Abbreviation	Function	Signal Format
PIN	Procedure interrupt negative	X011 0100
PIP	Procedure interrupt positive	X011 0101
PIS	Procedure interrupt signal	462 Hz for 3 s
PPS	Partial page signal	X111 1101
PPR	Partial page request	X011 1101
PRI-EOM	Procedure interrupt-EOM	X111 1001
PRI-EOP	Procedure interrupt-EOP	X111 1100
PRI-MPS	Procedure interrupt-MPS	X111 1010
RCP	Return to control for partial page	0110 0001
RNR	Receive not ready	X011 0111
RR	Receive ready	X111 0110
RTN	Retrain negative	X011 0010
RTP	Retrain positive	X011 0011
RTC	Return to Control	six EOLs
TCF	Training check	Zeros for 1.5 s
TSI	Transmitting subscriber identification	X100 0010
[. . .]	Alternative tonal signalling for Group 1 or 2	

3.7.2 Nonstandard Facilities Call

Valuable nonstandard proprietary features are permitted within the protocol for Group 3 fax machines. (See Section 3.8.7 for more information.) These features are invoked during handshake in a manner that will not interfere with the basic Group 3 service.

Nonstandard facilities (NSF) and called subscriber identification (CSI) are added ahead of DIS. NSF means the fax receiver has the ability to use proprietary features not covered by the Series T recommendations. After receiving NSF, the calling fax machine returns nonstandard setup (NSS) to lock in the called fax machine to the nonstandard operation specified. Some manufacturers had a private error-correction system, or 14.4 kb/s modem speed before these features were added as standardized options. Group 3 fax machines with NSS capabilities must also have standard capabilities to operate with other standard fax machines.

CSI sends a coded signal with the telephone number of the called fax machine. Some fax machines will display this number for the fax operator to check that they are sending to the correct unit, and the fax machine records the number in its electronic log. The sending fax machine uses transmit subscriber identification (TSI) to send its telephone number to the fax receiver.

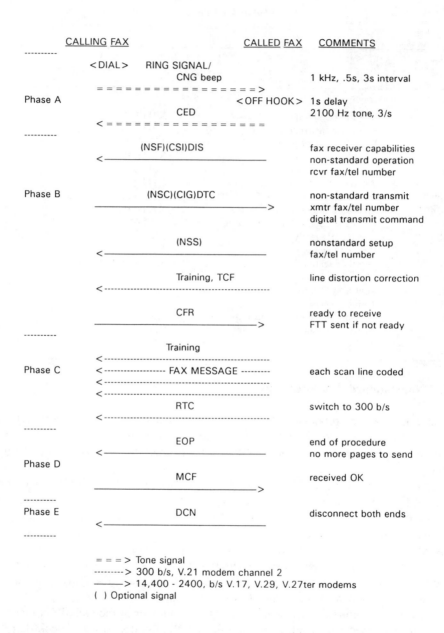

Figure 3.10 Polling called fax.

3.7.3 Polling Called Party

Polling allows a central fax machine to be programmed to call the sending fax machines sequentially and command each one to send documents from memory or its automatic document feeder. Polling is often used for an orderly sending of once-a-day information from many fax machines to a single fax machine at a central point.

Without polling it would be very difficult to prevent line-busy conditions at the central point. Many Group 3 fax machines have delayed calling programs with an automatic dialer that will allow polling at night when there are no operators around (see Figure 3.10).

After the central calling fax machine receives the called fax DIS response, it sends a nonstandard command (NSC) and the other fax machine takes over the session until it has sent all of the pages destined for the calling fax machine. Calling subscriber identification (CIG) is sent instead of TSI, with the telephone number coded in the same format. The subscriber identification codes may be checked by the transmitter to be sure the documents are being sent to the right caller.

3.7.4 Handshake Signal Formats

At the start of the initial handshake, the receiver uses its 300 b/s V.21 modem to send back information to the transmitter. Because this modem does not need a training signal to operate with a low error rate, the handshaking procedure is simplified. *High-level data link control* (HDLC) frames are used for the binary coded handshaking. An optional handshake at 2.4 kb/s is possible, but is seldom used. The following sequence is sent:

1. Preamble signal of flag fields (0111 1110) for 1 s precedes DIS, making sure the telephone line echo suppressors are operating in the right direction. Frame synchronization is also derived from this signal.
2. The first byte, the HDLC address field, identifies specific stations in a multipoint network. For calls on the PSTN, the code 1111 1111 is always used.
3. The HDLC control field is 1100 1000 for the last frame sent prior to an expected response from the distant station or 1100 0000 for other frames. The frame error-checking sequence is a two-byte signal calculated from the content of the data being sent. The receiving unit calculates the same digital number when there are no errors in the handshake signal data.

3.7.5 DIS/DTC Signal

DIS is a 300 b/s handshake signal sent by the called fax machine when it answers a call. It notifies the calling fax machine of its capabilities in standard, optional, and nonstandard specifications. The same codes are used for DIS from the fax receiver and the command DTC from the fax transmitter. The following options and possibly more are available:

- Modem types available
- Number of pels (dots) per scan line
- Number of pels per recording line
- Number of scanning lines per inch (or millimeter) in the paper feed direction
- Coding scheme for compression of the information to be sent
- Maximum page length
- Minimum time needed to record a scanned line at the fax receiver
- ECM or not
- Nonstandard mode or not
- Smaller page size (A5 and A6) Group 3 fax machines
- V.17 14.4 kb/s modem.

CSI, CIG, and TSI are each one byte, followed by one byte for a " + " and one byte for each digit of the international telephone number of the fax machine. The telephone number should be programmed into the fax machine after it is installed on the telephone line, and reprogrammed if moved to another telephone number. On receipt of this number, the other fax machine may display it, record it in its log, print it on received copy, or use it to screen calls. Another method sometimes used for subscriber identification is to send the desired information as a fax signal added to the page sent.

Upon decoding DIS, the calling fax machine automatically sends a burst of DCS signal, selecting the compatible features in the fax receiver to be used for this call. Appended to DCS is the training signal for the receiving modem, and a 1.5-s TCF signal (all 0s) to check whether the modem is receiving error-free bits. If these signals are received correctly, a CFR signal is sent from the fax receiver, indicating it is properly set and waiting for the fax signals. The calling station then again sends a training signal followed by the fax signals. At the end of the fax signals for one page, an RTC command is sent to switch back to the 300 b/s modem, followed by EOP. The fax receiver sends MCF to indicate the page has been received correctly. The fax transmitter notes a success in its log and sends DCN. Both fax machines then disconnect from the telephone line.

"It is acknowledged that existing equipments may not conform in all aspects to this recommendation. Other methods may be possible as long as they do not interfere with recommended operation" [2]. One example of this is the CED tone. Some fax machines have 1100 Hz for the first portion of the signal and 2100 Hz for the second part.

Table 3.6 lists the bit assignments including new features beyond the 40-bit Blue Book version handled by T.30 protocol. Older Group 3 fax machines do not have the extra features, but are compatible for the original options. The tentative assignments made for bits 41–49 may be changed so to add the higher resolution capabilities expected to be approved in October 1991. (See Appendix 2.)

Table 3.6
DIS and DTC Bit Settings

Bit Number	DIS and DTC	DCS
1	Transmitter-T.2 operation	
2	Receiver-T.2 operation	Receiver-T.2 operation
3	T.2 IOC = 176	T.2 IOC = 176
4	Transmitter-T.3 operation	
5	Receiver-T.3 operation	Receiver-T.3 operation
6	Reserved for future T.3 operation features	
7	Reserved for future T.3 operation features	
8	Reserved for future T.3 operation features	
9	Transmitter-T.4 operation	
10	Receiver-T.4 operation	Receiver-T.4 operation
11, 12, 13, 14	Data signaling rate	Data signaling rate
0, 0, 0, 0	$V.27_{ter}$ fall back mode	2400 bit/s/$V.27_{ter}$
0, 1, 0, 0	$V.27_{ter}$	4800 bits/s/$V.27_{ter}$
1, 0, 0, 0	V.29	9600 bits/s/V.29
1, 1, 0, 0	$V.27_{ter}$ and V.29	7200 bits/s/V.29
0, 0, 1, 0	not used	14400 bits/s/V.33
0, 1, 1, 0	reserved	12000 bit/s/V.33
1, 0, 1, 0	not used	reserved
1, 1, 1, 0	$V.27_{ter}$, V. 29 and V.33	reserved
0, 0, 0, 1	not used	14400 bit/s/V.17
0, 1, 0, 1	reserved	12000 bit/s/V.17
1, 0, 0, 1	not used	9600 bit/s/V.17
1, 1, 0, 1	$V.27_{ter}$, V.29, V.33 and V.17	7200 bit/s/V.17
0, 0, 1, 1	not used	reserved
0, 1, 1, 1	reserved	reserved
1, 0, 1, 1	not used	reserved
1, 1, 1, 1	reserved	reserved
15	Resolution = 8 × 7.7 1/mm (Note 13) and/or 200 × 200 pels/in (Note 15)	Resolution − 8 × 7.7 1/mm (Note 13) or 200 × 200 pels/in
16	Two-dimensional coding capability	Two-dimensional coding
17, 18	Recording width capabilities	Recording width
(0,0)	1728 pels for 215 mm	1728 pels for 215 mm
(0,1)	1728 pels for 215 mm and 2048 pels for 255 mm and 2432 pels for 303 mm	2432 pels for 303 mm
(1,0)	1728 pels for 215 mm and 2048 pels for 255 mm	2048 pels for 255 mm
(1,1)	Invalid (see Note 7)	Invalid
19, 20	Maximum recording length capability	Maximum recording length
(0,0)	A4 (297 mm)	A4 (297 mm)

Table 3.6 (cont'd)

Bit Number	DIS and DTC	DCS
(0,1)	Unlimited	Unlimited
(1,0)	A4 (297 mm) and B4 (364 mm)	B4 (364 mm)
(1,1)	Invalid	Invalid
21, 22, 23	Receiver time for printing a line	Minimum scan line time
(0,0,0)	20 ms at 3.85 or 7.7 l/mm	20 ms
(0,0,1)	40 ms at 3.85 or 7.7 l/mm	40 ms
(0,1,0)	10 ms at 3.85 or 7.7 l/mm	10 ms
(1,0,0)	5 ms at 3.85 or 7.7 l/mm	5 ms
(0,1,1)	10 ms at 3.85 l/mm: 5 ms at 7.7 l/mm	
(1,1,0)	20 ms at 3.85 l/mm: 10 ms at 3.85 l/mm	
(1,0,1)	40 ms at 3.85 l/mm: 20 ms at 7.7 l/mm	
(1,1,1)	0 ms	0 ms
24	Extend Field	Extend Field
25	2400 bit/s handshaking	2400 bit/s handshaking
26	Uncompressed mode	Uncompressed mode
27	Error correction mode	Error correction mode
28	Set to "0"	Frame size 0 = 256 octets
		1 = 64 octets
29	Error limiting mode	Error limiting mode
30	Reserved for G4 capability on PSTN	Reserved for G4 capability on PSTN
31	T.6 coding capability	T.6 coding enabled
32	Extend field	Extend field
33	Validity of bits 17, 18	Recording width
(0)	Bits 17, 18 are valid	Recording width indicated by bits 17, 18
(1)	Bits 17, 18 are invalid	Recording width indicated by this field bit
	Recording width capabilities	Middle 1216 elements of 1728 pels
34	1216 pels for 151 mm	
35	864 pels for 107 mm	Middle 864 elements of 1728 pels
36	1728 pels for 151 mm	Invalid
37	1728 pels for 107 mm	Invalid
38	Reserved for future	
39	Reserved for future	
40	Extend field	Extend field
41	Resolution = 8 × 15.4 l/mm (note 13)	Resolution = 8 × 15.4 l/mm (note 14)
42	300 × 300 pels/in	300 × 300 pels/in
43	Resolution = 16 × 15.4 l/mm (note 14) and/or 400 × 400 pels/in (note 16)	Resolution = 16 × 15.4 l/mm (note 14) and/or 400 × 400 pels/in
44	Inch-based resolution preferred (note 17)	0 = mm based resolution (note 17)
		1 = inch-based resolution
45	Metric-based resolution preferred (note 17)	Don't care

Table 3.6 (cont'd)

Bit Number	DIS and DTC	DCS
46	MSLT for resolutions above 8 pels/mm 0 = same tie as lower resolution (note 18) 1 = 1/2 time as lower resolution	Don't care
47	Selective polling	Set to "0"
48	Extend field	Extend field
49	Subaddressing capability	Set to "0"
50	Password capability	Set to "0"
51	Capable to emit data file	Not used
52	Reserved Facsimile Service Info (FSI)	Reserved Facsimile Service Info (FSI)
53	Binary File Transfer (BFT)	Binary File Transfer (BFT)
54	Document Transfer Mode (DTM)	Document Transfer Mode (DTM)
55	Editfact Transfer (EDT, per ISO 9735)	Electronic Data Transfer (EDT)
56	Extend field	Extend field
57	Basic Transfer Mode (BTM)	Basic Transfer Mode (BTM)
58	Reserved for future negotiation mechanism for data file transmission	Reserved for future negotiation mechanism for data file transmission
59	Capable to emit character file	Not used
60	Character mode	Character mode
61	Reserved for control document	Reserved for control document
62	Mixed Mode (Annex E, T.4)	Mixed Mode (Annex E, T.4)
63	Reserved for future negotiation mechanism for character file transmission	Reserved for future negotiation mechanism for character file transmission
64	Extend field	Extend field
65	Processable Mode 26 (T.505)	Processable Mode 26 (T.505)
66	Digital network capability	Digital network capability
67,68		
(0)	Half-duplex operation only	Half-duplex operation
(1)	Full and half-duplex operation	Full-duplex operation

Note on bit 28:

For ECM, set to "0."

For BFT, either "0" or "1" can be used to specify maximium frame size.

Notes to Table

1. T.2 fax units must have an index of cooperation (IOC) of 264.
2. T.3 fax units must have an index of cooperation (IOC) of 264.
3. T.4 fax units must have 297 mm recording paper length capabilities

4.

DIS or DTC frame capabilities	B/s, equipment operable at
$V.27_{ter}$	4800 or 2400
V.29	9600 or 7200
V.33	14400 or 12000
V.17	14400, 12000, 9600 or 7200

5. Recording width tolerances are + or −1%.

Table 3.6 (cont'd)

Bit Number	DIS and DTC	DCS

6. The standard DIS, DTC, and DCS field is 24 bits long. "Extend field" bit set to 1, adds 8 bits (32, 40, 48).

7. If DIS bits 17, 18 are received as (1,1), interpret as (0,1).

8. Bit 28 of DCS is valid only when bit 27 is set to 1 for error correction mode.

9. When bit 33 is set to 1 in DCS, the meaning of bit 15 is modified to mean vertical resolution is higher than 7.71/mm.

10. When the recording width is A4 only, the field consisting of bits 33–40 need not be present.

11. The optional T.4 error correction mode of operation requires 0 ms of the minimum scan line time capability. Bits 21–23 indicate the minimum scan line time, regardless of availability of the error correction mode. In the case of error correction mode, the sender sends DCS signal with bits 21–23 set to 1.1.1 indicating 0 ms capability. In the case of normal G3 transmission, the sender sends DCS signal with bits 21–23 set to the appropriateness according to the capabilities of the two machines.

12. T.6 coding capability specified by bit 31 is valid only when bit 27 (error correction mode) is set as a 1".

13. Recording width capabilities: 1728 pels for 215 mm, 2048 pels for 255 mm, 2432 pels for 303 mm.

14. Recording width capabilities: 3456 pels for 215 mm, 4096 pels for 255 mm, 4864 pels for 303 mm.

15. Bit 15, when set to 1, is interpreted by bits 44 and 45 as follows:

Bit 44	Bit 45	Interpretation
0	0	Invalid
1	0	200 × 200 pels/in
0	1	8 × 7.7 l/mm
1	1	200 × 200 pels/in and 8 × 7.7 l/mm

Bit 15 set to 1, without bits 41 through 46 being sent, indicates 8 × 7.7 l/mm

16. Bit 43, when set to 1 is interpreted by bits 44 and 45 as follows:

0	0	Invalid
1	0	400 × 400 pels/in
0	1	16 × 15.4 l/mm
1	1	400 × 400 pels/in and 16 × 15.4 l/mm

17. Bits 44 and 45 are used only in conjunction with bits 15 and 43. Bit 45 in DCS, when used, shall correctly indicate the resolution of the transmitted document, which means that bit 45 in DCS may not always match the selection of bits 44 and 45 in DIS/DTC. If a receiver indicates in DIS that it prefers to receive metric-based information (or vice versa), communication shall still take place. Such as selection will cause a small amount of aspect ratio distortion and possibly some reduction of reproducible area. Bits 44 and 45 do not require the apparatus to indicate on which bases the document was sent or received.

18. Also set bit 46 to 0 when MSLT is 5 ms for 7.7 l/mm or 200 pels/in. Bit 46 is set to 1 for fax machines whose printing mechanisms achieve standard vertical resolution by printing two consecutive, identical higher resolution lines. In this case, the minimum transmission time of the total coded scan line for the standard resolution is double the minimum transmission time of the total coded scan line for higher resolution. The minimum transmission time for the optional resolutions of 15.4 l/mm and 400 pels/in can be 1/4 that for the standard resolution.

19. The Binary File Transfer protocol is described in Recommendation T.434.

20. During file transfer only the transmitter initiates the maximum frame size of 64 or 256 octets.

21. When bits 31, 51, 53, 54, 55, 57, 59, 60 or 62 are set to "1," bit 27 shall also be set to "1."

Flexibility was provided by incorporating unassigned bits and by allowing extension of the field (bits 24, 32, and 40) to add new features. Some of these bits were assigned years after the standard was adopted (e.g., error-correction mode and V.17 modem).

3.8 GROUP 3 ENHANCEMENTS

3.8.1 Error-Concealment Techniques

The switched telephone network is prone to error when transmitting digital data. When such a transmission error occurs, a streak is typically created on the output page, which can be disturbing to the observer. The purpose of error-concealment techniques is to minimize the visual effect of transmission errors on the output copy. Error concealment is possible since an end-of-line code is transmitted between scan lines. If the receiver does not detect the EOL code at the expected location in the data stream, an error has likely occurred on the line following the last correctly received EOL code. Some examples of possible error conditions are:

- EOL occurs before 1728 pels have been written.
- More than 1728 pels have been written before EOL is received.
- No word in applicable code tables matches received bit pattern.
- Current line decoding references a run that does not exist in the previous line.

The effect of errors on output copy has been quantitatively measured by means of computer simulation; the simulation process is illustrated in Figure 3.11. To assist in interpreting these results, a new term, the error sensitivity factor (ESF), is used. The ESF is defined as the number of incorrect pels in the output image, resulting from transmission errors, divided by the number of transmitted bits in error. In other words, the ESF represents the effect of a typical transmission bit error on the picture.

Simulation runs were performed on the MH code and the MR code using the parameters shown in Table 3.7. As indicated in the table, the MR is twice as sensitive to errors as the MH even though an error-concealment technique was employed on the MR. This increased sensitivity is expected because the MR achieves greater compression by reducing redundancy in two dimensions. Figures 3.12 and 3.13 illustrate the output images from this simulation. The bit-error rate for this simulation is 0.7×10^{-3}. Note that the transmission errors have had a greater subjective effect on the MR image than the MH image. This is consistent with the ESF results.

Simulation runs were performed to compare the four different error-concealment techniques for the MR, which are described below.

Print White (PW): The first erroneous line is printed white, and all subsequent lines are printed white until a one-dimensional MH line is correctly received.

Print Previous Line (PPL): The first erroneous line (x) is replaced by the previous correctly received line $(x - 1)$, and all subsequent lines are replaced by $x - 1$ until a one-dimensional MH line is correctly received.

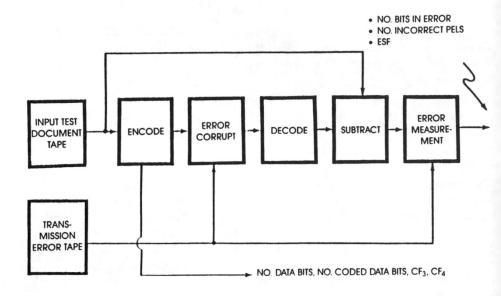

Figure 3.11 Block diagram of simulation process.

Table 3.7
Comparison of modified Huffman and modified read codes

	Test Parameters			Modified Huffman		Modified Read		
Test Doc.	Vert. Resol.	MSLT	Error File	BER $\times 10^{-3}$	ESF	K Factor	BER $\times 10^{-3}$	ESF
4	3.85	10	1	0.82	24.93	2	0.66	40.31
4	3.85	20	1	0.81	27.64	2	0.82	45.24
4	7.7	20	1	0.65	29.28	4	0.78	58.70
4	3.85	20	2	1.1	19.23	2	1.16	27.69
4	3.85	20	3	0.70	20.98	2	0.67	57.41
4	3.85	20	4	1.3	14.66	2	1.36	21.22
1	3.85	20	1	0.81	9.70	2	0.63	20.60
7	3.85	20	1	0.82	22.06	2	0.69	30.27
	Average ESF				21.06			37.68

L'ordre de lancement et de réalisation des applications fait l'objet de décisions au plus haut niveau de la Direction Générale des Télécommunications. Il n'est certes pas question de construire ce système intégré "en bloc" mais bien au contraire de procéder par étapes, par paliers successifs. Certaines applications, dont la rentabilité ne pourra être assurée, ne seront pas entreprises. Actuellement, sur trente applications qui ont pu être globalement définies, six en sont au stade de l'exploitation, six autres se sont vu donner la priorité pour leur réalisation.

Chaque application est confiée à un "chef de projet", responsable successivement de sa conception, de son analyse-programmation et de sa mise en oeuvre dans une région-pilote. La généralisation ultérieure de l'application réalisée dans cette région-pilote dépend des résultats obtenus et fait l'objet d'une décision de la Direction Générale. Néanmoins, le chef de projet doit dès le départ considérer que son activité a une vocation nationale donc refuser tout particularisme régional. Il est aidé d'une équipe d'analystes-programmeurs et entouré d'un "groupe de conception" chargé de rédiger le document de "définition des objectifs globaux" puis le "cahier des charges" de l'application, qui sont adressés pour avis à tous les services utilisateurs potentiels et aux chefs de projet des autres applications. Le groupe de conception comprend 6 à 10 personnes représentant les services les plus divers concernés par le projet, et comporte obligatoirement un bon analyste attaché à l'application.

II - L'IMPLANTATION GEOGRAPHIQUE D'UN RESEAU INFORMATIQUE PERFORMANT

L'organisation de l'entreprise française des télécommunications repose sur l'existence de 20 régions. Des calculateurs ont été implantés dans le passé au moins dans toutes les plus importantes. On trouve ainsi des machines Bull Gamma 30 à Lyon et Marseille, des GE 425 à Lille, Bordeaux, Toulouse et Montpellier, un GE 437 à Massy, enfin quelques machines Bull 300 TI à programmes câblés étaient récemment ou sont encore en service dans les régions de Nancy, Nantes, Limoges, Poitiers et Rouen ; ce parc est essentiellement utilisé pour la comptabilité téléphonique.

A l'avenir, si la plupart des fichiers nécessaires aux applications décrites plus haut peuvent être gérés en temps différé, un certain nombre d'entre eux devront nécessairement être accessibles, voire mis à jour en temps réel : parmi ces derniers le fichier commercial des abonnés, le fichier des renseignements, le fichier des circuits, le fichier technique des abonnés contiendront des quantités considérables d'informations.

Le volume total de caractères à gérer en phase finale sur un ordinateur ayant en charge quelques 500 000 abonnés a été estimé à un milliard de caractères au moins. Au moins le tiers des données seront concernées par des traitements en temps réel.

Aucun des calculateurs énumérés plus haut ne permettait d'envisager de tels traitements. L'intégration progressive de toutes les applications suppose la création d'un support commun pour toutes les informations, une véritable "Banque de données", répartie sur des moyens de traitement nationaux et régionaux, et qui devra rester alimentée, mise à jour en permanence, à partir de la base de l'entreprise, c'est-à-dire les chantiers, les magasins, les guichets des services d'abonnement, les services de personnel etc.

L'étude des différents fichiers à constituer a donc permis de définir les principales caractéristiques du réseau d'ordinateurs nouveaux à mettre en place pour aborder la réalisation du système informatif. L'obligation de faire appel à des ordinateurs de troisième génération, très puissants et dotés de volumineuses mémoires de masse, a conduit à en réduire substantiellement le nombre.

L'implantation de sept centres de calcul interrégionaux constituera un compromis entre : d'une part le désir de réduire le coût économique de l'ensemble, de faciliter la coordination des équipes d'informaticiens; et d'autre part le refus de créer des centres trop importants difficiles à gérer et à diriger, et posant des problèmes délicats de sécurité. Le regroupement des traitements relatifs à plusieurs régions sur chacun de ces sept centres permettra de leur donner une taille relativement homogène. Chaque centre "gèrera" environ un million d'abonnés à la fin du VIème Plan.

La mise en place de ces centres a débuté au début de l'année 1971 : un ordinateur IRIS 50 de la Compagnie Internationale pour l'Informatique a été installé à Toulouse en février ; la même machine vient d'être mise en service au centre de calcul interrégional de Bordeaux;

Figure 3.12 Modified Huffman, high resolution, 10 ms. MSLT, K-4, BER = 0.7×10^{-3}.

L'ordre de lancement et de réalisation des applications fait l'objet de décisions au plus haut niveau de la Direction Générale des Télécommunications. Il n'est certes pas question de construire ce système intégré "en bloc" mais bien au contraire de procéder par étapes, par paliers successifs. Certaines applications, dont la rentabilité ne pourra être assurée, ne seront pas entreprises. Actuellement, sur trente applications qui ont pu être globalement définies, six en sont au stade de l'exploitation, six autres se sont vu donner la priorité pour leur réalisation.

Chaque application est confiée à un "chef de projet", responsable successivement de sa conception, de son analyse-programmation et de sa mise en œuvre dans une région-pilote. La généralisation ultérieure de l'application réalisée dans cette région-pilote dépend des résultats obtenus et fait l'objet d'une décision de la Direction Générale. Néanmoins, le chef de projet doit dès le départ considérer que son activité a une vocation nationale donc refuser tout particularisme régional. Il est aidé d'une équipe d'analystes-programmeurs et entouré d'un "groupe de conception" chargé de rédiger le document de "définition des objectifs globaux" puis le "cahier des charges" de l'application, qui sont adressés pour avis à tous les services utilisateurs potentiels et aux chefs de projet des autres applications. Le groupe de conception comprend 6 à 10 personnes représentant les services les plus divers concernés par le projet, et comporte obligatoirement un bon analyste attaché à l'application.

II - L'IMPLANTATION GEOGRAPHIQUE D'UN RESEAU INFORMATIQUE PERFORMANT

L'organisation de l'entreprise française des télécommunications repose sur l'existence de 20 régions. Des calculateurs ont été implantés dans le passé au moins dans toutes les plus importantes. On trouve ainsi des machines Bull Gamma 30 à Lyon et Marseille, des GE 425 à Lille, Bordeaux, Toulouse et Montpellier, un GE 437 à Massy, enfin quelques machines Bull 300 TI à programmes câblés étaient récemment ou sont encore en service dans les régions de Nancy, Nantes, Limoges, Poitiers et Rouen ; ce parc est essentiellement utilisé pour la comptabilité téléphonique.

A l'avenir, si la plupart des fichiers nécessaires aux applications décrites plus haut peuvent être gérés en temps différé, un certain nombre d'entre eux devront nécessairement être accessibles, voire mis à jour en temps réel : parmi ces derniers le fichier commercial des abonnés, le fichier des renseignements, le fichier des circuits, le fichier technique des abonnés contiendront des quantités considérables d'informations.

Le volume total de caractères à gérer en phase finale sur un ordinateur ayant en charge quelques 500.000 abonnés a été estimé à un milliard de caractères au moins. Au moins le tiers des données seront concernées par des traitements en temps réel.

Aucun des calculateurs énumérés plus haut ne permettait d'envisager de tels traitements.

L'intégration progressive de toutes les applications suppose la création d'un support commun pour toutes les informations, une véritable "Banque de données", répartie sur des moyens de traitement nationaux et régionaux, et qui devra rester alimentée, mise à jour en permanence, à partir de la base de l'entreprise, c'est-à-dire les chantiers, les magasins, les guichets des services d'abonnement, les services de personnel etc.

L'étude des différents fichiers à constituer a donc permis de définir les principales caractéristiques du réseau d'ordinateurs nouveaux à mettre en place pour aborder la réalisation du système informatif. L'obligation de faire appel à des ordinateurs de troisième génération, très puissants et dotés de volumineuses mémoires de masse, a conduit à en réduire substantiellement le nombre.

L'implantation de sept centres de calcul interrégionaux constituera un compromis entre : d'une part le désir de réduire le coût économique de l'ensemble, de faciliter la coordination des équipes d'informaticiens; et d'autre part le refus de créer des centres trop importants difficiles à gérer et à diriger, et posant des problèmes délicats de sécurité. Le regroupement des traitements relatifs à plusieurs régions sur chacun de ces sept centres permettra de leur donner une taille relativement homogène. Chaque centre "gérera" environ un million d'abonnés à la fin du VIème Plan.

La mise en place de ces centres a débuté au début de l'année 1971 : un ordinateur IRIS 50 de la Compagnie Internationale pour l'Informatique a été installé à Toulouse en février ; la même machine vient d'être mise en service au centre de calcul interrégional de Bordeaux.

Figure 3.13 Modified read, high resolution, 10 ms. MSLT, K-4, BER = 0.7×10^{-3}.

L'ordre de lancement et de réalisation des applications fait l'objet de décisions au plus haut niveau de la Direction Générale des Télécommunications. Il n'est certes pas question de construire ce système intégré "en bloc" mais bien au contraire de procéder par étapes, par paliers successifs. Certaines applications, dont la rentabilité ne pourra être assurée, ne seront pas entreprises. Actuellement, sur trente applications qui ont pu être globalement définies, six en sont au stade de l'exploitation, six autres se sont u donner la priorité pour leur réalisation.

Chaque application est confiée à un "chef de projet", responsable successivement de sa conception, de son analyse-programmation et de sa mise en œuvre dans une région-pilote. La généralisation ultérieure de l'application réalisée dans cette région-pilote dépend des résultats obtenus et fait l'objet d'une décision de la Direction Générale. Néanmoins, le chef de projet doit dès le départ considérer que son activité a une vocation nationale donc refuser tout particularisme régional. Il est aidé d'une équipe d'analystes-programmeurs et entouré d'un "groupe de conception" chargé de rédiger le document de "définition des objectifs gionaux" puis le "cahier des charges" de l'application qui sont adressés pour avis à tous les services utilisateurs potentiels et aux chefs de projet des autres applications. Le groupe de conception comprend 5 à 10 personnes représentant les services les plus divers concernés par le projet, et comporte obligatoirement un bon analyste attaché à l'application.

II - L'IMPLANTATION GEOGRAPHIQUE D'UN RESEAU INFORMATIQUE PERFORMANT

L'organisation de l'entreprise française des télécommunications repose sur l'existence de 20 régions. Des calculateurs ont été implantés dans le passé au moins dans toutes les plus importantes. On trouve ainsi des machines Bull Gamma 30 à Lyon et Marseille, des GE 425 à Lille, Bordeaux, Toulouse et Montpellier, un GE 437 à Massy, enfin quelques machines Bull 300 TI à programmes câblés étaient récemment ou sont encore en service dans les régions de Nancy, Nantes, Limoges, Poitiers et Rouen ; ce parc est essentiellement utilisé pour la comptabilité téléphonique.

A l'avenir, si la plupart des fichiers nécessaires aux applications décrites plus haut peuvent être gérés en temps différé, un certain nombre d'entre eux devront nécessairement être accessibles, voire mis à jour en temps réel : parmi ces derniers le fichier commercial des abonnés, le fichier des renseignements, le fichier des circuits, le fichier technique des abonnés contiendront des quantités considérables d'informations.

Le nombre total de caractères à gérer en phase finale sur un ordinateur ayant en charge quelques 500 000 abonnés a été estimé à un milliard de caractères au moins. Au moins le tiers des données seront concernées par des traitements en temps réel.

Aucun des calculateurs énumérés plus haut ne permettait d'envisager de tels traitements. L'intégration progressive de toutes les applications suppose la création d'un support commun pour toutes les informations, une véritable "Banque de données", répartie sur des moyens de traitement nationaux et régionaux, et qui devra rester alimentée, mise à jour en permanence, à partir de la base de l'entreprise, c'est-à-dire les chantiers, les magasins, les guichets des services d'abonnement, les services de personnel etc.

L'étude des différents fichiers à constituer a donc permis de définir les principales caractéristiques du réseau d'ordinateurs nouveau à mettre en place pour aboutir à la réalisation du système informatif. L'obligation de faire appel à des ordinateurs de troisième génération, très puissants et dotés de volumineuses mémoires de masse, a conduit à en réduire substantiellement le nombre.

L'implantation de sept centres de calcul interrégionaux constituera un compromis entre d'une part le désir de réduire le coût économique de l'ensemble, de faciliter la coordination des équipes d'informaticiens; et d'autre part le refus de créer des centres trop importants difficiles à gérer et à diriger, et posant des problèmes délicats de sécurité. Le regroupement des traitements relatifs à plusieurs régions sur chacun de ces sept centres permettra de leur donner une taille relativement homogène. Chaque centre gérera environ un million d'abonnés à la fin du VIème Plan.

La mise en place de ces centres a débuté au début de l'année 197 un ordinateur IRIS 50 de la Compagnie Internationale pour l'Informatique a été installé à Toulouse en février , la même machine vient d'être mise en service au centre de calcul interrégional de Bordeaux.

Figure 3.14 Print white (7.7 lines/mm).

L'ordre de lancement et de réalisation des applications fait l'objet de décisions au plus haut niveau de la Direction Générale des Télécommunications. Il n'est certes pas question de construire ce système intégré "en bloc" mais bien au contraire de procéder par étapes, par paliers successifs. Certaines applications, dont la rentabilité ne pourra être assurée, ne seront pas entreprises. Actuellement, sur trente applications qui ont pu être globalement définies, six en sont au stade de l'exploitation, six autres se sont vu donner la priorité pour leur réalisation.

Chaque application est confiée à un "chef de projet", responsable successivement de sa conception, de son analyse-programmation et de sa mise en oeuvre dans une région-pilote. La généralisation ultérieure de l'application réalisée dans cette région-pilote dépend des résultats obtenus et fait l'objet d'une décision de la Direction Générale. Néanmoins, le chef de projet doit dès le départ considérer que son activité a une vocation nationale donc refuser tout particularisme régional. Il est aidé d'une équipe d'analystes-programmeurs et entouré d'un "groupe de conception" chargé de rédiger le document de "définition des objectifs globaux" puis le "cahier des charges" de l'application, qui sont adressés pour avis à tous les services utilisateurs potentiels et aux chefs de projet des autres applications. Le groupe de conception comprend 6 à 10 personnes représentant les services les plus divers concernés par le projet, et comporte obligatoirement un bon analyste attaché à l'application.

II - L'IMPLANTATION GEOGRAPHIQUE D'UN RESEAU INFORMATIQUE PERFORMANT

L'organisation de l'entreprise française des télécommunications repose sur l'existence de 20 régions. Des calculateurs ont été implantés dans le passé au moins dans toutes les plus importantes. On trouve ainsi des machines Bull Gamma 30 à Lyon et Marseille, des GE 425 à Lille, Bordeaux, Toulouse et Montpellier, un GE 437 à Massy, enfin quelques machines Bull 300 TI à programmes câblés étaient récemment ou sont encore en service dans les régions de Nancy, Nantes, Limoges, Poitiers et Rouen ; ce parc est essentiellement utilisé pour la comptabilité téléphonique.

A l'avenir, si la plupart des fichiers nécessaires aux applications décrites plus haut peuvent être gérés en temps différé, un certain nombre d'entre eux devront nécessairement être accessibles, voire mis à jour en temps réel : parmi ces derniers le fichier commercial des abonnés, le fichier des renseignements, le fichier des circuits, le fichier technique des abonnés contiendront des quantités considérables d'informations.

Le volume total de caractères à gérer en phase finale sur un ordinateur ayant en charge quelque 600 000 abonnés a été estimé à un milliard de caractères au moins. Au moins le tiers des données seront concernées par des traitements en temps réel.

Aucun des calculateurs énumérés plus haut ne permettait d'envisager de tels traitements.

L'intégration progressive de toutes les applications suppose la création d'un support commun pour toutes les informations, une véritable "Banque de données", répartie sur des moyens de traitement nationaux et régionaux, et qui devra rester alimentée, mise à jour en permanence, à partir de la base de l'entreprise, c'est-à-dire les chantiers, les magasins, les guichets des services d'abonnement, les services de personnel etc.

L'étude des différents fichiers à constituer a donc permis de définir les principales caractéristiques du réseau d'ordinateurs nouveaux à mettre en place pour aborder la réalisation du système informatif. L'obligation de faire appel à des ordinateurs de troisième génération, très puissants et dotés de volumineuses mémoires de masse, a conduit à en réduire substantiellement le nombre.

L'implantation de sept centres de calcul interrégionaux constituera un compromis entre d'une part le désir de réduire le coût économique de l'ensemble, de faciliter la coordination des équipes d'informaticiens; et d'autre part le refus de créer des centres trop importants difficiles à gérer et à diriger, et posant des problèmes délicats de sécurité. Le regroupement des traitements relatifs à plusieurs régions sur chacun de ces sept centres permettra de leur donner une taille relativement homogène. Chaque centre gérera environ un million d'abonnés à la fin du VIème Plan.

La mise en place de ces centres a débuté au début de l'année 1971 : un ordinateur IRIS 50 de la Compagnie Internationale pour l'Informatique a été installé à Toulouse en février ; la même machine vient d'être mise en service au centre de calcul interrégional de Bordeaux.

Figure 3.15 Print previous line (7.7 lines/mm).

L'ordre de lancement et de réalisation des applications fait l'objet de décisions au plus haut niveau de la Direction Générale des Télécommunications. Il n'est certes pas question de construire ce système intégré "en bloc" mais bien au contraire de procéder par étapes, par paliers successifs. Certaines applications, dont la rentabilité ne pourra être assurée, ne seront pas entreprises. Actuellement, sur trente applications qui ont pu être globalement définies, six en sont au stade de l'exploitation, six autres se sont vu donner la priorité pour leur réalisation.

Chaque application est confiée à un "chef de projet", responsable successivement de sa conception, de son analyse-programmation et de sa mise en œuvre dans une région-pilote. La généralisation ultérieure de l'application réalisée dans cette région-pilote dépend des résultats obtenus et fait l'objet d'une décision de la Direction Générale. Néanmoins, le chef de projet doit dès le départ considérer que son activité a une vocation nationale donc refuser tout particularisme régional. Il est aidé d'une équipe d'analystes-programmeurs et entouré d'un "groupe de conception" chargé de rédiger le document de "définition des objectifs globaux" puis le "cahier des charges" de l'application, qui sont adressés pour avis à tous les services utilisateurs potentiels et aux chefs de projet des autres applications. Le groupe de conception comprend 6 à 10 personnes représentant les services les plus divers concernés par le projet, et comporte obligatoirement un bon analyste attaché à l'application.

II - L'IMPLANTATION GEOGRAPHIQUE D'UN RESEAU INFORMATIQUE PERFORMANT

L'organisation de l'entreprise française des télécommunications repose sur l'existence de 20 régions. Des calculateurs ont été implantés dans le passé au moins dans toutes les plus importantes. On trouve ainsi des machines Bull Gamma 30 à Lyon et Marseille, des GE 425 à Lille, Bordeaux, Toulouse et Montpellier, un GE 437 à Massy, enfin quelques machines Bull 300 TI à programmes câblés étaient récemment ou sont encore en service dans les régions de Nancy, Nantes, Limoges, Poitiers et Rouen ; ce parc est essentiellement utilisé pour la comptabilité téléphonique.

A l'avenir, si la plupart des fichiers nécessaires aux applications décrites plus haut peuvent être gérés en temps différé, un certain nombre d'entre eux devront nécessairement être accessibles, voire mis à jour en temps réel : parmi ces derniers le fichier commercial des abonnés, le fichier des renseignements, le fichier des circuits, le fichier technique des abonnés contiendront des quantités considérables d'informations.

Le volume total de caractères à gérer en phase finale sur un ordinateur ayant en charge quelques 500 000 abonnés a été estimé à un milliard de caractères au moins. Au moins le tiers des données seront concernées par des traitements en temps réel.

Aucun des calculateurs énumérés plus haut ne permettait d'envisager de tels traitements.

L'intégration progressive de toutes les applications suppose la création d'un support commun pour toutes les informations, une véritable "Banque de données", répartie sur des moyens de traitement nationaux et régionaux, et qui devra rester alimentée, mise à jour en permanence, à partir de la base de l'entreprise, c'est-à-dire les chantiers, les magasins, les guichets des services d'abonnement, les services de personnel etc.

L'étude des différents fichiers à constituer a donc permis de définir les principales caractéristiques du réseau d'ordinateurs nouveaux à mettre en place pour aborder la réalisation du système informatif. L'obligation de faire appel à des ordinateurs de troisième génération, très puissants et dotés de volumineuses mémoires de masse, a conduit à en réduire substantiellement le nombre.

L'implantation de sept centres de calcul interrégionaux constituera un compromis entre d'une part le désir de réduire le coût économique de l'ensemble, de faciliter la coordination des équipes d'informaticiens; et d'autre part le refus de créer des centres trop importants difficiles à gérer et à diriger et posant des problèmes délicats de sécurité. Le regroupement des traitements relatifs à plusieurs régions sur chacun de ces sept centres permettra de leur donner une taille relativement homogène. Chaque centre gérera environ un million d'abonnés à la fin du VIème Plan.

La mise en place de ces centres a débuté au début de l'année 1971 : un ordinateur IRIS 50 de la Compagnie Internationale pour l'Informatique a été installé à Toulouse en février ; la même machine vient d'être mise en service au centre de calcul interrégional de Bordeaux.

Figure 3.16 Previous line/white (7.7 lines/mm).

L'ordre de lancement et de réalisation des applications fait l'objet de décisions au plus haut niveau de la Direction Générale des Télécommunications. Il n'est certes pas question de construire ce système intégré "en bloc" mais bien au contraire de procéder par étapes, par paliers successifs. Certaines applications, dont la rentabilité ne pourra être assurée, ne seront pas entreprises. Actuellement, sur trente applications qui ont pu être globalement définies, six en sont au stade de l'exploitation, six autres se sont vu donner la priorité pour leur réalisation.

Chaque application est confiée à un "chef de projet", responsable successivement de sa conception, de son analyse-programmation et de sa mise en œuvre dans une région-pilote. La généralisation ultérieure de l'application réalisée dans cette région-pilote dépend des résultats obtenus et fait l'objet d'une décision de la Direction Générale. Néanmoins, le chef de projet doit dès le départ considérer que son activité a une vocation nationale donc refuser tout particularisme régional. Il est aidé d'une équipe d'analystes-programmeurs et entouré d'un "groupe de conception" chargé de rédiger le document de "définition des objectifs globaux" puis le "cahier des charges" de l'application, qui sont adressés pour avis à tous les services utilisateurs potentiels et aux chefs de projet des autres applications. Le groupe de conception comprend 6 à 10 personnes représentant les services les plus divers concernés par le projet, et comporte obligatoirement un bon analyste attaché à l'application.

II - L'IMPLANTATION GEOGRAPHIQUE D'UN RESEAU INFORMATIQUE PERFORMANT

L'organisation de l'entreprise française des télécommunications repose sur l'existence de 20 régions. Des calculateurs ont été implantés dans le passé au moins dans toutes les plus importantes. On trouve ainsi des machines Bull Gamma 30 à Lyon et Marseille, des GE 425 à Lille, Bordeaux, Toulouse et Montpellier, un GE 437 à Massy, enfin quelques machines Bull 300 TI à programmes câblés étaient récemment ou sont encore en service dans les régions de Nancy, Nantes, Limoges, Poitiers et Rouen ; ce parc est essentiellement utilisé pour la comptabilité téléphonique.

A l'avenir, si la plupart des fichiers nécessaires aux applications décrites plus haut peuvent être gérés en temps différé, un certain nombre d'entre eux devront nécessairement être accessibles, voire mis à jour en temps réel : parmi ces derniers le fichier commercial des abonnés, le fichier des renseignements, le fichier des circuits, le fichier technique des abonnés contiendront des quantités considérables d'informations.

Le volume total de caractères à gérer en phase finale sur un ordinateur ayant en charge quelques 500 000 abonnés a été estimé à un milliard de caractères au moins. Au moins le tiers des données seront concernées par des traitements en temps réel.

Aucun des calculateurs énumérés plus haut ne permettait d'envisager de tels traitements.

L'intégration progressive de toutes les applications suppose la création d'un support commun pour toutes les informations, une véritable "Banque de données", répartie sur des moyens de traitement nationaux et régionaux, et qui devra rester alimentée, mise à jour en permanence, à partir de la base de l'entreprise, c'est-à-dire les chantiers, les magasins, les guichets des services d'abonnement, les services de personnel etc.

L'étude des différents fichiers à constituer a donc permis de définir les principales caractéristiques du réseau d'ordinateurs nouveaux à mettre en place pour aborder la réalisation du système informatif. L'obligation de faire appel à des ordinateurs de troisième génération, très puissants et dotés de volumineuses mémoires de masse, a conduit à en réduire substantiellement le nombre.

L'implantation de sept centres de calcul interrégionaux constituera un compromis entre d'une part le désir de réduire le coût économique de l'ensemble, de faciliter la coordination des équipes d'informaticiens; et d'autre part le refus de créer des centres trop importants difficiles à gérer et à diriger, et posant des problèmes délicats de sécurité. Le regroupement des traitements relatifs à plusieurs régions sur chacun de ces sept centres permettra de leur donner une taille relativement homogène. Chaque centre gérera environ un million d'abonnés à la fin du VIème Plan.

La mise en place de ces centres a débuté au début de l'année 197.. un ordinateur IRIS 50 de la Compagnie Internationale pour l'Informatique a été installé à Toulouse en février, la même machine vient d'être mise en service au centre de calcul interrégional de Bordeaux.

Figure 3.17 Normal decode/previous line (7.7 lines/mm).

Print Previous Line/White (PLW): This processing technique is a combination of the previous two. The first erroneous line (*x*) is replaced by the previous correctly received line (*x* − 1), and all subsequent lines are printed white until a one-dimensional MH line is correctly received.

Normal Decode/Previous Line (NDPL): In this case the first erroneous line is decoded and printed in the normal MH or MR manner up to the point in the line where the error is detected. From this point, the remainder of the first erroneous line is replaced by the corresponding pels in the "previous line." The resultant "correct" line is then used as a new reference "previous" line, and the process is repeated until an MH line is correctly decoded. This error-processing technique should be particularly advantageous in those instances where a transmission error occurs near the end (right-hand side of the page) of a scan line period. When this occurs it should be possible to decode correctly most of the scan line that was "hit" as well as most of the subsequent scan lines before a correct MH line is received.

Figures 3.14, 3.15, 3.16, and 3.17 illustrate the output images respectively resulting from these simulations.

3.8.2 Group 3 Error-Control Options

Standard Group 3 facsimile equipment employs no error-control technique in the classic sense. The periodic transmission of a MH line in the optional MR mode of operation is a type of forward error correction to prohibit the propagation of an error throughout the entire page. Another type of error control is that some fax machines will compute the number of lines in error at the receiver using the redundant EOL code, and request the retransmission of a page if the number of lines in error exceeds a threshold.

A more conventional error-control technique has recently been adopted by the CCITT as an option for Group 3 fax. When the option is employed in the MR mode, the K factor is set to infinity, thereby reducing the transmission time for good quality transmission lines. The transmission time is usually reduced by the error-control option because transmission may occur at a higher bit rate. Error control also has the obvious advantage of eliminating the error streaks in the output copy.

The CCITT has defined two possible error-control options in the Blue Book published in 1989. One option merely limits the effect of errors, but does not correct them. The second option employs true error-correction technology.

The error-limiting mode applies to one-dimensional MH coding. The first step is to divide the 1728 pels per line into 12 groups of 144 pels each. Each group is next classified to be either all white or nonwhite. A 12-bit code word at the beginning of each line identifies the white and nonwhite parts. The all-white groups are not encoded. The nonwhite groups are encoded separately by the standard MH. The intent of this option is to limit the effect of an error to half of a scan line rather than the entire scan line. The value of this option has yet to be proved in practice.

The error-correction mode is designed to be more universal in its application than the error-limiting mode, and therefore it has been implemented in many fax units. The design objectives for the error-control option were that the number of changes in the existing CCITT Recommendations T.4 and T.30 should be minimized, it should operate well in a burst error environment, and the overhead for error-free channels should be low. This option applies to both the MH and MR modes of operation. The error-control technique chosen by the CCITT is a half-duplex HDLC selectively repeating ARQ concept. The error control procedure is summarized below.

- The coded data stream is divided into HDLC "frames" of 256 bytes each.
- A redundant code is synthesized and transmitted with each frame, which permits the receiver to detect a transmission error in that frame.
- After the page is completely transmitted, the receiver requests the retransmission of the frames in error.
- The transmitter sends the bad frames.
- After four requests for retransmission of the same frame, the transmitter may stop or continue with optional modem speed fallback.

3.8.3 Dither Coding

About 20 million facsimile units are now operational, and sales are continuing at an increasing rate. This success can be traced to many causes, two of which are listed below.

The scanned image is first converted to binary pixels (black or white), which are easily compressed to minimize transmission time.

The printer is a binary device that writes only black or white dots. This has permitted the printer to be produced with high reliability and very low cost.

Most of the images transmitted through fax systems contain only black or white information (text, line drawings, etc.). Because the transmission system and printing system are binary, the output quality for documents of this type is excellent. When a gray-scale image is transmitted, however, the output image is usually severely distorted. The purpose of dither coding is to transmit gray-scale images through facsimile systems employing binary transmission and binary printing techniques with improved output quality.

3.8.3.1 The Basic Dither Process

The threshold circuit in a bilevel facsimile system is the key element in dither coding. For purposes of analysis, we can assume that conventional bilevel systems employ a fixed threshold at the midpoint between peak black and peak white. Figure 3.18(a) illustrates such a coding process. Note that an input gray level near the threshold is

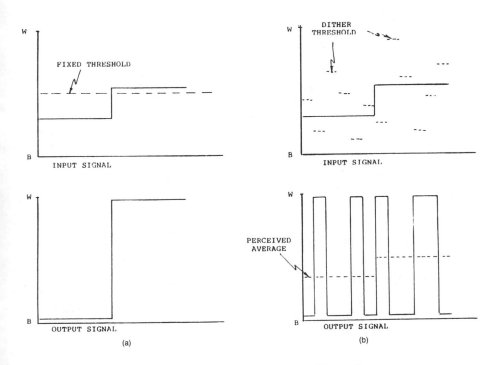

Figure 3.18 Dither coding: (a) conventional binary coding; (b) dither coding.

drastically altered in the output image. In dither coding, the threshold is varied, or dithered, in amplitude from pel to pel, as shown in Figure 3.18(b). If the threshold is dithered uniformly over the gray-scale range, the average value of the output image over a number of neighboring pixels will approximate the input gray value; the eye will tend to perform the averaging function, and the observer will perceive the input gray scale. A computer simulation study of dither coding has been performed in which clumped dither, ordered dither, and two enhancements were investigated. The results of this study are provided in Table 3.8.

3.8.3.2 Clumped Dither

The clumped dither compression technique is an electronic approximation of the photomechanical screening process. It employs a matrix of fixed thresholds, shown in Figure 3.19, which are arranged in such a way that a "dot" grows outward from the center as successively darker gray levels are encountered in low-contrast regions of the image [2]. The numbers in the matrix represent threshold values out of 256 possible brightness levels. The eight-bit gray level of each input pel is compared to one of the matrix thresholds; which threshold is used depends on the position of the pel in the image. Figure 3.20 shows how the irregular matrices interlock.

Table 3.8
Compression Results for Dither Coding Techniques (Bits/Pixel)

Coding Technique	House with Sky	House with Trees	Aerial Photo
Clumped	0.98	0.81	0.98
Clumped with plane coding	0.40	0.66	0.77
Ordered	1.25	0.99	1.10
Ordered with reordering	0.47	0.52	0.52

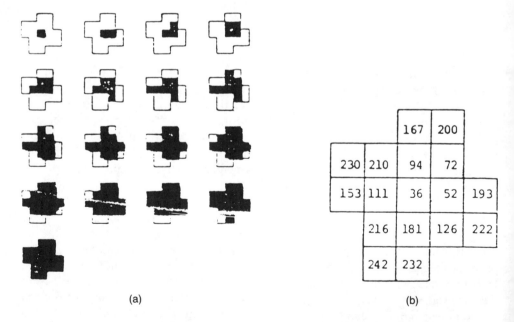

(a)　　　　　　　　　　　　　　　　(b)

Figure 3.19 Clumped dither matrix thresholds: (a) halftone dots in nondetail regions; (b) clumped dither matrix.

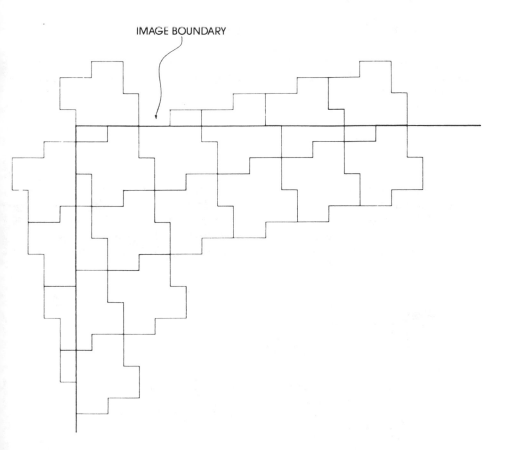

IMAGE BOUNDARY

Figure 3.20 Clumped dither matrix lattice.

3.8.3.3 Clumped Dither with Plane Coding

In the clumped dither with plane coding technique, the dithered image is separated into 17 planes, with each plane comprised of the pixels associated with one of the thresholds in the clumped dither matrix. The pixel in matrix position 1 of every clumped dither matrix is placed in plane 1; the pixel in matrix position 2 of every clumped dither matrix is placed in plane 2; and so on. Placing together all of the pixels compared to the same threshold, in most cases, increases the length of black or white runs, thus making the image more compressible. The 17 clump planes are then compressed by using Group 4 encoding. At the receiver, the planes are all decoded, and the dithered image is reconstructed from the clump planes by placing each pixel back in the position from which it was extracted at the transmitter. Clump plane separation provides enhanced compression, in most cases, with no effect on image quality. This technique, however, is more complex to implement than conventional clumped dither.

3.8.3.4 Ordered Dither

Ordered dithering employs an $n \times n$ matrix of fixed thresholds that is repeated throughout the image, in the same way as clumped dithering. The distribution of the thresholds within the matrix is designed to provide acceptable pseudogray-scale rendition and edge sharpness while producing a minimum of visible patterns or artifacts. The ordered dither matrix employed in this study is an 8×8 matrix in which the thresholds are arranged symmetrically, as shown in Figure 3.21. The threshold val-

25	19	11	27	24	18	10	2
9	1	3	21	8	1	2	20
7	7	5	13	16	6	4	12
31	15	23	29	30	14	22	28
24	18	10	26	25	19	11	27
8	1	2	20	9	1	3	21
16	6	4	12	17	7	5	13
30	14	22	18	31	15	23	29

Figure 3.21 Original matrix.

ues are related to a maximum of 32 shades of gray from black to white. The even-numbered thresholds (2–30) are arranged spirally in the upper right and lower left corners, and the odd-numbered thresholds (1–31) are arranged spirally in the upper left and lower right corners. This arrangement provides 32 pseudogray-scale levels with a pattern of four dots growing in each of the four corners of the matrix as successively darker gray levels are encountered in low-contrast regions of the image.

3.8.3.5 Ordered Dithering with Bit Reordering

If the ordered dither pixels, described above, are transmitted in the conventional raster pattern as shown in Figure 3.21, the length of the black and white rows usually will be short, and the compression will be poor. The purpose of the reordering technique is to transmit the pixels in a sequence where the contiguous transmitted pixels are more correlated and therefore more compressible. Figure 3.22 illustrates the reordering process.

1	3	5	7	6	4	2	1
9	11	13	15	14	12	10	8
17	19	21	23	22	20	18	16
25	27	29	31	30	28	26	24
24	26	28	30	31	29	27	25
16	18	20	22	23	21	19	17
8	10	12	14	15	13	11	9
1	2	4	6	7	5	3	1

Figure 3.22 Reordered matrix.

3.8.3.6 Test Results

The compression performance of the four dither coding techniques described above was measured by means of computer simulation. The compression algorithm used in the simulation is the MMR coding technique used in Group 4 facsimile equipment. The three images shown in Figure 3.23 were used in the simulations, and the compression results are summarized in Table 3.8. Output images were generated for the two coding techniques and the quality was found to be quite similar.

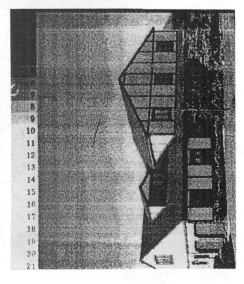

Figure 3.23 Test images.

3.8.4 EIA-232 Interface

Figure 3.24 is a functional block diagram of the typical facsimile machine indicating that the only I/O connection is a modem to interface with the PSTN. Table 3.9 indicates the three possible modes of operation for a conventional facsimile system: transmit, receive, and copy. Many facsimile manufacturers are offering an optional digital interface to connect directly with a local computer, digital network, crypto-graphic device, local scanner, or external modem. This digital interface is invariably accomplished in accordance with the EIA-232 standard. Figure 3.25 is a functional

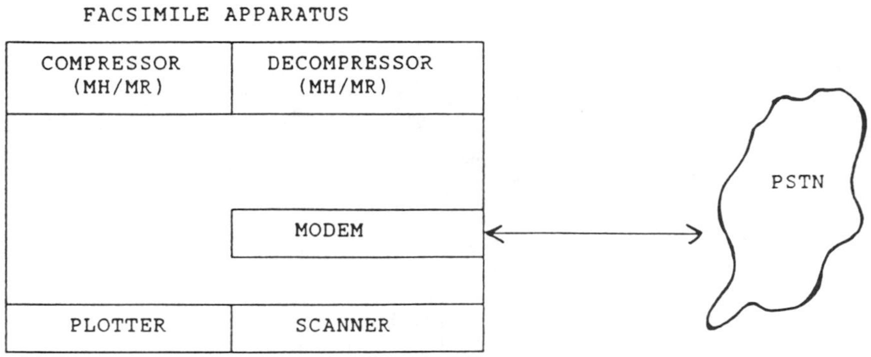

Figure 3.24 Typical facsimile machine.

Table 3.9
Functions of Facsimile Machines with EIA-232

	Function	Source	Destination	Input	Output
Without	Fax transmit	Scanner	Modem	Image	MH/MR
EIA-232	Fax receive	Modem	Plotter	MH/MR	
	Copy	Scanner	Plotter	Image	Image
	Plot	EIA-232	Plotter	MH/MR/image	Image
	Scan	Scanner	EIA-232	Image	
EIA-232	Transmit	EIA-232	Modem	MH/MR/image	MH/MR
	Receive	Modem	EIA-232	MH/MR	
	Compress	EIA-232	EIA-232	Image	MH/MR
	Decompress	EIA-232	EIA-232	MH/MR	
EIA-232	Print	EIA-232	Plotter	ASCII	Image
Plus character	Remote print	EIA-232	Modem	ASCII	MH/MR
Generator	Create image	EIA-232	EIA-232	ASCII	MH/MR/image

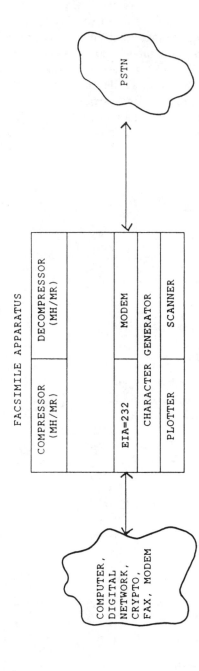

Figure 3.25 Facsimile machine with EIA-232.

block diagram illustrating the digital configuration with the EIA-232 interface. Table 3.9 lists six different modes of operation that can be accomplished by using the digital interface. In the transmit mode, imagery that originates in a computer is fed to the fax unit for transmission. In the receive mode, pictures received by the fax unit are fed directly to a computer, LAN, or cryptographic machine.

Another typical option frequently associated with the EIA-232 mode is the inclusion of a character generator as shown in Figure 3.25 and Table 3.9. In the remote print mode, the fax unit accepts ASCII character data from the local digital source, the character generator converts the data to raster format, and the MH/MR compressor prepares this signal for conventional fax transmission over the PSTN. The advantage of this mode as well as the transmit mode is that the input image is never scanned, and therefore the output image does not have the degradation associated with the scanning process.

It is unfortunate that no standard exists to define the signal protocol and frame that pass over the EIA-232 interface. Consequently, fax units from different manufacturers are not compatible over the digital interface.

3.8.5 High Resolution

The nominal resolution for Group 3 facsimile in the horizontal direction is 200 pels/in. A large fraction of Group 3 fax transmission employs the high-resolution option, which is 200 scan lines/in. in the vertical direction. Therefore, in this mode, the pels are essentially square: 200 pels/in. in both directions. Discussions have been held by the CCITT and domestic standards organizations about the possibility of extending the resolution of Group 3 fax beyond this present capability of 200 pels/in. It is likely that two additional resolutions will be selected: 300×300 pels because this is found in high-quality printers and 400×400 because this is double the basic 200×200 Group 3 resolution.

We should consider how the compression factor is affected by an increase in resolution. Figure 3.26 is a plot of the number of bits/page at 200 pels/in., and higher resolutions, for three of the standard CCITT documents. Notice that in each case the number of bits/page at 400 pels/in. is approximately double that at 200 pels/in. This occurs in spite of the fact that there are four times as many pels in the 400 pel/in. image relative to the 200 pel/in. image. This means that the compression ratio increases as the resolution increases, as shown in Figure 3.27. In general, the compression ratio doubles as the resolution doubles. The compression increases as the resolution increases due to the higher level of correlation and redundancy between adjacent pels.

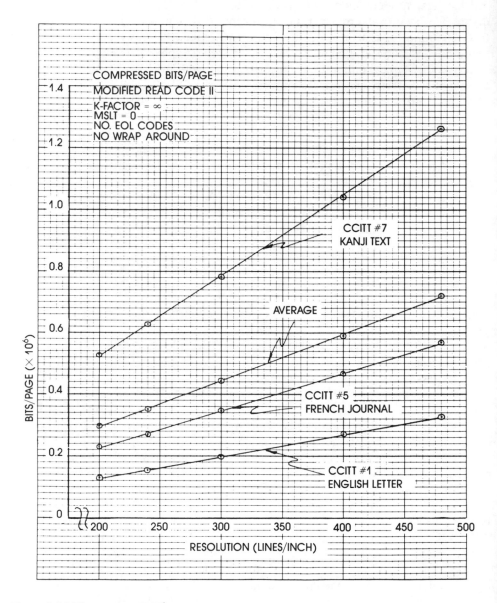

COMPRESSED BITS/PAGE
MODIFIED READ CODE II
K-FACTOR = ∞
MSLT = 0
NO. EOL CODES
NO WRAP AROUND

CCITT #7
KANJI TEXT

AVERAGE

CCITT #5
FRENCH JOURNAL

CCITT #1
ENGLISH LETTER

BITS/PAGE (×10⁶)

RESOLUTION (LINES/INCH)

Figure 3.26 Bits per page (×10⁶).

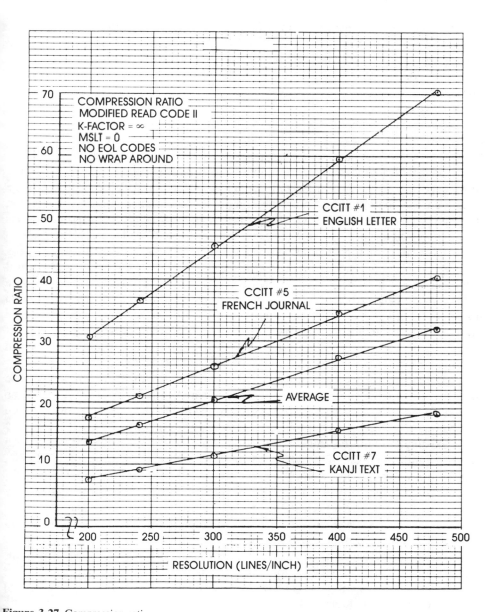

Figure 3.27 Compression ratio.

3.8.6 Small Page Size

The basic Group 3 standard is defined for the scanning and printing of an A4 page, which is 215 mm (8.5 in.) wide. The 1989 CCITT Blue Book defines two optional small page sizes that may be used for Group 3 operation. An A5 page is 151 mm (5.9 in.) wide and the A6 page is 107 mm (4.2 in.) wide. The primary purpose of these reduced page sizes for fax machines is to permit the development of small, inexpensive fax devices.

The CCITT recommendation not only defines the size of the I/O pages, but also the resolution that is to be used for various page sizes. Table 3.10 is from the CCITT recommendation defining the resolution in numerous modes of operation. The reader will note that it is permissible to mix page sizes, to transmit from any input page size (e.g., A4) to any other page size (e.g., A6). When different page sizes are used, these will be a corresponding reduction or enlargement at the output to ensure no data are lost. Table 3.10 defines system operation for all combinations of input and output page sizes. See Table 3.6 for the DIS and DTC bit settings to allow these new small page units to operate in one or more possible modes.

Provision is made for sending from a standard width (A4) transmitter with 8 pels/mm across an 8.5-in.-wide page to an A6 receiver with 16 pels/mm across a 4.25-in.-wide page. All information would be preserved, but the user might need a magnifying glass to read the small print size. Cost of the electronics required would probably be the same as for the A4 fax unit. An A5 fax unit that preserved all of the information would record on 7-in.-wide paper. No changes would be needed in existing Group 3 fax units to send in this manner to A5 or A6 fax units.

Alternatively, sending from an A4 transmitter to an A5 or A6 receiver can be done by throwing away pels at the transmitter to match the number of pels that the receiver prints. This method is similar to sending from A3 to A4 fax units. Figure 3.28 shows that copy received by this method has lower resolution.

Existing Group 3 fax units would not be able to throw away pels to match A5 or A6 requirements. The transmitter, however, could send a full line of 1728 pels, and the receiver could throw away the extra pels.

Sending from A5 to A5 or A6 to A6 fax units keeps the same narrower copy size without enlargement or reduction, providing both fax units have the same number of pels per line (see Figure 3.29). Sending from A5 or A6 fax units to an A4 unit can be done with the narrow page text centered on the A4 page.

Although this smaller paper size option has been defined by the CCITT for some time, very few machines employing the smaller paper sizes have appeared in the marketplace. It is still possible that very low cost systems of this type could be developed in the near future.

Table 3.10
Recommended Resolution

Interworking between equipments with A5/A6 and A4 facilities and between equipments with combinations of these facilities

Situation at transmission side				Terminal capabilities at reception side →				
§ 2.1 case	**Horizontal resolution**	**Vertical resolution**	**Pel process**	**b)**	**e)**	**g)**	**f)**	**h)**
			Horizontal resolution →	1728 pels/ 215 mm	864 pels/ 107 mm	1728 pels/ 107 mm	1216 pels/ 151 mm	1728 pels/ 151 mm
			Vertical resolution →	3.85 l/mm 7.7 l/mm	7.7 l/mm 15.4 l/mm	7.7 l/mm 15.4 l/mm	5.44 l/mm 10.9 l/mm	5.44 l/mm 10.9 l/mm
			Pel process →	Original 1728	864 1728 * .5 Note 1	Original 1728	1216 1728 * .70 Note 2	Original 1728
			DIS-DTC: DCS →	Bit 17 = 0 Bit 18 = 0 Bit 33 = 0	Bit 33 = 1 Bit 35 = 1	Bit 33 = 1 Bit 37 = 1	Bit 33 = 1 Bit 34 = 1	Bit 33 = 1 Bit 36 = 1
b)	1728 pels/ 215 mm	3.85 l/mm 7.7 l/mm	Original 1728	—	Reduced (A4 → A6)	Reduced (A4 → A6)	Reduced (A4 → A5)	Reduced (A4 → A5)
c)	864 pels/ 107 mm	7.7 l/mm 15.4 l/mm	864 * 2 Note 1	Enlarged (A6 → A4)	Equal (A6) Note 1	Equal (A6)	Enlarged (A6 → A5)	Enlarged (A6 → A5)
g)	1728 pels/ 107 mm	7.7 l/mm 15.4 l/mm	Original 1728	Enlarged (A6 → A4)	Equal (A6)	Equal (A6)	Enlarged (A6 → A5)	Enlarged (A6 → A5)
f)	1216 pels/ 151 mm	5.44 l/mm 10.9 l/mm	1216 * 1.42 Note 2	Enlarged (A5 → A4)	Reduced (A5 → A6)	Reduced (A5 → A6)	Equal (A5) Note 2	Equal (A5)
h)	1728 pels/ 151 mm	5.44 l/mm 10.9 l/mm	Original 1728	Enlarged (A5 → A4)	Reduced (A5 → A6)	Reduced (A5 → A6)	Equal (A5)	Equal (A5)

Note 1, 2

Note 1 – Bit 33 = 1 Transmit pel process = 432(W) + 864 + 432 (W)
Bit 35 = 1 Receive pel process extracts central 864 pels

Note 2 – Bit 33 = 1 Transmit pel process = 256(W) + 1216 + 256(W)
Bit 34 = 1 Receive pel process extracts central 1216 pels

(W) = white pels

THE SLEREXE COMPANY LIMITED

SAPORS LANE · BOOLE · DORSET · BH 25 8 ER

TELEPHONE BOOLE (945 13) 51617 · TELEX 123456

Our Ref. 350/PJC/EAC   18th January, 1972.

Dr. P.N. Cundall,
Mining Surveys Ltd.,
Holroyd Road,
Reading,
Berks.

Dear Pete,

    Permit me to introduce you to the facility of facsimile
transmission.

    In facsimile a photocell is caused to perform a raster scan over
the subject copy. The variations of print density on the document
cause the photocell to generate an analogous electrical video signal.
This signal is used to modulate a carrier, which is transmitted to a
remote destination over a radio or cable communications link.

    At the remote terminal, demodulation reconstructs the video
signal, which is used to modulate the density of print produced by a
printing device. This device is scanning in a raster scan synchronised
with that at the transmitting terminal. As a result, a facsimile
copy of the subject document is produced.

    Probably you have uses for this facility in your organisation.

                    Yours sincerely,

                    Phil.

                    P.J. CROSS
                    Group Leader - Facsimile Research

Registered in England: No. 2038
Registered Office: 60 Vicars Lane, Ilford, Essex.

Figure 3.28 Received copy—A6 from A4.

SAMPLE   DOCUMENT
(MT 5 TEST CHART NO.2)

IF you believe that their marketing
organization could be of help to you
in your current business, then this
could be an excellent deal where you
could not possibly lose and where there
would be a lot to gain. You could pay
the   book value down in your stock with
the additional half a million contingent
upon future earnings of Industries.
John Alden is a wealthy individual and the
kind of a guy that would be interested in a
deal with our stock.
I would urge you to have your accountants
look over the financials immediately and
come to some intelligent understanding as
to just what the picture looks like.

Figure 3.29 Received copy—A6 from A6.

3.8.7 Nonstandard Operation

The Group 3 facsimile standard permits a fax transmitter to request that the fax receiver switch to a nonstandard mode of operation if the receiver is equipped with the appropriate proprietary capability. This nonstandard mode of operation permits fax manufacturers to provide improved technology and service beyond that provided by the basic standard.

NSF (0000 0100) is used in the DIS signal to invoke nonstandard features between two fax machines made by the same manufacturer. CCITT Recommendation T.35 gives the details. NSF must be followed immediately by one byte of country code, provider code, and at least one more byte coded in any way desired to describe the nonstandard features to the other fax machine. Formerly these codes were not furnished to others. See Table 3.11 for U.S. provider codes.

The features specified by NSF are not recognized by fax machines made by other manufacturers. If handshake is completed in the NSF mode, the format for fax transmission could be changed for a proprietary mode of operation, for example, nonstandard compression algorithms, encrypted signals, higher speed modems, or for other purposes.

Table 3.11
U.S. Provider Code Assignments

Company Name	City	Provider Code
Adobe Systems	Mountain View CA	004400
AT&T Bell Labs	Middletown NJ	004A00
Bogosian Engineering	Fremont CA	004200
Brooktrout Technology	Wellesley Hills MA	006200
Castelle	Santa Clara CA	006600
Data Race	San Antonio TX	004C00
Fremont Communications	Fremont CA	004600
GammaLink Graphics	Palo Alto CA	006400
Hayes Microcomputer	Atlanta GA	004800
Hybrid Fax	Redwood City CA	006800
Murata Business Systems	Dallas TX	00A200
NetExpress	Vienna VA	008400
TRW Electronic Products	San Luis Obispo CA	004E00
Wang Laboratories	Lowell MA	008200
Xerox	Lewisville TX	009800

3.8.8 Encryption of Fax

Fax encryption devices (such as scramblers or privacy devices) available for business use can provide a very high degree of security. The digital fax signal that normally connects to the modem input when sending or output when receiving connects instead to an external encryption box. Two EIA-232 connectors are used, one for clear text and one for encrypted text. The box encrypts the digital signal to the modem when sending and decrypts the digital signal from the modem when receiving. At least one fax manufacturer is developing a fax machine with built-in encryption. With the better and more expensive encryption units, it would take a highest level workstation computer hundreds of years to break the code. Changing the code with time further decreases the chances of reading an intercepted fax message. One of the code systems available on a chip is the DES algorithm, approved by the U.S. government for U.S. business use within the United States and for selected international banking applications. Other algorithms are used alternatively.

The simple methods of the first paragraph are certainly not adequate for sending classified government information. Large government agencies devote much time and equipment to assuring that all government classified material including fax messages cannot be decoded and read by anyone other than the intended recipient. Fax machines used to send U.S. government classified material use special construction techniques and must have government approval.

The basic technique of encrypting a digital fax message is quite simple. Instead of sending the stream of bits that is normally fed to the modem input (clear text), each 0 or 1 in the bit stream is either passed through unchanged, or inverted so a 0 is sent as a 1, or a 1 as a 0. The decision whether to invert a particular bit or not is controlled "randomly" (see Figure 3.30). If truly random inversions were used, it would not be possible to decode the received fax signal. A pseudorandom pattern is used instead, but the pattern is so long that it is the same as "never" repeating. The receiving fax machine must have the same pattern to decode the received fax signals by again inverting the same bits. Identical patterns are generated from a pseudorandom number generator in both the sending and receiving encryption units by using the matching codes in each authorized receiving fax machine. If the code is changed, all encryption boxes must change at the same time and the new code must still be a secret.

Probably the easiest way to encrypt a Group 3 fax is to use a secure digital telephone that has a built-in data jack for the fax machine. The telephone plugs into

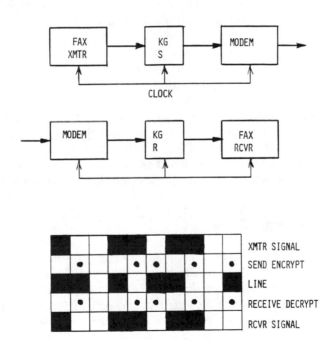

Figure 3.30 Digital fax encryption.

a regular telephone jack on the PSTN and the fax machine plugs into the data jack. The telephone, called STU III, is made in four different classes, depending on the degree of security authorized. The highest level of security is Type 1, for sending classified government documents. All of the classes make it extremely difficult and expensive to decode and display fax messages being sent even though the fax signals are intercepted and the interloper has a STU III telephone.

Type 4, the lowest security level, requires export approval for overseas use, but has the fewest restrictions on its use. It can be used by businesses worldwide to protect sensitive data from falling into unauthorized hands. It is not approved for sending U.S. government classified data.

Type 3 uses the data encryption standard (DES). This class of phone is limited to use within the United States with the exception of international fund transfer. Businesses such as banks and financial institutions are typical customers. Involvement in government programs is not required.

Type 2 (and Type 1) is controlled by the NSA (National Security Agency) and can be used by federal government contractors who need to send certain classes of government classified documents. The fax machine must be a special type that has been approved by the cognizant government agency for this use. The user of the phone is registered and is issued a special key. Use of the phone and the fax machine connected to it is generally limited to that person. Unless the STU III has SACS, the person called may answer the phone by voice before fax transmission starts and must remain there to receive the classified material. The phone must be locked up in a secure area at night and other times when not in use. The phone must only be operated in a secure environment that prevents interception of clear text signals before encoding. The secure phones will also operate with another secure phone at one level lower (Type 1 can work with Type 2 phones and so forth.)

Type 1 is for use only by authorized government personnel to send classified documents. Operating security restrictions are similar to those for Type 2 phones.

3.8.9 Fax/Phone Switch Boxes

Fax performs best when a separate telephone line is dedicated to its use. One advantage is that someone talking on the phone will not delay reception of important fax messages, but users who have only a small amount of fax traffic may want to consider a fax/phone switch box, or a fax machine with this feature built-in, to avoid the need for another line. When a call is received, the switch box connects the line to either the fax or the phone. It is fairly simple to access the phone line for placing an outgoing call by the telephone, fax machine, or PC. Without a fax switch, however, placing a call with a dial-pulse phone may confuse the fax or PC into thinking the pulses are ring signal from an incoming call and it will try to answer the call. As soon as it answers, the dial pulses are shorted and the voice call cannot be completed. Many different switch designs are available; some are complicated to use, some are unreliable, and some work reasonably well. Many low-cost fax machines now have switching built in, eliminating the need for a separate switch box.

Manual Transfer by the Receiving Party: Some fax installations avoid the complications of a fax switch by having the fax machine programmed to ring four or more times before answering. This gives time for answering the call if anyone is available or the fax machine will answer otherwise. If a fax call is answered by picking up the telephone, it is necessary to press a button on the fax machine to receive the fax call. With some systems, transfer after answering the phone can be made from the phone itself. The simplest and cheapest fax switches require the receiving party to press a button on the switch to transfer the call to the receiving fax machine. This simple manual switch is of little value. If it is in the fax position, a voice caller is greeted with the fax machine CED answer tone and the irritating (but distinctive) DIS signal.

Calling Party Manual Transfer: With tone dialing, one of the buttons on the caller's phone, often the # or *, makes the switch transfer the call to the fax machine. For pulse dialing, some fax switches claim the ability to have the caller dial a switch transfer command number, but this system may be unreliable. In the worst case, a caller may not be able to get through with a regular voice call. A few fax switches require the caller to say a certain word into the phone to transfer the call. This feature may be of value for a caller without tone dialing capability. Other fax switches require the caller to remain silent to perform the switch. This feature could cause an unintended switch to fax during a voice call. The caller must be told what to do when the fax switch answers the call because not everyone will know what to do in advance. A connection may be provided for a separate voice answering machine or answer message capability built into the fax switch.

Automatic Transfer of Received Call: Most, but not all, fax switches have the capability to detect CNG, the 1100-Hz tone sent by automatic calling fax units (and the manual fax units made in the last few years) when they are calling another fax. This signal alerts the switch that the incoming call is from a fax machine and connects it directly to the receiving fax machine.

The following additional features provided in some fax switches are worth considering:

Disconnect Detection: To prevent the phone line from accidentally being busied out when the caller has hung up or has been disconnected, the fax switch should automatically hang up under these conditions.

Barge-in Protection: This feature prevents someone from picking up a phone to make a call and disrupting momentarily or completely aborting the fax transmission. Optional lockout boxes for the phones are often required to provide this feature. If the fax machine has a telephone jack and all phones on this telephone number connect to telephone wires that originate at this jack, this feature usually is provided.

Access Code: Some fax switches allow an access code to be set to exclude all fax callers who do not know the code. It eliminates junk fax mail, but it also prevents reception of desired calls from anyone who does not have the code. It is similar to restricting your telephone callers to only those who enter a private code.

Night/Weekend Connection: Some fax switches can be set to connect all incoming calls to the fax machine while the office is closed. The timing of events in the switch box is important because the program must allow the receiving fax to answer before the 35-s timeout disconnects the calling fax machine. Many low-cost fax machines now have switching built in, eliminating the need for a separate switch box.

3.8.10 Soft Copy Fax Reception

Only recently has good readability been possible for received fax messages when viewed on the PC monitor. Although even the earliest PC-fax boards made it possible to show the received fax messages on screen, typed characters were almost impossible to read when the full line width was shown. Resolution of standard PC display technology was not adequate. Computer-generated ASCII characters could be read without strain when displayed in 80 columns across the screen, but not received fax pages. Each dot displayed for the internally generated computer font matches the optimum position for clarity of display. Fax, on the other hand, presents a much more difficult task. The random match between the scanning dot and the edge of a character causes much edge raggedness. Group 3 fax has 203 dpi across the page (1728 dots total) to print out sharp copy, while some PCs have only 320 dots across the screen. The only way to read such a fax on this type of display is to fill the screen with only a small portion of the page at one time. PC design has progressed to the point that higher resolution displays are common for the new PCs. The VGA display with 640 dots across the page is now the low-end standard, with 800 or 1024 dots across the page becoming the standard offering for PCs with 80386SX or better processor chips. This is a boon for PC-fax, making it unnecessary to print out the received page when the PC and the software provide high-resolution display of the fax image.

3.9 PC-FAX

A PC-fax board, installed in a personal computer vacant slot, allows it to emulate a Group 3 fax machine. The keyboard operator selects commands from a screen menu to go through the steps needed to transfer text or image files. Like a Group 3 fax, the PC automatically negotiates the highest sending speed possible, then sends. More time is usually needed before starting to send, however, than with a Group 3 fax. A document is composed and edited on the computer screen in the normal manner to make a computer file. TSR (terminate and stay resident) software provides a hot key to call up the PC-fax program directly from the computer applications program in use. Menu-driven screens guide the user through the necessary steps. The telephone number of the receiving fax machine is selected from a directory stored in the computer. Word processing, ASCII, and other computer files can be converted to Group 3 format, either in advance of calling or while being sent as a fax signal to the selected Group 3 fax machine. When sending faxes from a PC, the image sent does not exist as hard copy (see Figure 3.31).

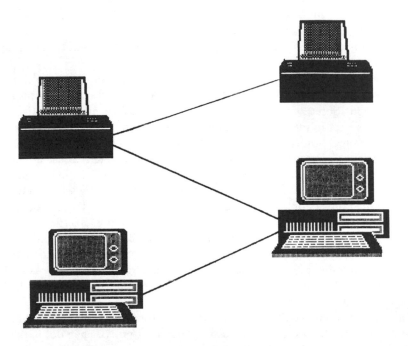

Figure 3.31 Use of PC-fax.

The items in the following description of PC-fax boards are not furnished by some PC-fax board designs. The modem incorporated on many PC-fax boards is the same CCITT V.29, V.27$_{ter}$, V.21 modem used in Group 3 fax units. It is programmed to attempt first to send at 9.6 kb/s, with the ability to step down to 7.2, 4.8, or 2.4 kb/s, if required by the telephone line characteristics. PC-fax boards with V.17, 14.4 kb/s modems may be available by the time this book is published. When a PC-fax receives the document is usually stored as a file on the computer disk. Received files may be viewed from the computer screen display as soft copy, or a hard copy can be made on a dot matrix, laser, or other bit-mapped printer. PC-fax units may compress the image with MH coding before storage. A page in storage typically takes 50 to 60K of memory, but up to 100K may be required. While a hard disk is not necessary for this service, without one, only a few pages can be stored. The computer can organize the documents in memory by dates, subjects, or originator to simplify search and retrieval.

Background operation of the computer with some PC-fax designs allows reception of facsimile copies without interruption of other work being done by the computer. One or more directory lists of telephone numbers can be stored in the computer for use with fax transmissions. These numbers can easily be retrieved for automatic calling for immediate or delayed transmission of fax documents. Delayed transmission may be specified to send at the time of lowest telephone line charges. Broadcast by sequential calling of a group of fax units may be used for automatically sending identical documents.

Security against unwanted viewing of the received document is good on a PC-fax. On most Group 3 fax units, the pages are stacked in a tray for any passerby to pick up and read. Some of the PC-fax and fax units have a mailbox option, where the document is kept in memory until accessed by means of a password. To prevent unauthorized interception and printing, the fax signal can be encrypted as it is passed from the applications program to disk storage. An intercepted signal could not be decoded without the proper encryption key (see Section 3.8.8). Finding the proper key by trial and error is almost impossible. Although some of the less expensive PC-fax units require conversion of files to Group 3 format before dialing the fax receiver, many PC-fax units will send ASCII files directly as Group 3 fax files. Non-ASCII word processing, spreadsheet, and graphic files may be sent in a similar manner. From the menu selection, the PC is given the print command for a particular printer specified by the PC-fax program. The fax signal addressed to the printer is redirected to a disk file. It has been stripped of control characters and stored as an ASCII file, which is then sent in Group 3 fax format.

The received copy quality is better when sent from a PC-fax board than a Group 3 fax machine. The PC-fax uses a character generator to place each dot in the matrix for a character in the optimum position for the typeface used (similar to the display on a PC screen). When a fax machine scans a character, the dot matrix formed depends on the exact character position related to the scan. The black dot pattern sent for a given character scanned a number of times will have different nonoptimum renditions. Figure 3.32 is a computer printout of a Group 3 scanned image. Notice that none of the fax-printed letters has the same pattern.

Integrated circuit (IC) chips for compressing the facsimile signals have both Group 3 and 4 standards, providing the capability for resolutions of 200, 300, and 400 dpi. To lower costs, most PC-fax boards use software for MH compression only. Costs to the user are usually higher though, since a longer time is needed to send documents.

Some fax boards incorporate 300 dpi as an alternative Group 3 system resolution. The 300-dpi laser and ink-jet printers or high-resolution dot matrix printers

Figure 3.32 White and black single pel on edge.

provide a better resolution copy between PC-fax board users when receiving documents scanned at 300 dpi. This feature, available now, could have a negative effect on the demand for Group 4 facsimile units. It may be difficult, though, to find a laser printer-compatible PC-fax board that will produce printing as sharp as a standard fax machine. Many PC-fax boards convert the 203-dpi received fax signal into 150 dpi on the laser printer rather than converting to 300 dpi.

A portable computer capable of mobile operation can be fitted with a PC-fax board for Group 3 communication in an automobile or other vehicle using a cellular phone system. See Section 11.1.5 for problems encountered when operating on cellular phone systems.

PC users wishing to send text files have been hampered by the lack of a universally accepted PC data communication standard. Users now can easily emulate Group 3 fax to send information to the 20 million Group 3 fax machines connected to the regular telephone network (PSTN). Most of these fax units are available 24 hours a day, like a regular telephone. Some PC-fax systems allow binary file transfer of computer data between PCs at 9.6 or 14.4 kb/s with the high-speed fax modems. This capability greatly reduces the telephone line charges compared to 1200 or 300 b/s with the commonly used Hayes-compatible modems. See Section 3.11 for information on the new standardized system for binary file transfer.

PC-fax boards offer some clear advantages over the Group 3 fax machines. These include:

1. The ability to print received fax copies on regular white paper rather than thermal paper. A 300-dpi laser printer is best, but even a good dot matrix printer will give satisfactory copy. Most fax machines record at 203 dpi on thermal sensitive paper, which has some handling and appearance problems. (Compared with plain paper fax, which is now becoming quite popular, there is no advantage to thermal sensitive paper.)

2. The copy can be viewed on screen by the user either as it is being received or when the transmission is completed. A high-resolution screen is required for satisfactory viewing unless an enlarging feature is used to observe a section at a time. Even the super VGA resolution of a 1024×768 screen gives less than half the resolution of a normal fax page and less than one-quarter that of fine resolution.

3. Computer-generated documents can be sent directly from the computer without first printing them out and then scanning them. The copy quality at the receiving fax machine is much better since edges of types and other markings are indexed to the fax signal rather than being random. A given typed character always has the same optimized matrix of dots produced by the computer. The same character when scanned at different positions on the page may have 10 or more different dot matrices, none of them optimum. Misalignment between

the scanning sample spot area and the edges of the markings accounts for the ragged appearance of scanned text.

4. Better security; printouts exist for only those authorized to see them.

Disadvantages of PC-fax include:

1. Existing documents cannot be sent unless a scanner is connected to the fax machine.
2. For PCs using a DOS operating system, there may be memory allocation problems that prevent things from working as expected. The computer may not have enough memory to load the PC-fax program or to run regular computer application programs after the software has been loaded. Even PC-fax programs that require only a small amount of memory after loading may take a large amount of memory while being loaded for use. Since modern word processing and other programs use a large portion of the basic 640 Kbytes low memory, where the fax software is also loaded, the PC can't load both programs. This may happen even if the PC has many megabytes of unused RAM in extended memory. When the PC-fax software is installed as memory resident (TSR), a memory manager software program may be tried to load it into high DOS memory (640 K to 1000 Kbytes). This might work, but there may not be enough room available in one contiguous memory slot.
3. For even simple transmissions, users must have some computer knowledge, whereas they can send via Group 3 fax machines with a minimum of effort (i.e., inserting the document into a tray and pressing a button or two).
4. Only a few combinations of PC-fax boards and software provide a selection of fonts or for sending computer generated imagery.

Cover sheets for the first page of a fax transmission can be generated automatically from memory, inserting a company logo. Some PC-fax adapters have the ability to discriminate between an incoming call of the telephone line. The fax board answers if the call is from a fax machine or the telephone rings if a voice call is received. It works in a manner similar to the one described in Section 3.8.9, which is based on detecting a CNG tone from the calling fax machine. Most PC-fax adapters will operate at a maximum speed of 9.6 kb/s and some of these boards cost less than $150. Background transmission capability is very desirable. The PC-fax adapter ideally should incorporate its own microprocessor to handle fast activities to free the host PC to regular computing chores while there is fax activity. If the host microprocessor is used for fax, other PC functions are stopped, turning the computer into an expensive fax machine.

Some companies offer a Group 3 fax adapter that connects between a computer and a laser printer and performs the same functions as a PC-fax board. Connection is made directly to the telephone line and memory in the adapter stores incoming faxes if the laser printer is in use. This memory is also utilized for sending Group

3 fax. Conversion of files sent from the PC is done in the adapter. Alternatively, when sending between the same type of units, character data from the PC (instead of Group 3 fax signals) can be sent to the receiving unit adapter and printed with the same 300-dpi resolution as a laser printer at the sending PC. Software provides the same flexibility as the high-level PC-fax boards.

The fax adapter can be installed with operation from a DOS prompt or with TSR PC memory of 10K to 100K, depending on the features wanted. Some PC-fax boards provide similar features when using a laser printer, but the fax adapter does not require removing the PC cover for installation of a PC card. This is a computer dedicated to sending and receiving Group 3 fax on up to four PSTN lines simultaneously. Multiple documents going to the same location are assembled and sent with a single call to maximize efficiency and lower phone costs. If one of the telephone lines being used for broadcast goes out of service, the task is automatically allocated to the remaining lines and notice is provided of the need for service. The document to be sent is entered via a keyboard. A multiline receive-and-print feature allows receiving directly to hard disk over four or six lines simultaneously and to print on a laser printer, either as received or on demand from memory.

3.10 CELLULAR RADIO FAX

Cellular radio allows automobiles and other vehicles to communicate with regular telephones, using one of 832 channels available in the 800-MHz band. Signals are broadcast between the phone's antenna and transceivers located within each cell's coverage area, a radius of 2 to 12 miles. To ensure continuous coverage, the cells overlap. A central computer switch, called a *mobile telephone switching office* (MTSO), monitors the signal quality on the channels and switches to another cell when the quality drops below a certain threshold. A brief loss of signal occurs during the switching, from 200 to 1200 ms. Callers often hear a low click during the switching, and the conversation continues normally. With fax in use, this will cause a streak about 1/16th in. across the page. The frequency of cell changing is unpredictable and fax pages may have no streaks, or up to 10 streaks per page. Switching may also result in a failure message at the fax transmitter, caused by too many received errors, or cause a disconnect. Cellular networks also produce lower quality transmissions because they are line-of-sight radio systems, subject to loss of signal, multipath, and fading due to physical obstructions, reflections from buildings, and distance. Use of the Group 3 fax error-correction mode is desirable.

With some limitations, cellular radio works very well for voice, but not as well for fax. Encryption of the fax signals may be important when sending sensitive information because programmable scanners can be set up to intercept cellular radio transmissions. Digital cellular radio may be much better, but in Europe and the United States, the competing digital systems still have not been standardized. The future of mobile fax with new cellular radio developments in the United States is not clear. Elimination of all technical restrictions on the types of radio technologies that can be used, including abandonment of current cellular compatibility requirements, was proposed by the Federal Communication Commission in 1987. There is no assurance that a cellular unit will work outside one's home region.

The time-division multiple access (TDMA) system, already adopted in Japan and many European countries, allows three users per channel instead of one user per channel with the current analog system. Some companies in North America were starting to produce equipment for TDMA digital cellular radio phone systems, but a different proposal is gaining supporters. The alternative code-division multiple access (CDMA) digital system should allow more than six times the capacity of the TDMA system, providing the extra channels that might be needed by fax in the future. CDMA has an individual code for each telephone and encryption to prevent eavesdropping. Extra CDMA cells can be added without requiring any changes to existing assignments of radio-frequencies or telephone numbers because all cells use the same radio-frequency. CDMA has been used by the military for many years.

3.11 ASYNCHRONOUS FACSIMILE DCE CONTROL STANDARDS

The purpose of these standards is to define a digital interface between data terminal equipment (DTE) such as a PC and Group 3 fax standards, allowing the DTE to access a Group 3 fax machine or other fax data communication equipment (DCE) for the functions of scanning, printing, and communication on the PSTN. The other DCEs include PC-fax boards that plug into a PC and external fax adapters.

Some fax boards have been furnished with the capability to use the high-speed Group 3 fax modems and ECM protocols for sending of binary data between computers, but different vendors used different interface techniques, making them incompatible with the PC software. Each fax modem vendor needed to develop its own applications software—a large job. The purpose of these standards is to define a common command language so vendors who write software for PCs can be sure their product will be compatible with multiple hardware vendors.

3.11.1 Background

A modem is data communication equipment (DCE) that allows data terminal equipment (DTE), such as a PC, to send digital signals over regular analog telephone channels (PSTN). The interface connection between the PC (DTE) and the modem (DCE) was standardized many years ago by the EIA as RS-232 (EIA-232-E in 1989) and by the CCITT as V.24, allowing PC manufacturers and modem manufacturers to build equipment that works together without having to customize the interface to match special characteristics between the devices. The connectors, circuit leads furnished, and electrical characteristics for each lead are specified. A shielded EIA-232 cable plugs into the RS-232 port on the computer and into the EIA-232 port of the modem (see Figure 3.33). EIA-574 describes the alternative 9-pin data connector commonly used on PCs.

The cable carries a serial asynchronous bidirectional data stream. Line drivers are required at each end of the cable to allow the devices being connected to be up to 50 ft apart (special cables allow greater distances). A power supply furnishing $+12$ V and -12 V is normally used for the line drivers. Modern serial interface standards use ± 5 volts.

When Group 3 digital fax standards were being developed, the set of modems needed was not available as a single device. The V.27$_{ter}$ 4.8 kb/s CCITT modem standard for use on the PSTN had just been adopted. The V.21 modem was available, but Group 3 needed only the return channel, for 300 b/s handshake signaling. The high-speed V.29 9.6 kb/s modem standard was being developed for use on 4-wire conditioned private telephone lines. Fortunately, CCITT Study Group XVII and the U.S. modem manufacturers assisted, and modem card sets with all of the wanted functions were available before the Group 3 fax standards were adopted. The modem card sets were incorporated inside the fax machine without line drivers or the other *bells and whistles* of a complete modem.

Those modem functions not easily available through the EIA-232 interface leads of a standard modem simplified the machine design, but there were no standards for the interface between the fax machine and the modem functions. The cost to the fax machine manufacturers of the first modem card sets (including 9.6 kb/s speed) was about 10% of what a 9.6 kb/s complete modem sold for at the time. Without this fortuitous combination, Group 3 fax may have been too expensive to succeed and the modem manufacturers may have lost their first large high-speed modem market.

The use of the PC for business communication increased greatly when the PC-fax board became available. The PC was then able to send and receive files to Group 3 fax machines. The technical name for the hardware covered in these standards is *fax adapter*. The term covers both *fax boards* and the *fax box* that are used in this book to distinguish between the types of fax adapters. The PC-fax board plugs into a vacant slot in the PC, directly interfacing the PC processor bus (see Figure 3.34).

An alternative arrangement uses as external box containing a fax modem set that plugs into the PC through the EIA-232 connector (see Figure 3.35).

The Asynchronous Facsimile Control Standards apply directly only to this arrangement. However, because a PC processor bus provides a character serial bidirectional data stream, PC-fax boards installed inside the PC are now using the same protocols, particularly if they also include V.22$_{bis}$ or V.32 serial modem services.

For sending ASCII files as fax pages, the PC generates a bit-mapped file as would be needed by a graphics printer. A character generator assembles, in memory, a row of characters across the page. The serial bit stream next generated is similar

Figure 3.33 PC communication interfaces.

```
PC      FAX BOARD            FAX BOARD      PC
DTE<====>DCE<=====PSTN=====>DCE<=====>DTE
```
PC bus   telephone line   PC bus

Figure 3.34 PC communication with a fax board.

```
PC          FAX BOX              FAX BOX          PC
DTE <=======> DCE <=====PSTN=====>DCE <=======> DTE
```
          cable   telephone line   cable
     EIA-232   EIA-232   EIA-232   EIA-232
     Interface Interface   Interface Interface

Figure 3.35 PC communication with a fax box.

to one from a fax machine scanner. An encoder provides modified Huffman digital code words from a look-up table. These words are sent over the PSTN by the modem. The sequence occurs in reverse at the receiver. Handshake commands and responses are generated, and control functions are performed.

With PC-fax boards, CCITT Recommendations T.4 and T.30 provided the standards for making PC files compatible with Group 3 standards and sending files to fax machines worldwide. There was no standard for how and which functions were provided by the computer, however, and each manufacturer had his own method of emulating Group 3 fax. Lack of standardization forced much customization of software. Both the software programs designed to run the PC-fax operation and the application programs with fax drivers were affected. The features provided by different PC-fax adapters varied widely, and adding any new feature was expensive.

The U.S. manufacturers of PC-fax boards prevailed upon the EIA TR-29 Facsimile Equipment and Engineering Committee to set up a subcommittee TR-29.2, Digital Facsimile Interfaces (Joe Deuir, Chair), to develop the standards needed. TR 29.2 is working on a set of standards described in this section.

Equipment is being manufactured that uses the Class 1 interface, and those for Class 2 should be available soon. These standards define an interface with an asynchronous serial bidirectional data stream between the PC (DTE) and a fax adapter (DCE) that contains a fax modem and other parts needed to emulate Group 3 fax operation on the PSTN. The data stream carries the Hayes AT command set commonly used for computer modems, with extensions for commands issued by the PC to configure and control the PC-fax adapter, and responses of the PC-fax adapter. It is expected that a CCITT standard will be based on this work. These standards restore the modem parts and protocols that were originally removed by Group 3 fax in the interest of cost and simplicity. The protocols can be used for interfaces to scanners, printers, LANs, SCSI, ANSI X3.1311, etc. Vendors who write software for PCs are now assured that their product will be compatible with multiple hardware vendors for PC-fax adapters and for other devices wanting to communicate with Group 3 fax machines. Protocols and procedures to adapt alternative communication schemes are beyond the scope of these standards. Three interface service classes (levels) in the communication path between the PC and the PC-fax adapter are being standardized as the functional partition.

A fax call is handled in the standard Group 3 protocol of five phases:

Phase A: Dialing and answering a fax call

Phase B: Selecting modem speed and matching fax specifications

Phase C: Sending fax signals for the page being copied

Phase D: Confirmation of fax page received successfully

Phase E: Disconnect phone line after last page.

3.11.2 Service Class 1 (EIA-578)

This is the simplest interface and is usually associated with a very small PC-fax adapter that would fit in a lap-top or portable PC. The PC-fax adapter provides interface with the PC, auto-dial functions, $V.27_{ter}$ (or optionally V.29 and V.17) modem functions for sending the fax data, V.22 with HDLC data formatting for T.30 commands and responses (handshaking), and PSTN interface through its LCU. It describes a set of services at the physical and data link layers: waiting, signaling, and HDLC data formatting. The DCE might be described as a tone generator/detector and data pump (sends and receives 1s and 0s with HDLC framing without any knowledge of their meaning).

The PC provides T.30 session management and the T.4 functions of MH/MR image coding and formatting of the data for each fax scanning line. These PC functions require substantial processing, so background operation of the facsimile function is difficult.

3.11.3 Service Class 2 (EIA-592)

In addition to the Class 1 functions, Class 2 includes a set of services described in CCITT T.30. The PC-fax board makes and terminates calls, manages the communication session, and transports image data. The PC prepares and interprets image data in compressed form as specified in CCITT T.4. Commands are sent from the PC to the fax adapter while it is in a command state. The Hayes AT command set is used, including extensions for fax commands. Service Class 2 also includes facilities establishing a data link protocol between the DTE and DCE to protect and recover from loss of data due to DTE system latency, multitasking, etc. Optional features include copy quality checking and fault conversions and control of scanners, printers, and local storage in fax machines.

3.11.4 Service Class 3

Service Class 3 was not ready for ballot when this book was published. In addition to the features provided in Class 2, the facsimile DCE converts image file data into CCITT T.4 compressed images for transmission, and reverses the conversion on reception. Tagged image file format (TIFF) and ASCII text are examples of file formats under study.

3.11.5 Group 3 Facsimile Apparatus Control (PN-1906)

PCs or other DTEs may now have the ability to interface with scanners, printers, and modems. Group 3 fax machines provide these functions, but there is no standard for the DTE to use these features. PN-1906 is developing a standard digital interface that allows DTE access to these functions. The scanner may provide the PC with imagery in various formats such as uncompressed bitmaps, modified Huffman, TIFF, pack bits, and/or GIFF formats. Formats printed on the fax machine may include TIFF, Epson, ASCII, Postscript, and/or HP Laserjet PCL, plus the standard facsimile formats. The PC should be able to control the fax machine and to provide or share storage for documents and phone numbers. Interworking will be provided for the above Service Classes 1, 2, and 3.

3.12 BINARY FILE TRANSFER

Binary file transfer (BFT) is a method of using the Group 3 fax protocols and high-speed modem to transfer computer files. A PC with a PC-fax board uses the same board for either fax or data transfer between computers. The Group 3 handshake, starting when the called computer answers a call, is all automatic. It is not necessary for the caller to have any knowledge of the capabilities of the PC being called except that it has BFT capability. Nothing has to be set by the caller to match the called machine; not bits per character, parity, or error correction used. The Group 3 fax ECM is a standard part of the BFT protocol. The protocols of Group 3 fax are extended to provide for the additional BFT function without affecting the Group 3 compatibility of existing Group 3 fax machines. The coding rules of BFT are technically aligned with ISO standard 8751, File Transfer, Access, and Management. A virtual file store describes a file system that is independent of its underlying physical hardware or operating system. Using BFT, a telematic service can transfer data files between apparatus for eventual storage on the real file store of the destination. BFT protocol is useful in transferring files in a teletex service transparent mode, or in a message handling service. This standard was prepared by EIA/TIA TR-29.1, Subcommittee on Binary File Transfer as SP-2225 (Phil Bogosian, Chair). As this book was written, BFT was undergoing final approval as an EIA standard. CCITT Study Group VIII has agreed to use the BFT standard for fax and teletex.

3.13 AUDIOGRAPHIC TELECONFERENCING TRANSMISSION

The CCITT and ETSI and EIA/TIA are developing somewhat different approaches for image transfer in teleconferencing systems. Neil Starkey of EIA/TIA TR-29 is the special CCITT rapporteur and editor of the EIA/TIA effort. EIA/TIA-586, Procedures for Audiographic Teleconferencing Transmission, should be issued before this book is published.[2] It defines the procedures for conducting a real-time audiographic conference between participants located at two or more locations interconnected by telecommunication networks. The protocol permits black-and-white, gray-scale, and color image transmission. The network is assumed to consist of synchronous channels of arbitrary capacity ranging from 2.4 to 2048 kb/s. Multiport image transmission and real-time interaction (draw, point, zoom, etc.) on the softcopy image are supported. The standard defines the communication protocol and is not hardware specific. Bit-mapped graphics are used at equivalent resolutions of 100 or 200 dots/in. Group 3 fax CCITT T.4 one- or two-dimensional image compression techniques may used with a K factor of infinity.

The ETSI Technical Committee is working on a standard that allows teleconferencing via the ISDN using one or two 64 kb/s channels. The communication devices that may be combined with speech are fax, still-picture television (SPTV), telewriter, or telematic terminal. Either point-to-point or multipoint communication will be used, depending on the audiographic teleconference needs. The physical layer multiplexing is provided by CCITT Recommendation H.221, providing a measure of compatibility with videoconferencing/videophone recommendations adopted by

---

[2]Standards proposal number 2087 is in the final stage of the EIA standardization procedures.

CCITT in 1990. For a basic service, only one 64 kb/s channel is available. Fax will have 8 kb/s and speech will have 48 kb/s. For special cases such as high-speed facsimile, a second 64 kb/s channel can, in principle, be used. It is possible to use the second 64 kb/s channel temporarily, on an on-demand basis, only during moments in the meeting when it is required. Not all Group 3 fax machines can be used for this service. The machine chosen must be capable of 2-wire private line operation and nonstandard facilities (NSF). An interface protocol adapter (IPA) connected between the network and the fax machine is programmed to adapt the facsimile protocol to the network requirements. Facsimile data at 7.2 or 4.8 kb/s is assembled into 1024-bit HDLC frames for network use. The frames are transmitted on the 8 kb/s multiplexed channel to the IPA at the receiving fax machine where they are converted into the Group 3 facsimile protocol. Sending may be to more than one fax machine simultaneously for a multipoint audiographic conference. If the sending fax has more pages to transmit, it must wait for responses from all receiving fax machines. As a substitute for the PSTN ringing signal of Phase A, the procedure interrupt signal (PIS) of 462 Hz is sent to the receiving fax machines for 3 s. Each receiving fax machine then responds using T.30 protocol, starting with the NSF signal. Phases B through D operate as specified in T.30. Phase E, call release, is not required.

The CCITT is working on a series of recommendations for audiographics conferencing. Recommendation F.710, defining the audiographics service, was adopted in 1990. It provides for real-time interaction for a broad class of black and white through full-color still images on a range of networks including ISDN, packet switched, and PSTN. Facsimile images are one class of images to be supported. SGVIII is now developing recommendations to implement the service. Four recommendations are anticipated: T.AGC is the real-time image transfer and interaction protocol; T.AGT and T.MCU specify the lower layer protocol stacks for the various networks for the audiographic terminal and multipoint control unit respectively. These recommendations will be aligned with the audiovisual series for audio and video conferencing providing for an integrated audio, graphics, and video solution on the ISDN.

REFERENCES

[1]   "V.17 Facsimile Communications Test," Report for CCITT from MCI, Rockwell, Xerox. EIA/TIA TR-29/91-27, May 1991.

[2]   CCITT Recommendation T.30, Fascicle VII.3, Note 2, p. 97.

[3]   J.C. Stoffel, *Graphical and Binary Images Processing and Applications,* Norwood, Mass.: Artech House, 1982, p. 295.

Chapter 4
Group 4 Facsimile

4.1 THE GROUP 4 STANDARD

The market for Group 4 is quite different from the stand-alone, person-to-person communication that Group 3 now covers so well. Group 4 is better suited to computer-controlled network communication with multiaddress, store-and-forward, and electronic mail (message) systems.

Although the CCITT adopted recommendations for Group 4 in 1984, work continues to complete the standardization. The recommendation specifies the OSI seven-layer model, but none of the U.S. networks exactly matches its requirements. Full compliance is planned in the future.

Some digital communication services offer Group 4 compatibility now, but worldwide connection to other parties is very limited. Operation of Group 4 machines on the regular telephone network (PSTN) is possible, but not in accordance with the Group 4 standards. The CCITT is still in the process of selecting a modem for the PSTN.

For the present, Group 4 will be limited to very specialized applications. Group 4 facsimile will not even start to replace Group 3 units until 1994. The regular telephone network is slowly being converted to an all-digital network that eventually may be a part of the ISDN. When the PSTN becomes the ISDN, Group 4 will have the same worldwide network availability that Group 3 enjoys now.

Groups 3 and 4 use the same techniques to process the picture signal before converting it to digital. The analog video output from the scanner is sampled and converted to a binary digital (black-white) signal. This is done by either a simple fixed-level slicing circuit or one that dynamically senses the background level. The Group 4 facsimile scanner and printer must be capable of storing at least one page of compressed data. Meeting this requirement should cause no problem because existing designs typically store 60 pages or more. Groups 1, 2, and 3 fax units did not include the traditional DTE/DCE interface because the modem was built-in. For Group 4 apparatus, a standard physical digital interface provides connection to the packet and circuit services of public data networks. In the future, the ISDN will be used for digital communication.

Computer Communications with Group 4: Group 4 facsimile is expected to usher in a new era in the facsimile business when ISDN becomes available everywhere. In addition to fax transmission to another user as in Group 3 facsimile, Group 4 will be an I/O device for a remote computer. There is now a limited degree of facsimile-computer interaction utilizing PC-fax on the PSTN. A few computer applications for Group 4 facsimile are discussed in the following:

Electronic Mail: The public data network can be accessed for the exchange of business mail.

Storage and Retrieval: Documents can be stored in a computer with availability for printing on a remote Group 4 fax unit.

Integration of Text with Graphics: Graphic data can be entered into a computer by a Group 4 scanner for use in a graphics and word-processing system. The operator will have the ability to add textual information or change the actual graphic image. The document could then be stored and distributed to Group 4 printers.

Optical Character Recognition (OCR) and Analysis of Graphic Data: Raw symbol and character data could be scanned by a Group 4 device and stored in a computer system, where pattern recognition could be performed.

4.1.1 The Seven-Layer OSI Model

The International Organization for Standardization (ISO) developed the seven-layer reference model of Open Systems Interconnection (OSI). The overall objective of the OSI is to define standards allowing systems to communicate. As new standards are developed, existing standards are retained where possible. Subcommittee 16 (on OSI interconnection) of Committee 97 started the standard-making project in 1977. The reference model became the international standard IS 7498 in October 1984.

OSI provides the framework to ensure that all communication standards developed are compatible. A system that obeys applicable OSI standards in its communication with other systems is termed an "open system," often referred to as a "distributed system" in the United States. The OSI open systems concept is based on the need for an application process such as a Group 4 fax or other device anywhere in the world to interact with any application process at another location. The protocols will make possible worldwide linkage of computers and terminals from different vendors, electronic-mail systems, Group 4 fax units, and other application processes. As a result, competitive products and lower prices are expected. Users will have a choice of vendors and a variety of communication equipment. Manufacturers and vendors will have improved productivity and a broader market base.

Communication between Group 4 fax units or with other devices (application processes) is broken down into seven subtasks called layers. Each layer groups certain related aspects of data communication (see Figure 4.1).

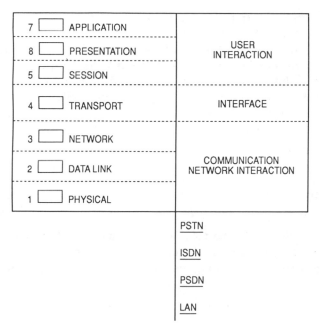

Figure 4.1 The OSI model.

A logical order was required for the continuum of functions involved, leading to the layering technique. Too many layers would make the structure overly complex, while too few would lead to the development of very complicated protocols. The decision on the structure was selected to be acceptable to the widest range of interests, both technically and politically. A seven-layer structure was developed and gained worldwide acceptance as the basis for the OSI architecture.

Each layer can be thought of as an envelope with the written information on the outside indicating where and how to deliver the contents. The actual data transmitted are in the innermost envelope. The seven envelopes used at the transmitting end are stripped off one at a time for each layer of the receiving end. The control information on the outside of each envelope is nondata information called *overhead*. This must be sent in addition to the data. For packet-switched networks, this overhead is quite high. Therefore, facsimile is not well suited to transmission over packet-switched networks. Architecture is still being developed for a complete family of interfaces and protocols for worldwide distributed information and telecommunication systems.

The following is an example of the type of service that may be provided under OSI. After initially programming the Group 4 fax unit, a letter could be typed with a "copies to" list. The fax unit looks up the calling numbers stored in its memory for the names on the "copies to" list and automatically sends to all of their offices.

If programmed into the receiving fax unit, the letter would be delivered to any location in the world where the recipient happened to be.

In the United States, OSI recently received a boost. As of 1990, all federal government purchasing of networks must conform to OSI standards, as specified in the Government Open Systems Interconnection Profile (GOSIP). Some analysts believe the federal purchasing mandate and the strong support for the model in Europe will make OSI networks commonplace by 1995.

Modifications of the original reference model reflect new services such as:

Connectionless-mode transmission

Security architecture

Naming and addressing

Management framework.

ISO specification IS 7498 is identical to the CCITT specification X.200 reference model of OSI developed by Study Group VII. Figure 4.2 shows some of the standards that are applicable to Group 4 facsimile and how they interface with other telematic services.

Layer 7—Application

The highest level, the application layer, is the user interface between Group 4 fax or other service and the OSI environment. The application process can be manual, such as operation of an automated banking terminal, a computerized process where a program running in a computer center accesses a remote database, or a physical process whereby a robotic arm is controlled remotely by a computer program.

A great amount of work is continuing on the following application layer standards:

- T.563 Terminal Characteristics for Group 4 Facsimile Apparatus
- T.521 Communications Application Profile BT0 for Document Bulk Transfer Using the Session Service Defined in Recommendation T.62bis
- T.503 A Document Application Profile for the Interchange of Group 4 Facsimile Documents
- Recommendation T.6 Facsimile Coding Schemes and Coding Control Functions for Group 4 Facsimile Apparatus.

Recommendations T.521, T.503, and T.563 appear in the new CCITT Blue Book as replacements for Recommendation T.5, General Aspects of Group 4 Facsimile Apparatus, as it is defined in the CCITT Red Book.

Layer 6—Presentation

The presentation layer protocol handles session establishment and termination requests, and it preserves the meaning of the data while resolving syntax differences.

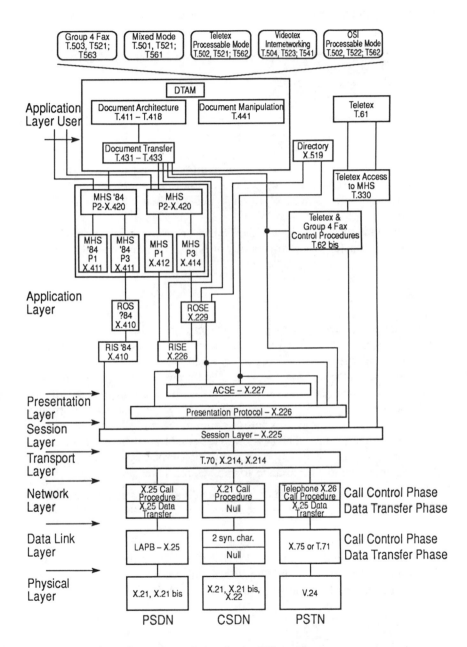

Figure 4.2 Group 4 facsimile recommendations in the OSI model.

The formats are selected for data and control signals. The most important standards currently in place are:

- X.226 Presentation Protocol Specification for Open Systems Interconnection for CCITT Applications
- X.208 Abstract Syntax Notation One (ASN.1)
- X.209 Basic Encoding Rules for ASN.1.

The ISO has counterparts to these standards. Recommendation X.226 specifies the procedure for transfer of data and control information from the presentation layer of the sending system to that of the receiving system.

Recommendation X.208 is used as a semiformal tool to define protocols and a mechanism for the transfer of user data. A number of simple types (i.e., integer, character, real) are defined. These simple types are then used to form more complicated ones.

Recommendation X.209 is a set of basic encoding rules used to derive the specification of a transfer syntax for values of types that have been defined by using X.208.

Layer 5—Session

The session layer protocol establishes, manages, and releases the communication connection. This layer provides functions such as the start and end of document transmission, acknowledgment of pages received, and error recovery if abnormal conditions are encountered. Documents may be transmitted in one direction or be part of a two-way exchange within the same session. Session protocol functions as a mediator between application processes. It synchronizes dialogue by binding and unbinding the application processes into a communicating relationship and helps to manage the exchange of data. The session layer combines different applications into a common language for calling another application process.

Recommendations of importance to the session layer are:

- X.215 Session Service Definition for Open Systems Interconnection for CCITT Applications. X.215 defines the services provided to the presentation layer by the session layer.
- T.62bis Control Procedures for Telex and Group 4 Facsimile Services Based on Recommendations X.215/X.225. T.62bis defines the set of rules for using the OSI session services and the additional requirements to conform to the control procedures for both teletex and Group 4 facsimile services.

Layer 4—Transport

The transport layer provides a communication path to other desired functions as a bridge between the application-related functions and the transmission-related functions. Additionally, it provides a consistent transport service in association with the lower three layers.

Functions performed by this layer are:

- Error recovery
- Error detection
- Flow control
- Multiplexing.

Recommendations of importance to the transport layer include:

- T.70 Network-Independent Basic Transport Service for the Telematic Services. T.70 defines the network-independent basic transport service applicable to both teletex and Group 4 facsimile terminals connected to the CSDN, PSDN, and PSTN. Transport layer procedures for ISDN are subject to further study.
- X.214 Transport Service Definition for Open Systems Interconnection (OSI) for CCITT Applications. X.214 defines the services provided by the transport layer to the session layer at their boundary.
- X.224 Transport Protocol Specification for Open Systems Interconnection for CCITT Applications. X.224 defines a common encoding and different classes of transport protocol procedures to be used with various networks and their quality of service. In addition, mechanisms are defined to enhance the quality of service as it relates to throughput rates, error rates, integrity of data requirements, and reliability requirements.

Layer 3—Network

Routing and relay functions through switched telecommunication media are the primary functions of the network layer. The means to establish, maintain, and terminate the network connections between systems is also under the network layer's control. Network connection is transparent to the transport entities, ensuring that service provided at each end of the network connection will be the same. This holds true even if the end-to-end connection spans several subnetworks.

Standards of importance to the network layer include:

- X.25 Interface Between Data Terminal Equipment (DTE) and Data Circuit Terminating Equipment (DCE) for Terminals Operating in the Packet Mode and Connected to Public Data Networks by Dedicated Circuit. X.25 defines mechanical, electrical, functional, and procedural characteristics to activate and deactivate the physical links between the DTE and DCE. In addition, it defines the packet layer procedures for the exchange of control information as well as for user data at the DTE-DCE interface.
- X.21 Interface Between Data Terminal Equipment (DTE) and Data Circuit-Terminating Equipment (DCE) for Synchronous Operation on Public Data

Networks. X.21 defines both the physical characteristics and call control procedures for a general-purpose interface between DTE and DCE employing synchronous transmission operating on public data networks.

Layer 2—Data Link

The major function of the data link layer is reliable transfer of all information over the physical transmission media. The maintenance and release of data link connections among all network entities is performed within this layer. Additionally, it is responsible for detecting and correcting errors that may occur in the physical layer and enabling the network layer to control the interconnection of data circuits within the physical layer.

Recommendations of importance to this layer include:

- X.75 Terminal and Transit Call Control Procedures and Data Transfer System on International Circuits Between Packet-Switched Data Networks. X.75 defines the physical, data link, and network layer protocols used for interworking between two packet-switched public data networks.
- T.71 LAPB Extended for Half-Duplex Physical Level Facility. T.71 defines the LAPB protocols at the data link layer for DTES operating in the packet mode to access a public data network or for two directly connected packet mode DTEs to communicate.

Layer 1—Physical

The physical layer deals with the transmission of a bit stream, regardless of its meaning, across a physical communication medium. This medium may be copper wires, optical fibers, or a radio link. The physical layer provides mechanical, electrical, functional, and procedural characteristics to activate, maintain, and deactivate physical connections to the transmission media. Connections may be either point-to-point or multipoint.

Recommendations of importance to this layer are:

- X.21bis Use on Public Data Networks of Data Terminal Equipment (DTE) Which Is Designed for Interfacing to Synchronous V-Series Modems. X.21bis defines the physical characteristics and call control procedures for a DTE, which operates with synchronous V-series modems to access a public data network.
- V.24 List of Definitions for Interchange Circuits Between Data Terminal Equipment and Data Circuit Terminating Equipment. V.24 applies to the interchange circuits at the interface between DTE and DCE for the transfer of binary data, control and timing signals, and analog signals. This recommendation applies to both synchronous and asynchronous data communication, data transmission on leased line service, and data transmission on switched network service.

4.1.2 Resolution

Resolution is the primary factor affecting quality of the output document as well as the number of bits required for transmission. Four resolutions were chosen for Group 4. Each has a horizontal and vertical tolerance of ±1%.

The 200 × 200 resolution was selected because it is the current high-resolution option for the Group 3 system. Most Group 3 systems manufactured today have this capability so its inclusion in the Group 4 system should help contribute to compatibility between Group 4 and Group 3 systems.

The 300 × 300 resolution is better for small typefaces and provides a higher quality of output images. The primary rationale for this resolution is that the human observer, even without the aid of optical magnification, can perceive more detail than is provided with the lower resolution. To the casual observer, the received document could pass as an original. This resolution matches the 300-dpi resolution of the laser printers generally used with PCs, making their use as Group 4 components relatively easy. Teletex compatibility requirements can also be satisfied with 300 lines/in.

The 400 × 400 resolution is required for good reproduction of fine detail, such as Japanese kanji characters. Group 4 has very high quality output images, providing a new and distinct service compared to Group 3. In a 400 lines/in. image, there are 78% more pels than in a 300 lines/in. image. Only one-third more bits are required to send the compressed image, however, since the compression ratio at 400 lines/in. is much greater. If the 400 lines/in. detail is needed, the relatively small increase in cost for communication and computer storage can usually be tolerated.

4.1.3 Three Classes of Group 4 Facsimile Apparatus

Teletex and Group 3 fax recommendations were adopted by the CCITT in 1980. Group 3 uses the public-switched telephone network, while teletex uses public data networks. When Group 4 fax specifications began, the CCITT insisted that the protocols developed for teletex be used for Group 4, and that the two services would communicate with each other. When Group 4 fax received teletex signals, it would decode the ASCII-like symbols and assemble them into a printing line in a manner similar to the 240 dots/in. teletex units. When sending from Group 4 fax units to teletex units, areas of the page containing symbols would be teletex coded for higher transmission efficiency.[1] Teletex supporters did not plan to use bit-mapped graphics with Group 4 coding. Because the fax supporters knew that most Group 4 users

---

[1]Only 8 bits per character are needed to send teletex, compared with about 90 to 180 bits to send the same information in Group 4 (8- × 10-in. page area). Teletex requires 80 characters/line × 60 lines/page × 8 bits/character = 2880 bits. Group 4 at 200 lines/in. requires 320,000 bits for the same area. Assuming a compression efficiency of 10:1, 32,000 bits are needed; 32000/2880 = 11.1. Group 4 at 400 lines takes only twice as many bits due to increase in compression efficiency.

CLASS	1	2	3
Pel-density of scanner-printer (pels/25.4 mm)	200	300	300
Pel transmission density (pels/25.4 mm)	200	300/200	300/200
Pel transmission conversion capability	not required	yes	yes
Mixed-mode capability	not required	not required	yes
Optional pel density of scanner-printer	300/400	400	400
Combined with pel transmission density (pel/25.4 mm)	400/300/200	400/300/200	400/300/200
Storage	not required	not required	yes

Figure 4.3 Characteristics of three classes of Group 4 fax units.

would not pay extra for teletex, recommendations were adopted for three classes of Group 4 fax units (see Figure 4.3).

Class 1 fax units send and receive facsimile coded documents. The only resolution required is 200 pels/in. (25.4 mm), but Class 1 fax units available today also have the higher optional resolutions of 300 and 400 pels/in. Recommendations T.6, T.503, and T.521 apply.

Class 2 fax units send and receive facsimile coded documents with Class 1 capabilities, adding 300 pels/in. as a mandatory requirement. In addition, Class 2 can receive teletex and mixed mode documents. Recommendations T.6, T.503, T.521, T.60, T.61, and T.561 apply.

Class 3 fax units send and receive facsimile coded documents with Class 1 and Class 2 capabilities. In addition, Class 3 can generate and send teletex and mixed mode documents. Recommendations T.6, T.503, T.521, T.60, T.61, and T.561 apply.

Three classes of Group 4 fax units are defined within the standard, but only Class 1 has a real chance for widespread implementation because Classes 2 and 3 may be eliminated.

4.1.4 Basic and Optional Coding Schemes

Recommendation T.6, Facsimile Coding Schemes and Coding Control Functions for Group 4 Facsimile Apparatus, details the coding schemes. The basic facsimile coding scheme for Group 4 apparatus is a two-dimensional code, which is very similar to that used for Group 3 facsimile. Optional coding schemes for both gray-scale and color images have been left for further study.

The Group 4 coding scheme, MMR, is a higher efficiency version of the Group 3 MR code and uses the same encoding tables. See Chapter 3 for a description of the various coding modes (pass, vertical, and horizontal). The position of each changing pel on the current coding line is encoded with respect to the position of a corresponding reference element situated on either the coding line or reference line that directly precedes the current coding line. After the current coding line has been encoded, it will become the reference line for the line directly beneath it. When coding the first line in a document, the reference line is an imaginary white line.

The reader will note that the code used for Group 4 has the following differences from the Group 3 code: The K factor is equal to infinity, the minimum scan line time is equal to zero, and no EOL codes are used.

The transport service for Group 4 facsimile can be provided by several types of network. These include the circuit-switched public data network (CSPDN), packet-switched public data network (PSPDN), public-switched telephone network (PSTN), and eventually the ISDN. The Group 4 facsimile apparatus will provide for automatic answering, transmission, reception, and clearing, regardless of the type of network used.

4.2 NETWORK-RELATED REQUIREMENTS

As the establishment of public networks for data transmission and ISDNs for integrated services grew, a need was seen for the development of standard "user classes of service." The user class of service details data transmission service with a standardized data signaling rate, call control signaling rate, and data terminal equipment operation mode.

4.2.1 Public-Switched Telephone Network

One advantage of the PSTN over other networks is its universal availability. The PSTN functions as the backbone of Group 3 facsimile apparatus and is viewed as a viable network for Group 4. One of the major disadvantages is that the system was designed to handle voice, not digital data. The rate at which data can be reliably transmitted is lower than over other types of network. The functional and procedural aspects of the interface have yet to be developed. Additionally, the modulation/demodulation schemes and the bit rates are still to be defined. If the Group 4 facsimile terminals are to transmit over the PSTN, they will probably require modems somewhat similar to those currently used for Group 3, but with higher speeds and improved performance.

4.2.2 Circuit-Switched Public Data Networks

The functional and procedural aspects of the interface are defined by CCITT Recommendation X.21. Bit rates are specified in Recommendation X.1, International User Classes of Service in Public Data Networks and Integrated Services Digital Networks (ISDNs). Group 4 fax has bit rates of 2.4, 4.8, 9.6, 48, and 64 kb/s for user classes of service 4 to 7 and 19. The signals in the call control phase are required to use International Alphabet No. 5.

4.2.3 Packet-Switched Public Data Networks

The functional and procedural aspects of the interface are defined by CCITT Recommendation X.25, which specifies that OSI layers 1, 2, and 3 be used for transmission over the PSPDN.

Recommendation X.1 specifies data signaling bit rates of 2.4, 4.8, 9.6, 48, and 64 kb/s, conforming to user classes of service 8 to 13. Because the signaling rates of 9.6 and below are the same as the Group 3 standard, compatibility between the Groups 4 and 3 apparatus should be easier to achieve.

4.2.4 Integrated Services Digital Network

The Integrated Services Digital Network (ISDN) is an internationally standardized extension of the ongoing conversion of the regular telephone network (PSTN) from analog to digital. The ISDN will provide an all-digital switched channel, end-to-end. The process started about 20 years ago when short-haul analog multiplexing systems like N-carrier began to have problems keeping up with the demand for telephone circuits. The quality of transmission had also degraded. The T-1 digital system was then introduced into the telephone plant in the Los Angeles area to handle regular voice calls. Two pairs of copper wires carry a 1.544 Mb/s signal for 24 voice channels. Today, telephone company central offices in most metropolitan areas use digital switching.

Instead of using 300- to 3000-Hz analog channels between a residential or small office customer and the central office, ISDN will provide 144 kb/s. Two full-duplex 64 kb/s channels plus one full-duplex 16 kb/s channel are planned.

ISDN is well suited to Group 4 fax communication. Existing Group 4 fax units must slow down to 48 or 56 kb/s to use existing digital channels. These channels are expensive, costing about $1000 per month as a connection fee, with an additional charge for each kilobit sent. Expensive lines are also needed to reach the telephone company's central office. Initially, charges for operation of fax units on the ISDN will probably be higher than existing PSTN channels.

What does this mean for the future of Group 3 fax? By using a voice telephone type codec, Group 3 fax can continue to be switched to worldwide destinations in the same way as voice. A 64 kb/s Group 3 interface would allow much higher speeds.

Currently ISDN is being offered in many areas as a tariffed service with usage restricted to small geographic zones. Many U.S. corporations are beginning to install ISDN for interoffice use. Not until 1995, however, will ISDN have replaced most of the existing telephone service and begun to offer a universal high-speed service for fax. Meanwhile, broadband ISDN is rapidly developing and will offer much higher speed channels.

4.3 DOCUMENT ARCHITECTURE TRANSFER AND MANIPULATION

4.3.1 Introduction

Group 4 facsimile is equipment that incorporates a means for reducing redundant information in a document signal prior to its transmission and generally assures error-free reception of the document. Group 4 facsimile uses a compression algorithm based on the MMR code. Unlike Group 3 facsimile, which was designed as analog devices for use over the PSTN, Group 4 facsimile was designed as digital devices for use over the ISDN.

During the 1984–88 study period, recommendations for telematic services were specified as separate entities; the 1988–92 study period saw a reversal in this idea. It was decided that the telematic services such as Group 4 facsimile and mixed mode of service should be integrated and based on a set of common recommendations. This new integrated approach is called *document architecture transfer and manipulation* (DATAM). DATAM is based on recommendations in three main areas: open document architecture (ODA) as specified in T.411; open document interchange format (ODIF) as specified in T.415; and document transfer and manipulation (DTAM) as specified in the complete T.430 series of recommendations. Similar work is ongoing within the ISO. Figure 4.4 is provided to show a graphical picture of the

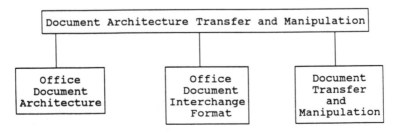

Figure 4.4 The DATAM relationships.

relationship of all these areas of work. Under this new approach every telematic service is viewed as an application of DATAM.

In addition, implementors would need to be familiar with Recommendation T.563, Terminal Characteristics of Group 4 Facsimile Apparatus; Recommendation T.521, Communication Application Profile BTO for Document Bulk Transfer based on Session Service (according to Rules defined in T.62bis); and Recommendation T.503, A Document Application Profile for the Interchange of Group 4 Facsimile Documents.

4.3.2 General Characteristics of DTAM

The T.430 series of recommendations defines a complete DTAM service and specifies a protocol within the application layer of the OSI model. DTAM is one of the many *specific application service elements* (SASE) in the application layer. The major role of DTAM is the creation of a communication environment that offers document transfer, document manipulation, document access, and document management. There are two ways in which to transfer documents, either directly or indirectly. The selection of indirect transfer requires use of the message handling system. The term *document manipulation* implies that the user can create, delete, or modify documents. DTAM also allows communication support functions through the use of the service of the session layer or through the use of association control service elements (ACSE) and the use of presentation layer services. Because it was necessary to retain backward compatibility, two modes of document interchange were introduced. The first is the transparent mode in which the presentation layer is not used, while the normal mode will utilize presentation layer services.

4.3.3 Communication Application Profile

A typical DATAM application profile will consist of both a communication application profile and a document application profile. To be in conformance with the recommendations, every application must be defined by a DATAM application profile. The communication application profile consists of three main parts: a particular service class, functional units, and communication support functions.

4.3.4 Service Classes

In general, the service class will indicate the type of document interchange to be used. At the present time, three types of classes are defined: bulk transfer, document manipulation, and bulk transfer with manipulation. Other service classes are being studied by the CCITT.

4.3.4.1 Functional Units

After deciding on a service class to be used, functional units must be defined. These units are used in the negotiation process. The most basic of these is the kernel, which is always required. Other available units are used to keep track of exception reporting and management. They include such things as a capability functional unit, data transmission functional unit, session management, and exception reporting. Other units are currently being considered.

4.3.4.2 Communication Support Functions

Most communication support functions being studied require the use of the ACSE and presentation services; other common application service elements are currently under study. One exception is that the document bulk transfer service class 0 can be directly mapped to session layer services.

4.4 OPEN DOCUMENT ARCHITECTURE PRINCIPLES

Documents within the ODA structure can be represented in three formats. First, the formatted form will only allow the receiver to present the document in the form as 536intended by the originator. Second, processible form will allow the receiver to edit and format the document as intended by the originator. Third, formatted processible form will allow the receiver to present as well as edit and reformat as the originator intended. The document architecture also consists of rules for defining the structure of the document as well as the representation of the document. Remember that the structural representation of the document describes the elements and their relationship. On the other hand, the descriptive representation will inform the recipient of how these elements are represented. These elements are better known as the *constituents* and are described by a set of attributes. The constituents are actually the information that is interchanged. The structural model will help to delimit portions within a document; delimit portions of a document that have logical meaning; use different coding types for different content types; and allow processing of the document.

4.4.1 Formatted Form

The formatted document architecture class includes a document profile and specific layout structure. Optionally, it may include the presentation styles and a generic layout structure (see Figure 4.5).

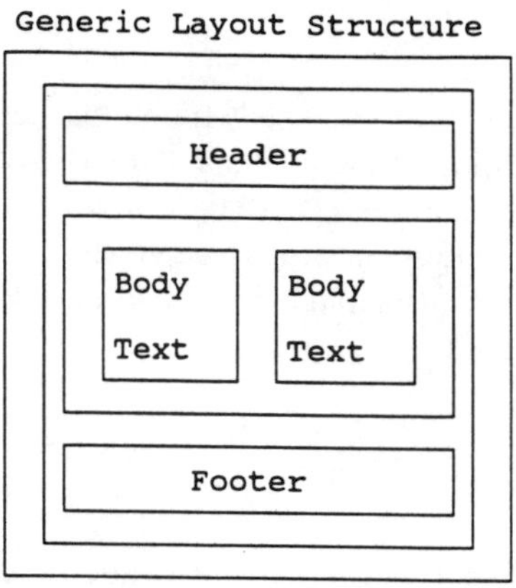

Generic Layout Structure

Figure 4.5 Generic layout structure.

4.4.2 Processible Form

The processible document architecture class includes a document profile and specific logical structure. Optionally it may include a generic logical structure, generic layout structure, layout styles, and presentation styles.

4.4.3 Formatted Processible Form

The formatted processible document architecture class includes a document profile, specific logical structure, specific layout structure, and generic layout structure. Optionally, it may include a generic logical structure, layout styles, and presentation styles.

4.4.4 Structural Model

Within the framework of the ODA model, the document is divided into two distinct parts, the document profile, which is used to describe characteristics for the document as a whole, and the document body. The document profile is not part of the structural model.

4.4.4.1 Logical and Layout Structure

The layout structure is formed by the following objects: block, frame, page, and page set. Logical objects are not classified; they are distinguished as either basic or composite. The logical structure is determined by the author, while the layout structure will be determined by the formatting process. In turn, the formatting process will be controlled by the attributes called layout directives. The layout directives are requirements that control such things as: all chapters start on new pages, that the title of a new section and a certain amount of its paragraph must be on the same page, or even the amount of indentation to be used.

4.4.4.2 Content Architectures

Three content architectures are used to structure the content of the basic logical layout object. These include character content architecture, raster graphic content architecture, and geometric graphics content architecture.

4.4.4.3 Descriptive Representation of a Document

A document is represented by a collection of constituents, which, in turn, is represented by a set of attributes. The following constituents are allowed:

- Document profile represented as a set of attributes that will detail the characteristics of the whole document
- Logical object description represented by a set of attributes that specifies an object within a structure
- Layout object description represented as a logical object description
- Logical object class description represented as a set of attributes specifying an object class within the document
- Layout object class description represented as a logical object class description
- Presentation style represented as a set of attributes that provides information on the format and appearance of the document
- Layout style represented as a set of attributes that will guide the creation of a specific layout structure and content portion description represented as a set of attributes that details a content portion within the document.

4.4.4.4 Attributes

In their simplest form, attributes are the property of documents or document constituents and provide information on the characteristics of that document. The attribute can also be used to show a relationship between one or more documents or document components. Attributes can be described as follows: document profile attribute, component description attribute, layout style, presentation style, and content portion description attribute. Furthermore, the component description attribute can be broken down into a shared attribute, logical attribute, or layout attribute.

Attributes can be classified as mandatory, nonmandatory, or defaultable and can only consist of data elements. One exception is the attributes belonging to the component description and layout styles that may contain an expression as their value. Allowable expressions include string, numeral, object identifier, and construction. If attributes for objects or content portion are defined as faultable, then rules are available to determine their values.

4.5 DOCUMENT PROCESSING MODEL

Document processing can be divided into three main categories: imaging process, layout process, and editing process. The document processing model itself is a conceptual view of document processing. It addresses only those things which are relevant to the document architecture.

4.6 EDITING PROCESS

The editing process allows document creation and document revision. Because the result is the same—a new document—both creation and revision are considered to be equivalent. Two types of processing are allowed, content editing and logical structure editing. The newly created or revised documents are said to be in the processable form and can then be used as input to the editing or the layout process.

4.7 IMAGING PROCESS AND LAYOUT PROCESS

The layout process is made up of two processes: document layout and content layout. The results of these two processes are used by the imaging process in presenting the document in a form perceptible by humans on some type of presentation medium.

The imaging process is responsible for presenting the document in a form perceptible to humans. This is accomplished either on paper or screen, it is not defined in the recommendations, and is left as a locally defined process.

4.8 APPLICATION PROFILE

As was stated previously, each application must have a document application profile that defines the parts of ODA that are used. In particular, the document application profile must have a document architecture level that defines the particular architecture class (i.e., formatted, processible, or formatted processible); a content architecture level that defines those features that pertain to a particular content architecture class (i.e., presentation attributes, coding attributes, and control functions); a document profile level describing its attributes and for each attribute its classification and permissible values; and the ODIF interchange format class.

4.9 MIXED MODE

4.9.1 General Characteristics

Equipment claiming to support the mixed mode of operation is required to support a set of basic features. In addition, the equipment can provide optional features, but these must be negotiated separately. For ease of use, when the term *document* is used it will mean one or more pages of data.

4.9.2 Basic Features

All equipment must be capable of creating, transmitting, and receiving documents that conform to the document application profile Mixed Mode.1, which is defined in CCITT Recommendation T.501. The equipment must also have the ability to interchange documents according to the application context defined in paragraph 7.1 of Recommendation T.561. This application content details such information as DTAM services, association control service elements, presentation services, and transport services.

4.9.2.1 Paper and Page Sizes

The equipment must be capable of handling the ISO A4 nominal page, and in addition it can support several optional nominal pages (see Table 4.1). The equipment must also provide the assured reproduction area of the ISO A4 page. In addition, if it supports other nominal pages, it must provide the guaranteed reproducible area associated with that page (see Table 4.1). Nominal pages are defined for paper output with a scale factor of one in the *basic measurement unit* (BMU), 25.4/1200 mm (1/1200 in).

For purposes of mixed mode documents, a page is considered to be a rectangular area that is used as the reference area for positioning and imaging the content of a document. The nominal page is equal to the ideal paper size used (see Table 4.2). A page may be equal to or less than the nominal page in relation to its physical paper format. All the pages defined in Table 4.2 describe the presentation of text information for the specified paper in both the vertical and horizontal image orientations.

Table 4.1
Guaranteed Reproducible Area

Page	Sizes		Status
ISO A4	width	: 9240 BMU	mandatory
	height	: 13200 BMU	
	top margin	: 472 BMU	
	left margine	: 345 BMU	
North	width	: 9240 BMU	optional
American	height	: 12400 BMU	
Letter	top margin	: 472 BMU	
	left margine	: 345 BMU	
ISO A3	width	: 13200 BMU	optional
	height	: 18480 BMU	
	top margin	: 472 BMU	
	left margine	: 345 BMU	
Japanese	width	: 11200 BMU	optional
Legal	height	: 15300 BMU	
	top margin	: 900 BMU	
	left margine	: 400 BMU	
Japanese	width	: 7600 BMU	optional
Letter	height	: 10200 BMU	
	top margin	: 900 BMU	
	left margine	: 400 BMU	

Table 4.2
Nominal Pages

Nominal Page	Sizes		Status
ISO A4	w:	9920 BMU (210 mm)	Mandatory
	h:	14030 BMU (297 mm)	
North American Letter	w:	10200 BMU (215.9 mm)	Optional
	h:	13200 BMU (279.4 mm)	
ISO A3	w:	14030 BMU (297 mm)	Optional
	h:	19840 BMU (420 mm)	
Japanese Legal	w:	12141 BMU (257 mm)	Optional
	h:	17196 BMU (364 mm)	
Japanese Letter	w:	8598 BMU (182 mm)	Optional
	h:	12141 BMU (257 mm)	

4.9.2.2 Receiving and Presenting Documents

All equipment claiming conformance to the mixed mode of operation must be capable of receiving documents that contain characters belonging to the teletex basic repertoire; or receiving documents that contain data encoded by the raster graphic coding scheme as defined in Recommendation T.6; or receiving documents that contain content encoded data using the teletex basic repertoire and the raster graphic encoding.

4.9.3 Nonbasic Features

Nonbasic features must be negotiated prior to the interchange of the mixed mode document. The most common nonbasic features are various paper sizes (see Table 4.2); and/or the ability to handle more than 31 received blocks for presentation as a single page of a document.

4.9.4 Characteristics Supported for Mixed Mode Documents

Mixed mode documents are classified as memoranda, letters, and reports and may contain characters and raster graphic data. The interchange of these documents is based on a document application profile defined in CCITT Recommendation T.501. Since the document must be in a formatted form, the intended recipient will only be allowed to display or print the document as the originator intended. The information that is interchanged falls within the following categories:

- *Page Format Features:* layout of each page, character content, and raster graphics layout and imaging features. This information will explain how the document content will appear within the pages.
- *Character Repertoire:* Character sets and control functions used within the document.
- *Raster Graphics Coding:* The representations of the raster graphics and the control functions used.

Furthermore, the creation of the document is independent from the document application profile. The mixed mode document results from a formatting process; therefore, it is the responsibility of the document application profile to allow the transfer of the complete layout characteristics. The content of a page can consist of either characters as used by any word processing system, and/or raster graphics as used in Group 4 facsimile.

As mentioned, the term *document* can mean one or more pages, each of which may contain a combination of characters and/or raster graphics. If the document contains a mixture of character and raster graphics, they must occupy separate blocks; each block is homogeneous. Each page in the document can contain several blocks, and each block has its own dimensions and location on the page. The blocks on a page can be positioned is such a way that they intersect either partially or fully. When the blocks intersect they share common areas, and since all blocks are transparent, the contents of the intersecting areas are combined. This is similar to the effect of laying overhead transparencies on top of each other and superimposing one image onto another.

4.9.4.1 Characters

Layout and Imaging Characteristics: The characteristics of each block are independent of other blocks, including such things as line spacing and character paths. The character content blocks contain information such as graphic characters and control functions. It is the control functions that define character and line spacing.

Line Spacing: In general, line spacing is the distance between successive lines of text. Values range from 3 lines per 25.4 mm up to 12 lines per 25.4 mm. The negotiable value for line spacing is 8 lines per 25.4 mm. Basic values are presented in Table 4.3. All values are based on a scale (ratio of a page size unit at the printer to the same unit at the scanner) of one.

Character Spacing: Character spacing is defined as the distance between successive characters on a single line of text. This spacing is generally based on 120 SMU providing 10 characters per 25.4 mm. Scaled measurement unit (SMU) is defined as BMU multiplied by scale factor. The negotiable values are defined in Table 4.4. All values are based on a scale factor of one. The first character may be a space and its position is defined by use of cartesian coordinates.

Character Presentation: Characters can be represented in four modes: normal rendition (default), underlined, italicized, and bold.

Table 4.3
Line Spacing Basic Values

SMU	*Lines/25.4mm (scale factor is one)*
100	12
200 (default)	6 (default)
300	4
400	3

Table 4.4
Character Spacing Negotiable Values

SMU	Characters per 25.4mm (scale factor is one)
80	15
100	6
200	12

4.9.5 Raster Graphics

4.9.5.1 Blocks

The blocks that contain raster graphics will be defined by the initial offset (by default, the left top corner) and the dimensions of the pixel array.

4.9.5.2 Pel Transmission Density

Tables 4.5 and 4.6 show the pel transmission densities for raster graphics.

Table 4.5
Pel Transmission Density Basic Values

SMU	Pels per 25.4mm (scale factor is one)
5	240
4	300

Table 4.6
Pel Transmission Density Negotiable Values

SMU	Pels per 25.4mm (scale factor is one)
6	200
3	400
2	600
1	1200

4.9.6 Specification of the Document Application Profile

The documents conforming to Mixed Mode.1 must at a minimum contain all required attributes. These include a document profile and layout object descriptions that represent a specific layout structure. In addition, it may optionally contain layout object class descriptions that represent a "partial" generic layout structure.

4.9.6.1 Layout Structure

The layout structure can be seen as having two distinct parts, generic and specific. The purpose of the generic layout structure is to provide information on predefined attribute values and content portions for objects in the specific layout structure. Additionally, the generic layout structure may also contain three different object classes, namely, the document layout root class, the page class, and the block class. All three are optional for the generic layout. Within the specific layout structure, three hierarchical levels are mandatory. These include the document layout root, page, and block.

Attributes Application and Classification: An attribute belongs to a document or to the component of a document and expresses a characteristic of that document or of the component. Each of these attributes will be assigned a name. The document layout root, page, and block all contain mandatory and optional attributes. These attributes are broken down into two types: shared attributes and layout attributes.

Shared attributes include mandatory information such as object type, object identifier, subordinates, and object class identifier. In addition, the shared attributes can also contain data on such things as default value lists, content portions, presentation style, and presentation attributes among others. All layout attributes are optional and include information on dimensions and positions. The document layout root has no layout attributes.

4.9.6.2 Content Architecture

The document application profile for Mixed Mode.1 defines two different content architecture levels: formatted character and formatted raster graphics. A complete listing of the graphic elements and coding types for the character content is contained in CCITT Recommendation T.61, while CCITT Recommendation T.6 provides the allowable coding types for the raster graphics content. The uncompressed mode of coding for raster graphics can also be invoked, but this must be negotiated and indicated in the document profile.

Presentation Attributes: Presentation attributes are all defaultable; the one exception is "pel spacing," which is mandatory. Allowable attributes for characters include character path, line progression, character orientation, initial offset, line spacing, character spacing, alignment, graphic character sets, and character rendition. Raster graphics attributes include the pel path, line progression, pel spacing, and initial offset.

4.10 GROUP 4 FACSIMILE

As discussed earlier, Group 4 facsimile consists of three classes. The Class 1 apparatus must be capable of sending and receiving documents containing facsimile encoded information. Class 2 apparatus must be capable of transmitting documents that are facsimile encoded and capable of receiving documents that are facsimile encoded, teletex encoded, and mixed mode. Class 3 apparatus must be capable of generating, transmitting, and receiving facsimile encoded, teletex encoded, and mixed mode documents.

In general, all three classes must, at a minimum, be capable of handling:

- The communication application profile for Group 4 facsimile and detailed in Recommendation T.521
- The document application profile for Group 4 facsimile and detailed in Recommendation T.503
- The A4/North American page for facsimile messaging
- The content, layout, and format of the document must be the same at the receiving terminal as it was at the transmitting terminal
- Scanning direction should be from left to right in both the transmitter and receiver
- Each and every terminal should have a unique identification

- The guaranteed reproduction of 196.6 × 281.46 mm for the ISO A4 page
- The MR code II as defined in Recommendation T.6 (1988)
- Bit rates of 2.4, 4.8, 9.6, 48 or 64 kb/s, depending on the network being used
- Class 2 and Class 3 machines must have, at a minimum, 128 octets of receiving storage
- The frame structure defined in the HDLC frame
- The apparatus must have the capability to negotiate optional functions during the handshaking procedure.

Pel transmission densities are given in Table 4.7. For point of reference, the center line is perpendicular to the scan lines and includes the point determined by the number of pels per line divided by 2. The raster point is the upper left corner of the ISO A4 page and occupies position (1,1). It is used as the starting point for character margins and positions.

Table 4.7
Pel Transmission Densities

	ISO A4	North American	ISO B4	ISO A3	Japanese Legal	Japanese Letter
Resolution (pels/inch)						
200	1728/2339	1728/2200	2048/2780	2432/3307	2018/2866	1728/2024
240	2074/2806	2074/2640	2458/3335	2918/3969	2458/3439	2074/2428
300	2592/3508	2592/3300	3072/4169	3648/4961	3072/4299	2592/3035
400	3456/4677	3456/4400	4096/5559	4864/6614	4096/5732	3456/4047
scan line length (mm) (P)	219.46	219.46	260.10	308.86	260.10	219.46
paper width (mm) (Q)	210	215.9	250	297	257	182
P − Q	9.46	3.56	10.10	11.86	3.10	37.46
Nominal paper (mm)	297	297.4	353	420	364	257

4.10.1 Group 4 Facsimile Communication Application Profile

The communication application profile used by Group 4 facsimile is BT_o. This means that the service class used is direct document bulk transfer; and the communication support function is a direct mapping to the session service. In addition, the following functional units are required: association use control, capability, document bulk transfer, token control, exception report, and reliable transfer mode 1. Because the communication support function is a direct mapping to the session service, it means no presentation layer services are used. This is known as the *transparent mode*. This also means that all DATAM services are mapped onto the application protocol data units (APDUs). From here, the APDU will be mapped onto the session services, and in turn the session services will be mapped onto the session PDU.

4.10.2 Group 4 Facsimile Document Application Profile

A typical document application profile for Group 4 facsimile is as follows:

document architecture level: formatted document

content architecture level: formatted raster graphics

document profile level: mandatory

interchange format class: ODIF class B

Group 4 facsimile does not require a logical structure because according to the criteria for formatted document architecture the only requirement is for a document profile and a specific layout structure. The specific layout structure will have only two hierarchical levels: document layout root and page.

4.11 FORMATTED RASTER-GRAPHIC CONTENT ARCHITECTURE

As mentioned in Section 4.10.2, Group 4 facsimile uses the formatted raster-graphic content architecture. This implies that a two-dimensional pictorial image is represented by picture elements (pels) in the form of a rectangular two-dimensional array. Pel positioning is accomplished through the use of a coordinate system with its horizontal and vertical axis parallel to the horizontal and vertical axis of the page coordinate system. The top left corner of the page is the origin of the coordinate system, the top of the page is the horizontal axis, and the left side of the page is the vertical axis. Scaled measurement units are used to identify points or to specify lengths.

4.11.1 Attributes

The formatted raster-graphic content architecture uses two type of attributes, presentation attributes and content portion attributes.

Presentation Attributes:

- *Pel Path:* The direction of the progression of successive pels along a line
- *Line Progression:* The direction of the progression of successive lines, relative to the pel path

- *Pel Transmission Density:* The resolution, the basic value is 200 pels/in.; however, this value is negotiable in the document profile
- *Initial Offset:* The position of the initial point relative to the basic layout object.

Content Portion Attributes:

- *Number of Pels/Line:* A defaultable attribute that specifies the number of pels on each line within a content portion
- *Number of Discarded Pels:* Also a defaultable attribute that represents the number of pels discarded at the beginning and end of each line
- *Coding Type:* A defaultable attribute represented by an ASN.1 object identifier indicating that MMR code II is used for coding
- *Compression:* A defaultable attribute indicating compressed or uncompressed encoding.

Pels will be imaged after the pels at the beginning of the line have been discarded, as specified in the attribute "number of discarded pels." The first pel in the array will be positioned at the initial point, as specified in the attribute "initial offset." If any part of the raster-graphic content extends beyond the boundaries of the basic layout object, they are ignored.

4.11.1.1 Group 4 Facsimile Document Profile

The document profile is used to provide information in the form of attributes about the document. The profile may be interchanged independent of the document body. The Group 4 facsimile document profile attributes are as follows:

Document profile descriptor—a mandatory set of attributes:

Specific layout structure—a mandatory attribute used if the document contains any layout object descriptions.

Document characteristics—an attribute set that contains:

Document application profile—indicates the particular document application profile that pertains to the document (i.e., Group 4, Class 1 is represented by the integer 2).

Document architecture class—for Group 4 facsimile this value is formatted document architecture.

Nonbasic document characteristics—a set of optional attributes including page dimensions, which contains the values of the layout objects of type page.

Raster-graphics coding attributes—set of attributes that in the case of Group 4 facsimile specifies compression, which, in turn, specifies if the code extension technique for uncompressed mode is present in a content portion.

Raster-graphic presentation attributes—a set of attributes that in the case of Group 4 facsimile specifies pel transmission density, which, in turn, specifies pel transmission density, pel spacing, and line spacing.

4.11.1.2 Group 4 Facsimile Component Description

Only shared and layout attributes are applicable to Group 4 facsimile. The shared attributes are as follows:

Object type—specifies whether the layout object is a root or page.

Object identifier—identifies an object uniquely within the content of the document. The attributes value is a sequence of integers. For Group 4 facsimile the first integer is equal to 1.

Content portion—specifies which content portions are associated with a page. Its value is a sequence of one or more integers.

Default value list—if specified for the root, the attribute will have default values for attributes for each subordinate page.

The layout attributes are as follows:

Presentation attributes—a set of attributes that apply only for the page; they are not applicable for the root. Pel path, line progression, pel transmission density, and initial offset have been previously defined (see Section 4.11.1). The content type attribute can be used as an alternative to the content architecture class attribute, but may only be used when the content architecture class is formatted. This is only used as an alternative to assure compatibility with former Recommendation T.73.

Dimension attribute—is defaultable and applicable only for the page. It consists of two parameters; horizontal dimension and vertical dimension. Both the vertical and horizontal dimension parameters have the subparameter fixed dimension, but the vertical dimension also can have another subparameter for variable page height.

4.11.1.3 Content Portion Attributes

Some content portion attributes such as type of coding, number of discarded pels, compression, and number of pels per line were defined earlier (see Section 4.11.1). The other allowable attributes are as follows:

Content information—this attribute is mandatory and is used for interchanging the actual content of the document. It is an octet string that represents a pel array encoded according to the value in the attribute "type of coding." This issue is to be further clarified as different recommendations assign it different meanings.

Content portion identifier—this attribute is a sequence of integers; the first integers indicate the basic layout object (page) to which the content portion is associated. The last integer refers to the content portion associated to the page.

4.12 OPEN DOCUMENT INTERCHANGE FORMAT (ODIF)

The interchange data elements contain a hierarchy of data structures and data items (constituents and attributes). All the descriptors consist of both simple and composite data items, the one exception is the content portion descriptor. This is represented by a text unit that has two fields. These fields are an attribute field and an information field. The attribute field will represent the attribute of the content portion; the information field represents content elements.

Two interchange format classes exist within the ODIF structure, Class A and Class B. Group 4 facsimile uses Class B. To comply with the rules for class B, documents must have a profile descriptor and a layout object descriptor (root and pages) and the associated text units. In Group 4 facsimile, every page is followed by its associated content portion. A typical data stream for Group 4 facsimile contains only one document profile descriptor, which is always the first interchange data element.

Chapter 5
Transmission of Facsimile

5.1 PUBLIC-SWITCHED TELEPHONE NETWORK (PSTN)

Universal availability is the main advantage of the regular telephone network (PSTN, which is also known as GSTN) compared to other networks. Appendix 1, Section A3 describes the development of the PSTN, including analog channels that are still used today.

For Group 3 digital fax, a modem built into the fax machine converts the digital fax signal to be sent into an analog (tone-type) signal that will pass through its limited bandwidth. The bandwidth available for data or fax transmission is less than that used for voice transmission. Each of the set of modems used in Group 3 fax places the carrier frequency near the center of the PSTN passband, and the modulation process generates matching pairs of sidebands above and below the carrier frequency. For good modem performance, the bandwidth needed equals the symbol (baud) rate plus 100 Hz (see Figure 5.1).

For the V.29 modem, the modulation keying rate is 1200 Hz (one-half the 2400-symbol rate). Significant sidebands are generated from the carrier frequency of 1700 Hz out to 500 and 2900 Hz (1700 ±1200 Hz). With V.27$_{ter}$, the bandwidth is narrower. The telephone channel must be of nearly constant transit-time delay to avoid envelope delay distortion. An allowance of 50 Hz is added at each end of the band, making the required telephone channel bandwidth 450 to 2950 Hz. The envelope-delay distortion from a telephone channel often causes more received-signal distortion than the amplitude frequency response of the channel. The distortions added by a switched telephone network call vary greatly between successive calls. Some channels could be left uncorrected and meet the modem performance requirements, but many could not. Fortunately, both of these distortions are minimized by the receiving-modem automatic equalizer after each telephone line circuit connection is made.

Although the customer interface is still analog, most of the PSTN is now digital, based on the T-1 system introduced many years ago. Voice signals are converted to digital signals that take 64 kb/s to send. This was more economical for the telephone companies than trying to extend the analog multiplexing technology. When

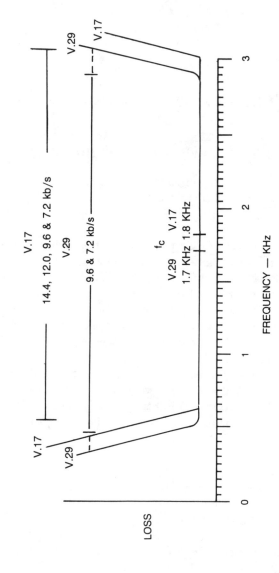

Figure 5.1 Group 3 bandwidth requirements.

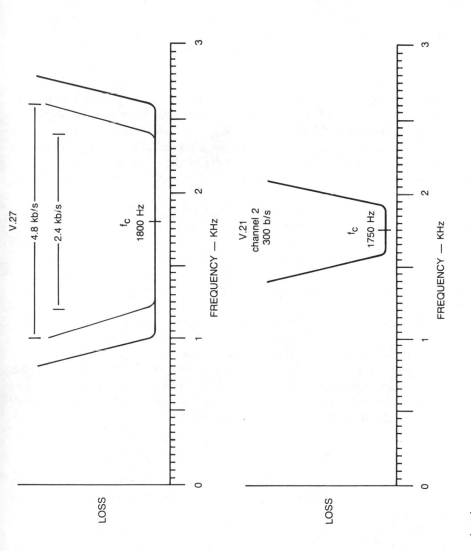

Figure 5.1 continued.

the fax process started using sophisticated modems such as the V.29 on the PSTN, strange things happened. The PSTN, capable of only 4.8 kb/s data transmission, was sending 9.6 kb/s fax signals. Digital signals generated inside the Group 3 fax machine were converted to analog signals by the modem to send over the PSTN. When the telephone company received these analog signals at their central office, they were converted back to digital, fitting into a digital voice channel of 64 (or 56) kHz. T-1 is also the building block for the digital telephone networks, including the ISDN.

The PSTN functions very well for Group 3 facsimile apparatus, but modems have not been selected for Group 4. With error-correction and a suitable modem, the PSTN could be used for Group 4. The maximum rate at which data can be sent on the PSTN is more than 19.2 kb/s, but this is still much lower than the speed available on digital networks. One of the major disadvantages of the PSTN is that the system was designed to handle voice, not digital data. The quality of the PSTN improves with time as older types of central office switches and noisy lines are replaced with newer types.

Today, most nighttime international calls are fax transmissions. The international carriers find it a waste of their facilities to send 4.8 or 9.6 kb/s fax on a 64, 40, or 32 kb/s digital channel. Equipment on these channels automatically detects fax calls and handles them in a different manner. Fax transmissions are demodulated to the original digital rate of 9.6 or 4.8 kb/s and occupy only that much of one digital voice channel. As many as six different 9.6 kb/s fax transmissions can now share a single voice channel. Until this remodulation equipment is modified, fax transmissions with the V.17 modem (up to 14.4 kb/s) are assigned the whole voice channel.

International carriers are not the only ones to take advantage of squeezing more fax into a telephone channel. Multiplexers are now available that allow business customers to place as many as eight fax calls into a single 64 or 128 kb/s channel between a pair of multiplexers. The Group 3 fax signals are handled at full speed, transparently, without dedicated fax-only bandwidth.

5.2 DIGITAL NETWORKS

Digital networks (sometimes called data networks) are essentially "error free." The probability of an error is so low that it can be ignored for all practical purposes. On existing digital channels, Group 3 and Group 4 fax machines operate at 64 or 56 kb/s. AT&T, MCI, and many other companies offer a 56 or 64 kb/s switched service that is being used for Group 4 fax. For a corporate user or anyone who needs a large number of channels, digital networks may be inexpensive for either Group 3 or Group 4 use. T-1 and fractional T-1 switched channels can offer high-grade channels at a low cost, especially when terminated in the company digital switchboard. SONET (Synchronous Optical Network) standards for 51 mb/s to 2.4 gb/s (planned), and broadband ISDN (BISDN), VSAT (very small aperture terminals), and many other satellite and other transmission options offer an almost endless method of connecting between fax machines. It is beyond the scope of this book to attempt coverage of all these options. For now, the PSTN still handles almost all connections between fax machines, and the ISDN 64 kb/s B channel is expected to absorb fax traffic gradually.

Discussed below are the two types of public data networks available for Group 4 use as standardized by the CCITT. They may be available in the future through the ISDN. Some years from now, even voice will operate through the ISDN rather than the PSTN as we know it today. For now, most CCITT data networks or other digital networks already in place must be accessed through an improvised digital connection.

5.3 CIRCUIT-SWITCHED PUBLIC DATA NETWORKS (CSPDN)

CCITT Recommendation X.21 bit rates (for Group 4 and other telematic services) are 2.4, 4.8, 9.6, 48, and 64 kb/s. In the United States, 56 kb/s is used to match the digital circuits available.

5.4 PACKET-SWITCHED PUBLIC DATA NETWORKS (PSPDN)

CCITT Recommendation X.25 bit rates (for Group 4 and other telematic services) are 2.4, 4.8, 9.6, 48, and 64 kb/s. OSI layers 1, 2, and 3 are used (see Chapter 4). Packet-switched networks designed for intermittent, short, bursty transmissions are not well suited for fax transmission. Fax is a steady one-way transmission that uses a very large number of packets per page. Some of the earlier packet networks found that fax saturated the network capacity.

5.5 INTEGRATED SERVICES DIGITAL NETWORK (ISDN)

ISDN is an internationally standardized all-digital channel, end-to-end. The conversion of the telephone plant to digital is an evolutionary process that started many years ago when the T-1 digital system was introduced to handle regular voice calls between telephone company central offices. Two pairs of copper wires carry a 1.544 Mb/s signal for 24 voice channels (64 kb per channel).[1] The local loops between the customer and the central office remain analog.

For ISDN, the 300- to 3000-Hz local loop channels will be converted to digital, providing 144 kb/s consisting of two 64 kb/s B channels plus one 16 kb/s D channel

---

[1]In Europe, a 2048 kb/s signal is used for 32 channels of 64 kb/s.

for small users. The 64 kb/s channel is circuit switched and well suited to Groups 3 and 4 fax communications. Although 64 kb/s will be used for the voice channel, charges for operation of fax units on the 64 kb/s ISDN may be higher initially than for existing voice channels. This 64 kb/s charge should eventually be less than that for a voice channel today. The 16 kb/s D channel is packet switched and not well suited for fax.

With ISDN, Group 3 fax can continue to be switched to worldwide destinations the same as voice by using a voice-type telephone codec. Group 3 with a 64 kb/s interface will soon allow much higher transmission speeds. Although ISDN availability is expanding, it will still be many years before ISDN will have replaced most of the existing telephone service and offer a universal high-speed service for fax. Broadband ISDN is rapidly developing, offering much higher speed channels, possibly even to the home.

5.6 LOCAL-AREA NETWORKS (LANs)

A PC and a PC-fax/LAN board can act as a fax gateway server to the PSTN. Computers and workstations on the LAN network can send to Group 3 fax machines on the PSTN through the PC-fax/LAN board for delivery of ASCII characters and graphics data (anything that can be sent to a printer). The PC-fax/LAN board has all of the functions of a high-level PC-fax board plus others, such as multiple-line PSTN calls to expedite sending of multiaddress messages.

This type of operation is better for sending to a fax machine than receiving from one, because handling of incoming fax messages has some problems. Addressing a recipient on a LAN network is not a normal function of a Group 3 fax machine and manual forwarding might be required. At least one PC-fax/LAN board, when operating on a network with Novell message handling software, can also receive facsimile messages and automatically distribute them on the network to the desired PC workstation. The incoming facsimile caller is prompted to use the standard telephone *dual-tone multifrequency* (DTMF) dialing buttons to enter the code for the fax mailbox at the recipient's workstation. The EIA/TIA TR-29 facsimile committee is considering DTMF as a short-term standard and several other approaches for incoming fax calls. LanFax software allows a message handling system (MHS) operating in a PC to send messages to standard Group 3 fax machines through a PC-fax board, operating as a gateway to the PSTN. The one PC acts as the MHS and fax server for the network. The fax server converts E-mail messages containing both text and graphics into Group 3 format.

Some LAN arrangements have an optical disk archiving of all fax traffic. The "write once read many times" (WORM) optical disk has a complete unerasable record of all transmissions to Group 3 fax machines. This kind of arrangement is good for bank and insurance applications. The network users can deliver ASCII text and

Epson-compatible graphics to unattended Group 3 fax machines. The PC-fax board may have a library of letterheads and signatures that can be automatically added to the message to build a complete letter form.

5.7 TRANSMISSION TIME-DELAY CONSIDERATIONS

5.7.1 Satellite Channels

Space-path lengths for radio-wave propagation on a single-hop satellite can cause a 1.2-s round-trip response time to commands sent. Double and triple satellite paths have been encountered. For a three-hop channel, presumably a worst case condition, about 3.6 s of dead time occurs every time a response is needed from the other fax machine. Some early digital 4.8 kb/s fax networks were set up and functioned properly on a three-hop satellite channel. Fortunately, the time delay of satellite channels was considered when the original Group 3 fax standards were being developed. In the handshake protocol, the number of turnarounds was limited and the response time-outs were set to be long enough to avoid disconnect problems. No turnarounds happen while a page is being sent. This time-delay problem was again respected when the Group 3 error-control mode was developed.

The delay problem gets worse for higher speed fax transmission such as the 64 kb/s for ISDN channels. Without satellite delay, Group 4 fax may need 3 s to send one page of fax data. Group 4 with the OSI protocol adds 6.3 s for a total of 9.3 s for sending one page. With Group 3 fax, 64 kb/s requires a total of 4.5 s, less than half the time. Of course this ratio reduces when more than one page is sent during the same session. Adding double-hop satellite delay times of the 10 Group 4 turnarounds for the one page example adds 24 more seconds! Furthermore the problem becomes far worse for the even higher speed channels now available.

5.7.2 Fiber Optics Channels

It is surprising to some that a similar time-delay problem may exist with long-haul fiber optics channels. Tests made from Switzerland to Australia showed the time delay was much higher than for copper channels, more like satellite time delays. This is unwelcome news for protocols like OSI that require many circuit turnarounds during a session.

Chapter 6
Scanning Technology

6.1 SCANNING PROCESS

The scanner is the part of a fax machine that converts the marks on the page being sent into electrical signals. A picture element is determined by the small spot of the image that covers one photosensor. The picture element is called a pixel when it contains gray-scale information, or a pel when it has only binary black-white information. Early scanners used only one photosensor that read a small spot of about 0.01 in. diameter. The page being sent was wrapped around a drum and the scanning spot traced a fine line as the drum rotated. The spot moved over 0.01 in. for each drum rotation, tracing a spiral about 8.5 × 100 × 11 in. long (= 9350 in.).

Instead of a single scanning spot, Group 3 fax machines use a stationary strip (array) of 1728 photosensors, one for each spot (or pixel) across the page. An electronic clock that ticks about a million times a second causes one photosensor to be read per tick. The whole page can be read in 5 to 10 s. The scanner reads sequentially, as one scanning line, all of the 1728 picture elements across the width of the page being sent. A stepper motor moves the page down and the next strip below is read. The first line starts in the upper left corner of the page. Wider sensor arrays of 2048 or 2432 pixels are used for the alternative wider page Group 3 fax machines.

6.2 CCD CHIP SCANNERS

The camera type of optics imaging system has a small charge-coupled device (CCD) photosensor chip where the 35-mm film would be in a camera. As with a camera, the lens cannot be very close to the page. At least 12 in. is required between the scanning line and the CCD chip. This distance controls the minimum size of the fax machine. The 8.5-in. page width matches the width of the 10:1 reduced-size image on the strip of 1728 photosensors. The scanning line position on the page is determined by the part of the image falling onto the photosensitive strip of the chip. These sensors see only a thin 0.005-in.-high line across the page (see Figure 6.1).

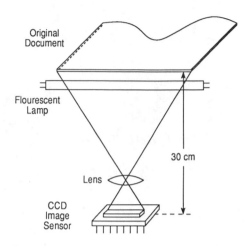

Figure 6.1 Camera type of CCD scanner.

Consider each photosensor of the 1728-element strip across the chip as a light-sensitive resistor connected in parallel with a small capacitor. The capacitor starts with a full voltage charge. If the image spot is white, the photosensor has a very low resistance that drains the voltage off the capacitor during an exposure time. If the image spot is black, the photosensor has a high resistance and the capacitor is not discharged.

A second 1728-element strip, near the photosensor strip is the CCD itself, an analog shift register (sometimes called a bucket brigade). This strip is divided with voltage gradient lines forming wells matching the photosensor elements. Between these strips is a strip of transfer gates (switches). The gates are open during the exposure time for each scanning line. Then the gates all close momentarily. The current in-rush to recharge the capacitors forms charge packets that represent each photosensor brightness in the CCD wells. A network of electrodes that form these wells is connected to different phases of the clock that controls the electronic scan, moving these charge packets in series to the output terminal. Each packet voltage represents the brightness for a particular photosensor, starting at the left end of the scanning line. Exposure of the image on the photosensor strip continues for the time between scanning lines, providing good sensitivity by allowing the longest time possible for the voltage to leak off.

After the 1728th pixel is sampled, a stepper motor moves the page down 0.01 in. and the process continues for the next scanning line. The photosensor capacitors are again charged and ready to accumulate a new line of data. The previous line in the analog shift register is transferred serially on clock pulses to the sensor's output where the successive charge packets are converted into an analog voltage. The output frequency may reach 20 MHz or more.

The amplitude of the picture signal is highest for white and lowest for black. Gray pixels have intermediate amplitudes. Each sensor is a pixel whose picture signal is connected in sequence to an automatic background control (ABC) circuit. For a gray or colored background, the gain of the ABC increases until its output is the same voltage as for a white background. Decrease in output signal amplitude caused by fall-off in brightness near the edge of the page is only partially compensated for by masking the light for the center of the line. Variations in sensitivity of the individual photosensor elements cause irregularities in the signal from the scan head. Without correction, vertical streaks would show in the received fax copy when sending a photograph, and there would even be a small effect on the quality of text. An electronic shading circuit corrects each pixel for a uniform background signal amplitude. Digital memory for each pixel controls the correction. This correction is very important for scanners that generate 256 shades of gray scale. Only the area near the scanning line is illuminated. As the paper moves past the scanning line, the other parts of the page are illuminated.

The analog picture signal is then changed to digital by a one bit per sample analog-to-digital (A/D) converter. A front panel control allows the operator to change the A/D threshold voltage, compensating for faded text or light markings on the page being sent. The output of the A/D converter is a digital signal with each input pixel converted to a one bit pel (black or white). This binary digital processing is necessary for efficient coding of the picture signal. The black-white effect on the page being sent is similar to that produced by an office copier.

6.3 CONTACT IMAGE SENSOR (CIS) SCANNERS

A major size reduction of Group 3 fax machines is an advantage when using a CIS scanner instead of the camera type of scanner described above. CIS uses a strip of photosensors 8.5 in. wide instead of a line of photosensors about 0.8 in. wide across a CCD chip. All of the scanner elements are contained in a small bar mounted to contact the page being scanned as it moves past. The scan bar also contains lamps for illumination of the scan line, optics (if any), the sensor array, and video signal processing circuitry. CIS scanners have the advantage of maintaining the exact dot position across the page and having the same sharpness of focus on the end of a line as in the center of the page being sent. The discussion of operation and circuitry given above also applies to CIS scanners. Either optics or full-contact imaging methods are used for CIS scanners (see Figure 6.2).

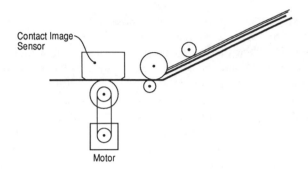

Figure 6.2 CIS scanner.

6.3.1 Optics CIS

An 8.5-in. narrow bar containing Selfoc™ fiber optics is mounted between the page being scanned and the photosensors. This is the same type of 1:1 optical imaging system used in some office copiers. Only about 5 cm is required between the sensor array and the page being scanned (see Figure 6.3).

The light source may be a fluorescent lamp mounted near the page being sent. In one design, the scanning line is directly above a fiber optics rod-lens array. It is focused with a 1:1 magnification onto the long image sensor strip below it. Each photosensor element is the same size as the pixel that it sees.

In an alternative arrangement, illumination of the line being scanned is provided by one or two rows of light-emitting diodes (LEDs) with built-in lenses. CIS scanners are also available in a moving scan-head design where the page to be sent is held face down on a glass plate and the scan head reads through the glass as it moves down the page (see Figure 6.4).

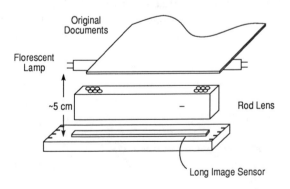

Figure 6.3 Contact image optics type of scanner.

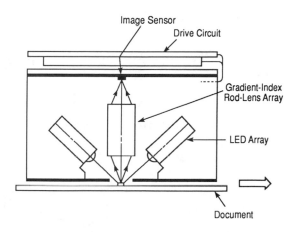

Figure 6.4 Contact image scanner.

The photosensor may be made from three 3-in.-wide silicon CCD or cadmium sulfide–cadmium selenide strips. The three strips are offset with overlap to allow for the mounting area beyond the sensors at the end of each strip. Analog memories fabricated with the CCD chips compensate for the offset. Signals from the strips that first see the scan line being read are stored until the paper-feed steps the same scan line into position to be read by the other strips. A manufacturing technique for mounting all CCD chips in a straight line developed by at least one company avoids the necessity for offset-compensation circuitry.

6.3.2 Full-Contact CIS

A full-contact CIS scanner is a lower cost design that may use amorphous silicon arrays. A continuous coating process makes a single array the width of the whole scanning line. The scan head has a very small hole through the center of each small photosensor element (see Figure 6.5).

An LED array for illumination of the scan line is on one side of the photosensor strip and the page being scanned is on the other side. Light from an LED passes through a photosensor hole to illuminate a very small spot (pixel) on the page being scanned. A transparent coating on the page side holds the paper a small distance from the sensitive side of the photosensor strip, allowing light from the illuminated spot on the page to diffuse and reach the sensitive area of the photosensor surrounding this hole. Practically none of the light reflected by one spot is picked up by adjacent sensors. The optical efficiency of this system is higher than the rod-lens

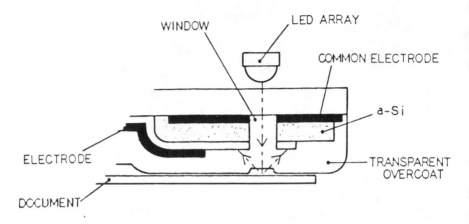

Figure 6.5 Full-contact CIS cross section.

optical imaging type. Amorphous silicon is less expensive, but the signal-to-noise ratio is only about 20 dB (borderline), compared to about 38 dB for the other sensors.

Self-contained scanners are available for use with PCs. They can be used with PC-fax cards, optical character recognition software, or for entering imagery from hard copy into computer memory for desktop publishing and other programs. When scanners first became available, most were based on facsimile standards with 203 dpi. Now most scanners for PCs also offer higher resolutions of 300 or 400 dpi.

Chapter 7
Printing Technology

Printing technology is a critical part of the quality of the output copy produced by a facsimile system. Most Group 3 fax machines use direct recording on thermal-sensitive paper, but plain paper recording methods (ink-jet, thermal transfer, xerographic) are becoming more common.

7.1 THERMAL PAPER FAX RECORDING

Recording directly onto heat-sensitive paper is the method used by most fax receivers today. The print head has a a comb-shaped array of wires with a row of very small resistor-element spots across the recording paper width; 1728 for 8.5 in., 2048 for 10 in., 2432 for 11.9 in.

The thermal recording paper touches this row of resistors. A pulse of current through a resistor causes it to become hot enough to mark the paper in a spot of about 0.005 in. diameter. The spot temperature must be changed from nonmarking temperature to marking temperature and return to nonmarking before the paper steps to the next recording line. The recording cycle may be 2.5 to 5 ms. In one design, 24 V at a power level of 0.5 W is applied to a marking resistor for about 0.6 ms. Marking temperature is about 200°F. Other head designs use 12 or 6 V.

Either thin-film or thick-film technology is used to make the print heads. Thin-film heads use a lower recording power and can be made with higher resolution. The head wires and integrated circuit elements are made in one compact head assembly (see Figure 7.1). Thick-film print heads have good immunity scratches and abrasive wear and enough resolution for Group 3 fax units.

The advantages of direct thermal recording include the following:

- Good readability of the recorded copy is produced with saturated sharp-edged black marks on an off-white background.
- The fax equipment and the recording paper costs are low.
- The fax equipment size is small. A small-volume print head design with the

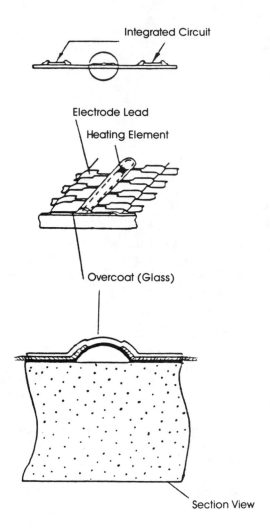

Figure 7.1 Thin-film thermal print head.

print driver electronics in an integral package with the print head wires makes this possible.

- There are no toner powders to be changed or to cause smudges. The only regular chore involved with fax equipment is changing the roll of recording paper, a very simple task.
- The print heads normally last the life of the fax machine without service calls or user maintenance.

The disadvantages of direct thermal recording are:

- The contrast of the recording deteriorates if thermal paper is exposed to light or heat. For archival records, an office copier print should be used even though a 5-yr copy life might be achieved with properly chosen paper type and favorable storage conditions.
- The paper curls and does not look or handle like regular white bond paper.
- The replacement cost of the thermal head may be up to half the original price of the fax machine. The thermal print head is one of the most sensitive components of a fax machine. For this reason, manufacturer's recommendations should be followed on which thermal recording papers will give good long-term results. In addition to producing good copy quality, the paper thickness must match the printer requirements. Abrasive materials may cause premature failure due to wear, and corrosive agents in the paper may be deposited on the print head.
- The following problem does not occur in most Group 3 fax machines, but may happen when a very small size thermal fax machine is used for high-volume applications. The thermal printing process uses low power while reproducing white areas, but when recording black all the way across the page, the print head alone may require 100 W or more to heat all wires at once. Under normal circumstances, this happens intermittently and the thermal mass of the print head assembly prevents overheating. Printing successive pages containing large amounts of black area might overheat the print head, causing warping or burn-out. To protect against this, a thermal sensor causes the print power to turn off until the head cools. A thermal fuse may also be used as backup, in case of failure of the thermal sensor logic to perform properly. The design of the print head and its drivers determines how much black can be printed before the power shuts off.

7.2 PLAIN PAPER FAX RECORDING

For the best fax recording quality, handling, and life of recording, plain paper fax recording is preferred. Plain paper looks and feels like a regular business document and doesn't have to be copied before use or permanent storage. The number of plain paper Group 3 fax machine models is growing rapidly now that the costs are lower. Five types of plain paper fax machines are described in this section.

7.2.1 Thermal-Transfer Recording

Thermal-transfer fax machines write on white paper instead of light gray thermal paper. Recorded copy handles about the same as copy from an office copier. Storage is not restricted by light or heat conditions as is the case for thermal paper. The print head is basically the same as the one used in thermal fax recorders.[1] A roll of white paper and a roll of black thermal-transfer film (often called ribbon) are used, with the film placed between the thermal head and the white paper (see Figure 7.2).

The black thermal-transfer film moves with the paper at the same rate, using the same quantities. The marking is made on white paper from a black pigment-impregnated wax coating (ink). Instead of impact transfer with carbon paper,[2] heat from the hot spots across the recording line causes black marks to be made on the white paper. The ink transfers completely to the white paper opposite the print-head wires and the transfer film has a negative record of all the pages recorded. This film roll can be retained for backup purposes, but it may be messy to handle. Before discarding this roll, consider whether the information it contains should be kept confidential.

Alternatively, new multipass thermal-transfer films produce more than one image from the same roll of film, thus lowering the cost of printing. Some of the newer fax machines use a stack of cut-sheet white bond paper instead of a roll of paper.

Recent advances in recording materials and printer design have been utilized in thermal-transfer fax machines to move from producing images of low to high quality. The sharp images have good moisture resistance and archival qualities.

Compared with direct thermal recording fax machines, the machine cost is higher and the size is larger. The cost of thermal-transfer recording materials varies from

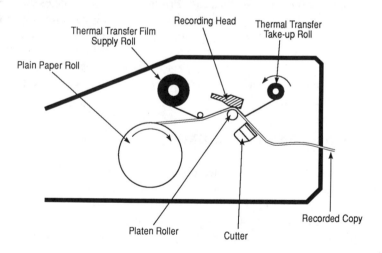

Figure 7.2 Thermal-transfer fax recording.

---

[1]Regular thermal paper can often be used as an alternative recording medium in thermal-transfer recorders.

[2]Thermal-transfer recordings are much sharper than carbon copies.

somewhat higher to about three times that of direct thermal recording. The overall reliability of the thermal-transfer fax machine may be less due to the mechanical take-up reel.

Early thermal-transfer fax machines required a very smooth (highly calendared) white recording paper. Originally, the black transfer ink would not mark in the valleys of bond paper, making a very spotty recording. The transferred ink has been made more viscous and fills in the rough spots for more even coverage of the entire paper marking area.

7.2.2 Laser Fax Xerographic Recorder

Xerography, the original form of electrophotography, was invented by Chester F. Carlson on October 22, 1938. His U.S. Patent 2,221,776 was issued two years later. Laser xerographic printers operating at 300 dpi are a well-established technology for office use in word processing, desk-top publishing,and now PC-fax systems. Similar laser printers, adapted to work at 400 dpi, are used as the recorders in almost all Group 4 fax machines. The quality of recorded copy is superior to that of thermal or thermal-transfer types used in Group 3 fax machines; however, the laser printer size and price have prevented it from making inroads into the Group 3 fax market.

Laser fax recorders are similar to office copiers, but the imaging is done by a fax signal that modulates a laser beam rather than direct optical imaging of a page to be copied (see Figure 7.3).

A small-diameter beam from a semiconductor laser is swept across a photo-sensitive semiconductor drum by a rotating polygon mirror, making one recording

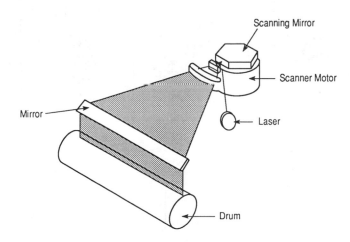

Figure 7.3 Laser fax xerographic recorder.

line per mirror face. An imaging lens system keeps the spot in focus. The drum rotates the height of one recording line for each mirror-face sweep. Some designs may use a photosensitive belt instead of a drum.

7.2.3 LED Fax Recording

An LED contact-type linear array is used in some Group 3 fax recorders instead of a laser and rotating-mirror system. This simplifies the recorder and increases its reliability by eliminating the rotating-mirror (see Figure 7.4).

An LED print head with 300 or 400 dpi is focused onto the photosensitive drum with a fiber optics rod-lens array. The drum has been charged by a high-voltage corona unit (electrostatic charge) before reaching the recording line. The charge is maintained in the dark, but is discharged at those points along the line exposed to light from the LEDs. The charge-pattern image remaining on the drum corresponds to the black marks on the page being sent by the fax transmitter. As this image passes the development box, black toner powder is picked up to reproduce a mirror-image

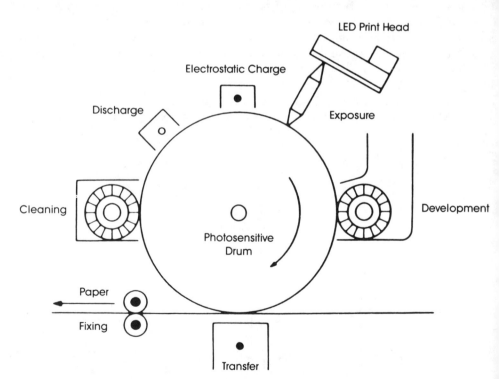

Figure 7.4 LED linear array recorder.

copy of the original. A sheet of paper is fed onto the drum surface to start in step with the page image. As the drum rotates, the sheet passes the transfer-corona station and the toner image transfers from the drum to the paper. The image is heat or pressure fixed to the sheet to form a permanent copy of the page sent. Recording widths of 8.5 in. and wider are available. The focus and spot size of the image are the same for all points (see Figure 7.5).

GLASS COVER

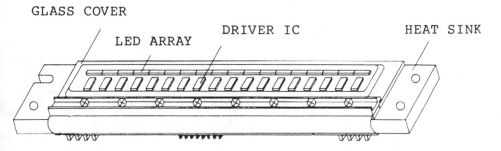

Figure 7.5 LED linear array print head.

7.2.4 Ink-Jet Fax Recording

Ink-jet recording, earlier tried for fax with little success, is now one of the lowest cost methods being offered. The received facsimiles are sharp and the plain paper avoids the curl and handling problems of thermal recording used by most fax machines. These fax machines should compete with the low-cost thermal fax machines. The resolutions up to 300 dpi offered on some models result in fax copy that compares favorably with that produced on a laser recorder. The plain paper used allows for the making of notes on the received copy with pen, pencil (erasable), or marker, and ink fading is not a problem with documents left out on the desk or filed. The recording power required is very low compared to laser, LED, liquid-crystal shutter, or thermal recording.

With all of the good features of ink-jet, the question arises as to why ink-jet fax machines have not been more popular than thermal recorders. Ink-jet fax machines were designed and limited numbers were built many years ago. Problems with the ink clogging, especially when left idle for a few days, and the messy job of handling the ink prevented them from being put into production. Again, before the Group 2 standard was in place, a few manufacturers did put ink-jet fax machines on the market, but they never became very popular and were withdrawn from sales.

What may have changed the situation now is the success of 300-dpi ink-jet printers for PCs. One of the prime reasons for this success is the incorporation of a replaceable cartridge that contains both the ink and the print jets. With the recent adoption of this type of printer for fax, a swing from thermal to ink-jet may occur, at least for the low- to medium-volume users. The ability to record either millimeter-based-resolution or inch-based-resolution on the same printer gives ink-jet a distinct advantage. The 300 dpi matches Group 4, and the 8 lines/mm matches Group 3, allowing the same fax machine to record both without size distortion. Many expect the new high-resolution Group 3 machines to have 300 dpi, not 304.8 dpi (12 lines/mm).

7.2.5 Liquid-Crystal Shutter Fax Printer

A liquid- crystal shutter (LCS) printer performs in the same manner as the 300-dpi LED printer described above. A linear-array strip of light elements is the same length as the recording paper width. The liquid-crystal elements selectively stop the light passing through them to write on the photosensitive drum. Very simple optics image the light spots on the photoconductive drum of the recorder. This type of print engine could be substituted for a laser printer in Group 3 facsimile designs. A typical LCS printer matches the LED print quality and produces 8 pages/min.

Chapter 8

Advanced Coding of Bilevel Images

8.1 OVERVIEW

Figure 8.1 is a diagram showing the hierarchy of compression techniques for the efficient coding of black-white or bilevel images. There are two broad categories of compression techniques: *information-preserving* (lossless) and *approximation* (lossy) techniques.

Information-preserving techniques may be defined as being lossless or reversible in the sense that the output image will be a perfect replica of the input image if there are no transmission errors. The two classes of compression techniques that preserve information are nonadaptive and adaptive. The nonadaptive techniques employ a coding algorithm that is independent of the statistics of the particular image being transmitted, while adaptive techniques employ an algorithm that is dependent on, and adapts to, the statistics of the image being encoded. Nonadaptive coding techniques are usually designed to compress the average or typical image very efficiently (e.g., text) and consequently are less efficient for the atypical image.

As indicated by Figure 8.1, most of the technical activity to date has been in the area of nonadaptive coding, which, in turn, is divided between those techniques that reduce redundancy in one dimension and those that reduce redundancy in two dimensions. The most well-known one-dimensional code is the modified Huffman code (MHC), which is the CCITT standard for Group 3 facsimile equipment.

The two different types of codes that remove redundancy in two dimensions are those that encode several scan lines simultaneously and those that encode each individual scan line on a line-by-line basis.

The two-line Weber code is an example of a multiple-line coding technique [1]. It is generally accepted that the more aggressive line-by-line techniques outperform the multiple-line techniques.

The two subclasses of line-by-line coding techniques are those that first perform a predictive function and those that do not. The prediction function is best explained by referring to Figure 8.2, which shows one possible rule for predicting the brightness of a pel based on the preceding pel in the same line and three adjacent pels in

INFORMATION PRESERVING

+ Nonadaptive
  • One-dimensional
  — Modified Huffman

  • Two-Dimensional
  — Multiple Line Coding
  — Line-by-Line Coding
    + Predictive
      • RLC Prediction Errors
      • RLC Prediction States
      • RLC Reordered Data
    + Nonpredictive
      • Modified Read
      • Modified Read II

+ Adaptive
  • Arithmetic Coding

APPROXIMATION

  • Interpolation
  • Feature Recognition
  • Symbol Recognition

Figure 8.1 Data compression techniques for black-white graphics.

State Number		Prediction	Probability of Correct Prediction	Probability of State	State Number	State Definition	Prediction	Probability of Correct Prediction	Probability of State
1	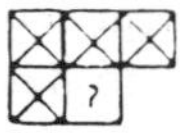	B	.96	.055	9	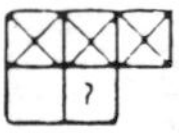	W	.63	.017
2	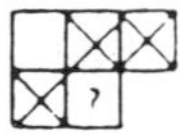	B	1.0	.0076	10	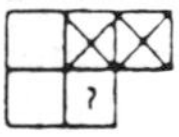	B	.71	.026
3	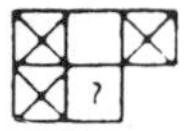	B	1.0	.0001	11	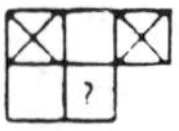	W	1.0	.0003
4	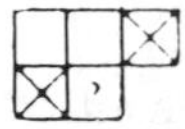	B	.99	.0033	12	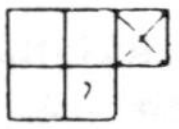	W	.85	.032

Figure 8.2 Four pel prediction algorithm.

State Number	State Definition	Prediction	Probability of Correct Prediction	Probability of State	State Number	State Definition	Prediction	Probability of Correct Prediction	Probability of State
5		B	.83	.0291	13		W	.84	.003
6		B	1.0	.0008	14		B	.86	.0015
7		W	.74	.027	15		W	1.0	.008
8		B	.55	.017	16		W	.99	.77

Figure 8.2 (cont'd)

the line above. In such a system, the original binary image is processed according to the prediction algorithm to form a new binary "image." Each pel in the new "image" is either a correct prediction or an incorrect prediction. The next question is how to process the new image of correct and incorrect predictions for transmission. Three alternatives have been proposed in the literature. The first performs a conventional run-length coding of the prediction image [2]. The second performs a run-length coding process on 16 different prediction images [3] each devoted to a separate prediction state in Figure 8.2. The third performs a reordering function prior to run-length coding [4]. In general, these predictive techniques do not perform as well as aggressive nonpredictive techniques.

The nonpredictive coding techniques directly process the imagery data on a line-by-line basis. The most well-known example of this compression technique is the modified read code (MRC), which is the optional code in Group 3 facsimile. (The compression algorithm is described in detail in Chapter 3.) This coding concept is based on the transmission of the location of black-white transitions relative to a corresponding transition on the line above.

The basic MR code is designed for facsimile transmission over the PSTN and between fax machines that are mechanically limited in their ability to advance the paper rapidly when transmitting a redundant portion of the page. For example, if a large portion of the page is white, it is frequently required to transmit "fill" bits because the fax machine is slower than the compressed data. The MR2 code is an adaptation of the basic MR code for transmission over data circuits with error control and between fax machines with image storage. Table 8.1 compares the characteristics of the two modified read codes.

Table 8.1

The difference between the Group 3 two-dimensional coding scheme and the Group 4 basic coding scheme.

Apparatus \ Item	First Line	K Parameter	Line Synchronization Code Word	End of Page	Fill Bits per Line	Pad Bits per Page	Run Length Longer Than 2623
G3	One-dimensional coding (MH)	K = 2 (standard res.) K = 4 (optional higher res.)	EOL + tag	RTC = 6 × (EOL + tag)	Variable-length string of "O"s	Not specified	Not specified
G4	Two-dimensional coding (MR) Note: reference line for first coded line is set to an imaginary white line	K: not specified all lines including the first line of a page are coded two-dimensionally	Not required	EOFB = 2 × EOL	Not required	Variable-length string of "0"s	Using the MUC(s) of 2560

An example of an adaptive information-preserving technique is arithmetic coding. This technique permits the more efficient compression of binary sequences as the statistics of the facsimile data changes [5,6].

Approximation Techniques

In the case of approximation techniques, the output binary image is usually not a perfect replica of the input binary image. Approximations are knowingly made for the intended purpose of achieving a higher compression ratio than can be achieved by those techniques that exactly reproduce the input image.

In the case of interpolation techniques, particular pels in the input image are purposely deleted from transmission. At the receiver, the brightness values of the missing pels are estimated from those adjacent pels that are transmitted. In the case of line interpolation, every other line is deleted from transmission, and the missing lines are replaced at the receiver by a line interpolation algorithm. (A brief description of such an algorithm is provided in Section 8.3.)

The ultimate compression technique, which reproduces an approximation of the input image, is a system that recognizes symbols such as alphanumeric text. A feature recognition system is very similar to symbol recognition; the primary difference is the complexity and size of the pattern that is recognized. In the case of feature recognition, the pattern that is recognized could be a portion of a symbol such as the cross bar of the letter t or the vertical bar in a the letter H. Figure 8.3(a) illustrates a set of five symbols sampled into binary pels. Figure 8.3(b) illustrates the same symbols after the binary pels have been processed by an algorithm that

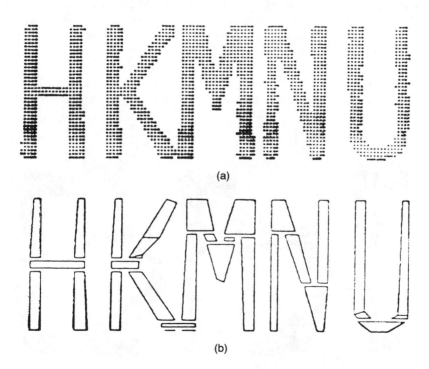

(a)

(b)

Figure 8.3 (a) Image definition by pels. (b) Image definition by quadrilateral features.

divides the symbol into quadrilateral features. A high degree of compression is achieved by transmitting merely the coordinates of the corners of the quadrilateral features.

The ultimate graphic compression technique is symbol recognition, whereby a large number of pels defining a symbol are transmitted by a short ASCII-like code. One basic concept describing this approach is *combined symbol matching* (CSM) [7] where the system adapts to the particular symbol font that is transmitted. This is done by first building up a library of characters at both the transmitter and receiver whenever a new symbol is encountered. When a subsequent symbol is found to match closely a symbol in the library, a short ASCII-like code is transmitted to the receiver. At the receiver, the corresponding bit pattern is retrieved from the library and printed. A basic requirement of symbol recognition systems is that the image must be divided into two parts, symbols and graphics. In the case of CSM, the graphic portions of the image are coded using the MR algorithm.

8.2 INPUT SPATIAL FILTERING

Figure 8.4 is an enlarged view of typographical characters illustrating the ragged nature of the edge of the image. Notice that the raggedness varies from character to character, indicating the complex and variable relationship between the paper fiber and the printing process. In the conventional printing process, this raggedness is obviously not visible to the eye due to its small size. Figure 8.5 illustrates how the scanning and spatial sampling process inherent in digital facsimile systems creates a much higher level of raggedness than existed in the original image. This digital

Figure 8.4 Enlarged view of typographical characters.

"noise" is not only harmful from an image quality point of view, but it also reduces the compressibility of the source image. Therefore, spatial filtering of the scanned fax signal prior to compression would be advantageous to improve the output picture quality and to reduce transmission time.

The performance of one particular simple spatially filter was measured by means of computer stimulation. The filter is illustrated in Figure 8.6 for one particular orientation and color combination. The three other orientations and four other color combinations are also included in the simulation. Figures 8.7 and 8.8 illustrate the input and output pixel image for such a filter. The compression for the filtered image was improved between 5 and 10% relative to the unfiltered image.

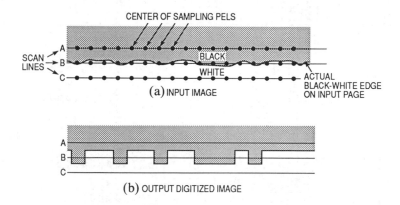

Figure 8.5 Digital input image noise.

ORIGINAL			OUTPUT		
B	B	B	B	B	B
W	B	W	W	W	W
W	W	W	W	W	W

Figure 8.6 Spatial filter.

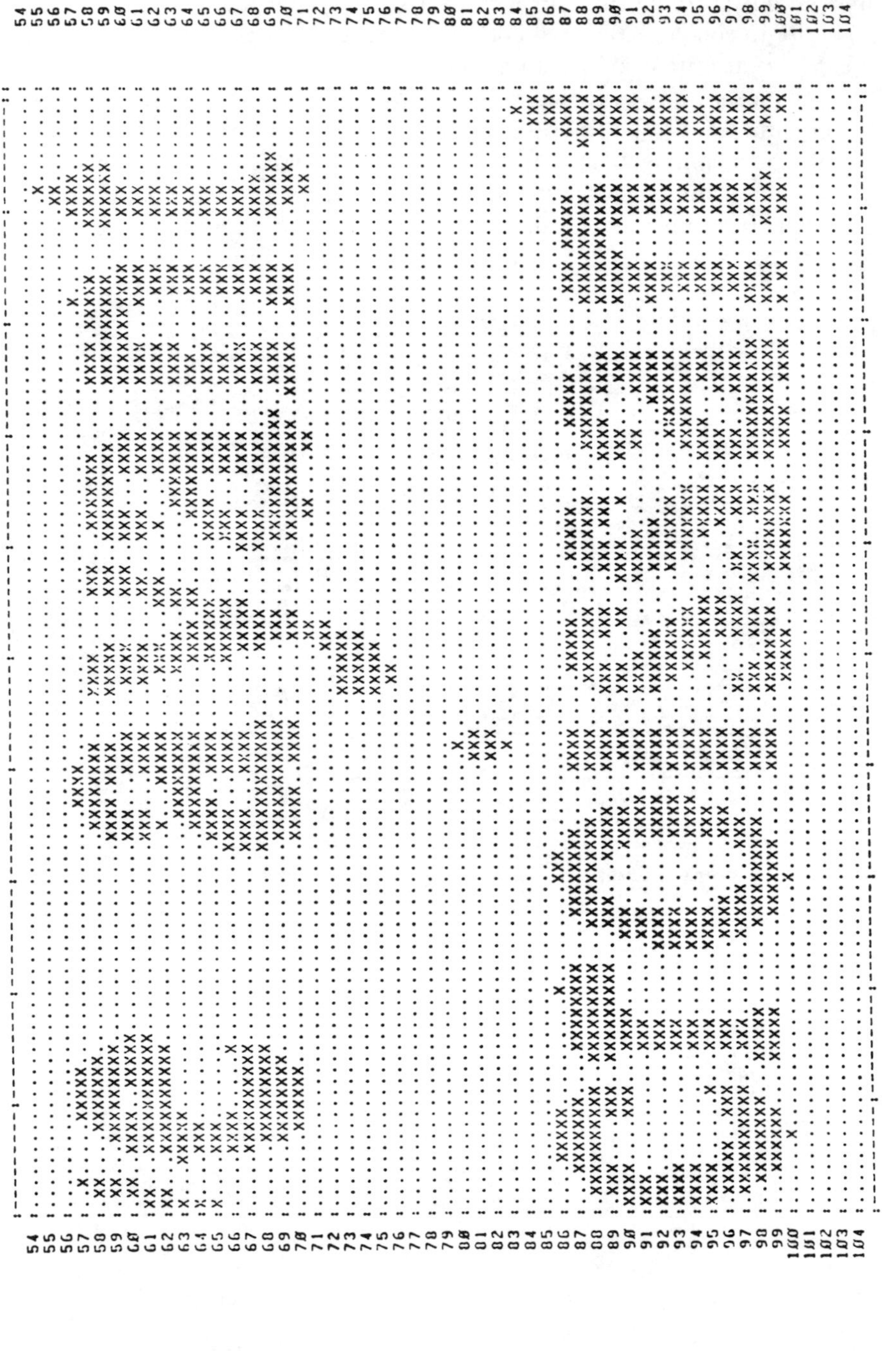

152

Figure 8.7 Unfiltered image.

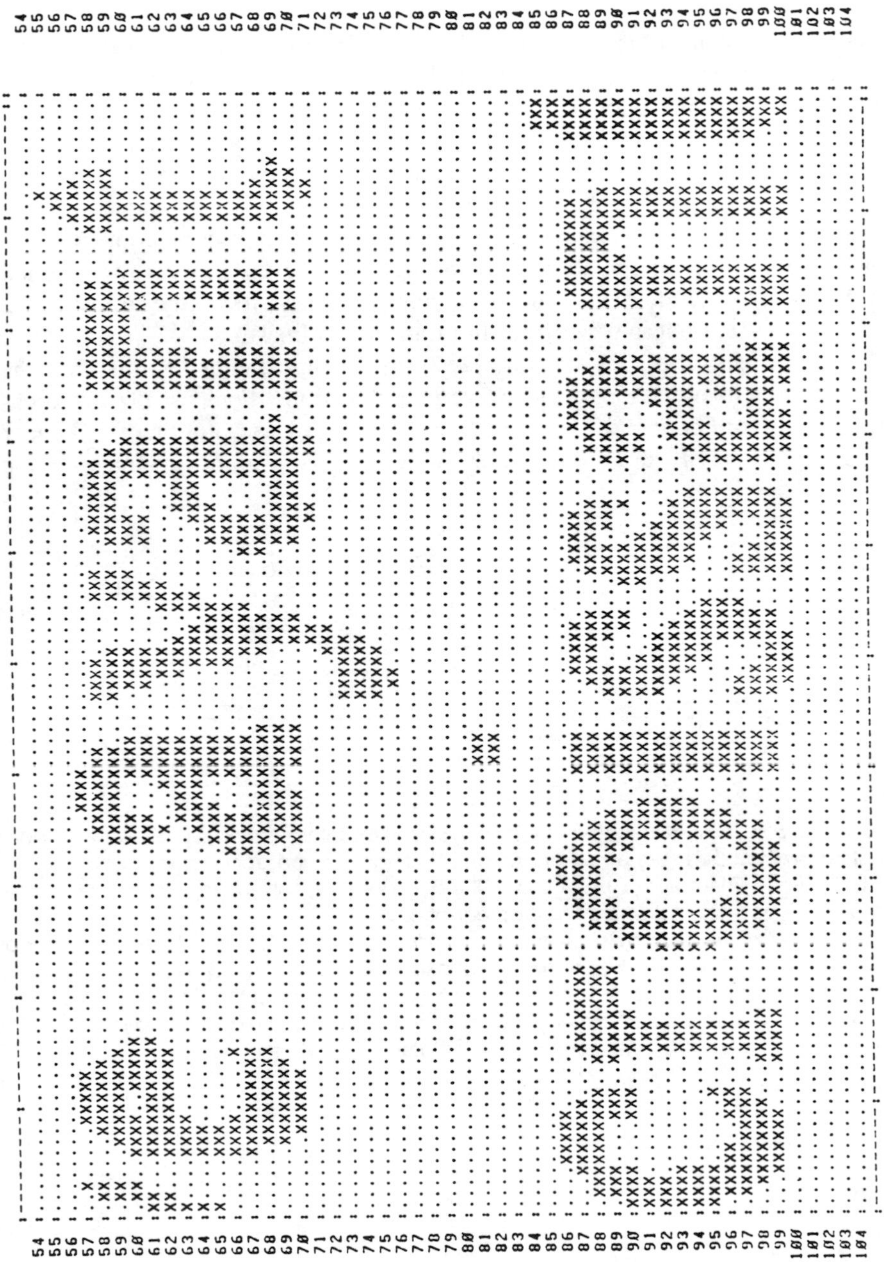

Figure 8.8 White and black single pel on edge.

8.3 INTERPOLATION

Source coding, a technique that reduces redundancy inherent in the input document, is the most common image compression technique. The modified Huffman and Modified Read codes are examples of source coding techniques. A fundamental characteristic of source coding is that the compression ratio is highly dependent on the complexity of the input document. Complex documents require more transmission time than documents containing little information. Interpolation techniques, on the other hand, achieve a fixed compression ratio independent of picture content. Consider the alternate line interpolation method, which achieves a fixed compression ratio of 2:1 by deleting alternate scan lines from transmission. At the receiver, the missing scan lines are interpolated from the transmitted lines.

Consider a typical digital facsimile system, which scans and prints with the same resolution in both the horizontal and vertical directions. For example, the high-resolution option for Group 3 facsimile equipment employs a resolution of 7.7 lines/mm in both directions. Figure 8.9 illustrates the general concept of line interpolation

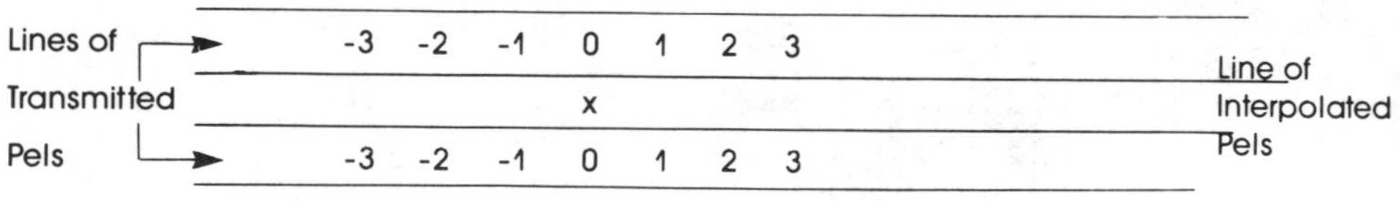

Lines of Transmitted Pels | -3 -2 -1 0 1 2 3 | Line of Interpolated Pels
x
-3 -2 -1 0 1 2 3

Designation of pairs of Transmitted Pels: P_{-3} P_{-2} P_{-1} P P_1 P_2 P_3

The pel to be interpolated is designated as x. The first step in the interpolation process is to consider the pair of transmitted pels (P_0) which are adjacent to x in the line above and below. If the P_0 pels are both black, interpolate x to be black. If the P_0 pels are both white, interpolate x to be white. If the two P_0 pels are of different color, adjacent pairs are examined to determine the color of the nearest pair where both pels are black or white. Pel x is interpolated to be the color of the nearest pair which is all black or all white. For example, if pairs P_{-2}, P_{-1}, P_0, and P_1 all have differing colored pels in each pair, but the pels in P_2 are both white, then x is interpolated to be white. If opposite colors are found equidistant from x, then x is interpolated to be white. For example, under the following conditions x is interpolated to be white:

P_{-2} — both black
P_{-1} ⎫
P_0 ⎬ — pairs have different colored pels
P_1 ⎭
P_2 — both white

Figure 8.9 Alternate line interpolation.

where each square represents one pixel in the input and output images (e.g., 1/200 in. × 1/200 in.). As shown in the diagram, every other line of pixels is transmitted, and the lines not transmitted are interpolated at the receiver.

In Figure 8.9, the pixel labeled "x" is being interpolated using the transmitted information from the lines above and below. The interpolation scheme differs from source coding in two respects. First, the compression ratio is fixed at 2:1 regardless of the redundancy of the input image. Second, the interpolation techniques does not reproduce the input digital image exactly, and thus errors will occasionally be made.

The above discussion views the proposed system from a data compression perspective. We may also consider the interpolation proposal from an "image enhancement" viewpoint. Figure 8.10 illustrates the typical "stairstep" distortion in a conventional digital facsimile system when scanning a black-white edge, which is nearly parallel with the scanning track. This ragged edge distortion is very visible to the naked eye and significantly reduces the acceptability of digital facsimile. We can enhance the appearance of the output image by artificially creating, or interpolating, twice as many scan lines on the output copy as were scanned and transmitted. If this were done, the size of the ragged stairstep distortion would be reduced to half, and the image would be more pleasing to the eye. The proposed interpolation algorithm would automatically position the stairstep transitions on the interpolated lines in the

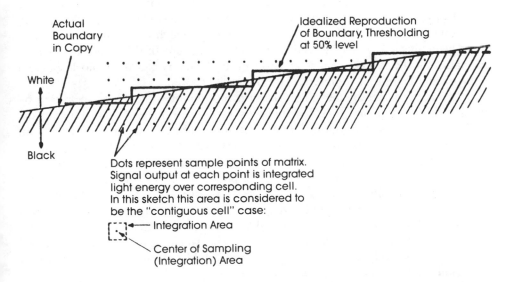

Figure 8.10 Staircase.

optimum position—halfway between the steps on the above and below transmitted lines.

8.4 PATTERN RECOGNITION

A large fraction of the pages transmitted through facsimile systems contain primarily textual information. Several investigators have proposed pattern recognition techniques to detect symbols, such as text in an OCR-like manner, and to transmit the location and identification of the patterns using a short, efficient, ASCII-like code. Conventional OCR techniques are not feasible in the facsimile environment due to the large number of fonts that could be encountered and to the uncontrolled nature of the fax signal. However, it is feasible to consider an adaptive OCR-like system that develops a library of characters as the page is scanned. The first work in this pattern recognition area was identified as CSM [7]. More recent work has been performed by AT&T, culminating in a technical contribution to the CCITT in 1983. The remainder of this section describes the AT&T technique and its performance.

A facsimile image is examined line by line. When a black pel is located, a *pattern isolator* surrounds connected pels in order to extract the entire pattern of which the pel is a member. The pattern is decomposed into $M \times M$ sub-blocks called *symbols*. In many cases, a symbol will be an isolated pattern that fits entirely within the $M \times M$ block. The incoming symbol is matched with already identified symbols stored in a library. If a match is detected, information about the position of the symbol in the image and its location in the library is coded. If no match is found, the incoming symbol is added to the symbol library, which is assumed to be empty at the beginning of the coding and is gradually built up. In this case, an accurate description of the symbol and its position in the image is coded. A block diagram of the coding algorithm is presented in Figure 8.11.

The performance of the AT&T pattern recognition system was measured by means of computer simulation. Compression ratios were measured for three of the CCITT test documents at four different resolutions. The compression of the pattern recognition system is approximately three times that for Modified Modified Read.

This higher compression is not achieved without a cost in picture quality. Figure 8.12 illustrates the pixel printout for the bottom of CCITT document number 1 as it would be printed for a lossless compression system such as MR2. Figure 8.13 shows the comparable image produced by the pattern recognition system. Notice that the letters e and s have all been recognized to be the same character. Note, however, that the characters on the input document are very small, much smaller than typed characters. It is likely that the misrecognition would not affect the readability or intelligibility of the document at all.

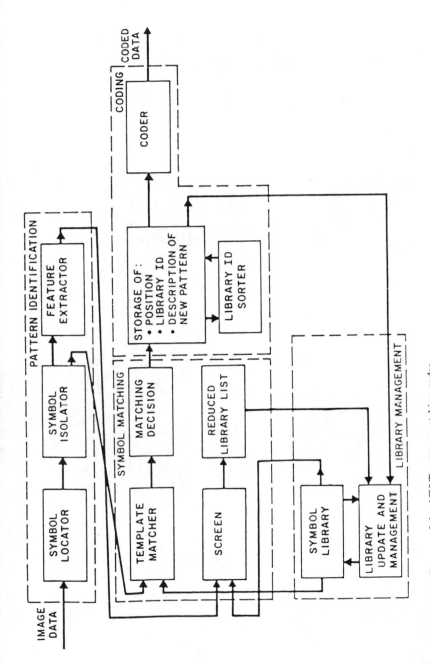

Figure 8.11 Block diagram of the AT&T pattern matching coder.

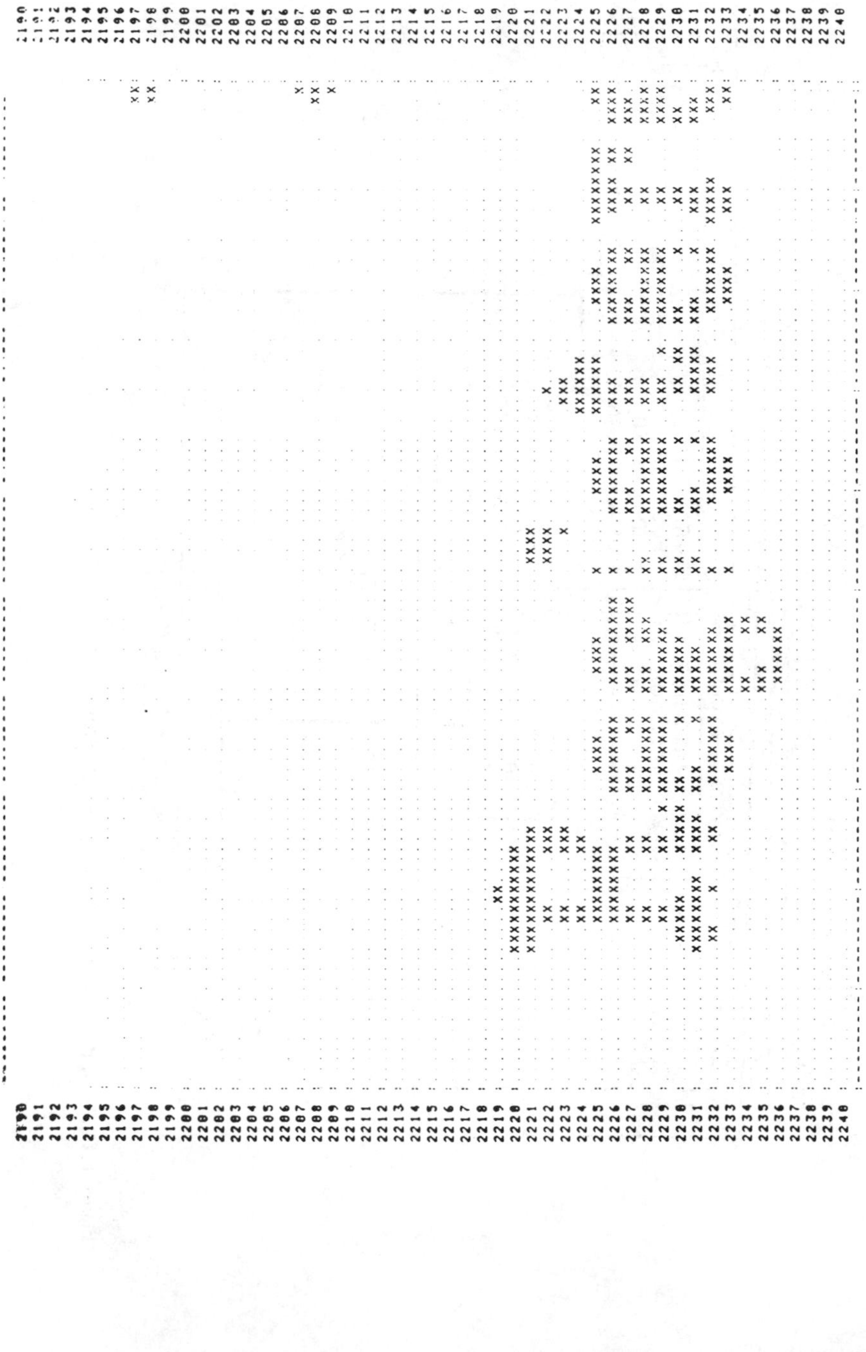

Figure 8.12 Original input image: CCITT document number 1; 200 lines/in., bit image printout.

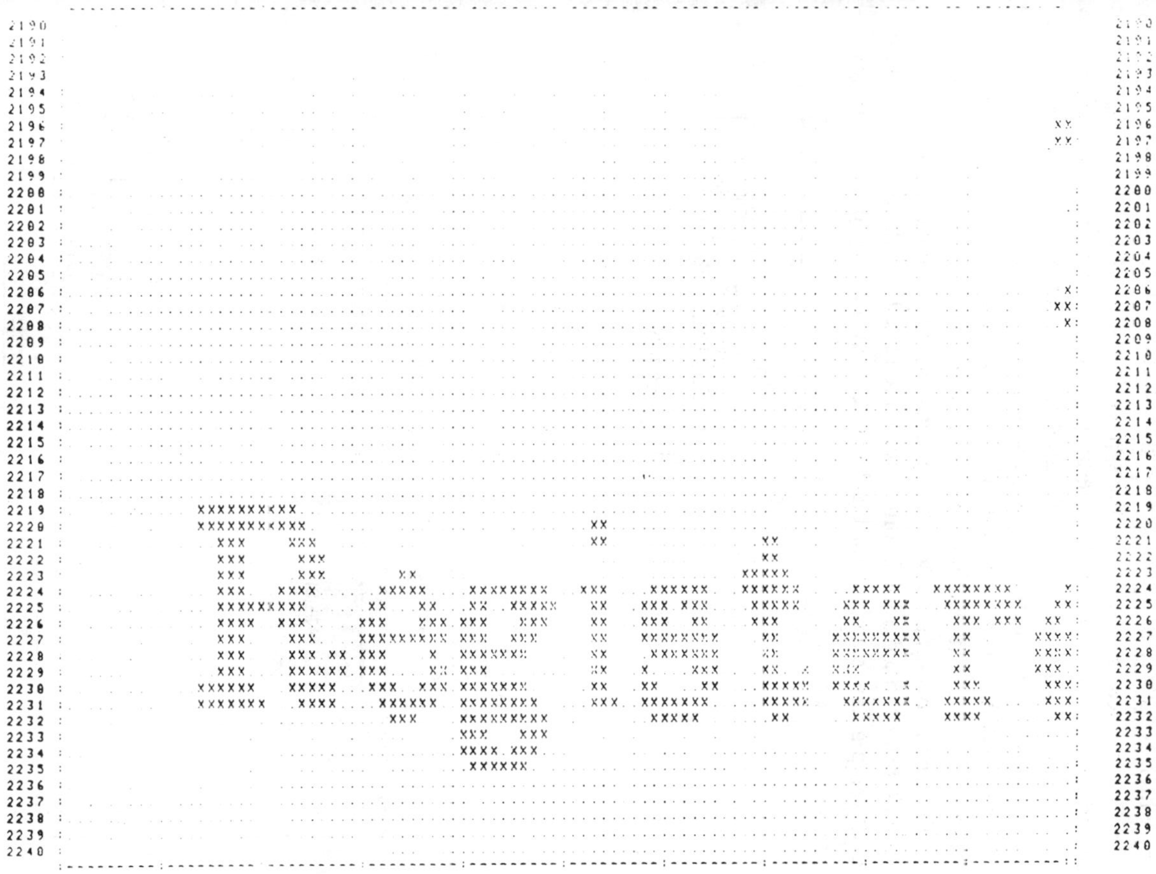

Figure 8.13 Output image: CCITT document number 1; 200 lines/in., bit image output, reject threshold of 4.

8.5 ADVANCED GROUP 4 CODING FOR BILEVEL IMAGES

The basic coding scheme for Group 4 facsimile is a two-dimensional line-by-line technique, which is merely an extension of the Modified Read algorithm for Group 3 facsimile. A great deal of activity by the standards organizations is directed toward improved coding of bilevel images relative to this existing standard. Most of the new work on compression addresses facsimile applications that differ from the conventional message fax. In one case, the Open Document Architecture (ODA) will be used for narrowly defining the structure of mixed mode documents. This would be used primarily where the documents originate in a computerized publishing environment rather than operating on scanned raster data. In a second scenario, the ISO and the CCITT have formed a joint committee called the Joint Bi-level Image Group (JBIG) to develop a new standard for black-white imagery. The primary application

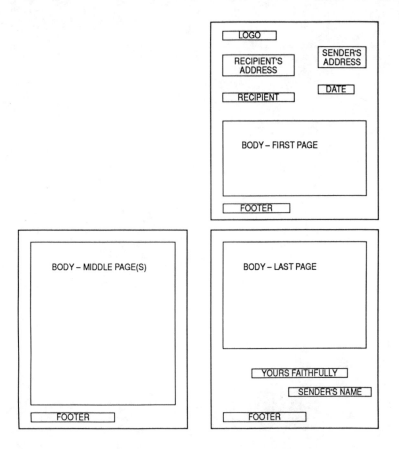

Figure 8.14 Example of a layout structure for a document called "letter."

of this algorithm will be the exchange of bilevel images over the ISDN with considerable emphasis on access by CRT terminals rather than printers. Since the JBIG standard will have considerable impact on the future of facsimile, it is discussed separately in Section 8.6.

Figure 8.14 is an example of a layout structure of a letter as defined by the ODA. A coordinate system has been defined for a page based on basic measurement units (BMUs), where there are 1200 BMUs per inch and the point of origin is the upper left-hand corner. An image is defined by locating blocks and frames of image data on the page as illustrated in the figure. The ODA is extremely efficient for image compression because no data are transmitted for the blank parts of the page. A high level of compression is also achieved because text information is usually inserted by key stroke, permitting the definition of a character by the highly efficient ASCII code. The ODA also provides for the ability to define graphic imagery by means of vectors rather than by raster, yielding an additional degree of compression for graphics.

8.6 THE JBIG CODING ALGORITHM

8.6.1 Overview

In 1988, an experts group was formed to establish an international standard for the coding of bilevel images. The JBIG is sponsored by the ISO (IEC/JTC1/SC2/WG9) and the CCITT (SG VIII). The JBIG has developed a draft standard entitled "Progressive Bi-level Image Compression Standard" and much of the material in this section is derived from this document.

The JBIG standard defines a method for compressing a bilevel image (that is, an image that, like a black-and-white image, has only two colors). Because the method adapts to a wide range of image characteristics, it is a very robust coding technique. On scanned images of printed characters, observed compression ratios have been from 1.1 to 1.5 times as great as those achieved by the modified modified read (MMR) encoding of CCITT Recommendations T.4 (G3) and T.6 (G4). On computer-generated images of printed characters, observed compression ratios have been as much as five times greater. On images with the gray scale rendered by halftoning or dithering, observed compression ratios have been from 2 to 30 times as great.

The method is bit-preserving, which means that it, like the CCITT T.4 and T.6 recommendations, is distortionless and that the final decoded image is identical to the original.

The JBIG standard provides for both sequential and progressive operation. When decoding a progressively coded image, a low-resolution rendition of the original image is made available first, with subsequent doublings of resolution as more data are decoded. Progressive encoding has two distinct benefits. One is that one common database can efficiently serve output devices with widely different resolution capabilities. Only that information in the compressed image file that allows reconstruction to the resolution capability of the particular output device need be sent and decoded. Also, if additional resolution enhancement is desired for, say, a paper copy of something already on a CRT screen, only the needed updating information has to be sent.

The other benefit of progressive encoding is that it provides subjectively superior image browsing (on a CRT) over low-and medium-rate communication links. A low-resolution rendition is rapidly transmitted and displayed, with as much resolution enhancement as desired then following. Each stage of resolution enhancement builds on the image already available. Progressive encoding makes it easy for a user to recognize quickly the image being displayed, which, in turn, makes it possible for that user to interrupt quickly the transmission of an unwanted image. Six successive stages of a progressive display are illustrated in Figure 8.15. The

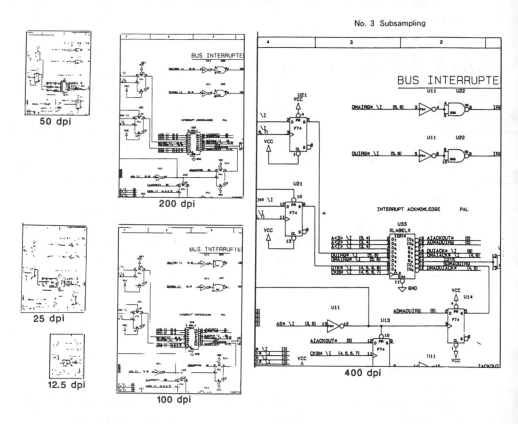

Figure 8.15 Stages of a progressive display.

resolutions are 12.5, 25, 50, 100, 200, and 400 dots/in. when referred to the original page.

Although the primary goal of this recommendation is bilevel image encoding, this standard can be used effectively for multilevel image encoding by simply encoding each bit plane independently as though it were itself a bilevel image. When the number of such bit planes is limited, such a scheme can be very efficient while at the same time providing for progressive buildup in both spatial refinement and gray-scale refinement. The remainder of this discussion assumes a bilevel image.

8.6.2 Stripes and Data Ordering

When it is necessary to distinguish progressive coding from the more traditional form of image coding in which the image is coded at full resolution from left to right and top to bottom, this older form of coding will be referred to as sequential. The advantage of sequential coding over progressive coding is that no frame buffer is required. Progressive coding does require a frame buffer because lower resolution images are used in coding higher resolution images.

The JBIG standard provides for images to be encoded either progressively or sequentially and then later they can be decoded either progressively or sequentially. The total information describing the image is independent of the method of encoding and the expected method of decoding. All that changes with a switch from compatible-progressive to compatible-sequential encoding is the order in which parts of the message are created by the encoder. All that changes with a switch from compatible-progressive to compatible-sequential decoding is the order in which these parts are used by the decoder.

Compatible progressive/sequential coding is achieved by breaking an image into smaller parts before compression, the parts being created by dividing the image in each of its resolution layers into horizontal bands called *stripes*. Figure 8.16 shows such a decomposition when there are three resolution layers with four stripes per layer.

A progressive decoder most naturally decodes in the order

1,2,3,4,5,6,7,8,9,10,11,12.

The most natural order for a sequential decoder is

1,5,9,2,6,10,3,7,11,4,8,12.

A stripe has a vertical size that is typically much smaller than that of the entire image. As an example, a stripe may be 8 mm high, yielding approximately 35 stripes for a page in a business letter.

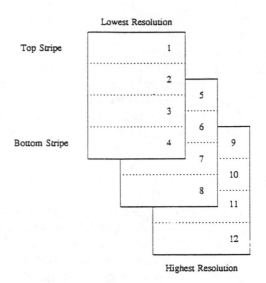

Figure 8.16 Decomposition in the special case of three layers and four stripes.

8.6.3 Design Concept

Figure 8.17 is a functional block diagram of the JBIG encoder. Although conceptually there are D differential-layer encoders as shown in this figure, some implementations may choose to use recursively one physical differential-layer encoder.

Differential-layer Encoder

Each of the differential-layer blocks of Figure 8.17 is identical in function, hence only a description of the operation at one layer is needed. For such a description,

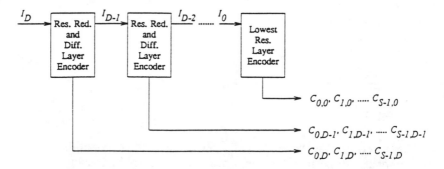

Figure 8.17 Decomposition of encoder.

only two resolution layers are involved. For simplicity in the remainder of this section, the incoming image will be referred to as the "high-resolution" image and the outgoing image as the "low-resolution" image.

The differential-layer encoding block of Figure 8.17 can itself be decomposed into sub-blocks as shown in Figure 8.18. Not all sub-blocks need be used in all systems. The acronyms that are frequently used for the blocks in this figure are given in Table 8.2.

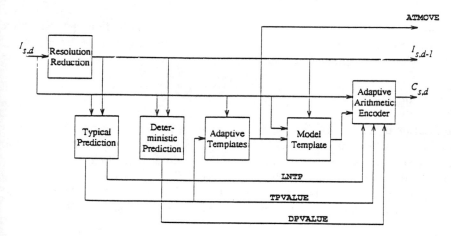

Figure 8.18 Differential layer encoder.

Table 8.2
Acronyms Used in Figure 8.18

ACRONYM	MEANING
RR	Resolution Reduction
TP	Typical Prediction
DP	Deterministic Prediction
AT	Adaptive Templates
MT	Model Templates
AAE	Adaptive Arithmetic Encoder
AAD	Adaptive Arithmetic Decoder

The RR block performs resolution reduction. This block accepts a high-resolution image and creates a low-resolution image with, as nearly as possible, half as many rows and half as many columns as the original.

An obvious way to reduce the resolution of a given image by a factor of 2 in each dimension is to subsample it by taking every other row and every other column. Subsampling is simple, but creates images of poor subjective quality, especially when the input image is bilevel.

For bilevel images containing text and line drawings, subsampling is poor because it frequently deletes thin lines. For bilevel images that contain ordered dithering to render gray scale, subsampling is poor because grayness is not well preserved, especially if the dithering period is a power of 2, as is frequently the case.

This recommendation suggests a particular resolution reduction method which has been carefully designed, extensively tested, and found to achieve excellent results for both dithered gray scale and lines.

Typical Prediction

The typical prediction block provides some coding gain, but its primary purpose is to speed implementations. TP looks for regions of solid color and when it finds that a given current high-resolution pixel for coding is in such a region, none of the processing normally done in the DP, AT, MT, and AAE blocks is needed. On text-type images, TP usually makes it possible to avoid coding over 95% of the pixels. On dithered images, processing savings from TP are significantly smaller.

Deterministic Prediction

The primary purpose of the DP block is to provide coding gain. On one particular set of test images, it provided a 7% gain, which is thought to be about typical.

When images are reduced in resolution by a particular resolution reduction algorithm, sometimes a particular current high-resolution pixel to be coded can be inferred from the pixels already known to both the encoder and decoder; that is, all the pixels in the low-resolution image and those in the high-resolution image that are causally related (in a raster sense) to the current pixel. When this occurs, the current pixel is said to be *deterministically predictable*. The DP block flags any such pixels and inhibits their coding by the arithmetic coder.

Model Templates

For each high-resolution pixel to be coded, the MT block provides the arithmetic coder with an integer called the *context*. This integer is determined by the colors (binary levels) of particular pixels in the causal high-resolution image, by particular pixels in the already available low-resolution image, and by the *spatial phase* of the pixel being coded. Spatial phase describes the orientation of the high-resolution pixel with respect to its corresponding low-resolution pixel.

Adaptive Templates

The AAE block is an entropy coder. It notes the outputs of the TP and DP blocks to determine if it is even necessary to code a given pixel. Assuming it is, it then notes the context and uses its internal probability estimator to estimate the conditional probability that the current pixel will be a given color. Often the pixel is highly predictable from the context so that the conditional probability is very close to 0 or 1 and a large entropy coding gain can be realized.

Maintaining probability estimates for each of the contexts is a nontrivial statistical problem. A balance must be struck between obtaining extremely accurate estimates and the conflicting need to quickly adapt to changing underlying statistics.

REFERENCES

[1]   Hochman, D., and D.R. Weber, "Dacom Facsimile Data Compression Techniques," *Proceedings International Conference Communications,* 1970, pp. 20.14–20.21.

[2]   Federal Republic of Germany, "Two-Dimensional Coding Scheme," CCITT SGXIV Document Number 82, March 1979.

[3]   Xerox Corporation, "Proposal for an Optional Two-Dimensional Coding Apparatus," CCITT SGXIV Document Number 84, April 1979.

[4]   Netravali, A.N., and F.W. Mounts, "Ordering Techniques for Facsimile Coding: A Review," *Proc. IEEE,* Volum 68, No. 7, July 1980, 796–807.

[5]   Langdon, G.G., Jr. "An Introduction to Arithmetic Coding," *IBM Res. Devel.,* Volume 28, No. 1, March 1984, 135–149.

[6]   Pratt, W.K., et al., "Combined Symbol Matching Facsimile Data Compression System," *Proc. IEEE,* Volum 68, No. 7, July 1980, 786–796.

[7]   Langdon, G.G., Jr and J. Rissanen, "Compression of Black-White Images with Arithmetic Coding," *IEEE Trans. Comm.* Volume COM-29, No. 6, June 1981, 85–867.

Chapter 9
Coding Gray-Scale and Color Pictures

9.1 OVERVIEW

The compression of bilevel black-white images was reviewed in Chapter 8. The purpose of this chapter is to discuss techniques for coding continuous-tone gray-scale images and color pictures. Figure 9.1 is a functional block diagram of a generic system that digitally transmits images over a communication channel. At the transmitter, the input analog signal is first filtered such that the upper cutoff frequency of the signal is B cycles/s. The filtered signal is next sampled at a rate of at least 2B samples per second (the Nyquist rate) to avoid aliasing distortion. Each sample is defined as a pixel, which is commonly encoded with 8-bit accuracy because this precision is required to avoid any visible distortion in the output image. At this point the bit rate is typically 16B b/s, which may exceed the bit rate of the transmission channel (C b/s). The purpose of the compressor is to reduce the 16B bit rate by reducing the pixel-to-pixel redundancy inherent in the image. The channel coder (e.g., modem) processes the binary compressed signal for efficient transmission over the communication channel. The compressor is commonly referred to as a *source coder* (signal source) in contrast to the channel coding process. As shown in Figure 9.1, the functions at the receiver are the inverse of those at the transmitter.

   Figure 9.2 is a functional block diagram of a generic compression system illustrating the various compression techniques that could be applied to video signals. The diagram shows that any image compressor can be viewed as having four sequential functions: signal conditioner, signal processor, quantizer, and variable length coder. The purpose of the signal conditioner is to prepare the input uncompressed signal for the subsequent coding process. The *signal processing* (SP) function is probably the heart of the overall compression subsystem. In the case of predictive coding, the SP performs the prediction function. In the case of transform coding, the SP performs the transform function. In these two particular cases, the output of the SP is a prediction error signal and transform coefficients, respectively. In all cases the SP output signal is quantized for transmission. The output of the quantization process is a series of binary codes or words, each defining a single pixel or

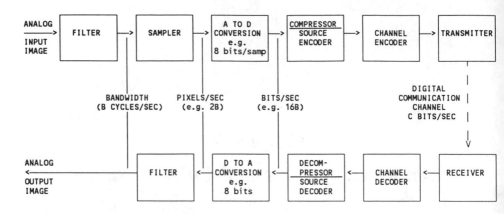

Figure 9.1 A generic system for the digital transmission of images.

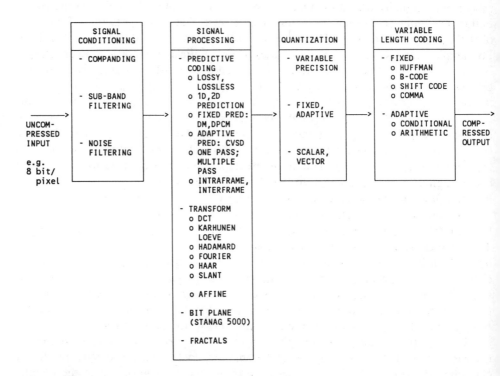

Figure 9.2 Functional block diagram of a generic video compression system.

block of pixels. These codes are not equally probable, i.e., redundancy exists. At this point variable length coding (VLC) is employed to reduce this redundancy. Short codes are assigned to likely events, and longer codes are assigned to unlikely events. VLC is a lossless, transparent process that does not degrade the coding accuracy.

Predictive coding is a basic workhorse compression technique that encodes a picture pel by pel. In this technique the brightness value of each new pel is predicted based on previously coded information that has been transmitted. The actual brightness value of the new pel is subtracted from the predicted value and the differential error signal is quantized for transmission. A significant bit rate reduction can be achieved by predictive coding for two reasons: first, the error signal is statistically more redundant than the original pels; second, the eye is less sensitive to coarse quantization of the error signal than the original PCM pels. A wide range of predictive coding systems is based on different designs for the quantizer (fixed or adaptive) and for the predictor (one dimensional or two dimensional prediction).

In the other major category of coding techniques, the image is divided into blocks of pels, which are encoded rather than transmitted on a pel-by-pel basis. Transform coding and vector quantization are examples of coding techniques that encode blocks of pels. In the case of transform coding, a block of pels is transformed into another domain called the *transform domain* prior to quantization and transmission. Significant bit rate reductions can be achieved in transform coding for two reasons: First, a large fraction of the coefficients can be deleted from transmission without affecting the picture quality; second, the transform coefficients can be encoded with less accuracy than the original pixels without severely affecting picture quality.

The conventional scalar quantization process is accomplished in two steps: First, the range of possible input values is divided into subranges or subsets; then a single representative value is printed or displayed at the output when an input value falls within a particular subrange. With vector quantization, the same two operations occur, not in one-dimensional scalar space, but in an N-dimensional vector space. This technique is discussed further in Section 9.7.

The CCITT and ISO standards organizations have formed a joint committee to develop a standard gray-scale coding technique for a wide range of applications such as Group 4 facsimile, freeze-frame TV, and videotex. This Joint Picture Encoding Group (JPEG) illustrated in Figure 9.3 has rigorously compared several competing algorithms such as the discrete cosine transform and predictive coding. The primary objective of the group is to develop a standard for a progressive coding algorithm for the rapid distribution of pictures over the 64 kb/s ISDN channel. A draft standard for the JPEG algorithm has been prepared and is discussed in Section 9.9.

The signal conditioning and the VLC functions are universally used in all compression systems. Therefore, they are discussed first in Secs. 9.2 and 9.3, respectively. Five coding algorithms that are of particular importance are presented in Secs. 9.4 through 9.8, and issues related to color facsimile are discussed in Section 9.10.

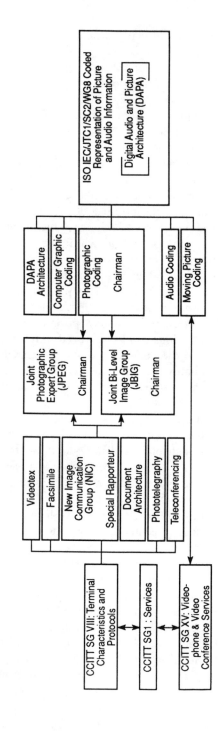

Figure 9.3 Organization of photographic standardization.

9.2 SIGNAL CONDITIONING

Signal conditioning techniques can be cascaded with each other and with the subsequent coding techniques. Sub-band filtering could be advantageous because the signal may have different properties in the various frequency bands, which could be most efficiently encoded by different compression algorithms. Companding is the name for a general process wherein the transfer function of the input signal is adjusted for optimum compression—not too small, but not too large such that limiting is caused. This gain adjustment may appear trivial, but it is difficult to do well. If the input transfer function is linear, modification (companding) of the signal is usually desirable so that low-level signals are encoded more precisely than high-level signals. This is commonly done to match the logarithmic characteristic of the eye.

9.3 VARIABLE LENGTH CODING

Variable length coding (VLC), also called entropy coding, is a technique whereby each event is assigned a code that may have a different number of bits. To obtain compression, short codes are assigned to frequently occurring events and long codes are assigned to infrequent events. The expectation is that the average code length will be less than the fixed code length that would otherwise be required. If all events are equally likely, or nearly so, then VLC will not provide compression.

All codes considered must be uniquely decodable; that is, there must be only one way that a concatenation of VLCs can be decoded. In addition, the code should be instantaneous; that is, each code word should be decoded without reference to subsequent code words. Taken together, these requirements mean that no code word can be the beginning of another code word. For example, we may not have 01 and 0110 as code words, since the second code word starts with the first code word. In decoding, it is not known whether 01 is the first code word, or just the start of the second code word.

A major advantage of VLC is that it does not degrade the signal quality in any way. That is, the reconstituted signal will exactly match the input signal so that if the signal is adequately described by a series of events, using VLCs to communicate them to the decoder will not change the events. Therefore, the system is transparent to the VLC used.

The disadvantage of VLCs is that they only provide compression in an average sense. Therefore, sometimes the code could be longer for a specific section of signal. This characteristic gives rise to the need for a buffer to match the variable rate of bit generation with the fixed bit rate of the communication channel, and a control strategy to prevent long-term overflows or underflows of the buffer. Also the establishment of frames or packets of data becomes more difficult with VLCs.

Seven VLCs are discussed here. They are comma codes, shift codes, B codes, Huffman codes, conditional codes, arithmetic codes, and two-dimensional codes.

9.3.1 Comma Code

The comma code is the simplest of the VLCs. It assigns to each event a different length of code, starting at 1. A particular bit polarity marks the end of the code word. For example:

Code
0
10
110
1110
11110
111110
.
.
.

The advantage of the comma code is that it is simple to generate and decode, requiring only counters to count the number of 1s. However, this code rarely matches the statistics of the events accurately, so it is used primarily where simplicity of implementation is important.

9.3.2 Shift Code

In the case for which the probabilities of the events decrease monotonically as the magnitudes increase, a great simplification can be obtained by the use of a systematic VLC, such as a shift code. In this code, each code word consists of a series of subwords, each of length L bits. The first subword is capable of conveying 2L values, one of which is a shift that indicates that the value of the code word is contained in the following subword. In this way, any length of code word can be obtained by concatenating a number of subwords together.

The following are examples of the beginnings of shift code tables for L = 1, 2, and 3, where a subword of all 1s indicates a shift.

L = 1	L = 2	L = 3
0	00	000
10	01	001
110	10	010
1110	1100	011
11110	1101	100
111110	1110	101
1111110	111100	110
11111110	111101	111000
111111110	111110	111001
1111111110	11111100	111010
11111111110	11111101	111011
.	.	.
.	.	.
.	.	.

9.3.3 B Code

Another variable length code that is systematic is the B code. Again the code consists
of a sequence of subwords, each of length L. But in this case, one bit of the subword
is used to designate whether another subword is to be added to the code word. Therefore, the remaining L − 1 bits in the subword can be used as part of the code. For
L = 1, the B code also reduces to the comma code.

The following are examples of the beginning of B code tables for L = 1, 2,
and 3:

L = 1	L = 2	L = 3
**********	* * * *	* * *
0	00	000
10	01	001
110	1000	010
1110	1001	011
11110	1100	100000
111110	1101	100001
1111110	101000	100010
11111110	101001	100011
111111110	101100	101000
1111111110	101101	101001
11111111110	111000	101010
.	111001	101011
.	111100	110000
.	111101	110001
	10101000	110010
	10101001	110011
	10101100	111000
	.	111001
	.	111010
	.	111011
		100100000
		.
		.
		.

In this table, the * marks the columns containing the continuation bits, where a 1
indicates continue and a 0 marks the last subword of the code word. This version
of the B code is instantaneous. In another version, the continuation bit is the same
value for all subwords in the code word, but alternates with each succeeding code
word. That version is not instantaneous.

The B code is best suited to cases for which the probabilities drop off slowly,
since the number of codes available increases geometrically with increasing code
length.

9.3.4 Huffman Code

The Huffman code is a VLC that provides the shortest average code length for a given distribution of input probabilities. The method for generating the code is well known, but a distribution of input probabilities, either theoretical or measured, is required before the code words can be calculated. If the actual distribution differs from the one used to calculate the code, then the average code length may not be less than other codes. If a large enough sample can be obtained to measure the distribution accurately, the Huffman code may be an attractive choice. In any event, it provides a reference against which other codes can be compared if the distribution is measured on the image being coded.

9.3.5 Conditional VLCs

In general, the most likely sample values to be encoded are near 0, and therefore the small values are given the shortest codes. However, 0 is the most likely sample value only in the absence of information about other samples. If the values of neighboring samples are known, then the distribution of the current sample value can be markedly changed. In the simplest case, only the previous sample is used. Although, in principle, other samples can be used for each value of the previous sample, the frequency of occurrence of each of the current samples can be obtained, and a set of VLCs devised for each. Since both the encoder and decoder know the value of the previous sample, decoding can take place without significant delay.

9.3.6 Arithmetic Coding

In arithmetic coding, the frequency of occurrence of the symbols to be coded is continuously measured by both the encoder and decoder. In the resulting code, the correspondence between the events and specific bits is not one to one. Arithmetic codes can be generated at a rate of less than one bit per event, whereas a Huffman code requires at least one bit per event. Since arithmetic coders adapt dynamically to the statistics of the image being transmitted, the compression is generally superior to that for conventional nonadaptive VLCs.

9.3.7 Two-Dimensional VLC for Coding Transform Coefficients

A VLC has recently been developed that is particularly designed to code transform coefficients. It is a two-dimensional code where the two dimensions are: (1) the number of zero-value coefficients in a row (usually from a zigzag scan) and (2) the value of the next nonzero coefficient. This VLC is a likely code to be employed in the JPEG standard (Section 9.9).

9.4 PULSE CODE MODULATION (PCM)

In pulse code modulation (PCM) coding, the signal is sampled at the Nyquist rate, each sample is quantized to 2^m levels, and each level is represented by a binary word m bits in length. At the decoder, these binary words are converted into a series of amplitude levels, which is low-pass filtered. Since each sample is encoded independently of its neighbor, no redundancy is reduced, and PCM is used as a reference to measure the performance of bit rate reduction techniques. The PCM coding precision typically used for this reference is 6 to 8 bits per pel because it is this precision which assures that no visible degradation will occur in the picture. Figures 9.4, 9.5, and 9.6 illustrate the type of contouring distortion that occurs when the coding precision is limited; they show 2-bit, 3-bit, and 4-bit precision, respectively.

The eye is logarithmic in its sensitivity to brightness distortion; that is, it is equally sensitive to equal percentage changes in brightness. For this reason the PCM quantization is typically nonlinear, with the size of the quantizer steps increasing with brightness. This nonlinear companding improves the picture quality for a given number of bits per pel.

Figure 9.6 illustrates the picture quality for conventional 4-bit PCM coding. A contouring type of distortion is visible and is somewhat disturbing because the eye

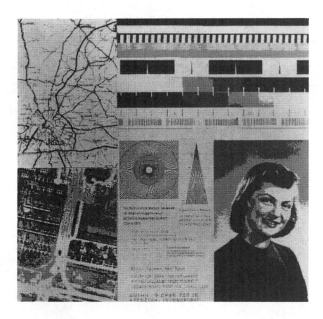

Figure 9.4 Two-bit PCM encoding.

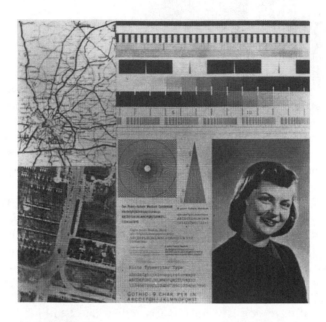

Figure 9.5 Three-bit PCM encoding.

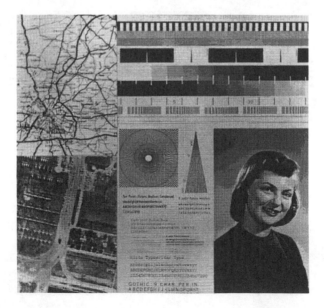

Figure 9.6 Four-bit PCM encoding.

is particularly sensitive to low-frequency noise. The visibility of the distortion can be reduced by adding a low-level pseudorandom high-frequency noise to the signal prior to encoding and subtracting the same noise at the receiver after decoding. The distortion associated with this technique, know as *dither coding,* is concentrated in the higher frequency region, which is more acceptable to the eye. Figure 9.7 illustrates the quality of a 4-bit PCM dither-coded picture.

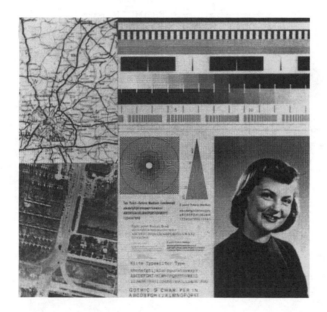

Figure 9.7 Four-bit PCM dither-coded picture.

9.5 PREDICTIVE CODING

PCM transmits each pel as an independent sample without taking advantage of the high degree of pel-to-pel correlation existing in most pictures. Predictive coding is a basic bit rate reduction technique, which does reduce this pel-to-pel redundancy. Figure 9.8 is a block diagram illustrating the basic predictive coding process. A predictor predicts the brightness value of each new pel based solely on the pels that have been previously quantized and transmitted. The predicted brightness value is subtracted from the actual brightness value of the new pel resulting in a bipolar prediction error signal. This error signal is quantized and transmitted. This quantization process can vary over a wide range of complexities. The most common technique is conventional pel-by-pel scalar quantization. However, transform coding or

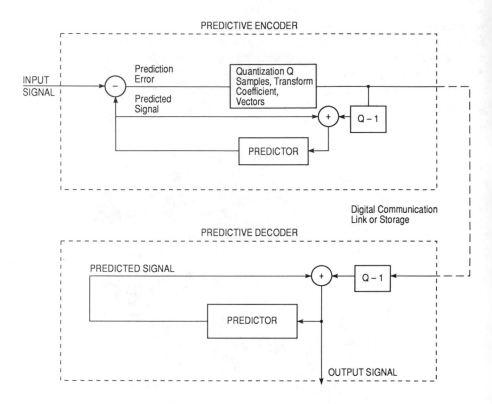

Figure 9.8 Block diagram of a generic predictive coding system.

vector quantization can also be employed. The quantization can be fixed or it can adapt to the data. The quantizer can also vary over a wide range of accuracies. If 1-bit quantization is employed, the system becomes the well-known *delta modulation* technique. If the predictive quantizer employs multiple bits per pel, the technique is commonly defined as *differential PCM* (DPCM). At the receiver the inverse of the quantization process is performed and the decoded error signal is added to the predicted value to form the output signal for viewing. The output signal is fed to the predictor to be used for prediction of the next pel. Referring back to the predictive encoder, the reader will note that the transmitted signal is decoded at the transmitter using exactly the same decoding process used at the receiver. The predictive encoder can be viewed as a servo loop, which continually forces the decoded output signal to be as close as possible to the input signal.

Figure 9.9 illustrates the transfer function of a typical 3-bit DPCM predictive coder. The quantizer is usually nonlinear because the eye is very sensitive to small changes in low-detail portions of a picture (small prediction error), but the eye is

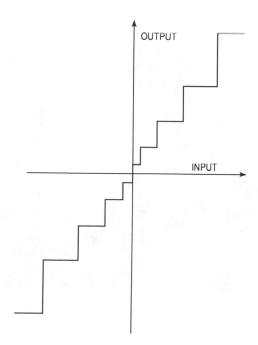

Figure 9.9 Quantizer for predictive encoder.

insensitive to coarse quantization of high-contrast edges (large predictive error). The design of this quantizer is a compromise between conflicting objectives. The quantizer precision should be fine, particularly for small error signals, to keep the background granular noise in the output picture at an acceptably low level. On the other hand, the quantizer steps must be large enough, particularly the largest increment, so the output can respond reasonably well to high-contrast changes in the input picture. If the largest increment is too small, slope overload occurs resulting in picture blurring. Figure 9.10 is an illustration of the prediction error signal for a delta modulation system that exhibits severe slope overload.

Figure 9.11 is a picture coded using DPCM with 2-bits/pel precision. Note that high-contrast vertical edges are slightly blurred due to the slope overload characteristic. Figure 9.12 is also 2-bit DPCM, but in this case two-dimensional prediction is employed rather than one-dimensional. Note that the vertical edges are sharper due to the more sophisticated predictor.

One fundamental characteristic of bit rate reduction techniques such as predictive coding is that, as redundancy is reduced, the compressed signal is more sensitive to errors in the transmission channel. To illustrate this point, Figure 9.13 shows the output picture for 5-bit PCM transmission if the bit error rate is 10^{-2}. Figure 9.14

Figure 9.10 Severe slope overload.

Figure 9.11 Two-bit delta modulation encoding.

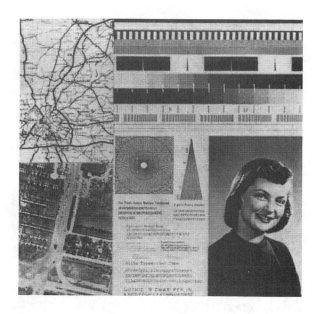

Figure 9.12 Two-bit H-V delta modulation encoding.

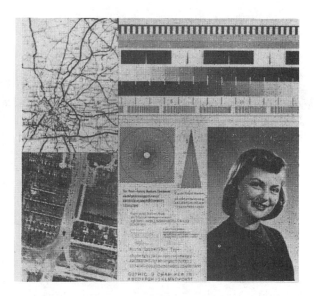

Figure 9.13 Five-bit PCM transmission. (Error rate $= 10^{-2}$.)

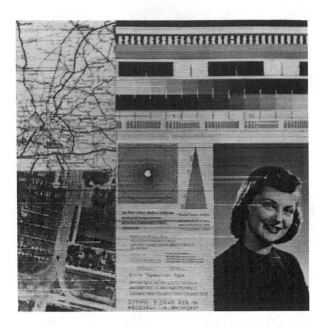

Figure 9.14 One bit HIDM encoding with data link noise. (Error rate $= 10^{-3}$.)

shows the output picture quality for a delta modulation system if the bit error rate is 10^{-3}. Clearly, the delta modulation scheme is much more sensitive to errors.

9.6 TRANSFORM CODING

Transform coding algorithms, generally speaking, operate as two-step processes. In the first step, a linear transformation of the original signal (separated into sub-blocks of $N \times N$ pels each) is performed, in which signal space is mapped into transform space. In the second step, the transformed signal is compressed by encoding each sub-block through quantization and variable length coding. The reconstruction operation involves performing an inverse transformation of each decoded, transformed sub-block. The function of the transformation operation is to make the transformed samples more independent than the original samples, so that the subsequent operation of quantization may be done more efficiently.

The transformation operation itself does not provide compression; rather, it is a remapping of the signal into another domain in which compression can be achieved more effectively. Compression can be achieved for two reasons: First, not all of the transform domain coefficients need to be transmitted in order to achieve acceptable picture quantity. Second, the coefficients that are transmitted can be encoded with reduced precision without seriously affecting image quality.

9.6.1 Transformation Techniques

Transforms that have proven useful include the Karhunen-Loève, discrete Fourier, discrete cosine, and Walsh-Hadamard transforms. The Karhunen-Loève transform (KLT) is considered to be an optimum transformation, and for this reason many other transformations have been compared to it in terms of performance. However, the KLT has certain characteristics that make it less than ideal for image processing. These include the necessity to estimate the covariance matrix before processing in both row and column operations. Also, the actual eigenvector determination must be carried out to generate the basis matrix. These drawbacks would not be significant if the efficiency of the KLT was much greater than that of other transforms. However, for data having high interelement correlation, the performance of other transforms (such as the discrete cosine transform) is virtually indistinguishable from that of the KLT, and thus usually does not warrant its added complexity.

The discrete Fourier transform is one of the few complex transforms used in data coding schemes, but disadvantages arise from using a complex transform for data coding. The most obvious is the storage and manipulation of complex numbers. Again, as in the case of the KLT, this complexity issue would not be a factor if the performance of the DFT was significantly greater than that of other transforms. However, other transforms that are less complex perform better than the DFT.

The discrete cosine transform (DCT) is one of an extensive family of sinusoidal transforms. In their discrete form, the basis vectors consist of sampled values of sinusoidal or cosinusoidal functions that, unlike those of the DFT, are real number quantities. The DCT has been singled out for special attention by workers in the image processing field, principally because, for conventional image data having reasonably high interelement correlation, DCT performance is virtually indistinguishable from that of other transforms that are much more complex to implement.

The three transforms mentioned previously have basis functions that are either cosinusoidal, i.e., the Fourier and discrete cosine, or are a good approximation of a sinusoidal function, such as KLT. The Walsh-Hadamard transform is an approximation of a rectangular orthonomal function. The actual transform consists of a matrix of $+1$ and -1 values, which eliminates multiplications from the transform process. The elimination of multiplications is a significant property, since the aforementioned transforms require real or complex multiplications. However, the Walsh-Hadamard transform does not provide the excellent performance that the discrete cosine transform provides.

Since the discrete cosine transform is universally accepted as the preferred transform for image coding, we will provide more detail on its implementation. The execution of the discrete cosine transform algorithm requires the division of an image into a series of $N \times N$ sub-blocks of pixels. Each sub-block is transformed by a two-dimensional $N \times N$ discrete cosine transform process as follows:

$$[T] = [C] \cdot [D] \cdot [C]^T$$

where $[T]$ is the transformed sub-block, $[C]$ is the DCT basis matrix, and $[D]$ is the input data sub-block ($[C]^T$ is the transpose of the DCT basis matrix). The DCT basis matrix coefficients were determined from the following relation:

$$C_{ij} = C_0 \cdot \sqrt{(2/N)} \cdot \cos[i \cdot (j + 0.5) \cdot (\pi/N)]$$

where $C_0 = 1/\sqrt{2}$ for $i = 0$, $C_0 = 1$ otherwise, and $i = j = 0$ to $N - 1$. Figure 9.15 illustrates the basis functions for an 8×8 DCT. This transformation converts each $N \times N$ sub-block of pixels into an $N \times N$ matrix of transform coefficients, which consists of one DC coefficient and $(N \times N - 1)$ AC coefficients. The sum

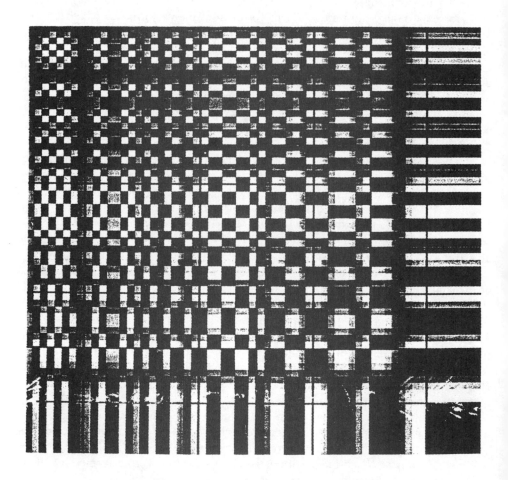

Figure 9.15 DCT basis function.

of the squares of all of the AC coefficients in a given transform matrix is known as the AC energy of that transform matrix.

9.6.2 Coding of Transform Coefficients

As explained in the previous section, the DCT is usually used when pictures are transmitted using transform techniques. This transformation merely creates a set of coefficients equal in number to the original set of pels. At this point no compression has been accomplished except that the original set of pels with uniformly high redundancy has been decorrelated, and the information has been compacted in the lower spatial frequency coefficients. The purpose of this section is to address the second part of the two-step process: how to encode the transform coefficients for transmission.

The first step in the coding process is to determine which coefficients are to be transmitted and which are to be deleted. Figure 9.15 illustrates the set of 64 transform coefficients corresponding to an 8 × 8 block of pels to be coded.

Coefficient number one is the DC coefficient, which is a measure of the average brightness of the block. Coefficients in the top row measure spatial frequency content in the horizontal direction. Coefficients in the left column measure frequencies in the vertical direction, and all others measure various combinations thereof. In general, most of the energy is contained in the low-frequency coefficients with relatively little signal strength in the high-frequency coefficients.

Figure 9.16 shows a simple example of how each 8 × 8 block is coded. Figure 9.16(a) shows the original block to be coded. The block has a constant slope or shading from the upper left corner to the lower right. Without compression, this would take 8 bits to code each of the 64 pixels, or a total of 512 bits. First, the block is transformed, using the two-dimensional DCT, giving the coefficients of Figure 9.16(b). Note that most of the energy is concentrated into the upper left-hand corner of the coefficient matrix.

Essentially, the DCT is performed by multiplying the input block by each of the 64 basis functions shown graphically in Figure 9.15. The results of each of these multiplications, also 8 × 8 arrays, are summed to give the 64 transform coefficients. In the upper left-hand corner of Figure 9.15, the first basis function is constant over the block, and therefore gives rise to the DC value of the input block. At the opposite corner, the basis function is a checkerboard and will give significant coefficient values only if there are elements of this pattern in the input block. Of course, the coefficients are, in practice, calculated by a chip in a more efficient manner than described here.

Next, the coefficients of Figure 9.16(b) are quantized with a step size of 6. [The first term (DC) uses a step size of 8.] This produces the values of Figure 9.16(c), which are much smaller in magnitude than the original coefficients and most of the

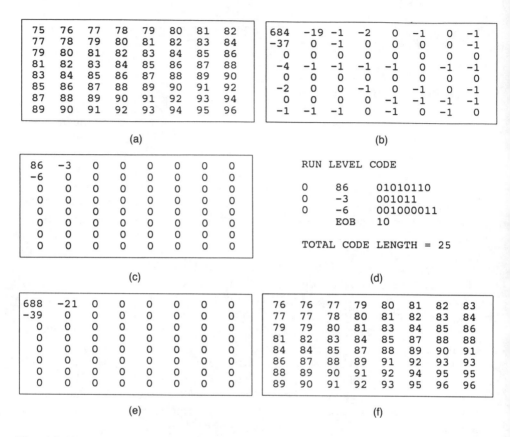

Figure 9.16 Sample block coding: (a) original block (8 × 8 × 8 = 512 bits); (b) transformed block coefficients; (c) quantized coefficient levels; (d) coefficients in zig-zag order and variable length coded; (e) inverse quantized coefficients; (f) reconstituted block.

coefficients become zero. The larger the step size, the smaller the values produced, resulting in more compression.

The coefficients are then reordered, using the zigzag scanning order of Figure 9.17. All zero coefficients are replaced with a count of the number of 0s before each nonzero coefficient (RUN). Each combination of RUN and VALUE produces a VLC that is sent to the decoder. The last nonzero VALUE is followed by an end-of-block (EOB) code. The total number of bits used to describe the block is 25, a compression of 20:1. The code in Figure 9.16(d) is based on the two-dimensional variable length code (CCITT Recommendation H.261) shown in Table 9.1.

The following additional examples illustrate the coding process. In examples 1, 2, and 3, the codes are obtained directly from Table 9.1. For examples 4, 5, 6, and 7, the combinations of run length and level cannot be found in Table 9.1, so the escape code is used, together with the binary representation of the run length (6 bits) and the twos-complement representation of the level.

Example Run

EXAMPLE	RUN LENGTH	LEVEL	CODE
1	0	3	001010
2	0	−3	001011
3	26	−1	0000 0000 1101 11
4	32	−1	000001,100000,11111111
5	60	2	000001,111100,00000010
6	60	−2	000001,111100,11111110
7	60	−86	000001,111100,10101010

At the decoder, the step size and VALUE's are used to reconstruct the inverse quantized coefficients, which, as shown in Figure 9.16(e), are similar to, but not exactly equal to, the original coefficients. When these coefficients are inverse transformed, the result of Figure 9.16(f) is obtained. Note that the differences between this block and the original block are quite small.

Figure 9.18 shows a slightly different example that demonstrates more clearly some of the features of DCT coding. In this example, in addition to shading, the block contains a checkerboard pattern that matches the highest order basis function. This causes the last coefficient to be transmitted. There are 60 zero-value coefficients (in the zigzag order) between the previous nonzero coefficient and the last one, so the run length is 60. The last coefficient is coded as a 6-bit escape code (000001), a 6-bit run code (111100) [6010], and an 8-bit level code (00000010) [210], as shown at the bottom of Table 9.1.

1	2	6	7	15	16	28	29
3	5	8	14	17	27	30	43
4	9	13	18	26	31	42	44
10	12	19	25	32	41	45	54
11	20	24	33	40	46	53	55
21	23	34	39	47	52	56	61
22	35	38	48	51	57	60	62
36	37	49	50	58	59	63	64

Figure 9.17 Scanning order in a block.

Table 9.1
Two-Dimensional Variable Length Code
(CCITT Recommendation H.261)

Run	Level	Code
	EOB	10
0	1	1s IF FIRST COEFFICIENT IN BLOCK
		(*Note*—Never used in INTRA macroblocks)
0	1	11s NOT FIRST COEFFICIENT IN BLOCK
0	2	0100 s
0	3	0010 1s
0	4	0000 110s
0	5	0010 0110 s
0	6	0010 0001 s
0	7	0000 0010 10s
0	8	0000 0001 1101s
0	9	0000 0001 1000 s
0	10	0000 0001 0011 s
0	11	0000 0001 0000 s
0	12	0000 0000 1101 0s
0	13	0000 0000 1100 1s
0	14	0000 0000 1100 0s
0	15	0000 0000 1011 1s
1	1	011s
1	2	0001 10s
1	3	0010 0101 s
1	4	0000 0011 00s
1	5	0000 0001 1011 s
1	6	0000 0000 1011 0s
1	7	0000 0000 1010 1s
2	1	0101 s
2	2	0000 100s
2	3	0000 0010 11s
2	4	0000 0001 0100 s
2	5	0000 0000 1010 0s
3	1	0011 1s
3	2	0010 0100 s
3	3	0000 0001 1100 s
3	4	0000 0000 1001 1s
4	1	0011 0s
4	2	0000 0011 11s
4	3	0000 0001 0010 s

Table 9.1 (cont'd)

Run	Level	Code
5	1	0001 11s
5	2	0000 0010 01s
5	3	0000 0000 1001 0s
6	1	0001 01s
6	2	0000 0001 1110 s
7	1	0001 00s
7	2	0000 0001 0101 s
8	1	0000 111s
8	2	0000 0001 0001 s
9	1	0000 101s
9	2	0000 0000 1000 1s
10	1	0010 0111's
10	2	0000 0000 1000 0s
11	1	0010 0011 s
12	1	0010 0010 s
13	1	0010 0000 s
14	1	0000 0011 10s
15	1	0000 0011 01s
16	1	0000 0010 00s
17	1	0000 0001 1111 s
18	1	0000 0001 1010 s
19	1	0000 0001 1001 s
20	1	0000 0001 0111 s
21	1	0000 0001 0110 s
22	1	0000 0000 1111 1s
23	1	0000 0000 1111 0s
24	1	0000 0000 1110 1s
25	1	0000 0000 1110 0s
26	1	0000 0000 1101 1s
	ESCAPE	0000 01

NOTE:
DEFINITION OF S
0 = positive level
1 = negative level
The remaining combinations of (RUN, LEVEL) are encoded with a 20-bit word consisting of 6 bits ESCAPE, 6 bits RUN and 8 bits LEVEL.

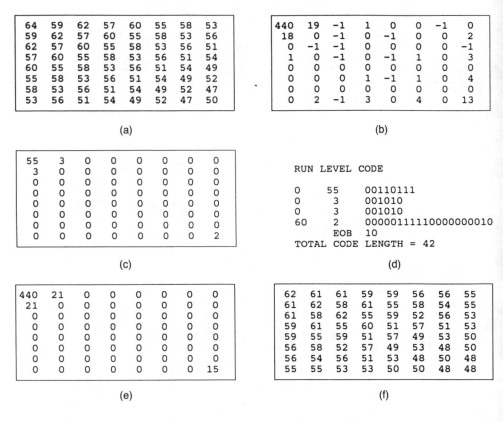

Figure 9.18 Example of DCT coding: (a) original block; (b) transformed block coefficients; (c) quantized coefficient levels step size = 6; (d) coefficients in zig-zag order and variable length coded; (e) inverse quantized coefficients; (f) reconstituted block.

Two types of distortion appear in transform-coded pictures: truncation error and quantization errors. Quantization errors are noise-like, whereas truncation errors cause a loss of resolution. In practice, the truncation threshold and quantization precision must be adjusted experimentally to achieve the maximum compression and acceptable picture quality. In general, transform coding is preferable to predictive coding for compression to bit rates below 1 or 2 bits/pel for single pictures. However, in those applications where cost and complexity are important issues, the choice between these two algorithms may be less clear.

9.7 VECTOR QUANTIZATION

Vector quantization begins by dividing an image to be transmitted into rectangular blocks of pixels, all blocks having the same dimensions. The transmitter compares each block with a large library of typical blocks, called a *code book,* and selects the library block that best approximates the block to be transmitted. The transmitter then encodes and transmits the index to the selected library block. The receiver, equipped with a copy of the code book, decodes the index, retrieves the selected library block, and inserts it into the output image.

This process is called vector quantization because, both theoretically and computationally, each block is treated as a vector. The vector representation of a block can be thought of as laying out all the gray-scale values of the block pixels in a single string, that of the upper-left pixel first, and of the lower-right last. Such a string of numbers comprises a vector in k dimensional space, where k is the number of pixels in the block. When the block is treated in this manner, the entire body of mathematical knowledge of vector analysis and multidimensional analytical geometry can be brought to bear on the vector quantization problem. In the balance of this discussion, the terms *block* and *vector* will be used interchangeably, with block referring to a rectangular array of pixels in an image, and vector referring to the representation of these pixels as a string of numbers.

All of the variations of vector quantization require a trade-off between image quality and data compression. In the theoretical limit of zero distortion, the code book would contain vectors representing all possible blocks. An exact match would always be found. Distortionless transmission would, however, entail an enormous code book and little data compression, even with optimal coding. At the other extreme, a code book containing few vectors (representative blocks) would yield large compression ratios, but poor image quality. The objective of any vector quantization system design is, therefore, to achieve the best compromise among code book size, data compression, and received image quality.

A review of published papers reveals many variations on the vector quantization theme. Gersho [1] presents a mathematical treatment of the problem. The code book is, in effect, the vector quantizer in that it "quantizes" the multidimensional vector "space" into a finite set of representative vectors. Gersho goes on to explore the partitioning problem and concludes that the only practical way to design the quantizer (select the vectors to be included in the code book) is to take advantage of vector clustering.

The basic vector clustering algorithm was thoroughly developed by Linde, Buzo, and Gray [2]. This algorithm, known as the LBG algorithm, takes advantage of the fact that the vector representations of image blocks tend to cluster in the vector space. A code book containing vectors representing the cluster centroids offers the best compromise between code book size and received image quality. The method consists of using a long sequence of "training" vectors to design the code book. Gray and Linde [3] explain and compare several variations on the LBG code book generation method and compare the resulting performances of Gauss-Markov sources. In particular, the authors show that tree-assisted code book searches allow the use of code books much larger than those practical with exhaustive searches at the expense of a suboptimal code book. The performance is only slightly degraded with respect to the exhaustive-search approach. Huang and Woods [4] discuss predictive vector quantization, which consists of a combination of predictive filtering and vector quantization. The purpose of the predictive filtering is to remove redundancy before vector quantizing the residue. A vector quantization method that offers great promise of good compression and low distortion is described in Japan Annex 4 [5]. This method combines DPCM and vector quantization. Other references include Helden and Boekee [6] and Gersho and Ramamarthi [7].

Vector quantization, in all its forms, requires a large code book of vectors from which one is selected for each block to be transmitted. Therefore, two very important issues are code book search and code book generation. The two basic search methods are *exhaustive* and *tree-assisted*. The exhaustive method is guaranteed to select the code book vector that best matches the input vector. This method is practical, however, only for very small block sizes because the search is much faster. A binary tree search begins with a choice between two code book vectors that act as "keys" to the next search level. The selection of one of these keys leads to another two-way choice, which leads to a better approximation of the input vector, which leads to yet another two-way choice, etc. This method, though much faster than the exhaustive search, may fail to find the best match, because once a two-way choice has been made in a given tree level, the search may be directed to a subtree that does not contain the best match. The general m-way tree search, in which an m-way choice is made at each decision level, gives better performance as the value of m increases, at the expense of longer search time. The exhaustive search is the limiting case of one M-way decision, where M is the total number of code book vectors.

The code book generation objective is a code book that gives low image distortion while minimizing the code book size. Minimizing the code book size is important, not only to minimize memory and search time, but also to achieve high compression ratios.

All code book generation methods reported in the literature are variations on the LBG method. In principle, if we knew the statistics of all images to be transmitted, we could generate a code book analytically. The most commonly used method consists, however, of using a large number of training vectors, with each training vector representing a "typical" image block.

The following is a summary of the LBG code book generation method. Assume, for the moment, a partially optimized code book. Each training vector "belongs" to a code book vector in that the training vector matches the code book vector at least as well as it matches any other. (Ties are broken in various ways depending on the specific method used.)

The code book is updated to make each code book vector the centroid of the set of training vectors that belong to it, thus minimizing the average distortion with respect to that set of training vectors. The update may, however, cause some of the training vectors that belonged to a given code book vector before the update to belong to a different code book vector afterward. Another iteration is therefore performed to compute new centroids, and the code book is updated again. This process is repeated until no further improvement is possible or the improvement is less than some specified value.

This iterative method of code book improvement leads to a local minimum of average distortion. A slight perturbation of the code book vectors gives greater distortion. This method leaves the possibility that some large change to the code book might give even less distortion; hence, the local minimum is not necessarily the global minimum (best possible code book for the training vector set).

Code book generation begins with one code book vector, which is the centroid of all the training vectors. This vector is then split into two vectors very close to each other. The splitting objective is to make the numbers of training vectors belonging to the two code book vectors approximately equal. The code book is then optimized, as described above. The two (now optimized) vectors are then split into four, and optimization is repeated. The process is continued until a code book of the required size is achieved.

The typical block size employed in vector quantization systems is 4 × 4 pels, and the bit rate reductions that can be achieved are comparable to transform coding. However, the vector quantization technology, particularly in the area of code book generation and search, is not fully mature and consequently few operational systems have been implemented. Nevertheless, vector quantization will probably play a significant role in gray-scale coding in the future.

9.8 BIT PLANE CODING

Most of the picture coding techniques described in previous sections are inexact in that they do not usually transmit an exact replica of the original PCM picture. Bit plane coding (BPC) is a lossless coding technique that does exactly reproduce the input image. BPC requires the storage of at least one complete scan line at the transmitter prior to encoding and at the receiver after decoding. Consider the case where a 4-bit PCM image is to be transmitted. In BPC the 4 bits for all the pels in a scan line are not transmitted pel by pel, but sequentially in accordance with the coding precision. First, all the most significant bits of all the pels in the line are transmitted. This is defined to be the most significant bit "plane." Then the second most significant bit plane is transmitted, and so on until all four bit planes are transmitted. Bit rate reduction is achieved because each plane is encoded for transmission using a binary image compression technique as presented in Chapter 8. At the receiver, all planes are reassembled in the normal multibit-per-pel word structure such that the image can be printed pel by pel. Figures 9.19 through 9.22 show the bit planes for a 4-bit PCM picture. Notice how the less significant bit planes are more noisy and difficult to compress then the most significant bit planes. This particular image was transmitted with an average of 0.6 bits/pel by using the modified read code to compress each plane. This yields a compression of 6.7:1. Compression can be improved

Figure 9.19 One-bit PCM.

Figure 9.20 Second most significant bit.

Figure 9.21 Third most significant bit.

Figure 9.22 Least significant bit.

further if the 4-bit planes are defined as a gray code rather than using the conventional binary code.

The NATO countries have adopted a standard for coding gray-scale images known as *Stanag 5000*. Pels are transmitted using the two-line wobble pattern illustrated in Figure 9.23. The coding technique is the 4-bit BPC concept described above. Each pel is defined using the gray code in Figure 9.24 rather than the conventional binary code. Compression is increased further by adaptively reducing the

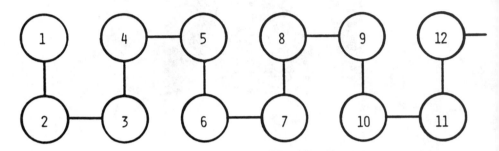

Figure 9.23 Two-line wobble scan.

Intensity Level	Normal Binary				4-bit Gray Code			
0	0	0	0	0	0	0	0	1
1	0	0	0	1	0	1	0	1
2	0	0	1	0	0	1	0	0
3	0	0	1	1	0	1	1	0
4	0	1	0	0	0	0	1	0
5	0	1	0	1	0	0	0	0
6	0	1	1	0	1	0	0	0
7	0	1	1	1	1	0	1	0
8	1	0	0	0	1	0	1	1
9	1	0	0	1	0	0	1	1
10	1	0	1	0	0	1	1	1
11	1	0	1	1	1	1	1	1
12	1	1	0	0	1	1	1	0
13	1	1	0	1	1	1	0	0
14	1	1	1	0	1	1	0	1
15	1	1	1	1	1	0	0	1
	1	3	7	15	3	4	4	4

Figure 9.24 Four-bit gray codes.

resolution in particular portions of a bit plane. Each 2 × 2 matrix of pels within the wobble scan (see Figure 9.25) is examined to determine whether high detail or low detail is present. If little detail is present, the block of 4 pels in transmitted as a single pel. The criteria for use of the low-resolution mode is provided below.

- *Bit plane 1 (most significant):* low resolution never used
- *Bit plane 2:* Low resolution used if transition threshold is not exceeded
- *Bit plane 3:* Low resolution used if transition threshold not exceeded or if bit plane 2 uses low resolution
- *Bit plane 4:* Low resolution always used.

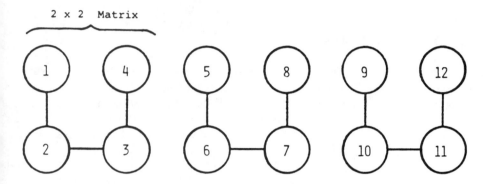

Figure 9.25 Pels used for autoresolution

9.9 JPEG CODING ALGORITHM

9.9.1 Overview

The Joint Photographic Experts Group (JPEG) is an ISO/CCITT working group in the process of developing an international standard, Digital Compression and Coding of Continuous-tone Still Images, for general-purpose, continuous-tone (gray-scale or color), still-image compression. The aim of the standard algorithm is to be general purpose in scope to support a wide variety of image communication services such as facsimile. JPEG reports jointly to both the ISO group responsible for Coded Representation of Picture and Audio Information (ISO/IEC JTC1/SC2/WG8) and to the CCITT Special Rapporteur group for Common Components for Image Communication (a subgroup of CCITT SG VIII). This dual reporting structure is intended to ensure that the ISO and the CCITT produce compatible image compression standards.

The JPEG draft standard specifies two classes of encoding and decoding processes, lossy and lossless processes. Those based on the DCT are lossy, thereby allowing substantial compression to be achieved while producing a reconstructed image with high visual fidelity to the encoder's source image. The simplest DCT-based coding process is referred to as the *baseline sequential process*. It provides a capability that is sufficient for many applications. Additional DCT-based processes extend the baseline sequential process to a broader range of applications. In any application environment using extended DCT-based decoding processes, the baseline decoding process is required to be present in order to provide a default decoding capability. The second class of coding processes is not based on the DCT and is provided to meet the needs of applications requiring lossless compression (e.g., medical x-ray imagery). These lossless encoding and decoding processes are used independently of any of the DCT-based processes.

9.9.2 The Baseline System

Baseline system is the name given to the simplest image coding/decoding capability proposed for the JPEG standard. It consists of techniques well known to the image coding community, including 8 × 8 DCT, uniform quantization, and Huffman coding. Together these provide a lossy, high-compression image coding capability, which preserves good image fidelity at high compression rates. The baseline system provides sequential buildup only.

The baseline system codes an image to full quality in one pass and is geared toward line-by-line scanners, printers, and Group 4 facsimile machines. Typically, the processing starts at the top of the image and finishes at the bottom, allowing the recreated image to be built up on a line-by-line basis. One advantage is that only a small part of the image is being buffered at any given moment. Another feature stipulates that the recreated image need not be an exact copy of the original, the idea being that an almost indistinguishable copy of the original is just as good as an exact copy for most purposes. By not requiring exact copies, higher compression, which translates into lower transmission times, can be realized. Together, these features are known as *lossy sequential coding or transmission*.

Figure 9.26 shows the main procedures for all encoding processes based on the DCT. It illustrates the special case of a single-component image (as opposed to multiple-component color images); this is an appropriate simplification for overview purposes because all processes specified in this international standard operate on each image component independently.

In the encoding process, the input component's samples are grouped into 8 × 8 blocks, and each block is transformed by the forward DCT (FDCT) into a set of 64 values referred to as *DCT coefficients*. One of these values is referred to as the *DC coefficient* and the other 63 as the *AC coefficients*.

Each of the 64 coefficients is then quantized using one of 64 corresponding values from a quantization table (determined by one of the table specifications shown

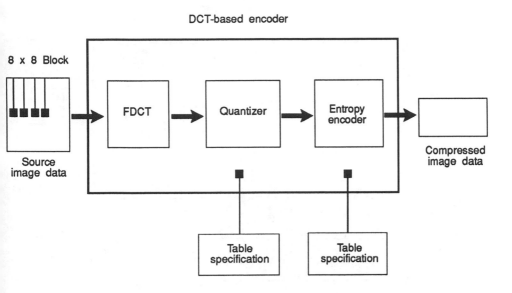

Figure 9.26 DCT-based encoder simplified diagram.

in Figure 9.26). No default values for quantization tables are specified in this international standard; applications may specify values that customize picture quality for their particular image characteristics, display devices, and viewing conditions.

After quantization, the DC coefficient and the 63 AC coefficients are prepared for entropy encoding. The previous quantized DC coefficient is used to predict the current quantized DC coefficient, and the difference is encoded. The 63 quantized AC coefficients undergo no such differential encoding, but are converted into a one-dimensional zigzag sequence, which is common for DCT coding.

All of the quantized coefficients are then passed to an entropy encoding procedure, which compresses the data further. Since Huffman coding is used in the baseline system, Huffman table specifications must be provided to the encoder, as indicated in Figure 9.26.

Huffman coding has two forms: fixed and adaptive. Fixed Huffman coding assumes that coding tables can be generated in advance from test images and then used for many images. In adaptive Huffman coding, the encoder analyzes an image's statistics before coding and devises Huffman tables tailored to that image. These tables are then transmitted to the decoder. Then the image is coded and transmitted. On receipt, the decoder can reconstruct the image using the previously transmitted, tailor-made, Huffman tables.

Figure 9.27 shows the main procedures for all DCT-based decoding processes. Each step shown performs essentially the inverse of its corresponding main procedure

DCT-based decoder

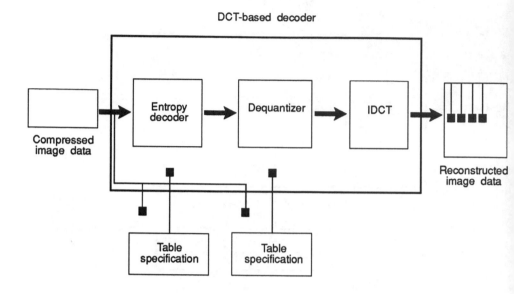

Figure 9.27 DCT-based decoder simplified diagram.

within the encoder. The entropy decoder decodes the zigzag sequence of quantized DCT coefficients. After dequantization, the DCT coefficients are transformed to an 8×8 block of samples by the inverse DCT (IDCT). For DCT-based processes, two alternative sample precisions are specified: either 8 or 12 bits per sample. The baseline process uses only 8-bit precision.

9.9.3 Extended System

Extended system is the name given to a set of additional capabilities not provided by the baseline system. Each set is intended to work in conjunction with, and to build on, the components internal to the baseline system in order to extend its modes of operation. These optional capabilities, which include arithmetic coding, progressive buildup, *progressive lossless* coding, and others may be implemented singly or in appropriate combinations.

Arithmetic coding is an optional, "modern" alternative to Huffman coding. Because the arithmetic coding method chosen adapts to image statistics as it encodes, it generally provides 5 to 10% better compression than the Huffman method chosen by JPEG. This benefit is balanced by some increase in complexity. Progressive buildup, the alternative to sequential buildup, is especially useful for human interaction with picture databases over low-bandwidth channels. For progressive coding, a coarse image is sent, then refinements are sent, improving the coarse image's quality until the desired quality is achieved. This process is geared toward applications such as image databases with multiple resolution and quality requirements, freeze-frame teleconferencing, photovideotex over low-speed lines, and database browsing. Three different, complementary, progressive extensions exist: spectral selection, successive approximation, and hierarchical.

Progressive lossless refers to a lossless compression method that operates in conjunction with progressive buildup. In this mode of operation, the final stage of progressive buildup results in a received image that is bit-for-bit identical to the original (though the possibility exists that this mode might become a *pseudo-lossless* capability, which would guarantee only that output pixels would be within one level of the original pixels).

The JPEG draft standard includes the requirement that the baseline system be contained within every JPEG-standard codec that utilizes any of the extended system capabilities. In this way, the baseline system can serve as a default communications mode for services, allowing encoders and decoders to negotiate. In such cases, image communicability between any JPEG senders and receivers that are not equipped with a common set of extended system capabilities is assured.

9.9.4 Lossless Coding

Figure 9.28 shows the main procedures for the lossless encoding processes. A predictor combines the values of up to three neighborhood samples (A, B, and C) to form a prediction of the sample indicated by X in Figure 9.29. This prediction is then subtracted from the actual value of sample X, and the difference is losslessly entropy-coded by either Huffman or arithmetic coding.

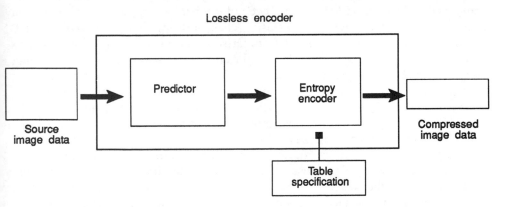

Figure 9.28 Lossless encoder simplified diagram.

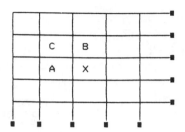

Figure 9.29 Three-sample prediction.

9.10 COLOR FACSIMILE

Very little color facsimile equipment is available in the marketplace today. Several reasons exist for this lack of activity including the complexity and cost associated with color scanning and printing as well as the inherently long transmission time. Another key issue hindering the development of color fax is the lack of standardization. The number of system parameters requiring standardization is manifold: color components, transmission sequence, bilevel versus continuous-tone, and finally the coding algorithm. Each of these issues is discussed in the following sections.

9.10.1 Color Components

Transmitting color in the facsimile world is not straightforward; a color space transformation from the scanned colors to the printed colors must occur either before or after a facsimile's transmission. In general, fax color scanners scan documents using red, green, and blue light (RGB); while fax color printers typically use cyan, magenta, and yellow inks (CMY). These two color schemes (or color spaces) represent different color mixing laws with opposing characteristics. RGB represents the additive color mixture law and is used primarily in television, CRTs, etc.; whereas CMY represents the subtractive color mixture law and is used primarily in printing, painting, etc. For example, mixing together equal amounts of red, green, and blue light produces the color white; while mixing together equal amounts of cyan, magenta, and yellow inks produces the color black. Therefore, producing an accurate color facsimile requires transforming from the RGB to the CMY color space either before or after facsimile transmission.

If the transformation can occur either before or after facsimile transmission, then either color space can be used to represent the facsimile during transmission. However, one of the two color spaces might be better than the other at providing quick document interchanges. In addition, other color spaces might provide even quicker document interchanges. Unfortunately, they might require color space transformations both before and after facsimile transmission.

It is useful to compute the transmission time required for a page transmitted in the RGB format. Consider the following hypothetical parameters for a continuous-tone color facsimile system:

Resolution 200 pels/in.

Page size 8.5 × 11 in.

Transmitted bits/pel (compressed) 2

Color signals (e.g., RGB) 3

Transmission bit rate 9600 b/s

Transmission time 39 min.

The long transmission time of 39 min points out one of the primary reasons that color facsimile has been introduced slowly in the marketplace. However, transmitting the three color signals with full bandwidth is wasteful because the eye is incapable of perceiving high-resolution color. Transmitting a full-resolution luminance signal (Y) supplemented by two low-resolution chroma signals would be more efficient. This concept is now employed in the two major commercial TV transmission standards. Table 9.2 summarizes the relative bandwidths of these standards where B is the luminance bandwidth.

Table 9.2
Relative Bandwidths

	NTSC Standard	PAL Standard (Europe)
Luminance	(Y)B	B
Chroma	(I) B/2	(U) B/3
Chroma	(Q) B/6	(V) B/3
Total	1.67 B	1.67 B

The reader will note that both TV standards transmit the three signals in the reduced channel capacity of 1.67 B rather than 3 B with a net compression of 1.8. In general, employing the European YUV components for transmission is more convenient than YIQ because the two chroma components have an equal bandwidth. YUV has also been standardized by CCIR Recommendation 601 and has been used by the JPEG committee in their test program.

9.10.2 Transmission Order of the Color Space Components

At least five ways are available to order a color space's components for scanning, transmission, and printing. Using a particular ordering (interleave format) of a color space's components significantly affects transmission duration times. These five formats are the pel, line, block, blocky line, and plane interleave formats. Their names correspond to five different resolutions of a color document.

Plane: A page of a color document consists of p planes; one for each color space component.

Pel: Smallest unit on a plane that may be scanned or printed. A plane consists of $n \times m$ pels.

Line: A line consists of a row of pels on a plane. There are n pels in a line, and there are m lines on a plane.

Block: A block consists of $q \times r$ pels. There are $(n \times m)/(q \times r)$ blocks on a plane.

Blocky line: A blocky line consists of a row of blocks on a plane. There are m/r blocky lines on a plane.

The interleave formats have the following definitions:

Pel: For each pel, the color space component values are contiguous. (For example, the red, green, and blue components of pel 1 are followed by the red, green, and blue components of pel 2, and so on.)

Line: For each color space component, all values corresponding to each pel on the line for that component are contiguous. (For example, the red, green, and blue components of line 1 are followed by the red, green, and blue components of line 2, and so on.)

Plane: For each color space component, all values corresponding to that component are contiguous. (For example, the red, green, and blue page components.)

Block: For each block, the color component values are contiguous. (This is similar to the pel interleave format.)

Blocky line: For each color space component, all values corresponding to each block on the blocky line for that component are contiguous. (This is similar to the line interleave format.)

9.10.3 Bilevel Color Systems

Bilevel color facsimile systems are attractive because they can be inexpensive, offer short document interchange times, and provide color facsimiles with good quality.

By using the least expensive color printer and color scanner technologies, inexpensive bilevel color facsimile systems can be constructed. Suitable bilevel color printer technologies are thermal wax transfer, drop-on-demand ink-jet, and bubble ink-jet. They provide consistent results at a reasonable price. Other bilevel color technologies such as dot matrix and electrophotographic are either too slow, too expensive, or give inconsistent results.

Most color scanner technologies are already inexpensive and usually provide continuous-tone values (8 bits/pel/color). Although bilevel equipment needs bilevel values, converting from continuous-tone values to bilevel values is a relatively simple process. Secondly, by performing a continuous-tone–to–bilevel conversion in the transmitter (scanner), document interchange durations can be minimized; fewer bits per pixel need be coded and transmitted.

A bilevel color facsimile system will probably include these features:

- Compliance with established CCITT recommendations
- Compliance with other telematic services' color space standards
- Compliance with other telematic services' interchange color space and interleave format standards
- Minimum document interchange durations
- Minimum amount of storage (memory) required
- May interchange documents with bilevel monochrome facsimile equipment or other telematic services
- Uses the pel or line interchange interleave format
- Has a document interchange duration of approximately 100 s.

9.10.4 Continuous-Tone Color Systems

Today, the major limiting factor for continuous-tone color facsimile systems is the available printer technologies; they are expensive. It is hoped that they will eventually become inexpensive, and good examples are the cycolor and continuous ink-jet technologies. Color scanner technologies are not a major limiting factor. As mentioned before, most of them already provide continuous-tone values (8 bits/pel/color) inexpensively.

Altogether, the most feasible print technologies for continuous-tone color facsimile systems include cycolor, electrophotographic, continuous ink-jet, thermal dye diffusion transfer, and thermal dye sublimation transfer. Of these, cycolor now appears to be one of the best candidates for an inexpensive system. Its technology is in the paper, and the paper may be processed quickly using unsophisticated and inexpensive equipment. Because the equipment is simple and because the paper comes in rolls, facsimile systems using this method would probably be reliable and maintenance-free, just like most existing Group 3 equipments.

A continuous-tone color facsimile system could include these features:

- Compliance with established CCITT recommendations
- Compliance with other telematic services' color space standards
- Compliance with other telematic services' interchange color space and interleave format standards
- Minimum document interchange durations
- Minimum amount of storage (memory) required
- Uses the line interchange interleave format

- Uses 8 bits/pel for each color space component (prior to compression)
- Has a minimum required memory storage of a line.

9.10.5 Color Fax Compression

As explained in Section 9.9, one of the major objectives of the JPEG algorithm is the compression of color facsimile signals. The baseline JPEG coding technique (8 × 8 pixel DCT followed by Huffman coding) would be applied to each of the three color components to be transmitted. The color components will consist of a wideband luminance supplemented by two reduced-bandwidth chroma signals. A good example of such a component set is Y, U, V, which is the TV standard employed in CCIR Recommendation 601.

It is useful to compute the transmission time of a color fax page over a standard ISDN B channel (64 kb/s). The assumptions for the computation are as follows:

Page size 8.5 × 11 in.

Luminance resolution Y 9 × 106 pixels (300 pixels/in.)

Chroma resolution UV 4.5 × 106 pixels (150 pixels/in.)

Total pixels 13.5 × 10^6 pixels

Compressed bits/page 6.75 × 106 bits (JPEG, 0.5 b/pixel)

Transmission rate 64 × 10^3 b/s

Transmission time 100 s.

If the page size were reduced to 4 × 5 in., the transmission time is reduced to approximately 20 s.

REFERENCES

[1] Gersho, A., "On the structure of vector quantizers," *IEEE Trans. Info. Theory* IT-28(2), 157–166 (March 1982).

[2] Linde, Y., A. Buzo, and R.M. Gray, "An algorithm for vector quantizer design," *IEEE Trans. Commun.* COM-28(1), 84–95 (Jan. 1980).

[3] Gray, R.M., and Y. Linde, "Vector quantizers and predictive quantizers for Gauss-Markov sources," *IEEE Trans. Commun.* COM-30(2), 381–389 (Feb. 1982)

[4] Huang, H.-M., and J.W. Woods, "Predictive vector quantization of images," *IEEE Trans. Commun.* COM-33(11), 1208–1219 (Nov. 1985).

[5] "Component vector quantization," Annex 4 of CCITT Study Group VIII, Geneva, 1–12 December 1986.

[6] Helden, J., and D.E. Boekee, "Vector quantization using a generalized tree search algorithm," *Proc. 5th Symp. Information Theory in the Benelux,ri Aalten, pp. 21–27 (May 1984).*

[7] *Gersho, A., and B. Ramamurthi, "Image coding using vector quantization," Proc. ICASSP, Paris (1982).*

Chapter 10
Fax Test Charts

Before availability of the standardized fax test charts described here, each company used its own test charts, and it was difficult to compare performance of nonstandard fax machines with nonstandard test charts. Today, both the fax machines and the test charts are standardized. With new fax machine performance standards, new higher resolution and color charts have been developed. The following test charts are for testing both fax equipment performance limitations and transmission channel characteristics. Fax machine manufacturers can use the test charts to measure the level of performance achieved in a new design and to assure the quality of production line fax machines. Users may find the charts helpful in comparing brands and models of fax machines. Periodic testing will assure that the desired performance level is maintained over the long run.

10.1 IEEE CHART 167A

Developing definitions of facsimile terms, test procedures, and test charts has been among the functions of the Institute of Electrical and Electronic Engineers (IEEE) and its earlier organizations IRE and AIEE since the 1940s. The first IRE facsimile test chart was issued in 1955. Thirty-five years later, after many updates and reissues, this chart is still widely used for testing performance of fax, electronic imagery devices, office copiers, and other photographic systems (see Figure 10.1).

This chart has a high degree of precision and accuracy of reproduction to allow measurement of equipment performance and transmission channel performance. A full range of continuous-tone gray scale is achieved from paper white to a saturated black density of 1.8. The wide variety of test patterns makes it easy to spot transmission problems and loss of resolution. Although some of the patterns may appear to be redundant, each one is better than others for a particular resolution measurement or distortion evaluation. The original chart was assembled from favorite test patterns from each member of the IRE Facsimile Committee. It was expected that

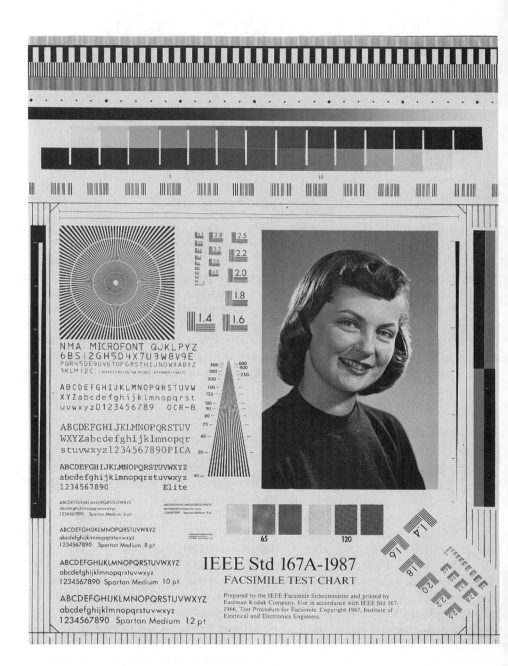

Figure 10.1 IEEE Facsimile Test Chart 167A.

after all of the patterns were assembled on one chart, many could be eliminated, but each one was defended and none was eliminated. Patterns 14A and 14B are copies of the National Bureau of Standards (NBS) Microcopy Resolution Test Chart without the three lowest resolution patterns. The highest resolution NBS pattern corresponds to 36 lines/mm (914 lines/in.), but the contrast of this pattern is low and the lines are broken. Even the microdefects in some of the patterns are useful for testing. Users are able to spot instantly distortions of the received copy gray scale by looking at the picture in the test chart.

The Eastman Kodak secretary, whose picture appears in all issues of the chart, little realized that her likeness would be spread worldwide on more than 30,000 facsimile test charts. Each chart as it was used made many more fax copies until her image is universally recognized and associated with facsimile test patterns. Thirty-three years of reproducing test charts from the master negative has degraded her photo so much that it may not be possible to get further use of this picture. The last printing of this test chart can still be purchased from the IEEE Service Center, 445 Hoes Lane, P.O. Box 1331, Piscataway, NJ 08855-1331. Ask for SH10959, list price $18.00.

10.2 CCITT FAX TEST CHART NO. 1

In 1960 the CCITT issued Recommendation T.20 for Test Chart No. 1 (see Figure 10.2). The recommendation states:

> . . . that it will be a great advantage to use a standardized test chart to check the quality of facsimile transmissions and that such a chart would provide the receiving office with a reliable and rapid means of checking the quality of test transmissions according to uniform principles and of making comparisons between different transmission results in a precise way. This chart has been designed for measuring the quality of both picture and black-and-white transmissions and it enables the apparatus used and the communication channels to be judged by means of objective measurements, the results of which may be expressed in code.

> The chart size is 4.33 × 9.84 in. (110 × 250 mm). Gray-scale performance is checked by a 15-step density pattern and the photograph. Black-white patterns measure single-line and multiple-line resolution up to 6 lines/mm (152 lines/in.). Other patterns will show analog facsimile distortions caused by telephone lines and equipment design. A second edition was issued in October 1968. The main change is in the photograph used. The CCITT had requested permission to use the "IEEE girl photo," but the IEEE thought it might be confusing since the photo was almost a trademark.

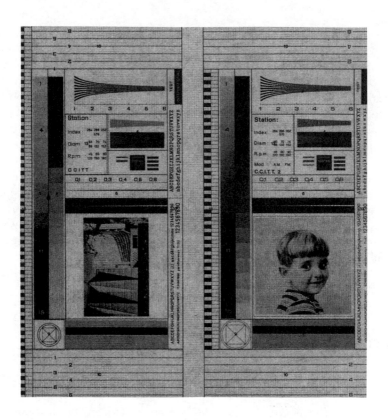

Figure 10.2 CCITT Test Chart No. 1.

10.3 CCITT FAX TEST CHART NO. 2

In 1980 the CCITT issued Recommendation T.21 for Test Charts No. 2 and No. 3. The recommendation states:

> . . . that a standardized test chart to check the quality of document facsimile transmissions will have great advantages. Owing to the development of international document facsimile transmission services, a great variety of characters and symbols, including ideographic symbols, are involved and must be taken into consideration.

The size is 8.23 × 11.69 in. (210 × 297 mm) based on the ISO A4 international paper size, instead of 8.5 × 11 in. as used in North America. The edge-to-edge pattern width is only 8.25 in., narrower than that provided by some Group 3 fax units. These charts for checking the quality of document facsimile transmissions were issued at the same time as the Recommendation T.4 for Group 3 facsimile.

Test Chart No. 2 is a "transmission test chart" with patterns for quantitative evaluation of distortion and character groups for evaluation of readability (see Figure 10.3).

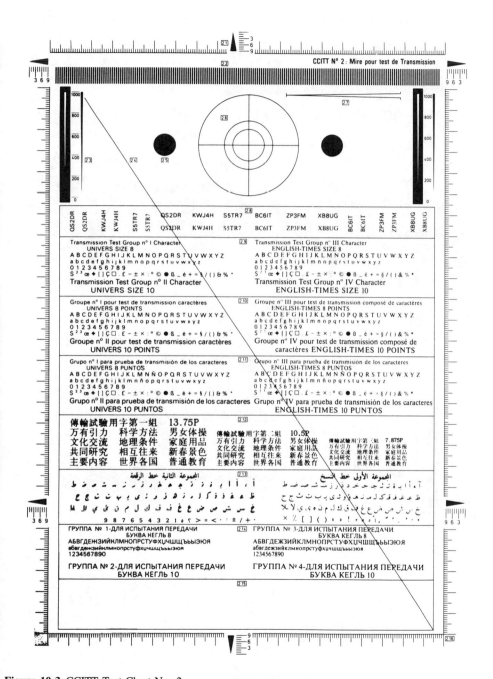

Figure 10.3 CCITT Test Chart No. 2.

214

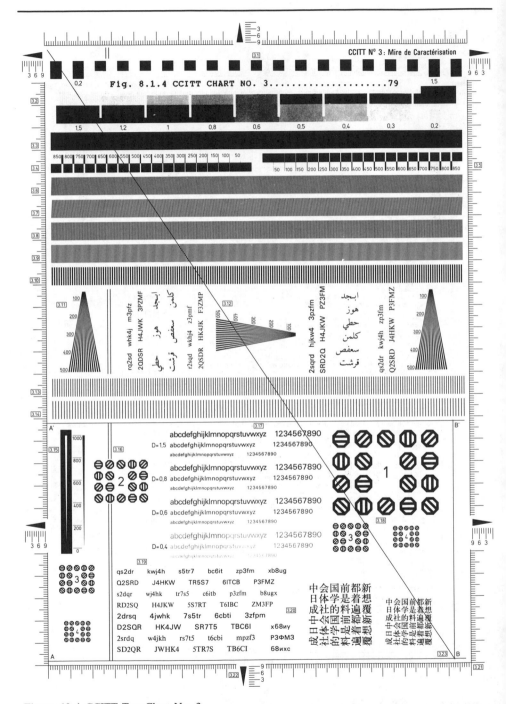

Figure 10.4 CCITT Test Chart No. 3.

It contains test patterns for measuring lost margins and resolution. The four borders framing the chart are calibrated in millimeters, allowing direct measurement of distortions in length on horizontal and vertical lines. The circle will reproduce as an oblong shape if there is a paper feed rate error. Measurement of the border length will confirm such an error. The diagonal line through the patterns may show steps or white streaks if there are errors in the received picture data. Printing the previous line for MR coding errors will show as a step in the diagonal line. Most of the chart consists of text and characters in English, French, Spanish, Chinese, Arabic, and Russian.

10.4 CCITT FAX TEST CHART NO. 3

Test Chart No. 3 is a "characterization test chart" for evaluation of the technical quality parameters of the fax units. This chart helps technicians maintain the fax machine by detecting faults, making adjustments, and calibrating performance. Patterns 3.4 and 3.5 show the system performance with thin, isolated, black lines on white and white lines on black. For the same line width, isolated lines (as in type) will usually reproduce better than black-and-white patterns of equal width as in patterns 3.6 through 3.11. Pattern 3.6 has alternating lines corresponding to the Group 3 horizontal resolution of 203/in. (8/mm). These lines are tilted 2 deg from vertical, allowing alignment and misalignment with the photosensors as the chart moves through the scanner. A decreasing density character set allows for determination of the limits of reproducible density and for checking the effectiveness of the scanner adaptive threshold (see Figure 10.4).

10.5 CCITT GROUP 3 TEST IMAGES

To determine which code words should be shortest, when designing the modified Huffman code tables, eight test pages—each with different languages and content—were used (see Figure 10.5). Test image No. 1 [Figure 10.5], a short business letter, is frequently used by sellers for measuring the time taken to send a page. The time listed does not include the initial handshake, which takes about 15 s, or the few seconds between pages.

When designing the modified Huffman code tables, eight test pages with different languages and content were used to determine which code words should be shortest. It should be noted that CCITT is in the process of including these eight reference documents in a recommendation. These images were scanned and a histogram made showing the number of times that each white run length and each black run length occurred. The modified Huffman design code assigned short code words to those runs that occurred most frequently.

The CCITT does not recognize these test images as official standards, and does not have them for sale. They have become *de facto* standards, however. Some sets

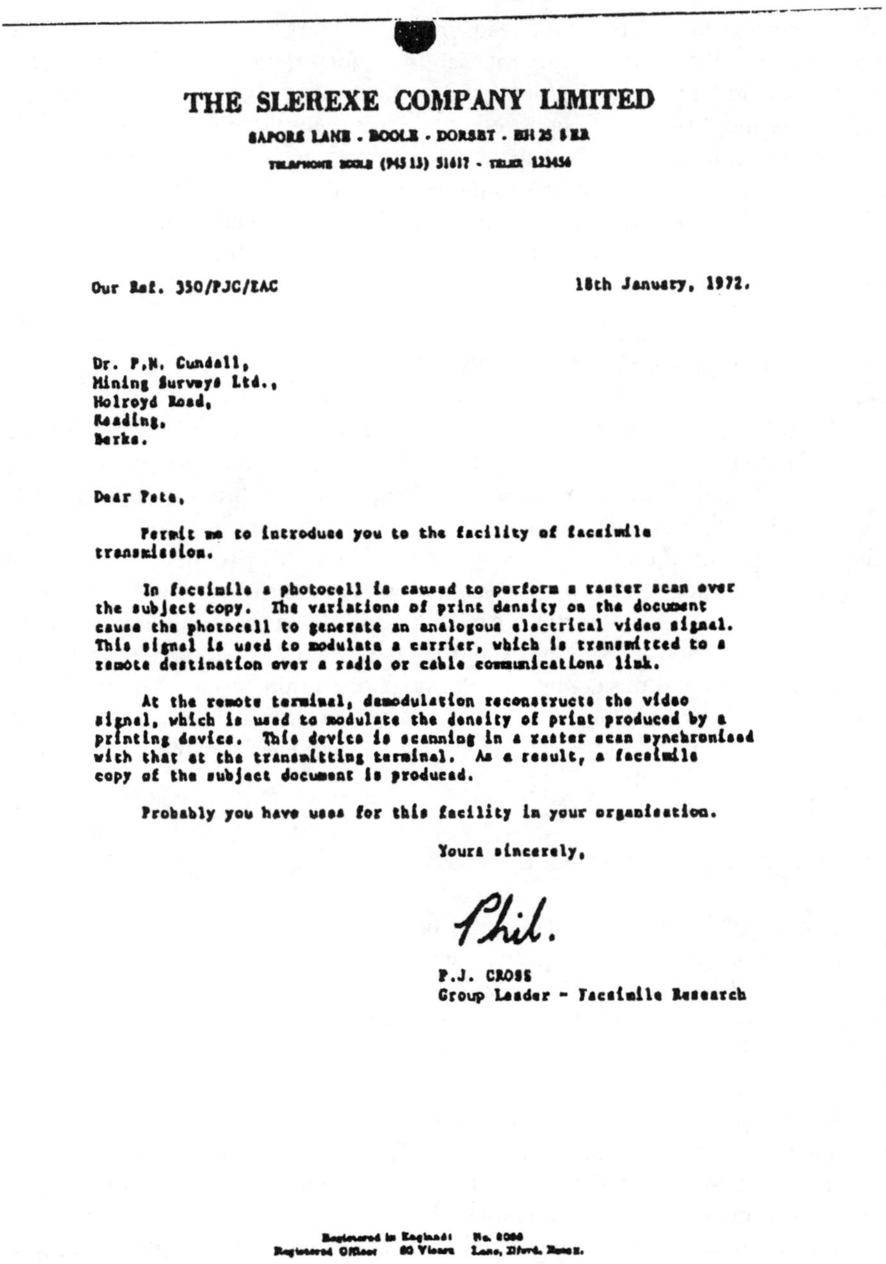

THE SLEREXE COMPANY LIMITED

SAPORS LANE · BOOLE · DORSET · BH 25 8 ER

TELEPHONE BOOLE (945 13) 51617 · TELEX 123456

Our Ref. 350/PJC/EAC   18th January, 1972.

Dr. P.N. Cundall,
Mining Surveys Ltd.,
Holroyd Road,
Reading,
Berks.

Dear Pete,

   Permit me to introduce you to the facility of facsimile
transmission.

   In facsimile a photocell is caused to perform a raster scan over
the subject copy. The variations of print density on the document
cause the photocell to generate an analogous electrical video signal.
This signal is used to modulate a carrier, which is transmitted to a
remote destination over a radio or cable communications link.

   At the remote terminal, demodulation reconstructs the video
signal, which is used to modulate the density of print produced by a
printing device. This device is scanning in a raster scan synchronised
with that at the transmitting terminal. As a result, a facsimile
copy of the subject document is produced.

   Probably you have uses for this facility in your organisation.

                                        Yours sincerely,

                                        Phil.

                                        P.J. CROSS
                                        Group Leader - Facsimile Research

Registered in England: No. 2088
Registered Office: 60 Vicars Lane, Ilford, Essex.

Figure 10.5 CCITT Group 3 test images. Test image No. 1, business letter.

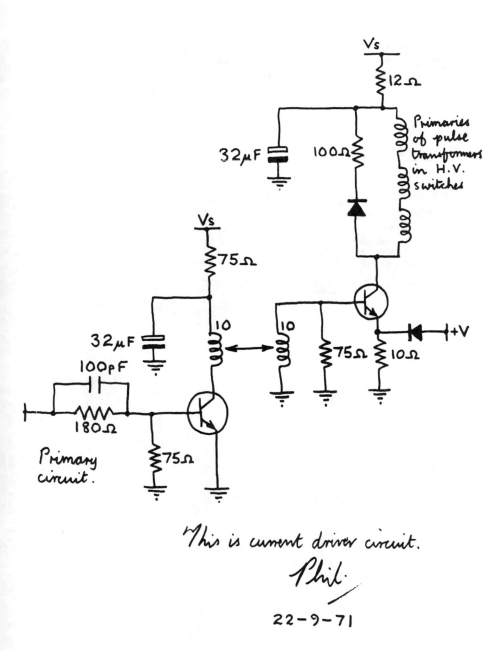

Vs

12Ω

Primaries
of pulse
transformers
in H.V.
switches

32μF

100Ω

Vs

75Ω

32μF

100pF

10

10

75Ω

10Ω

+V

180Ω

Primary
circuit.

75Ω

75Ω

This is current driver circuit.

Phil.

22-9-71

Figure 10.5 continued Test image No. 2, pencil sketch and handwritten comment.

ÉTABLISSEMENTS ABCDEFG
SOCIÉTÉ ANONYME AU CAPITAL DE 300 000 F
20, RUE DU XVUTRSTBSL F 00000 NTBCLAG
Tél. : (35) 24.46.32 Adr. Tg. : NRVLJRQLM
Télex : 31596 F IN : 718490070257
Transporteur (ou Transitaire)
M M. DUPONT Frères
8 quai des blcdfsh F 0000 NTBCLAG

Mot directeur				
CLASSEMENT		FACTURE INVOICE	Exemplaire 15	
CODE CLIENT Z 04399		DATE 7-7-74	NUMÉRO 06	FEUILLET 01
Votre commande		du 74-2-2uméro 438		
Notre offre AZ/B7		du 74-1-1uméro 12		

LIVRAISON

5, rue XYZ

99000 VILLE

FACTURATION

12, rue ABCD BP 15

99000 VILLE

DOMICILIATION BANCAIRE DU VENDEUR

PAYS D'ORIGINE   PAYS DE DESTINATION

CODE BANQUE	CODE GUICHET	COMPTE CLIENT	CONDITIONS DE LIVRAISON DATE 74-03-03

LICENCE D'EXPORTATION   NATURE DU CONTRAT (monnaie)

ORIGINE	TRANSPORTS DESTINATION	MODE	CONDITIONS DE PAIEMENT (échéance, %...) FAB
Pays 1	Etat 2	Air	

MARQUES ET NUMÉROS MARKS AND NUMBERS	NOMBRE ET NATURE DES COLIS : DÉNOMINATION DE LA MARCHANDISE NUMBER AND KING OF PACKAGES: DESCRIPTION OF GOODS	NOMEN- CLATURE STATISTICAL No.	MASSE NETTE NET WEIGHT MASSE BRUTE GROSS WEIGHT	VALEUR VALUE DIMENSIONS MEASURE- MENTS
74.21.456.44.2 A	1 Composants	U 123/4	5 kg 8 kg	1400 X 13x10x6

QUANTITÉ COMMANDÉE ET UNITÉ QUANTITY ORDERED AND UNIT	N° ET RÉF. DE L'ARTICLE	DÉSIGNATION	QUANTITÉ LIVRÉE ET UNITÉ QUANTITY DELIVERED AND UNIT	PRIX UNITAIRE UNIT PRICE	MONTANT TOTAL TOTAL AMOUNT
2	AF-809	Circuit intégré	2	104,33 F	208,66 F
10	S8-T4	Connecteur	10	83,10 F	831,00 F
25	ZI07	Composant indéterminé	20	15,00 F	300,00 F

Costs	Débours	Inclus	Non inclus
Packing	Emballages		92,14
Freight	Transport		
Insurance	Assurances		
Total Invoice amount	Montant total de la facture		1431,80
Installment	Acomptes		
NET TO BE PAID	NET A RÉGLER		1431,80

Figure 10.5 continued Test image No. 3, invoice.

L'ordre de lancement et de réalisation des applications fait l'objet de décisions au plus haut niveau de la Direction Générale des Télécommunications. Il n'est certes pas question de construire ce système intégré "en bloc" mais bien au contraire de procéder par étapes, par paliers successifs. Certaines applications, dont la rentabilité ne pourra être assurée, ne seront pas entreprises. Actuellement, sur trente applications qui ont pu être globalement définies, six en sont au stade de l'exploitation, six autres se sont vu donner la priorité pour leur réalisation.

Chaque application est confiée à un "chef de projet", responsable successivement de sa conception, de son analyse-programmation et de sa mise en oeuvre dans une région-pilote. La généralisation ultérieure de l'application réalisée dans cette région-pilote dépend des résultats obtenus et fait l'objet d'une décision de la Direction Générale. Néanmoins, le chef de projet doit dès le départ considérer que son activité a une vocation nationale donc refuser tout particularisme régional. Il est aidé d'une équipe d'analystes-programmeurs et entouré d'un "groupe de conception" chargé de rédiger le document de "définition des objectifs globaux" puis le "cahier des charges" de l'application, qui sont adressés pour avis à tous les services utilisateurs potentiels et aux chefs de projet des autres applications. Le groupe de conception comprend 6 à 10 personnes représentant les services les plus divers concernés par le projet,et comporte obligatoirement un bon analyste attaché à l'application.

II - L'IMPLANTATION GEOGRAPHIQUE D'UN RESEAU INFORMATIQUE PERFORMANT

L'organisation de l'entreprise française des télécommunications repose sur l'existence de 20 régions. Des calculateurs ont été implantés dans le passé au moins dans toutes les plus importantes. On trouve ainsi des machines Bull Gamma 30 à Lyon et Marseille, des GE 425 à Lille, Bordeaux, Toulouse et Montpellier, un GE 437 à Massy, enfin quelques machines Bull 300 TI à programmes câblés étaient récemment ou sont encore en service dans les régions de Nancy, Nantes, Limoges, Poitiers et Rouen ; ce parc est essentiellement utilisé pour la comptabilité téléphonique.

A l'avenir, si la plupart des fichiers nécessaires aux applications décrites plus haut peuvent être gérés en temps différé, un certain nombre d'entre eux devront nécessairement être accessibles, voire mis à jour en temps réel : parmi ces derniers le fichier commercial des abonnés, le fichier des renseignements, le fichier des circuits, le fichier technique des abonnés contiendront des quantités considérables d'informations.

Le volume total de caractères à gérer en phase finale sur un ordinateur ayant en charge quelques 500 000 abonnés a été estimé à un milliard de caractères au moins. Au moins le tiers des données seront concernées par des traitements en temps réel.

Aucun des calculateurs énumérés plus haut ne permettait d'envisager de tels traitements.

L'intégration progressive de toutes les applications suppose la création d'un support commun pour toutes les informations, une véritable "Banque de données", répartie sur des moyens de traitement nationaux et régionaux, et qui devra rester alimentée, mise à jour en permanence, à partir de la base de l'entreprise, c'est-à-dire les chantiers, les magasins, les guichets des services d'abonnement, les services de personnel etc.

L'étude des différents fichiers a donc permis de définir les principales caractéristiques du réseau d'ordinateurs nouveaux à mettre en place pour aborder la réalisation du système informatif. L'obligation de faire appel à des ordinateurs de troisième génération, très puissants et dotés de volumineuses mémoires de masse, a conduit à en réduire substantiellement le nombre.

L'implantation de sept centres de calcul interrégionaux constituera un compromis entre : d'une part le désir de réduire le coût économique de l'ensemble, de faciliter la coordination des équipes d'informaticiens; et d'autre part le refus de créer des centres trop importants difficiles à gérer et à diriger,et posant des problèmes délicats de sécurité. Le regroupement des traitements relatifs à plusieurs régions sur chacun de ces sept centres permettra de leur donner une taille relativement homogène. Chaque centre "gérera" environ un million d'abonnés à la fin du VIème Plan.

La mise en place de ces centres a débuté au début de l'année 1971 : un ordinateur IRIS 50 de la Compagnie Internationale pour l'Informatique a été installé à Toulouse en février ; la même machine vient d'être mise en service au centre de calcul interrégional de Bordeaux.

Figure 10.5 continued Test image No. 4, very dense document.

Cela est d'autant plus valable que $T\,\Delta f$ est plus grand. A cet égard la figure 2 représente la vraie courbe donnant $|\phi(f)|$ en fonction de f pour les valeurs numériques indiquées page précédente.

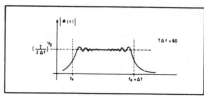

Fig. 2

Dans ce cas, le filtre adapté pourra être constitué, conformément à la figure 3, par la cascade :

— d'un filtre passe-bande de transfert unité pour $f_0 \leqslant f \leqslant f_0 + \Delta f$ et de transfert quasi nul pour $f < f_0$ et $f > f_0 + \Delta f$, filtre ne modifiant pas la phase des composants le traversant ;

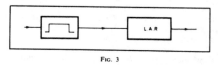

Fig. 3

— filtre suivi d'une ligne à retard (LAR) dispersive ayant un temps de propagation de groupe T_R décroissant linéairement avec la fréquence f suivant l'expression :

$$T_R = T_0 + (f_0 - f)\,\frac{T}{\Delta f} \quad \text{(avec } T_0 > T\text{)}$$

(voir fig. 4).

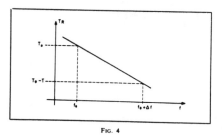

Fig. 4

telle ligne à retard est donnée par :

$$\varphi = -2\pi \int_0^f T_R \, df$$

$$\varphi = -2\pi \left[T_0 + \frac{f_0 T}{\Delta f} \right] f + \pi \, \frac{T}{\Delta f}\, f^2$$

Et cette phase est bien l'opposé de $\underline{/\phi(f)}$,

à un déphasage constant près (sans importance) et à un retard T_0 près (inévitable).

Un signal utile $S(t)$ traversant un tel filtre adapté donne à la sortie (à un retard T_0 près et à un déphasage près de la porteuse) un signal dont la transformée de Fourier est réelle, constante entre f_0 et $f_0 + \Delta f$, et nulle de part et d'autre de f_0 et de $f_0 + \Delta f$, c'est-à-dire un signal de fréquence porteuse $f_0 + \Delta f/2$ et dont l'enveloppe a la forme indiquée à la figure 5, où l'on a représenté simultanément le signal $S(t)$ et le signal $S_1(t)$ correspondant obtenu à la sortie du filtre adapté. On comprend le nom de récepteur à compression d'impulsion donné à ce genre de filtre adapté : la « largeur » (à 3 dB) du signal comprimé étant égale à $1/\Delta f$, le rapport de compression

est de $\dfrac{T}{1/\Delta f} = T\,\Delta f$

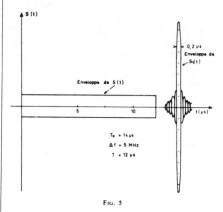

Fig. 5

On saisit physiquement le phénomène de compression en réalisant que lorsque le signal $S(t)$ entre dans la ligne à retard (LAR) la fréquence qui entre la première à l'instant 0 est la fréquence basse f_0, qui met un temps T_0 pour traverser. La fréquence f entre à l'instant $t = (f - f_0)\,\dfrac{T}{\Delta f}$ et elle met un temps

$T_0 - (f - f_0)\,\dfrac{T}{\Delta f}$ pour traverser, ce qui la fait ressortir à l'instant T_0 également. Ainsi donc, le signal $S(t)$

Figure 10.5 continued Test image No. 5, printed technical drawings and mathematical equations and notation.

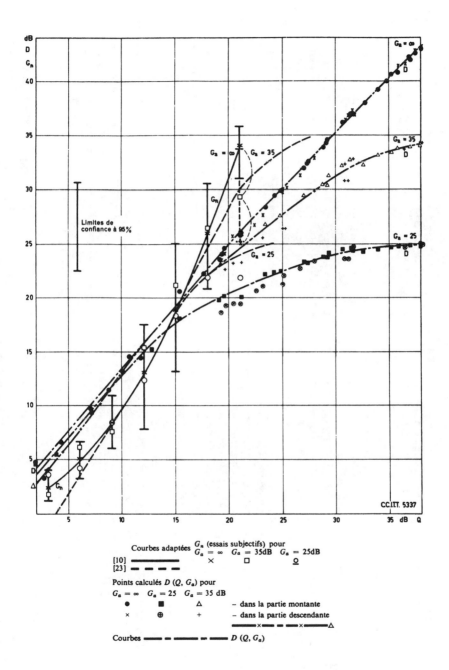

Figure 10.5 continued Test image No. 6, chart.

CCITTの概要

沿革

CCITTは、国際電気通信連合（ITU）の四つの常設機関（事務総局、国際周波数登録委員会、CCIR、CCITT）の一つとして、ITUの中でも、世界の国際通信上の諸問題を真先に取上げ、その解決方法を見出して行く重要な機関である。日本名は、国際電信電話諮問委員会と称される。

CCITTの前身は、CCIF（国際電話諮問委員会）とCCIT（国際電信諮問委員会）である。CCIF（1924年にヨーロッパに「国際長距離電話通信諮問委員会」が設置され、これが1925年のパリ電信電話会議のとき、正式に、「国際電話諮問委員会」として万国電信連合の公式機関となったものである。CCITは、同じく1925年の会議のとき、CCIFと併立するものとして設置された。

そして、CCIFは、1956年の12月に第18回総会が開催されたのち、併合されて現在のCCITとなった。このCCIFとCCITが解散した直後、第1回のCCITを開催し、第2回総会は、1960年にニューデリーで、第3回総会は、1964年、ジュネーブで、第4回総会は、1968年、アルゼンチンで開催された。

CCIFとCCITが合併したのは、有線電気通信の分野、とくに伝送路について電信回線と電話回線とを技術的に分ける意味がなくなってきたこと、各国とも大体において、電信部門と電話部門は同一組織内にあること、CCIFの事務局とCCITの事務局の合併による能率増進等がおもな理由であった。

CCITは、上述のように、ヨーロッパ内の国ぐにによって、ヨーロッパ内の電信・電話の技術・運用・料金の基準を定め、あるいは統一をはかってきたので、現在でも、その影響を受け、会合参加国は、ヨーロッパの国が多く、ヨーロッパで生起する問題の研究が多い。たとえば、1960年のCCITT勧告の中で、配慮する距離は約2,500kmであったが、これはヨーロッパ内領域を想定したものである。

しかしながら、1956年9月に敷設された大西洋横断電話ケーブルは、大陸間電話通信の自動化および半自動化への技術的可能性を与え、CCITTがこの問題を取り上げるに及び、CCITTの性格は高次、汎世界的色彩を実質的に帯びるに至った。この汎世界的性格は第2次世界大戦後ますましく大きくなったアジア・アフリカ植民地の独立に伴ってITUの構成員の中にこれらの国が加わり、ITUの中に新しい意見が導入されたことにも起因して、技術面、政治面の双方から導入されてきた。

た。CCITTの汎世界化は、1960年の第2回総会がニューデリーで開催されたことにもあらわれている。この総会までは、CCIT・CCIFのいずれにしろ、アメリカやアジアで総会が開催されたことがなく、CCITT委員長も、ニューデリー総会の準備文書で、この点には注目すべきであるとのべている。

任務

ITUは、全権委員会議、主管庁会議、主管庁電気通信条約を始めとして、七つの機関をもち、それぞれの機関の権限と任務は国際電気通信条約に明記されている。そこで条約を参照してみるならば、CCITTの任務は、つぎのとおりとなっている。

「国際電信電話諮問委員会（CCITT）は、電信および電話に関する技術、運用および料金の問題について研究し、および意見を表明することを任務とする。」（1965年モントルー条約第187号）

「各国際諮問委員会は、その任務の遂行に当たって、新しい国または発展の途上にある国における地域的および国際的分野にわたる電気通信の創設、発達および改善に直接関連のある問題について研究し、および意見を作成するように妥当な注意を払わなければならない。」（同第188号）

「各国際諮問委員会は、また、関係国の要請に基づき、その国内電気通信の問題について研究し、かつ、勧告を行なうことができる。」（同第189号）

上記第187号と第188号にいわれる「意見」とは、フランス語のAvisから訳したもので、英語的には「勧告（Recommendation）」となっている。CCITTの表明する意見は「国際法的には強制力をもたないものであって、この点が、条約、電信規則、電話規則等各国を拘束する力をもっているものと異なる。もっとも意見と称しても、技術的分野では、電信規則のごとき、実際にある機器の仕様を定める場合には、多くの国の意見が統一されたこの「意見」に従わなければ、円滑な国際通信を行なう場合各国が直面する問題について、具体的意見を表明するもので、たとえば、大陸間ケーブルで大陸間通話を半自動化しようとする場合、その信号方式や取り扱う通話の種類およびその料金は、どのようにするかを研究して意見を表明する。したがって、CCITTの活動は、つねに時代の最先端を行くもので、CCITTの活動方向は、その時々世界の国際通信の活動方向であるともいえる。

この意見は、また、電信規則以下のその他の規則のごとく、数年以上の間隔をもって開催される主管庁会議というような大会議の決定をまたなくても表明することができ、また、その改正も容易であるので、現在のように進歩の早い国際通信界では、関係国の意見を統一した国際的見解としては非常に便利である。

Figure 10.5 continued Test image No. 7, Japanese text.

memorandum

FROM:		TO:
A. P. Sprggs Research		G. V. Smith Project Planning
TEL:	EXTN: 2041	DATE: 1-9-71

We know that, where possible, data is reduced to alphanumeric form for transmission by communication systems. However, this can be expensive, and also some data must remain in graphic form. For example, we cannot key-punch an engineering drawing or weather map.

) think we should realise that high speed facsimile transmissions are needed to overcome our problems in efficient graphic data communication. We need research into graphics data compression.

Any comments?

Albert.

Figure 10.5 continued Test image No. 8, handwritten note on printed memorandum sheet.

in use are multiple-generation copies that are not as sharp as the original ones and will give slightly different transmission times. The images Nos. 1, 4, 5, and the Delta Facsimile Test Chart have been scanned at resolutions of 200, 240, 300, 400, and 480 lines/in. and recorded on magnetic tape. One 2400-ft reel of 9-track tape at 1600 b/in. in IBM standard EBCDIC format contains these 20 binary images.[1]

10.6 CCITT HIGH RESOLUTION AND COLOR TEST CHARTS

When the CCITT decided that a color test chart would be needed for development and testing of Group 4 color fax, the U.S. National Communications System (NCS) volunteered (and was assigned) to undertake this task. It was determined that four new charts would be needed:

1. A black-white chart with higher resolution than then available to test the 400 dpi (and possibly higher) resolutions.
2. A monochrome test chart with more gray scale steps than then available to check color and black-white fax performance on shadings between black and white.
3. A full color test chart by the four-color screen type printing process to test performance on color materials from business publications.
4. A full color, nonscreened, test chart produced by photographic color printing to check performance of color photographs without screen dots.

The first two charts, now CCITT T.22, are suitable for testing both Group 4 and Group 3 fax, especially the new high resolution options. The third (color) chart has also been approved to proceed toward the production printing stage. The photographic color test chart has progressed to conceptual sample prints.

10.6.1 CCITT Test Chart No. 4—Black-White Facsimile Test Chart BW01

This monochrome test chart with black-white patterns has only text and line work printed on high-gamma photographic paper for optimum sharpness and high contrast without fogging the white areas next to black markings. The overall size of the printed chart is 222 × 298 mm (8.75 × 11.75 in.) to allow for maximum paper size tolerances. The patterns that make up the chart are defined below (see Figure 10.6):

1. Border of four scales with millimeter markings. The arrows near the ends of the top border are 8.5 in. apart and centered on the page.
2. Black bar across full page width and a scale in inches across the top, starting from 0 in the middle of the page with 0.1-in. scale markings. The border at the left side of the chart is also marked in inches.

---

[1]This diskette can be obtained from National Communication System, Attn: NT, 701 South Court House Road, Arlington, VA 22204-2198.

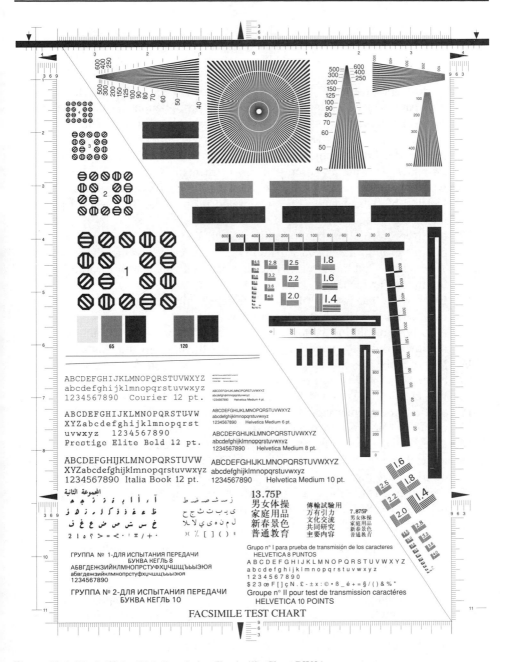

Figure 10.6 Black-White High Resolution Facsimilie Chart BW01.

3. Four patterns of truncated fan-type multiple-line pattern with low taper rate. The larger two are calibrated in black plus white lines per inch, and the smaller ones are calibrated in microns.

4. Gurley type Pestrecov star pattern with circles of 50, 100, and 200 lines/in. This pattern is better for detecting some moiré phenomena than pattern 3.

5. Alternating black and white lines. Upper pattern is 150 lines/in., inclined at 3 deg from vertical. The lower pattern is 200 lines/in., inclined at 2 deg from vertical. The angle is to allow the lines to drift through a match and a mismatch with the photosensor array elements.

6. Black-white bar patterns of 100, 150, 200, 300, 400 and 600 lines/in.

7. Isolated black and white lines calibrated in microns. The vertical pattern is inclined at 5 deg from vertical.

8. NBS-type resolution pattern calibrated in line pairs (black plus white) per millimeter with the smallest patterns near the center of the chart.

9. Tapered isolated black and white line patterns with the line width calibrated in microns or inches.

10. Black-white bar pattern of five black plus white bars per inch.

11. Parallel lines inclined at 5 deg from vertical.

12. NBS-type resolution pattern calibrated in line pairs (black plus white) per millimeter with the smallest patterns near the edge of the chart.

13. Diagonal line for checking irregularities in vertical pitch. Printed fax line with errors will show breaks or steps of this line.

14. ISO character hexagonal line patterns for readability testing.

15. Halftone dot screens of 10, 50, and 90% black. The 65 and 120 are the number of dots per inch measured at a 45-deg angle.

16. Line crossing pattern. The center-to-center line separation is 0.15 in. on the left end and 0.05 in. on the right end. The number of scanning line crossings of both lines multiplied by 10 is the vertical line pitch in lines per inch.

17. Text in English, Arabic, Chinese, Russian, Spanish and French. English text is in 12, 10, 8, 6, 4, and 2 point sizes.

10.6.2 CCITT Test Chart No. 5—Continuous-Tone Facsimile Test Chart CT01

This continuous-tone test chart is printed on low-gamma photographic material that preserves the complete gray-scale between paper white and black for continuous-tone photographs. It is designed to be used for testing both fax machines with gray-scale capability and fax machines that send signals for black-white only. The black-white threshold setting of the fax machine scanner can be set very accurately with this chart. The patterns that make up the chart are defined below (see Figure 10.7):

1. Stepless continuous-tone strip from black on the left to white on the right.

2. Stepless continuous-tone strip from white on the left to black on the right.

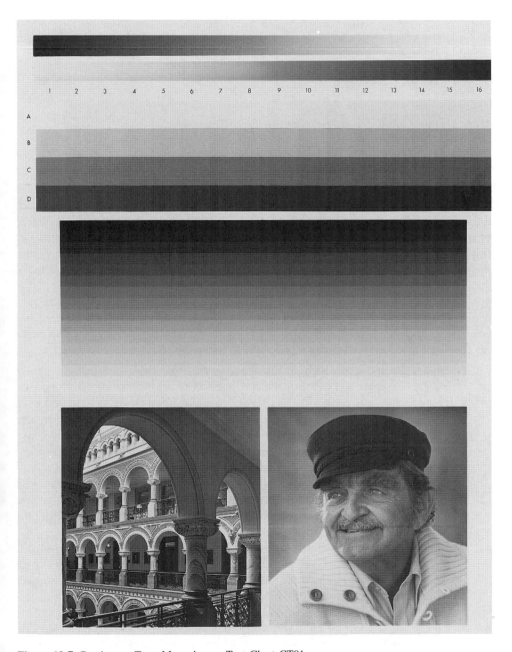

Figure 10.7 Continuous-Tone Monochrome Test Chart CT01.

3. Density step tablet with 48 steps of 0.5-in. squares in three rows of 16 steps.
4. Uniform density strips across the page with 15 steps (plus white).
5. Continuous-tone photograph.
6. Continuous-tone photograph.

10.6.3 Four-Color-Printing Facsimile Test Chart 4CP01

This chart is for testing color facsimile equipments that send four-color screen printed material such as that used in brochures, business reports, and magazines.

The 4CP01 chart is printed from four-color separation negatives using the 3-M Matchprints process, one of types used in the color printing industry to check the quality of the color separations before setting up the color printing presses. These charts may be available later in a high quality four-color version in gravure or offset four-color printing. The pattern sharpness is adequate for testing facsimile equipments up to 600 dpi, but not as sharp as in the B/W chart. The patterns that make up the chart are defined below.

This chart will be submitted for Resolution 2 accelerated standardization procedures at the next meeting of Study Group VIII. A test run in offset printing has been made and the standard will contain only minor changes. The patterns that make up the chart are described below:

1. Border of four scales with millimeter markings. Red arrows near the ends are 8.5 inches apart and centered on the page. The top border is red (solid magenta and yellow printing). The right border is green (solid yellow and cyan printing). The left border, also marked in inches, is blue (solid cyan and magenta printing). Bottom border, three segments—cyan, magenta, & yellow.
2. Black bar at the top across full page width and a red scale in inches under it, starting from 0 in the middle of the page with .1 in. scale markings.
3. Gurley type Pestrecov Star of solid, non-screened, tapered width lines with circles of 50, 100, and 200 lines/inch (same as Black-White Facsimile Test Chart BW01). The pattern is divided into four segments. Clockwise from the left are C, M, Y, K.
4. Eighteen colors with eight intensities for each color, for a total of 144 different color patches. Two-color printing color primary patches are used for seven of the intensity columns. Column 8 has 25% black added to give warmer tones. Each row between the primaries has a fixed ratio of two printing primaries as the 175-line screen dot percentages decrease in steps.
5. Twelve light color patches selected from the Macbeth color chart plus text and isolated line patterns in the same color. Line widths of the line patterns are .04, .01, and .005 in. (1.016, .254, and .127 mm). Half of the lines are slanted 1 in 10 to provide random match between the scanning line sample and the pattern. The edges of the typeface provide a similar function.

6. Black text simulating magazine text that might be on the same page as a screened color photo. The following Postscript fonts are used: headline— Bookman .40″ bold, heading— Helvetica .18″, 1st paragraph—New Century Schoolbook .13″, 2nd paragraph—Avante Garde .14″, footnote—Helvetica Narrow .09″. This note is repasted in 4-point type and in 2-point type.

7. Solid unscreened blocks of printing ink colors. Starting at the left—Cyan, Magenta, Yellow, Red (magenta + yellow), green (yellow + cyan), blue (cyan + magenta). These are solid patches of the primary printing inks and two-color combinations. The last block is black.

8. Color patches for a combination of black and each of the printing color primaries to show darker colors not covered elsewhere in the chart. These patches were selected to give good steps to the eye. The left three patches are 100% primary overprinted by 60, 40, or 20% black dots. The next three are primary/black combinations of 60/20, 40/20, and 20/20% dots.

9. Three sets of screened gray scales with 90, 75, 50, 25, 10, and 5% dots. The first row is an 85-line screen. The next rows are 175- and 133-line screens.

10. Photograph, *Toys* showing facial tones and wide color range.

11. A computer generated simulation of spheres with shadings for three-dimensional effect.

12. Graphics image from a magazine cover showing a three-dimensional effect.

13. The five-step CMY gray scale may be used to check the color balance of the printing inks.

10.6.4 Continuous Tone Color Facsimile Test Chart PC01

This chart is for testing color facsimile equipments that send continuous-tone color material of original art or produced by photography. A preliminary chart was generated, but completion of the layout is planned after approval of the four-Color-Printing Facsimile Test Chart 4CP01. The layout of the two charts will be similar. The PC01 chart will be printed without screening on color positive photographic paper.

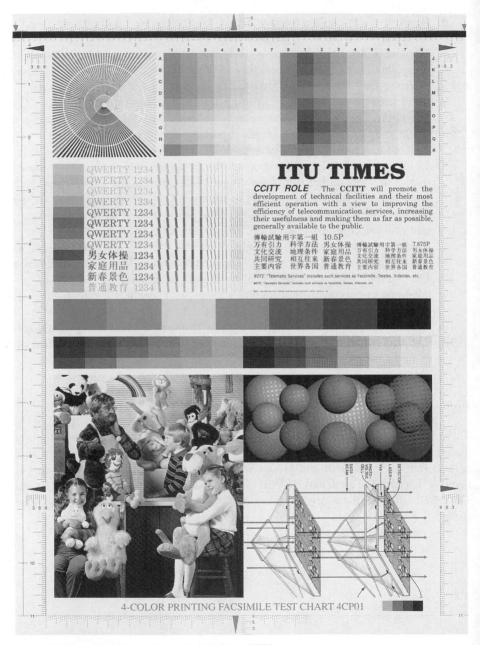

Figure 10.8 Four-Color Printing Facsimile Test Chart 4CP01.

Chapter 11
The Fax Market

11.1 DEVELOPMENT OF THE FAX MARKET

Good copy quality for office facsimile started with digital facsimile, six years before the CCITT digital fax standards existed. These digital fax machines, designed and manufactured by Dacom, were sold by Dacom in the United States and later by Kalle in Europe. Customers generally preferred them over the analog fax machines, but the price and size limited their sales so that they did not make large inroads into the business fax market. A few other digital facsimile units were designed later but each company had its own proprietary algorithm for compression of the facsimile data and could send only to others of its own manufacture. The need for a digital facsimile standard instead of competing, incompatible units soon became evident.

As the CCITT recommendations for Group 3 fax (T.4 and T.30) were nearing completion in 1979, some U.S. manufacturers jumped the gun and started making what they thought were Group 3 fax machines. They could see a good market, but unfortunately the standard had a few more changes added before it was officially adopted. It may have been good for the fax industry though, insofar as these machines served as a beta test group and probably saved the industry from some problems when manufacture of standard Group 3 fax machines started. Group 2 fax was dominant, and many thought it would continue to be so for many years due to its much lower price and simple design compared with Group 3. The digital Group 3 fax machines, priced at $12,000 to $15,000 each, sold somewhat slowly at first.

For the first 100 years there was no real fax market. There were more people who worked on fax development than the number of machines used for more than demonstrations. Table 11.1 shows significant items in development of fax markets.

In 1941, the small number of fax units made were for newsphoto use. Sales were made by press associations, such as Associated Press or United Press.

In 1943, Order No. 1041-MPD-43 for 300 fax units was placed with Times Facsimile Corporation by the U.S. Army Signal Corps for facsimile transceiver FX-1B, part of facsimile equipment RC-120. For receiving photos on film or photographic paper, the FX-1B could be operated in a portable "dark tent" with light-tight

Table 11.1
Development of Fax Markets

First 100 Years	No Fax Market
1941	Newsphotos — Manufacturers Sell Fax to Press Associations
1948	Telegram Messages by Fax Western Union 40,000 to 50,000 Units
1943	Fax for Photos/Messages Sell to U.S. Government
1965	Magnavox Telecopier Office Fax Xerox & Magnavox Marketing 25,000 Ordered
1975	100,000 Office Fax in USA
1980	Group 3 Standard Set Company Salesmen Retail Sales Channels
1987	Critical Mass Reached Fax Sales Explode!!! 8 Million Group 3 FAX
1991	Better Group 3 Performance Sales Continue High 20 Million Group 3 Fax

arm holes. The film was loaded on the drum, and the controls were operated without seeing what you were doing. When a second source did not meet performance standards, follow-on orders were obtained with little marketing effort.

In 1948, Western Union had 40,000 to 50,000 Deskfax™ units in service. The telegram-size page was wrapped around a drum and held there by rolling metal "garter springs" over it. Deskfax was designed and manufactured by Western Union and furnished to their telegram service customers.

In 1965, Xerox placed an order with Magnavox for 25,000 telecopier units with an option for 25,000 more. This started substantial marketing efforts for sales of fax to business customers. Loading a page for sending or receiving on the telecopier was as easy as opening and closing a door. The telephone handset was placed on a small box to match its microphone and speaker connected to the fax unit. The fax unit now talked and listened for fax tones on the telephone line (called acoustic coupling). This made the regular telephone line usable for office fax units. A wired-in connection by the Bell System (DCTE 602) was costly, impractical, and little used.

In 1975, after many other U.S. manufacturers increased their sales efforts, 100,000 fax units had been sold. Marketing and sales were usually done directly by the manufacturer. Some joint-venture companies were set up and later bought by the Japanese who then switched to their own product names for selling.

In 1980, manufacturing was shifting rapidly to Japan, but selling was still mainly through national sales organizations. In Europe and North America, the marketing of Japanese-produced facsimile units was often through original equipment manufacturing (OEM) channels using companies that had earlier designed and manufactured their own fax units.

Digital technology improved and as more complex circuits became available on chips, the difference in manufacturing costs between the Group 2 analog fax and the digital Group 3 fax became smaller and smaller. Group 3 fax sales soon overtook Group 2 fax. Manufacture of Group 2 fax was phased out rapidly, but many Group 2 units were still in use. Group 3 sales escalated at a high growth rate, and in 1987 sales started to skyrocket. Selling channels expanded to add distributors, dealers, department stores, discount houses, and catalog merchandisers. More than half of the U.S. Group 3 fax units were sold by the National Office Equipment Dealers Association (NOMDA) members. Direct sales accounted for one-third, and the rest were sold through distributors and wholesalers. In Western European countries fax equipment was sold mainly by the PTTs (Post, Telegraph, and Telephone, government organizations). The PTT selling role is still strong in some countries such as Holland and Switzerland, but other selling channels have become dominant elsewhere in Europe. Marketing became easier as businessmen realized they needed fax units. By this time many Japanese companies were selling fax through their own European and American companies.

In 1988 the number of Group 3 units in service increased by 81% in just one year for North America and increased by 156% in Western Europe. The worldwide growth of Group 3 fax units was 75%. The percentage growth rates have decreased, but the number of Group 3 fax machines in use totaled about 20 million in 1991. The Group 4 fax units for North America had an early temporary spurt with the sale of units to Federal Express for their now defunct electronic courier service. Group 4 fax sales are still limited to very large businesses and are still only a few tenths of 1% of sales in the United States. New enhancements that give Group 3 fax the ability to provide Group 4 fax features at much lower costs should hold down Group 4 sales for some time.

In the previous edition of this book, we used 1988 statistics on the penetration of fax units into the business telephone lines. The ratios between United States and

Japan were 1:5 and we foresaw a promising market in North America. So far in 1991, our prediction is holding, with the U.S. percentage having risen from 4 to 10%, and with the Japan percentage remaining constant. The top percentage may never equal that of Japan, however, because of language differences. The conversion into ASCII code necessary for PC use is far more complicated for the 4000 Japanese ideograms than for the 26-letter Roman alphabet used in the United States.

11.2 FAX MARKETS IN NORTH AMERICA

Major U.S. companies selling OEM fax units are AT&T, Harris/3M, Pitney Bowes, Radio Shack, Telautograph, and Xerox. This has not changed much in the last two to three years, but the number of Japanese-owned companies has increased greatly. Including other selling channels, more than 60 brands of fax are available (see Chapter 12). OEM sellers in the United States often compete for sales directly with the Japanese supplier.

By 1991, the models that sold the highest volume were desk top, some taking little more space than a modern office telephone. User-friendly automatic operation coupled with the continuing rapid drop in selling price have been responsible for the huge success of fax. The lowest priced Group 3 fax machines cost about 3% of the units introduced at the end of 1980!

Sending documents by fax is surely the fastest way and is usually the cheapest as well. Because information is transferred faster and unnecessary talking eliminated, fax is more economical than a telephone call. Before a courier service could come to pick up a document, fax delivery has been completed. Delivery costs for fax start at 10 cents or less (sometimes free) for local calls.

In the United States, coast-to-coast fax costs about 60 cents for two pages during business hours, or less than a dollar for five pages. Compare this cost with courier or express mail service, and consider also that these services both require the private user to drop off the document for sending. Night fax, at rates less than half daytime, still delivers earlier than couriers. The prime advantage of fax, however, is immediate delivery. There is really no comparison between Group 3 fax and delivery costs with courier services and telex. Although the costs of sending fax compared with mail or courier are most advantageous for a few pages, sending even a 25-page document may be cheaper by fax.

Newspapers, magazines, and business reports are jumping on the fax bandwagon. This article in the *Sarasota* (Florida) *Times* on February 19, 1991 is typical:

> Facsimile machines remain primarily business machines in America, though more are being purchased for home use. And more machines are being purchased, period: a projected 2.2 million in 1991, up from 1.7 million in 1990 and 1.4 million in 1989. This is in contrast to the 70, 000 machines sold in 1983. California (of course) leads the way in American

fax use, followed by New York, Florida and Illinois. Faxless executives and entrepreneurs across the nation have learned that if they're not in this burgeoning communications loop, they're out—out in the cold. . . . The resulting communication revolution has further shrunk the globe. European businesses, Day says, use fax even more that their American counterparts.[1] Far Eastern [and Middle Eastern] nations such as China and Japan, with languages and alphabets that make computer coding difficult, find it essential.

Although thermal recording fax machines are still far in the lead for the numbers of machines in use and the number of machines sold, the number of fax models featuring plain paper is proliferating due to lowered costs. Plain paper fax (from a low base number) now has a higher growth rate than thermal fax. Laser fax has become available in competitive Group 3 fax, whereas it was formerly limited to expensive Group 3 fax units with Group 4 enhancements. Lower prices for laser print engines (also used in Group 3 fax) were the result of high volume production of computer printers. The high cost of supplies, which in the past limited sales of thermal fax recorders, are now competitive. Recently introduced ink-jet fax recorders are another low-cost alternative.

The number of plain paper fax machine placements more than doubled in one year from 1989 to 1990 according to the July issue of *Today's Office* magazine (p. 12). Growth of plain paper fax is expected to continue a rapid rate.

11.2.1 PC-Fax Board Market

For years, exchanging text and graphic information between PCs required rather complicated settings to match the specification variables needed for sending and receiving via PC modems. These constraints can be bypassed with add-in PC-fax boards that enable the PC to transmit and receive faxes. Computer-generated documents are converted to electronic signals for rapid fax transmission to a Group 3 fax or another PC-fax. The fax protocols automatically match the specifications to optimum for each session. Markets for these boards exist both among PC users who occasionally want to send to fax machines and those who have high-volume transmission requirements that can be met less expensively by PC-fax adapters than by stand-alone machines. Such applications, which are attracting an increasing number of system integrators, including the following:

- *LAN fax servers:* A local-area network fax server can facilitate sharing of PC-fax boards and dedicated phone lines from any PC or workstation on its net,

---

[1]This is easily seen, since there are so many different languages in an area about the size of the United States.

thus substantially reducing the cost of providing computer fax capabilities to individual users.

- *E-mail networks:* Any location on a network served by a fax machine can receive electronic mail via fax gateways. A user simply sends an electronic mailgram to the gateway along with the fax machine's phone number. The gateway then converts the mailgram to fax format and transmits it to the designated fax machine. Major customers for E-mail gateways include large organizations and commercial E-mail service providers.
- *Fax store-and-forward:* With this process, an incoming fax is received, stored on disk, and later redirected to another fax machine. A major application for these systems is enhancing phone service. For example, cellular phone companies can offer customers with mobile fax machines the capability to receive faxes even when they are away from their vehicles. The cellular phone company can automatically store incoming faxes addressed to such customers and then forward the fax when they return to their vehicles.
- *Integrated fax/voice response:* These systems enable anyone with access to a fax machine to retrieve information from a computer database. For example, hot lines to request literature can be based on an integrated voice-response system. A caller to the hot line is instructed by voice prompts to select a desired literature item and enter a fax number from a DTMF telephone. The system then faxes the selected literature to the user. The FCC reports the number of fax registrations in the U.S. more than doubled from 1989 and ending in October, 1991. This increase is a result of the development of PC-fax boards. The number of U.S. applications for Part 68 registrations tripled in 1991. CAP International expects fax board shipments, estimated at 60,000 units worth $28 million in 1989 to grow at a 57% compound annual rate through 1993, when annual shipments are expected to reach 372,000 units and be worth $208 million.

11.2.2 Cellular Fax Market

Statistics on cellular phone use in the United States have shown a growth from 2 million in 1989 to almost 6 million by the end of 1990. By 1995, there could be 20 million. Although some users are sending fax over cellular systems, the process isn't as reliable or simple as might be expected. See Chapters 3 and 12 for more information.

11.3 FAX MARKETS IN EUROPE

The completion of the European Community process is expected to affect greatly the marketing of fax products in Europe. In the past, the customer in Europe paid almost twice as much for a fax machine as in the United States. If this ratio changes significantly as expected, it should be a driving force for a new surge of European fax sales. Protectionist policies requiring equipment to be made (at least partially) in the country where sold should no longer be in effect.

One of the negative factors that made things more difficult has been the differences between countries regarding fax equipment registration for use on the PSTN. The PTTs, who have been a major sales factor, will be compelled to buy their fax machines to meet common, publicly known type approval tests. The fax machine suppliers will have "one-stop" testing for all European countries. All conforming fax equipment must be allowed to connect to the PSTN. However, national historic peculiarities may be added to the purchase orders and slow down the process.

About half of the four billion dollar equivalent total European transmission revenues in 1990 were from the United Kingdom, Germany, and France. These revenues are growing about 50% per year. The traffic in transmissions to locations outside Europe is growing rapidly and sending to the United States alone could reach revenues of one billion by 1993.

11.4 FAX MARKETS IN JAPAN

11.4.1 Group 3 Fax

While the number of Japanese fax machines in service is still increasing rapidly, the number of units sold per year is declining. From 1986 to 1990, the number of fax machines in use almost tripled to 4.3 million at the end of 1990. Over the same time period, the sales per year of new fax machines increased about 80%, but the increase was only 10% from 1988 to 1990. Fax machine sales seem to be approaching a plateau of less than 1.5 million units per year. Figure 11.1 shows these trends.

Note that the number of units in service increases much less than the previous year's units plus sales for the year. This is because older fax machines are being replaced. The number of fax machines sold for replacement now exceeds those sold for new installations. In 1986, 120,000 fax machines were replaced, whereas in 1990, replacements accounted for 690,000 fax machines.

In Japan, facsimile is in virtually all of the 10,000 offices with 300 or more employees. Of the 130,000 offices with 50 employees or more, 95% have fax machines. About 85% of the million offices with between 10 and 50 employees have fax machines. In the 6 million smallest offices with under 10 employees, only about 35% have fax.

Facsimile has become a commodity in the Japanese market. The low-end fax machine models produced in high volume have the same features as the more expensive ones produced in medium volume and there usually is no compelling reason to buy one brand over another. If a new feature is added by one manufacturer, it is soon available from others. An example is a built-in telephone answering device. This option was offered by one company, but is now available from almost all companies. The life cycle of the product is very short and features available only on

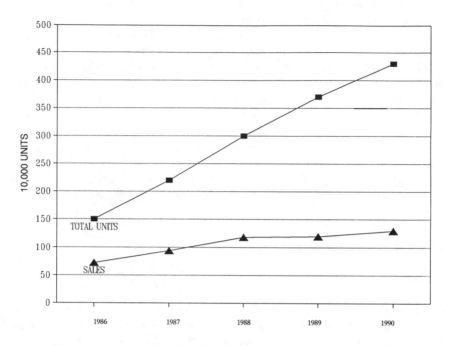

Figure 11.1 Japanese fax market.

mid-priced units today are found on low-cost fax machines tomorrow. Some companies are starting to offer an even lower priced class of fax machines with practically no bells and whistles. These facts do not seem to discourage additional companies from entering the market. Perhaps they are impressed by the phenomenal growth rate of facsimile.

Thermal printing technology has been used almost exclusively in Group 3 fax machines since the 1980 Group 3 standard. Plain paper recording, used in some models, is much preferred by the user, but a much higher price has limited its use. With the much lower priced laser printers available today, there is renewed interest in plain paper fax recording. The success of LED printers and the lower cost ink-jet printers is inducing fax machine manufacturers to bring out more plain paper models. The thermal-transfer plain paper fax machines seem to be making little headway in the market.

The largest potential market for new fax machines is in the 38 million homes in Japan. Estimates vary, stating that from 40,000 to 150,000 Japanese homes already have fax machines. With the flattening of yearly sales of fax machines to medium- and large-size businesses, it is no wonder that the home market is being examined. There have been a number of earlier attempts to penetrate this market in

Japan. One of the latest was the A5 size (5.9-in.-wide page) and A6 size (4.25-in.-wide page) Group 3 fax machines. Brochures showed teenagers using these small size fax machines in conjunction with telephone calls to their peers. After being marketed in Japan for about a year, these smaller fax were tried in the United States, but couldn't garner any interest, probably because the price was almost as high as the lowest price full-size Group 3 machine. Also, the need for such a fax machine was not perceived by the American public. It is assumed the small-size units had a similar fate in Japan. In an earlier Japanese experiment, fax signals broadcast by TV stations on a noninterfering basis with television signals were received at home. The fax machines did not meet Group 3 standards and a viable service never developed.

The Japanese now feel they need a new concept to develop the home market and are trying a new type of multiplexed TV broadcast-digital facsimile system. The fax receiver meets Group 3 fax standards with normal page size and fine resolution (8 pels/mm horizontal $\times$ 7.7 lines/mm vertical). The sending speed is equivalent to 9.6 kb/s. This is obtained using 16 kb/s transmission with four-phase differential phase modulation of the fax signal on a 70.804-kHz subcarrier, with FM modulation of the main voice carrier.

Initially at least, the TV receiver will not have to be modified because the fax receiver will have its own electronics for reception of the TV signal when connected to the same cable system or TV antenna. It will also be possible to use a standard Group 3 fax machine connected to the regular telephone line and to a TV broadcast adapter for alternative reception. Another kind of terminal uses a Group 3 fax built for both TV fax broadcast and for reception from the telephone line. The fax receiver may be furnished with a soft copy display instead of printing out the information. Alternatively, the receiving terminal may use a PC for soft copy display and its printer for making copies of the pages selected. The differences between the new TV-fax system and teletext (videotex), which has been tried for displaying page images in a number of countries, are great. The number of characters per page using TV-fax is 2000 to 4000 compared with 120 to 480 with the earlier systems. TV-fax has the advantage of receiving sharp full-page copy simultaneously with TV reception. The printed material may be a supplement to the TV program; for example, recipes from a program on cooking or detailed maps from a travel program. By using a preset program number, the fax may be set to receive unrelated information scheduled for broadcast, such as closing stock market prices. There may be a charge for specialized information furnished by fax.

11.4.2 Group 4 Fax

The Japanese have been trying to ensure that Group 3 fax is not enhanced enough to compete seriously with Group 4 fax. They probably have more Group 4 fax machines in service than any other country. There were about 4800 Group 4 fax machines in service by March 1990 (see Table 11.2).

Table 11.2
Group 4 Fax in Japan

March	1990	1991	1992	1993	1994	1995
	4,800	15,000	45,000	90,000	150,000	225,000

Group 4 fax will depend heavily on the ISDN network and Japan expects about 30% of the ISDN lines to be for fax use. Small users will have the INS NET64 DSU interface, providing 2B (64 kb/s) +1 D (16 kb/s) channels. The B channels can be used independently like two telephone lines. One might be used for voice and the other for Group 4 fax operating at 64 kb/s. The D channel can be used independently as a packet network connection for a digital terminal such as a computer. The line fee is 5400 yen ($40)/month for 2B+D in office use or 4600 yen ($34)/month for home use. The message fee is 10 yen (7.5 cents)/min.

Larger users will find the INS NET1500 to be more economical. This interface is used primarily between digital switchboards and operates at 1.5 Mb/s. Connection to the individual users is made from the digital switchboard by furnishing 2B+D channels as in the INS NET64 service. Between switchboards, there are 23 B (64 kb/s) channels + 1 D (64 kb/s) circuits. The line fee is 45,000 yen ($330)/month and the communication fee is 60 yen (45 cents)/min on the 1.5 Mb/s interconnection between switchboards.

11.5 FAX MARKET IN KOREA

Starting in 1970, some fax machines were imported from Japan for use on private line networks in Korea, but connection to the PSTN was not allowed until 1983. Manufacture of fax machines within Korea did not start until 1978 when Ricoh of Japan started Sindo Ricoh. Other Japanese companies then started manufacturing fax in Korea, taking advantage of the lower labor rates. Sanyo started using Dae Woo manufacturing facilities in 1980. NEC and Matsushita started with Goldstar as the manufacturer in 1981. Toshiba started with Samsung in 1983, and Xerox started its own Korean plant in 1984. In 1990 Korea had 13 different facsimile manufacturers, including Hyundai, Hwasung, Lotte (for Canon), Liker, and Iljin.

Korean development of its own fax machines began in 1986, with announcement of the first G2/G3 products in 1988. In 1989, 90,000 fax machines were manufactured, with 285,000 expected in 1990 and 500,000 in 1991. More than 50% of the fax machines made in 1990 were for the personal fax market. This type of fax has an automatic document feeder with up to five sheets of paper and gray-scale sending capability, but no automatic paper cutter. Their standard grade fax machine (35% of the market) has automatic dialing and an automatic paper cutter. The mid-grade fax machine, with 10% of the market has an automatic phone/fax switch, an ADF with 10 to 30 sheets of paper, and accommodation of the B4 copy size. About 3% of the fax machines are high end, with broadcasting capability, multipage memory, an error-correcting mode, plain paper recording, and a full 328-ft roll of recording paper. Many of the key parts of the fax machine (thermal print head, contact image sensor, modem, laser printer, and CCD chip) are sourced from outside Korea, but plans exist for them to be made in Korea later.

For the near-term future, a shift in marketing from sales in the United States to sales in Europe is planned. The major markets are the United Kingdom, Germany, France, Italy, and Spain. The European common market is seen as a chance for outstanding growth in 1992.

Chapter 12
Fax Customer Advice

12.1 HINTS TO FAX BUYERS

When buying a fax machine, knowing which features will be most helpful for the particular needs of the company can save money. It is also advantageous to know what the other offered features do. The fax machine will probably be used much more than initially estimated. This fact should be considered when deciding on the size of recording paper roll needed and whether the fax needs its own separate phone line. In offices with heavy fax traffic, fax calls often exceed those for voice conversations. If possible, plan on using a separate phone line for your fax machine. In the United States, the Group 3 fax machine plugs into a standard RJ-11 telephone jack that would normally be used for a telephone. If a telephone is not part of the fax machine, it usually has an RJ-11 jack for plugging in a telephone. Many of the fax machines sold today have built-in automatic dialers, but a phone should still be part of each installation. The phone is for dialing other fax machines, but it can be used for voice conversation when there is no fax traffic. The Group 3 fax machine should be left powered up and connected to the telephone line so it can automatically receive fax traffic at any time. It's like having instant Federal Express delivery any time someone anywhere in the world wants to send.

If the phone line must be shared with voice use, look for a fax machine that connects to it only when a fax call is detected. Make sure the fax you buy sends a CNG (calling) beep tone for both automatic and manual calls. Without CNG, a fax receiver on a shared voice line may not answer the call. It is best if the fax receiver or fax/phone switch box detects the first CNG (calling) tone and immediately answers the fax call. Some detect the CNG tone only after a preset number of rings, but this is little better than those that eventually answer with fax handshake even though no CNG tone is sent.

The extra convenience and cost savings of automatic features such as dialer, document feeder, broadcast, polling, and paper cutter should be well understood. Some manufacturers offer methods of locking out undesired fax transmissions to your fax machine by means of software that stores in memory only approved fax senders' numbers.

The fax market is continually being flooded with new Group 3 fax models that may or may not have the features you need. Features once considered only for high-priced multi-user machines are now offered in low-priced units. It is becoming difficult to pick out different sets of fax features for personal, departmental, or mail-room use. Competition has forced high-end features into low-end units. Features such as relay broadcast are not needed for applications that do not send to large numbers of locations, and the personal fax user usually won't buy an expensive laser fax machine. The key is to determine which features you really want and ignore the others. Consider the following items:

Automatic Document Feeder: A document feeder can be a timesaver if you send more than one page at a time. Even Group 3 fax machines selling for less than $500 have an automatic document feeder for five pages.

Cellular Radio Fax: Cellular phones are more like FM police radios than regular telephones and have little in common with regular phones. The Group 3 fax machine is designed for connection to a 2-wire PSTN telephone line using an RJ-11 jack. If you want to send fax over a cellular system, try to get a phone with the familiar RJ-11 phone plug and its 2-wire circuitry. Some vehicular phones and transportable phones (which weigh about 4 to 8 lb) have an RJ-11 jack built in. The smaller portable phones weigh much less, but may not have a way to interface to a fax machine. The few vehicular and portable cellular phones that come with an RJ-11 jack require manual operation, and the installation of some phones requires making connections inside the handset. Portable facsimile machines may operate on batteries or plug into the cigarette lighter socket.

An outgoing call cannot be made automatically from the fax machine. It is dialed instead from the cellular phone. After connection to the called party, the cellular phone is then switched over to the RJ-11 and the transmit button is pressed on the fax machine. After making the fax transmission, the call must be manually disconnected. There is no automatic answer of an incoming fax call by the fax machine.

As an alternative, a special interface box can be installed between the fax machine and the cellular phone. This box provides the same conditions as a regular RJ-11 jack connected to the PSTN: simulated ring signal on incoming calls, dial tone for outgoing calls, and battery between tip and ring leads of the jack.

The Group 3 fax ordered should have the CCITT optional error-correcting mode (ECM), which should help to overcome some of the cellular radio transmission problems. Of course, this feature works only when operating with another Group 3 fax that has the same feature. However, ECM will not correct for any loss of signal that a cellular system might encounter. Buildings, mountains, and trees can block a signal.

Installation and Training: Some dealers include installation and training in the purchase price for the fax machine. If you are trying to save money, these functions might be handled by someone in your organization. Fax machines that have their own telephone number should be programmed to answer an incoming call at the start of the first ring. This procedure eliminates unnecessary waiting on a fax call and doesn't disturb the called office. Where a telephone line is shared between fax and voice, the phone may ring five times before being answered by the fax machine, allowing time to answer a voice call. A better arrangement is to have a fax machine or a switch box that will automatically determine whether the incoming call is fax or voice.

Plain Paper Fax: Slippery, shiny, spiraling paper output was one of the less appealing features of most fax machines in the 1980s. The expensive high-end laser fax machines were an exception. More and more of the 1990s fax machines are writing on plain paper as the recording techniques needed are becoming much less expensive. Alternatives are now available for those who think a Group 3 laser fax machine still costs too much. Section 7.2 gives details on five kinds of plain paper fax machines.

For those who already have a laser printer, it is a natural choice to receive Group 3 faxes on plain paper. Some PC-fax boards allow an existing PC and laser printer combination to add fax. There are also devices that connect to, or install in, a laser printer with at least 1 Mb memory to print received fax messages. Ranging in price from $400 to $1000, these are a cost-effective way to overcome the thermal paper annoyance.

Although 300 dpi laser printers should make sharper fax copies than 203 dpi Group 3 fax machines, don't count on it. With the typical method employed, the fax 203 dpi received data is changed into 150 dpi for the laser printer, with each laser dot being printed twice. The Group 3 fax machine gives sharper copy. On the other hand, standalone Group 3 laser fax machines may have a good algorithm that prints at 203 dpi or prints two dots at 400 dpi. These fax machines give sharper copy with the superior laser printing technique.

In another arrangement, a box connected between the PC and the laser printer can receive faxes even when the PC has its power off. It allows the laser printer to be shared between the PC and fax printing, and has memory for storing PC pages while it is printing fax.

PC-fax Boards: For users who often fax information prepared on a computer, the addition of a PC-fax board to the PC will likely be cost and time effective. It is often better to send the fax directly from the computer rather than print the page and then fax it. The received fax page is sharper and it's a faster operation. To have a complete Group 3 fax sending capability, the PC-fax must have a scanner or even a low cost thermal fax machine for faxing documents that are already printed.

For fax reception, a high-resolution printer is usually needed, since reading received faxes on a computer screen is cumbersome. Only a portion of one page can be seen at one time on the screen of most computers. The PC should be capable of receiving a fax at any time. This usually means the PC power must be left on, since automatic boot up of the computer on ring signal may take too long. If the PC will be used for normal computing while receiving fax, make sure the PC-fax board allows fax transmission and reception without slowing down the computer operation too much. The price of a page scanner is often more than an inexpensive Group 3 fax machine. Purchase of a supplementary fax machine may be a better investment than a scanner for some PC-fax board users.

The optimum combination of a PC-fax board with the other components needed for Group 3 fax emulation depends upon the needs of the user. For example, where a high resolution printer is not available, the PC-fax board plus Group 3 fax machine may be best. Connecting the fax machine to a second phone line (even one shared with voice) would allow automatic fax reception and the ability to send fax from sheets of paper when needed without slowing down the main fax sending operation. The fax machine can be used as a scanner for the PC and might also print out edited image files. Sharpness of the recorded copy is better on the Group 3 fax machine than on the best quality 7×9 matrix printer.

In another example, a scanner for the PC is already available and the computer printer has adequate resolution. Scanners generally have 300 dpi to match the resolution of the popular laser printers. If the resolution is higher than the 203 dpi of Group 3 fax, the image file can be converted by the PC to this resolution. With a scanner, the user can enter headers and signatures into computer memory. These files may be chained to a text file to generate letters, reports, and other business documents which look like they were typed on letterhead stationery and signed before sending. Image editing programs can be used to edit fax image files displayed on the PC screen. These programs can be used to compose a page combining graphics and text before sending. They can also be used to modify received fax documents. (See Chapter 3 for more information.)

Another alternative offered is a combination scanner, PC-fax board, and printer sharing device with page memory. Faxing between like devices can be done at the full 300 dpi laser printer resolution. This combination can also be used as a high print quality laser office copier, but in one of these combinations it is not possible to use the scanner to input imagery to the computer. See Section 3.9 for more information on PC-fax boards.

Page Size: Most users need the capability to handle full-size 8.5- $\times$ 11-in. pages or A4 size pages. Two smaller page sizes for Group 3 fax machines introduced a few years ago are not very popular and it is unlikely you will see one. Copies of documents sent from the standard size A4 units and recorded on A5 units are reduced in size, but can still be read if the original print is no smaller than 12 point (10 characters per inch typewriter size). The Group 3 fax units with A6 half-width recording paper are of very limited use when operating with standard page size fax units. An A6 fax machine is most useful when operating with another A6 unit in a special application where small page size is acceptable. (See Section 3.8.6 for more information on A5 and A6 fax units.)

Paper Cutter: Even some low-end fax machines now have an automatic paper cutter. When a number of pages are received on a fax without a paper cutter, a banner of paper many feet long will be on the floor by the fax machine waiting to be cut by hand.

Paper Roll Size: Most low-end units have a 60- to 98-ft-long roll of recording paper. If this length is too short for the number of copies you expect to receive between convenient changing times, look for a model with 148- to 164-ft intermediate length rolls or a standard-feature fax machine with a full 328-ft roll length. Paper curl near the end of short rolls may be annoying. Wider paper rolls for recording wider doc uments are available for alternative use on some fax machines.

Prices: New fax models arrive very rapidly as models that have been marketed for a year or so are discontinued. Features are added or dropped. Brand names are a mixture of fax machines sold by the manufacturer, catalog and store OEM brands, and OEM brands sold through distributors and dealers. A particular fax model may be available directly from the manufacturer's sales staff or from competing sales channels, often at a lower price. In other cases, the same fax machine has a different name for each seller. The price spread is rather large, as might be expected, and discounts are available on many models. Low-end discounted fax units sell for less than $500, some under $400. There is a continuous spectrum of Group 3 fax models from the low-end units, now with more than the bare essentials, but not good for high-volume applications, to the high-end units with enhanced features. The lowest prices often are from sellers who are not authorized dealers, offer no help on how to set up the equipment, and sell gray market goods with no factory warranty.

Reliability: Reliability is generally very good, with most fax units not requiring service for more than a year. Plain paper fax units have more mechanical parts that may malfunction, reducing reliability somewhat.

Resolution: Fine resolution of 203 lines/in. $\times$ 198 lines/in. is usually available on even the lowest price fax units. It provides better clarity of fax copies for pages with fine print and should be insisted upon.

EIA-232 Digital Connection: This is one feature very few users need. (See Section 3.8.4 to find out how EIA-232 can be used.) Those who just call other fax units on the regular telephone network (PSTN) do not have any need for it. Unless you are sure you need it, don't pay extra for it.

Seconds per Page: Most suppliers quote the time taken to send CCITT Test Image No. 1. (Fig. 10.5) in standard resolution. Pages with more lines of printing or more detail take longer to send. Modem speed, minimum scan line time, the MH or MR coding method, and other factors affect this time. The time quoted will exclude the automatic handshake time of about 15 s before the first page is sent. When buying fax for a number of locations that communicate with each other, consider Group 3 fax units with V.17 modems (operate at 14.4 kb/s, 50% faster than V.29). The extra cost may be saved in lower telephone line charges and in fewer fax machines needed.

(See paragraph 3.6).[1] Time per page listed varies from 6 to 45 s for Test Image No. 1. Low-end fax units usually take longer than a standard fax machine to send or receive a page.

Service Contract: Before signing a service contract, establish the guaranteed maximum response time offered.

Warranty: Warranties vary from 90 days to 2 years.

Brand names of fax machines sold in the United States include the following: Adler Royal, AEG Olympia, AT&T, Audiovox, Avatex, Brother, Canon, CMB America, Citifax, Cobra Electro, Dynascan, Emerson, Extel, Fujitsu, Gestetner, Harris/3M, Hitachi America, Konica, Lanier, Medbar, Minolta, Mita, Mitsubishi, Muirhead, Murata, NEC America, Nissei, Nitsuko, Northwest Bell, Okidata, Olivetti, Olyfx, Omnifax, Pactel, Panafax, Panasonic, Pitney Bowes, Radio Shack, Relisys, Ricoh, Royal Imaging Systems, Samsung, Sanyo, Savin, Sharp, Southwestern Bell, Tatung, Teli, TIE, Toshiba, Trans-Lux, and Xerox. More than 60 brands of fax are available.

12.2 HINTS TO FAX USERS

Automatic Dialer: Enter the numbers you send faxes to as individuals and for groups you will send the same message to. This is a timesaver and you'll avoid wrong numbers.

Automatic Document Feeder: Use this feature to send more than one page and you won't waste time waiting for each page to be sent. If the pages you want to send are on onion-skin paper or dog-eared, make an office copy to send and avoid the possibility of jamming your original in the fax machine. Some fax units have a five-page document feeder. To avoid a paper jam, don't exceed the limit or put in thick sheets.

Calling a Fax on a Shared Voice Line: If a voice recorder answers the call, it may be necessary to wait until the beep tone stops before pressing the SEND button. If heard by your fax machine, the answer machine beep tone may prevent your fax from sending by locking it into receive mode.

Cleaning the Fax Machine: Kits are available for the occasional cleaning your fax machine may need. If the recording has streaks, the print head can be gently cleaned with alcohol. If the automatic document feeder sometimes fails to pull in the page being sent, the scanner section paper rollers probably need cleaning. The kit has a simple method of doing this without opening the fax machine.

---

[1]Some fax units made before 1991 have a higher speed proprietary mode of operation under the NSF option that reduces the time per page and may reduce the handshake time. This enhanced speed works only when sending between similar units from the same manufacturer, but will fall back to standard mode when working with another Group 3 fax.

Fax Form Design: Avoid using screen dot patterns, because they greatly increase transmission time. Avoid background blocks of different color or gray shading than the overall page, because this may cause the fax receiver to print black blocks, or miss printing in some blocks.

Fax Number Listing: Use your fax number on your business card and in your advertising material to generate additional business. These listings will be seen by your existing and potential customers. A listing in a fax directory might bring additional desirable business contacts, but it may also bring junk fax mail.

Fine Mode: Use this higher resolution mode when sending small type, when the received fax copy will be used in a report, or when you want to make a good impression. Some people use fine mode all the time. If your fax machine has MR coding, it does not take much longer.

Location of Fax: Some complaints are reported of time wasted by having to wait in line for the fax machine. This problem is often caused by not having enough fax machines in the right places. Picture an office with a few telephones in a separate phone room, and the length of a waiting line for their use! Locating a fax machine in your own or your secretary's office will give you instant fax communication without mailroom delays. Having your own fax not only saves time spent trying to find a fax that isn't in use, but avoids wasting time tracking down documents that were faxed to you. It also prevents your received documents from being on view to everyone who walks by. Consider upgrading to a fax model that has a built-in memory mailbox with a security number if confidential documents are to be received.

Overseas Calls: Take advantage of the time zone differences. For example, a fax sent from the United States at the end of the workday will be received in Japan just before the recipient arrives for work (the next morning there). The recipient can tend to tasks during the workday and have time to generate a fax reply to transmit at the end of the workday in Japan. It will be waiting in the sender's fax machine the next morning, thereby gaining a whole business day.

Paper Supply: When leaving at night, make sure there is enough recording paper for overnight fax reception.

Polling: Use a polling code when leaving documents in the fax machine to be sent later upon a polling command from someone else. Otherwise they could be sent to the wrong party.

Phone Line for the Fax: A separate fax phone line with its own number, terminated in an RJ-11 jack, is usually best. The separate line cuts down on fax and phone competing with each other. Although they both use the telephone network, fax and phone are separate services. When sending a document of many pages, the user should not have to wait to make or receive important phone calls. This line should not be a switchboard extension. The operator, necessary to complete a switchboard call, won't be around after working hours. One of the fax advantages is 24 hour availability for sending documents to the fax machine. If you can't afford two phone lines, consider buying a fax machine with an integrated fax/phone switch, or a separate fax/phone switch box. The switch box plugs into your telephone jack. Both the telephone and the fax machine plug into jacks on the switch box. When a call is received, the switch box connects the line to either the fax or the phone.

Power: A separate power circuit for the fax machine is recommended. This prevents putting the fax out of business when the circuit breaker is tripped by overload from an electric heater or other power-hungry device. Keep the fax power turned on 24 hours, seven days a week, so it is always ready to receive. This allows use across time zones or when the fax sender is working late. Standby power is usually about 15 W. A plug-in power and telephone line filter like those sold for computers is a good investment, but the power and telephone lines should be unplugged during severe thunderstorms, if possible.

Recording Costs for PC-Fax Card Users: A fax page can be recorded with a dot matrix or ink-jet computer printer for about one cent per page or five cents for a thermal paper fax machine. Sharpness of recording will suffer unless a high-resolution printer is used. With a laser printer, the total supplies cost, including toner cartridges, is almost the same as for a thermal paper.

Thermal Recording Paper: WARNING. Use of the wrong thermal recording paper can gum up the thermal head in the fax machine. Using low-temperature papers made for small, low-power fax machines in a standard fax machine would surely cause problems. It could even cause permanent damage. The paper thickness must match the fax printer requirements. The thermal print head is one of the most sensitive components of a fax machine and may cost up to half the original price of the machine if it has to be replaced. For these reasons it is a good idea to follow the manufacturer's recommendations on what thermal recording papers will give good long-term results. Don't use the cheapest paper unless the fax manufacturer approves its use. Abrasive materials may cause premature thermal head failure due to wear, and deposits of corrosive agents will cause streaks or prevent recording.

Originals: If your originals don't feed through the fax machine properly, try to avoid sending pages right after they are made on an office copier. This problem usually happens with a copier that has high usage. A volatile coating on the paper used in the copier may be the culprit. Thermal paper fax copies also do not feed very well if it is necessary to retransmit received documents. Automatic document feeders often fail to send thermal paper without feed problems.

12.3 APPLICATIONS AND MISAPPLICATIONS OF FAX

The applications of fax are now no longer the novelty of only a few years ago when the idea of faxing in a sandwich order to the delicatessen or soliciting blind dates rated a feature news story. By communicating faster and more accurately than voice, fax has become as essential as the telephone. The fax and the phone may be idle much of the time, but both are indispensable. For most desks, a fax machine is likely to get much more use than a desktop PC or a LAN terminal. E-mail is useful for those who are comfortable with a keyboard, but many are not. Hotels are now providing rooms with an extra jack for the business guest to plug in a portable fax, or will loan a fax for use during the stay. A late document from the office is often waiting at check-in.

More and more executives and even their employees find a fax machine in the home makes work easier, faster, and allows almost impossible deadlines to be met. Fax applies to all businesses that have any written communication. Fax has changed the way business is conducted, making possible some enterprises that wouldn't otherwise exist. One application in this category is instant delivery of data sheets and similar material. Call a computer database and press the telephone buttons to enter the proper code. If you don't know the code, a voice announcement gives a menu of selections available. Press the receive button on the fax machine and the requested material will be spewing out within seconds.

Some misapplications for fax are obvious, such as junk fax, treated separately below. Somewhat less offensive, but still objectionable, is printing a computer-generated document and then sending it on a fax machine instead of using the PC-fax board. Of course, things are different if a copy is needed by the sender. Faxing a thick document that has no time sensitivity is also wasteful. The fax line is tied up preventing more productive use.

Another misapplication is faxing computer-generated text that at the receiving end must be stored in computer format or edited before use. OCR (optical character recognition) software can be used for the task of conversion, but it is more error-intensive to read fax-received characters than printed material. It is much easier to fax it from the computer than to send it by a PC data modem. No decisions need be made regarding modem speed, type of error correction, bits/byte, parity bits, number of stop bits, and other protocol settings used by the other PC; however, computer to computer binary file transmission can be 10 to possibly 40 times faster than using fax with the same modem speed.

Yet another misguided use can occur when computer-generated text is sent via PC-fax if the received data must be converted to be machine readable. To rekey it into the PC at the receiving terminal is time-consuming and error-prone. Even less productive use of time happens when users print out the document at the sending end and then transmit via a standard fax machine for rekeying at the other end.

Fortunately, a much better method is at hand. The new binary file transfer standard for use between computers with PC-fax boards sends with the simplicity of a Group 3 fax transmission (no user protocol matching). The speed is accelerated by use of the fax modem, 9.6 or 14.4 kb/s, and can be made even faster with binary text compression protocols.

12.4 DOCUMENT SECURITY AND ENCRYPTION

Many users do not realize that documents sent by fax to a certain person are readily seen by others. The receiving fax machine is often where others pass by and some people are probably reading fax mail not addressed to them. If fax documents are being sent that shouldn't be seen by others, a number of ways are available to assure privacy. The simplest technique is to locate the fax machine in a locked office where unauthorized personnel have no access. Another privacy method is to use a fax receiver with an electronic mailbox. The received fax documents are not printed as received, but are stored in memory. The correct password must be entered in order to print them. Possibly one of the above methods provides all the protection required to assure privacy, but this is not so if the information would be very damaging in the wrong hands. Fax machines that use thermal-transfer recording have another security problem. The roll (called ribbon) of carbon paper, thrown away as each roll of white and carbon paper is replaced, has a complete recording of all fax pages received.

Compare fax with a voice telephone call where it is very easy to listen in by picking up another telephone on the same line. Another Group 3 fax machine connected to the same line would interfere with the intended fax machine initial handshake and probably neither fax machine would receive anything. However, a fax machine can be modified by a knowledgeable person to copy all faxes sent or received on the fax/telephone line to which it is connected. This makes it possible to copy fax messages even in a different location by wire-tapping techniques. It is not necessary to connect physically to a telephone line to intercept the fax signals. Many telephone and fax calls are sent by microwave transmission or by satellites where the signals can be picked up with the proper receiving equipment. Cellular radio transmissions can be picked up on a standard communications-type radio receiver. Computers can be used to ferret out and select only fax calls, or even fax calls to a particular fax/telephone number. Foreign governments are believed to have sophisticated monitoring stations that do this.

Fax encryption devices (also known as scramblers or privacy devices) that can provide a very high degree of security are available for business use. The digital fax signal that normally connects to the modem input when sending, or output when receiving, connects instead to an external encryption box. Two EIA-232 connectors are used, one for clear text and one for encrypted text. The box encrypts the digital signal to the modem when sending and decrypts the digital signal from the modem when receiving. At least one fax manufacturer is developing a fax machine with a built-in encryption device. With the better and more expensive machines, it would take a highest level workstation computer hundreds of years to break the code. The DES algorithm, approved by the U.S. government for U.S. business use within the United States, or other private algorithms are used. The simple methods mentioned above are certainly not adequate for sending government information classified secret or for any other government classified material. Large government agencies devote much time and equipment to assuring that all government classified material including fax messages cannot be decoded and read by anyone other than the intended recipient. Fax machines used to send U.S. government classified material use special construction techniques and must have government approval. The elaborate and very expensive methods needed here are not available for regular business use (see Section 3.8.8). Probably the easiest way to encrypt Group 3 fax is to use a secure digital telephone that has a built-in data jack for the fax machine. The telephone plugs into a regular telephone jack on the PSTN and the fax machine plugs into the data jack. A call is made to another fax machine that has the same class secure phone. The telephone, called STU III Class 1 or Class 2, costs about $1000, which seems very reasonable compared to other alternatives.

12.5 JUNK FAX MAIL

When the first edition of this book was published, junk fax was just becoming a problem. As more and more fax machines have come into use, more and more fax receivers are becoming clogged with unsolicited and unwanted material in the form of advertising brochures, politicians' propaganda, etc. Not only is this the same nuisance as junk mail (sent at the senders' expense), but it costs the recipient for paper, toner, and lost machine time.

Junk fax mail may have started innocently enough as an extension of normal fax communications for the purchase of paper and supplies. The supplier started sending unsolicited flyers of specials and other fax items. Delicatessens and sandwich shops started to receive noon pickup orders sent from nearby offices. Then the delis began sending out menus with daily specials, ready for the customer the first thing in the morning. A fax with stored telephone numbers can make the calls before normal work hours. The telephone numbers need be entered only once into the fax machine's telephone directory. For sending the daily menus, the pages to be sent are first scanned to enter them into the fax unit's memory. A few key strokes then set up the automatic calling and sending. PC-fax cards make it much easier to send junk fax mail. The sender does not even need to print out the pages before sending. He is also no longer limited to 100 numbers for sending junk fax mail, but can send to thousands. Separate phone number lists can be kept in the PC for different types of mailings. If the list becomes too large to handle with one PC and one phone line, a fax service such as MCI Fax can do it, calling many fax units simultaneously. As far as undesired junk fax mail is concerned, the situation has recently taken a disturbing turn. One PC-fax card seller now offers a floppy disk mailing list of other fax users along with the PC-fax card. The package can be programmed to send a mailing directly from the PC to all fax numbers on the list. The floppy disk distribution of specialized fax users means that the sender has all the fax telephone numbers collected for him and has only to transfer the list to his computer hard disk.

Even an unlisted number may find its way onto one of these fax floppies for sale. This practice may eventually be self-regulating because users will avoid doing business with those who send junk fax mail.

Federal lawmakers are responding to consumers' complaints with proposed legislation that would prohibit unsolicited advertising over telephones and fax machines. One bill would create a nationwide master list for consumers opposed to receiving computerized calls or unwanted faxes. A 1990 House bill was passed but was opposed by the Bush administration. Hong Kong Telephone was one step ahead of the United States and suspended service to two of its customers when they ignored requests to stop tying up fax users' lines with ads. Fax machines are now available with junk fax countermeasures. One fax has "selective rejection" that allows up to 50 calling fax numbers to be programmed for rejection. Some are programmed to receive only from designated fax machines. Receiving units can be programmed to hang up the phone if the calling party identification doesn't match authorized stored identification.

Several states have passed legislation to curtail this abuse of fax facilities. Ironically, an impetus to passage of these laws was provided when the governors' fax machines were jammed with messages from opponents of the bill!

12.6 GROUP 3 FAX AND PC-FAX BOARD FEATURES

The following list discusses features available in Group 3 fax machines with comments on what they really do and under what conditions they might be helpful. The first section lists standard and optional Group 3 fax machine features that will work even between machines of different manufacture. Many of the features are available even on the low-cost fax machines. The design of Group 3 fax equipment changes very rapidly with most suppliers bringing out more than one new model every year. Even as prices are lowered, more features are added to the low-cost models. Models that are dropped from the line may not be very old at all, but may be more expensive to manufacture. The consumer seems to be getting more for the money each year. For these reasons, the ratings in the following table should be considered only indicative of Group 3 fax machines. Many features are automatic and are designated in the feature names in the alphabetical listing below. A Group 3 fax feature is designated with an F and a PC-fax feature with a P.

F P Alternative Number Calling: The document may be sent to an alternative fax machine if the called fax machine is in use. When setting up the list of telephone numbers for fax machines to be called, an alternative number may be entered just after listing the regular number. Some fax machines are programmed to try the regular number one time, then if busy, try the alternative number. If the alternative number is busy, the regular number is tried again a specified number of times at a specified interval.

F Background Control, Automatic: When sending a page, the same results are obtained for gray or colored backgrounds as for white. The ABC circuit adjusts the background signal level to be the same as white before digitizing it to black-white. This saves the operator from trying to guess the proper setting.

F P Batching: To reduce the number of fax calls made for sending during the day, various users can scan their documents into memory for delayed start sending at night or the end of the day. All documents to one fax number will then be sent in one call. Multiple destinations may be specified for one or more documents.

F Book Scanning Mode: This feature allows a book to be placed on the glass plate top of the fax machine and scanned. Some units also have an automatic document feeder for sending documents.

F P Broadcasting: Many fax machines with this feature allow documents to be scanned rapidly and stored in memory for sending sequentially to many different locations. Other fax machines require leaving the pages to be sent in the automatic document feeder. Most fax machines of this type can only be programmed to send to a single station. Some fax machines use special dialing cards to allow different documents to be sent to different fax machines. Some units allow documents entered into memory during the day to be automatically sorted for delayed sending of all documents for one destination in one phone call. Different combinations of the same documents can be programmed for different destinations.

F P Bulletin Board: A set of documents is entered into memory for polling by any fax caller who wants a copy. The same set is sent to each polling caller until a new set is entered into memory.

F P Callback Message: A short fax message requesting a voice call from the other operator can be sent by pushing a button.

F P Calling Tone (CNG): CNG is a beep tone sent by the fax transmitter every 3 s (1100 Hz for 0.5 s) when calling another fax machine. When answering a ring signal, it will be heard on a telephone, indicating that a fax machine is calling (not a voice call). For shared telephone lines that are answered by lifting a telephone receiver, pressing the START button of the fax receiver when CNG is heard will switch it on to record the fax message. Some fax receivers designed for shared telephone line use recognize CNG and start without human intervention. Unfortunately, if there is no CNG, the telephone will ring for a voice call. Not all fax machines send CNG, but automatic calling ones dial fax numbers stored in memory and must send CNG. Most newer model fax machines always send CNG, whether in automatic send mode or not. An alternative to buying a fax machine that recognizes CNG is to add a voice/fax switch box. Most voice/fax switches recognize CNG and will then ring the fax machine instead of the telephone.

F P Compression Coding, Modified Huffman: This run-length coding scheme is mandatory for Group 3.

F Compression Coding, Modified Read: This optional two-dimensional coding scheme sends fax pages about one-third faster than modified Huffman coding.

F Compression Coding, Modified Modified Read: This two-dimensional coding scheme sends fax pages much faster than modified read coding. It is standard for Group 4 fax machines and is a recognized option for Group 3 fax machines. It may be used in combination with the optional Group 3 ECM.

F Copy Mode: A document may be copied instead of being faxed by pressing the COPY button. The fax machine then sends to its own printer. This function can also be used to check whether the fax machine will pick up pencil or other light markings, before sending the fax transmission.

F P Copy Size Reduction: Some fax machines have the capability of sending from wider pages, usually 10 to 12 in. wide. Standard 8.5-in.-wide pages are also sent without wasting the wider border space. The number of pels per scan line is automatically set as the document feeder guides are adjusted for paper width. When sending wide pages to another fax machine that has 8.5-in.-wide paper, the original is reduced in size to fit the narrower recording paper width. Most fax transmitters throw away pels from the wider page, causing a reduction in resolution. At least one PC-fax for a laser printer has size reduction options.

F P Cover Sheet, Automatic: The cover sheet is generated in the fax machine and sent as the first page. The sheet may contain the destination name, calling telephone number, and one of six different stored messages.

F P Date/Time: A clock in the fax machine generates date and time numbers that are added to the top of each page sent and appear in the journal.

F P Delayed Polling: (See the Polling option first.) A timer in the receiving fax machine can be programmed to delay calling until the time when all of the documents at the sending fax machine should be ready. Some fax machines can be programmed to poll many fax transmitters one after the other in one setup, providing overnight reception (e.g., orders for morning delivery from a bakery).

F P Delayed Transmission: A timer in the fax machine can be programmed to delay calling until the telephone rates are low or a particular person will be in the receiving office. This is particularly useful for large time zone differences where no one is at the receiving end during business hours at the sending station. (See the Broadcasting option.)

F P Dialing, Automatic: The phone numbers of fax machines called can be stored in memory and used for sending fax transmissions by pressing one or two buttons.

F P Dialing Groups: The dialing groups of fax numbers are programmed on a single key for serial broadcast transmission of documents. A number of groups can be set up on different keys.

F P Disconnect, Automatic: The fax machine automatically disconnects from the phone line after the last page is sent or after a page sent is not received properly. This keeps the fax line open when the fax is not in use. All fax machines have this feature.

F Document Feeder, Automatic (ADF): A tray is provided to drop in the documents to be sent. It is not necessary to hand feed one page at a time or to wait at the fax machine while the pages are sent. Five-page capacity is common on very small fax machines, and 30 on a full-size fax.

F Document Feeder, High Capacity: Thirty-page ADF capacity is common. These ADF units are generally more reliable and the range of page thicknesses handled is wider than the five-page units. Paper jams and multiple page feed errors are less likely.

F P Encryption Interface: The facsimile data stream can be encrypted to be completely unintelligible to a fax receiver not having the proper code. This prevents the sending of sensitive information to the wrong party and thwarts unauthorized eavesdropping. A set of two EIA-232 interfaces is furnished for an external encryption unit and the internal modem is used. The encryption algorithm must be the same and the codes used must match for sending and receiving encryption units. (See Section 3.8.8.)

F P Error-Correction Mode (ECM), CCITT: This standardized Group 3 option produces error-free fax copies even though there are some errors in the received data stream. ECM breaks the picture signal into HDLC blocks and automatically retransmits the blocks of a page received with errors. The receiving fax machine assembles an error-free page in memory by replacing the error blocks with retransmitted error-free blocks. If there are no errors, this option takes about 5% longer than standard Group 3 transmission time.

F P Fine Resolution: The optional vertical resolution of 196 lines/in. prints smaller type sizes with good clarity. This option is furnished with almost all fax machines.

F Group 1 Fax Compatibility: Group 1 and North American 6-min fax machines have been obsolete for a number of years, making this feature useless. Despite this, compatibility is still offered on some Group 3 fax machines. This feature may cause problems sending to Group 3 fax machines. Since Group 1 fax has no required handshake from the receiving fax, the transmitter might start a transmission in the 6-min mode to no receiver.

F P Group 2 Fax Compatibility: If the fax machine called is Group 2 (obsolete design), the page will be sent with Group 2 protocol. This feature becomes less useful each year as more and more Group 2 units are retired.

F P Handshake, Automatic: Group 3 units have many different features that must be matched between the transmitter and receiver. The electronic handshake takes care of this automatically and selects the fastest transmission possible between the two units.

F P Header Print: The date, time, and phone number of sender is printed at the top of each page received.

F Indicators for Status or Errors: Errors in proper performance of the fax machine or telephone line may be indicated by audible alarms, an error lamp, or a character display. The display may also show operating instructions, optional settings, call progress, and other items.

F P Identification of Sending Party: The sender's fax (telephone) number may be printed at the top of the page along with the company name, time, date, and page number. The fax number may also show in the front panel character display and the journal if the optional CCITT signal CSI or CIG is sent.

F Interpolation: This technique fills in, at the fax receiver, an extra line between scanned lines to make standard-resolution recorded copy look almost as good as fine resolution. Some fax machines also fill in dots between scanned dots along the scanning line. An algorithm uses adjacent pels to determine whether to make a receiver-added pel black or white.

F P Journal: A record is made in memory for each document sent or received. This record indicates the date for the journal entry, time of transmission, phone line connection time, identification of the other fax machine, number of pages, identity of other party, and confirmation of receipt. Any problem will be noted. The journal may automatically print out each day, when there are 32 entries, or on request.

F P Keyboard Programming: A keyboard containing letters of the alphabet is very useful for entering the company name or other identification for the sending fax machine or PC-fax (to be printed at the top of each page). Some fax keyboards are simplified by having two letters on each key. The second letter is entered by pressing the key twice. Another keyboard application is entering names associated with the fax numbers for automatic dialing. The PC monitor or a small screen on the fax machine shows the letters entered.

F Light/Dark/Normal Control: This control allows the operator to compensate for light or heavy markings of the page being sent when necessary. Most pages are sent satisfactorily with the "normal" (default) setting.

F Mailbox, Personal: When travelling your office fax machine can be programmed to forward received fax messages to another fax machine. Alternatively, with a fax machine in a hotel or other location, up to 30 received fax pages stored on the fax machine at home or office may be retrieved by entering an access code and a series of commands.

F P Memory: Most fax machines with memory will store up to 30 pages being sent, but some store many more pages. The fax machine user can quickly scan the documents into memory before starting to send them, and then return the originals to file. The actual sending can be immediate or delayed to send automatically at a later time. Sending faxes at night provides lower telephone rates. Fax machine memory can also be used to receive faxes. The transmission time for a document is shorter, since there is no delay for the fax machine printing operation (0-ms scan time). PC-fax has the same features as the fax receiver, but the number of pages stored, controlled by the PC memory, can be very large even at 50 kbytes per page.

For PC-fax, the memory requirement per page sent may be 1/20th as much as that of a fax machine, but for receiving, memory requirement is the same as that of a fax machine. The wide disparity of memory requirements is caused by the necessity to store received faxes in compressed bit map format, but for sending, fax pages can be stored in ASCII character format.

F P Modem High Speed Options: The optional 14.4 kb/s V.17 modem and the 9.6 kb/s V.29 modem provide faster sending speeds and thus lower phone line costs. The cost difference between the mandatory 4.8 kb/s and the optional 9.6 kb/s modem is now quite small and competition is forcing even low-cost fax machines to have 9.6 kb/s capability. Speeds up to 25.6 kb/s may eventually be available.

F P Modified Read Coding: This optional coding scheme sends pages about 30% faster than the modified Huffman coding. The MR code is more complex and thus more expensive. Low-cost 8-bit microprocessor chips are too slow, and special coding chips are too expensive for low-price fax machine models and most PC-fax cards. You would find the extra cost to be worth it.

F P On-hook Dialing: Fax machine numbers stored in memory can be called and the transmission started by pressing one button. Some faxes have a speakerphone so progress of the call can be monitored until the fax transmission starts.

F One-Touch Buttons: These allow items associated with each destination, such as telephone number, resolution, and transmission time, to be stored and recalled by one button. A different set of transmitting conditions can be associated with each number on the list.

F P Out of Paper Reception: The fax unit continues to receive pages into memory when the recording paper runs out. Some fax machines can store only a few pages.

F P Page Numbering: Each page of the received document is automatically numbered. Some fax machines also print "END" on the last page.

F P Page Retransmission: If the receiving fax machine sends a negative acknowledgment (too many received errors for acceptable fax copy), the page is resent automatically.

F Panel Display: An LCD display with 20 or 40 characters guides the operator in use of the fax machine and reports error messages.

F Paper Cutter: This very desirable feature automatically cuts received pages and stacks them in the receive tray. Without a cutter, a long banner of paper spills on the floor if documents are received while the fax machine is unattended. The time saved can easily pay for the extra cost. If, however, only a few pages a day are received, a cutter is probably not needed.

P PC Operating System Compatibility: Most PC-fax cards have either DOS or Macintosh operating system compatibility. Some PC-fax cards will operate in computers with other operating systems such as Concurrent DOS, SCO Xenix 285, SCO Unix 386, and AT&T Unix V.

F Photograph Transmission (or Gray Scale): Pictures are continuous tone and should have 5 to 8 bits of information per picture element, depending on the application. Group 3 fax is a digital system that sends only black or white information for each picture element with compression coding selected for black-white information. The Group 3 compromise allows pictures to be sent to any Group 3 fax machine, but the results are poor. The fax transmitter encodes the signal to represent gray-scale shades by clumps of pels, which imitate the photo screening process used by newspapers. The quality is even poorer than desk-top publishing systems, which use almost twice as many picture elements per square inch. Photos also take much longer to send since many short coding runs are generated. A page may take 5 min or longer to send. Most PCs lack photograph handling capability, but a scanner with the capability to screen photographs might be used to enter photographs in PC memory and then send them by fax.

F P Plain Paper Recording: Fax machines that record on plain paper provide copies that look and handle like those from an office copier. The number of fax machine models that use plain paper recording is increasing. Lower costs for laser and ink-jet printers have helped this trend. (See Chapter 7 for more details on the different types of plain paper fax machines available.)

F P Polling: This feature allows a called fax machine to transmit automatically, documents intended for the calling fax machine. Polling is especially useful when many fax machines must send documents to a single receiving fax in a short period of time. If polling were not used, each sender would be competing with others to access the fax receiver, leading to many busy signals and frustration. Polling is often done at night when the fax machines called are unattended.

To prevent unauthorized access to waiting documents, a polling code is usually required. With some fax machines, telephone numbers of those fax machines that have permission to poll are in memory, and polling requests from others are ignored. An alternative method is to assign one or more polling system numbers that could be called by a large number of fax machines.

F P Reception, Automatic: The Group 3 fax machine should be left with the power always on, ready for unattended reception 24 hours. This feature allows fax communication even if the two fax machines are not in the same time zone, especially useful between overseas locations.

F P Redial, Automatic: If the called fax machine is busy, it is called again in 1 to 10 min. The time is programmable in some fax machines.

F P Remote Terminal Identification (RTI): The non-CCITT name for the other party's telephone number sent during handshake. (See CSI, CIG, TSI in Figures 3.8 and 3.10).

F P Retransmission, Automatic: Pages not received successfully can be automatically resent from memory.

F Signal Processing: The received copy quality can be improved by this seldom offered enhancement. Isolated specks can be removed from the page being sent and aliasing (edge jitter) can be reduced by signal processing.

F Speakerphone: This built-in feature is the same as a speakerphone in a separate telephone instrument.

F P Step-down Modem: If the modem fails to train at its highest bit rate, it automatically steps down to the next lower bit rate and tries again. This feature is found in virtually all fax machines.

F P Step-up Modem Operation: This allows the modem to step up to a higher sending rate between pages if the error rate is low and the modem is running at a slow rate. An isolated noise burst during training signal could have caused this low-speed condition.

F Talk/Fax: The Group 3 CCITT protocol has special signaling codes for voice request to alert a person near the other fax machine by a ringing-like tone from the fax machine. If this Group 3 talk function is used before sending fax copies, the TALK button is pressed after the 2100-Hz answer tone is heard. A few seconds signaling delay then occurs before the phones are connected. Talk function can be invoked whenever the two fax machines are connected without interrupting the page being sent. The command is delayed and sent between pages.

F Telephone Built-in: A phone may be furnished as a part of the fax machine, since it takes little extra room and makes it easy to switch between telephone and fax. Operation of the fax machine and the phone are basically the same when a separate phone is used instead of the Group 3 system described in the Talk/Fax option. It is not necessary to send a fax if the phone is used for a voice call.

F P Transaction Report: A confirmation of reception is printed out at the fax transmitter after a document has been sent. A strip of paper less than 2 in. long typically contains the date, starting time, telephone line number of the called fax machine, time the telephone line was connected, pages sent, and whether the pages were received OK. The OK is printed only if all pages were received with almost no perceptible degradation of the fax copy. The facsimile receiver counts the number of facsimile lines received with errors and if a threshold number is not exceeded, returns an acknowledgment signal. This threshold is usually set by the fax machine manufacturer, and may be 64 or more lines per page. Most fax machines store this same information in memory and print out a summary page at least once a day. (See the Journal option.)

F Transmission Reservation: If the fax machine is receiving when the operator wants to send, the document can be placed in the automatic document feeder and handled almost the same as if the fax machine were not being used. After the document is scanned into fax memory, the originals can be put back in the files. When the fax is no longer busy, it will automatically transmit from memory.

F P Transmit Terminal Identification (TTI): Sender's name prints on top of each page sent.

F P Turnaround Polling: This feature allows the calling station to poll a fax machine and then automatically send documents to it. A built-in timer may allow this feature to be combined with the Delayed Polling option.

F User Identity Cards: Credit card size identity cards can restrict use of a fax machine to card holders. They also list the users in the journal and can automatically sort out usage costs by department.

F Verification Stamp: Each page sent is automatically stamped on the back of the sending page after the fax receiver handshake confirms that it was received.

F Voice Announcements: Both the sender and recipient are notified of the communication status by voice announcement from the fax machine.

F Voice Answering Machine: If a voice call (but not a fax call) is received, this feature works like a regular voice answering machine. It responds to the call with a prerecorded outgoing message and records the caller's voice message.

F Voice/Fax Switching: A received call rings the telephone if a voice call is received or the fax machine if a fax call is received. An automatic transfer switch built into the fax machine determines whether the incoming call is from a fax machine or is a voice call. If the call is from an automatic calling fax machine, the CNG beeps between ring signals are detected and the call is switched to the fax machine. The CNG tone may not be present for automatic fax calls from some PC-fax cards. For a manual call, the logic used may differ between different models. One design inserts CNG tone beeps when the sender's START button is pressed. On a manual fax call, the receiving fax machine may automatically answer after a preset number of rings. If the call is answered on the telephone, the fax sender is told to press the START button to start the receiving fax machine.

F Voice/Fax Transfer: A single telephone line may be shared for alternative voice use or fax reception. This feature allows the voice telephone to be located away from the fax machine. After answering an incoming call, a fax call can be transferred to the fax machine by pressing a button or two on the DTMF telephone.

F Voice Request: If the sending operator wants to talk after sending, an alarm can be set to ring at the receiving fax machine after transmission is complete. This feature is of no use for normal fax transmission, but might be used by someone who is new to fax. It is seldom needed after users become familiar with fax operation. Alternatively, the receiving station operator can set a calling station alarm for operation at the end of the page being sent. Some fax machines will automatically print out a callback request if the other party fails to answer.

F Wide Paper Recording: This feature allows the use of recording paper wider than 8.5 in. for receiving full-width copies from wide-paper-sending fax machines. Often, either of two recording paper widths can be loaded.

F Wide Paper Sending: This feature, sometimes called size-reduction mode, allows pages wider than 8.5 in. to be sent to a standard-width recording fax for a reduced size copy. The automatic document feeder of the transmitter is arranged to send without copy reduction if the ADF paper guides are set for 8.5 in. Wide-paper pages will automatically be sent without reduction when sent to a wide-paper recording fax machine.

12.7 NONSTANDARD GROUP 3 FAX FEATURES

The following NSF features work only with the same type or compatible types of fax equipment made by the same manufacturer. For instance, super fine resolution offered by two different manufacturers usually will not be compatible.

F Automatic Resolution Control: Using NSF, a page will be sent with fine resolution where there are fine details and with normal resolution elsewhere. This saves transmission time when compared to sending the entire page in the high-resolution mode.

F P Confidential Reception (or Confidential Mailbox): To prevent received fax documents being seen (or taken) by anyone who walks by the fax machine or printer for PC-fax, confidential transmission can be used. Instead of printing out the document as received, it is stored in memory at the receiving machine. The receiving machine may show that a confidential document has been received. A password reserved for the intended recipient is entered at the fax transmitter before sending. The same code must be entered at the receiver to print out the document. A separate password is required for each recipient. For use of confidential reception, the receiving fax machine must be one from the same manufacturer and must have this special storage capability.

F EIA-232 Interface: The use of this digital interface is not defined as a standard for fax and is not needed by most users. Some manufacturers offer it as an extra cost option for connection to computers for fax picture signals or for printing ASCII characters on the fax machine. One should make sure both the fax machine and the unit it connects to are coordinated by the manufacturer. (See Section 3.8.4.)

F P Encryption, Built-in: This feature encrypts the fax signal for sending between similar-model fax machines of the same manufacturer. If the fax signal is intercepted, it cannot be converted into plain text and printed on another fax machine.

F Error-Free Mode, Proprietary: This NSF feature, was offered by some manufacturers before the CCITT had an error correction option. It should not be confused with the error-correction mode (ECM), now a standardized Group 3 option. The newer fax machines use ECM, providing error-free communication with fax machines made by any manufacturer.

F P Password Answer: Fax units can be set with one or more passwords to prevent the fax communicating with unauthorized parties. This is particularly useful in polling. For a station communicating only with a given set of fax machines, a password will block reception of junk fax mail.

F Photograph Transmission, Proprietary: An NSF compression algorithm is used to reduce the transmission time for sending photographs to other fax machines of the same manufacture. The coding efficiency of the Group 3 fax algorithms is much poorer than an algorithm designed for photographs. (See the Photograph Transmission option in the previous section.)

F P Relay Broadcast: This feature uses another fax machine to assist in sending the same documents to multiple destinations. The relay fax receives documents into memory and then transmits to many other fax machines. Because the documents are stored in memory rather than being sent again from recorded fax copies, the original fax copy quality is maintained. A group code for a number of fax machines is stored in the relay fax machine. Sending to many relay fax machines makes it possible to broadcast a document to hundreds of other fax machines in a much shorter time than sending from only one fax. Relay broadcast can also save substantial telephone line charges when the relayed fax transmissions are local calls. This is especially so when overseas calls are made. Only the more expensive fax machines have this feature, but even the least expensive units made by the same manufacturer often can relay through the expensive one. The relay fax machine usually has previously stored in memory the telephone numbers to which it will retransmit.

F P Relay Broadcast Command: This feature commands compatible receiving Relay Broadcast (above) to retransmit fax messages received into its memory to another calling group of fax machines.

F Remote Diagnostics: The supplier's diagnostic service center can call a malfunctioning fax machine and read its diagnostic codes to assist the technician in identifying and solving problems quickly.

F Super Fine: An NSF optional resolution of 203 × 392 lines/in. gives better results when sending gray-scale images such as photographs. It also increases the sharpness of printed text. The 392 lines/in. is achieved by stepping the page through only

1/392 in. per scan line. The size of the pels may still be 1/196 in. high, giving overlap in the paper feed direction, not true 392 lines/in.

F Ultrafine: A few fax machines have an optional mode of true higher resolution of about 400 lines/in., both horizontally and vertically with a laser printer at the receiving end.

F White Space Skipping: This NSF method sends faster by skipping lines that are all white, but works only with compatible fax machines of the same manufacturer.

Chapter 13
Facsimile Services

Fax users who do not own fax machines must rely on facsimile service providers to keep up with modern business demands for faster delivery of documents. Fax service providers for these users range from small shops to hotels, telephone companies, and PTTs. The sender goes to a local shop offering fax services and waits while the document is transmitted. If the fax recipient has a fax machine, delivery is completed. If the recipient does not have a fax, the document is sent to a shop nearby the destination and a telephone call is made to the recipient. Both sending and receiving parties pay a fee. These services send more documents to fax owners than the total documents they receive for delivery. For a fax owner to send a fax to a nonowner, he may have to rely on the recipient to obtain the fax number to call, but there is a separate business of selling specialized quarterly telephone directories of fax copy shops and others who will handle the fax copy in another city. Bureaufax or Postfax operators (mainly in Europe) have directories for their offices (see Figure 13.1).

Value-added facsimile services, provided by a number of companies, offer fax broadcast of documents, store-and-forward message handling, and E-mail distribution by fax. The U.S. fax services market is expected to top $500 million by 1992 and then flatten out before 1995 as more small users get their own fax machines and more large businesses provide their own enhanced fax services.

13.1 BUREAUFAX

In many countries, government agencies are responsible for the post office, telegraph, and telephone (PTT) services. Bureaufax was developed under CCITT Recommendation F.170 for PTT use as a fax service to replace the telegram. It used Group 2 fax machines, and later changed to Group 3. It is offered by the PTTs in 68 countries for fax message transmission (see Table 13.1).

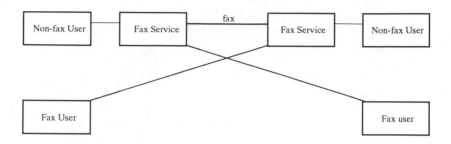

Figure 13.1 Fax delivery services.

A person wanting to send a *faxgram* uses a standard form for the message. Bureaufax became very successful, with a large increase in traffic continuing through 1985. This period corresponds to the period in which customers discovered the convenience of fax. Then a slowdown in growth rate corresponded to a rapid increase in Group 3 fax sales, including sales to former users of the service. Bureaufax has been useful in stimulating interest in fax, but now is less important as business owners have their own fax machines and send most of their traffic on regular telephone lines (PSTN).

Table 13.1
Bureaufax Countries

Antigua	Germany	New Guinea
Argentina	Greece	New Zealand
Australia	Guadeloupe	North Korea
Austria	Guyana	Norway
Bahrain	Hawaii	Panama
Belgium	Hong Kong	Peru
Bermuda	Iceland	Phillippines
Brazil	Indonesia	Portugal
Canada	Israel	Réunion
Cayman	Italy	Singapore
Chile	Ivory Coast	Spain
Costa Rica	Japan	Sri Lanka
Cyprus	Kuwait	St. Pierre and Miquelon
Denmark	Luxembourg	Sweden
Egypt	Macao	Taiwan
Fiji	Maldives	Thailand
Finland	Malta	Trinidad and Tobago
France	Martinique	Turkey
French Guyana	Netherlands	United Kingdom
French Polynesia	New Caledonia	United States

13.2 PTT FAXPOST

FAXPOST is a public fax service primarily for international communication to or from customers who do not have Group 3 fax units. More than 100 countries participated in this service in August 1987. Like Bureaufax, this service has been largely replaced by Group 3 fax or inexpensive express mail service. Intelpost, operated by the U.S. Postal Service through an interface in Miami, Florida, failed to develop any volume of fax messages.

13.3 U.S. POSTAL SERVICE AND HOTELECOPY

FaxMail is a joint program of the U.S. Postal Service and Hotelecopy, providing fax service in most major cities. Self-service fax machines are located in post offices and in hotel lobbies. In hotels, and some large post offices where the lobbies are open 24 hours, FaxMail can be used anytime. Users type in answers to questions that appear on a computer screen. An auxiliary telephone allows the user to call an operator for assistance. Charges for the service are paid by major credit card and have a 3-min minimum (good for several pages). The price, similar to that for express mail, is more than paid-for fax services provided by most retail shops.

FaxMail supplements Hotelecopy, a service started earlier and used by major hotel chains in the United States. With Hotelecopy, documents are sent to or received from one of the participating hotels by a Group 3 fax machine on the regular telephone network (PSTN). Hotels have a captive audience of business travelers who need to keep in touch with the home office. Fax documents with items needing the traveler's attention can be waiting upon check-in. Copies of reports left behind can be quickly relayed if suddenly needed. With fax transmission, order numbers and other data will not become garbled. Fax documents can also be exchanged with customers and suppliers for rapid completion of business transactions. Hotel users of fax services receive many more faxes than they send. As more and more business transactions depend on fax, the need for hotel fax services increases. Some hotels increase their fax revenues by offering delivery to nearby recipients who do not have fax units. The hotel will then have a bell hop hand-deliver it. Walk-in service is also available to private individuals and those few businesses who don't have their own fax units. Wade Helms, EVP and general manager of Hotelecopy, explains: "One of the great advantages to locating the service in a hotel is that it's open 24 hours and it's always safe to walk into." The service caught on rapidly, and now covers hotels in 50 states plus the Caribbean islands.

13.4 TELEPHONE COMPANY FAX SERVICES

Many of the telephone companies offer specialized fax services. Broadcast service sends documents to one or thousands of Group 3 fax machines in a short time.

Automatic retry and delivery confirmation is usually provided. Customer fax number lists may be kept on file by the company providing the service. A major advantage of this service for the sender is that phone lines are not tied up for long periods of time. Mailbox service with passwords provides subscribers with security and the ability to retrieve received fax messages while traveling.

AT&T Enhanced Fax: This service provides fully automated global store-and-forward fax capabilities. In addition to the above features, it includes automatic forwarding of fax documents to any Group 3 fax specified, deferred delivery of fax documents at an exact time, and service access provided from a touch-tone telephone by a toll-free number. The cost of the service is 60 cents/page domestically and about $1 to $5 per initial page for international calls (additional pages cost about half).

DHL Worldwide Express: This is an overnight electronic document delivery service using 400 lines/in. fax units to send customers' documents. The plain paper laser fax unit is compatible with Group 3 and Group 4 fax units. The system is designed to use the X.25 protocol on the NetExpress Communications, Inc., international packet-switching network. The company has operating agreements with the national telecommunication administrations of 13 foreign countries. Access to the U.S. network is through nodes in certain cities. The NetExpress network will also handle Group 4 transmissions.

MCI Fax: MCI Fax is a premium connection service for MCI customers to send by Group 3 fax to U.S. and overseas Group 3 users connected to the PSTN. A dedicated, digital, optical fiber network designed for 9.6 kb/s is used for domestic and international facsimile transmission. Connection to the office or home is provided by the local exchange carrier who uses his own copper telephone pairs and charges. Office-hour rates are about 25 to 35 cents/min in the United States and higher on overseas calls. Fax rates are higher than for a regular MCI voice call. Other services such as broadcast to many fax users and store-and-forward are offered.

SNET FaxWorks: The documents to be faxed by FaxWorks are sent to the telephone company as Group 3 fax, telex, or electronic mail.

Some resellers of long-distance telephone line service are trying to compete with low-cost transmission services that bypass long-distance phone companies. Gemfax, as an example, offers a fax switching service that sends the customer's fax document from its store-and-forward computer to one or many Group 3 fax units worldwide. Another entrepreneur, Public Fax Inc. of Orange, California, is selling shared use of their 800 number to public facsimile service operators.

13.5 ADDITIONAL FAX SERVICES

Many print shops, copy shops, drug stores, and stationery stores offer to send and receive faxes. These small businesses invested in Group 3 fax units and started charging about $5/page to send one page and about half that for additional pages. Some are organized as franchises and will send to other associated shops for pickup by the person needing the received copy. Some services pick up and deliver fax documents. By having local letter couriers do this work, they avoid the expense of their own delivery system. Others sell franchises for self-service public fax booths. With easy access at any time, the customer doesn't have to wait for a shop to open in the morning or worry about finishing his document before the shop closes.

13.6 ELECTRONIC MAIL WITH GROUP 3 FAX DELIVERY

Many public E-mail systems (EMS) now use Group 3 fax units for message delivery. Messages in low-order ASCII characters are received from subscriber data terminals, PCs, mainframes, or a telex. The system then converts the message to Group 3 fax format and sends it to the customer's Group 3 fax unit over regular telephone lines (PSTN). A message can be distributed to hundreds of recipients with just one call. The EMS systems can send, but not receive, fax messages. Any communicating terminal, such as a PC, may be used to send messages for delivery via Group 3 fax units. Some of the EMS will also receive Group 3 fax messages for relay to multiple fax addresses, similar to MCI Fax discussed in Section 13.4. Many of these systems charge by the half page with prices between 35 cents and $1 for the first page. Additional pages are about two-thirds as much. The telephone line charges may be additional. There is usually an additional monthly fee of $10 to $25.

Among companies providing this service in the United States are:

AT&T Mail, EasyLink

E-FAX Communications

Electronic Courier Systems

Gemfax New Facsimile Switching Network

MCI Mail Fax Dispatch (MCI is owner of RCA Globecom and Western Union International)

Syscom WORD*FAX

US Sprint SprintMail

US West Message-Net

ViTel International ViTelefax

Western Union

Chapter 14
The Future of Fax

In 1944, when the 100th anniversary of the telegraph was being celebrated, the *New York Times* heralded it as an "outstanding invention" that along with radio has brought about the "shrinking of the planet" and is "part of the technological unification of mankind."

In 1992, one year short of the 150th anniversary of facsimile, "fax" dominates the business world's means of communication, and could well have been substituted for "telegraph" if the *Times* were to publish any such tribute again. The telegraph has long been obsolete; fax, the sleeping giant, is shrinking the planet in ways not even conceived in 1944.

14.1 THE FUTURE OF GROUP 3 FAX

Group 3 Stand-Alone Fax: Group 3 fax with a configuration similar to the current one will be in great demand for many years. The laser printer fax devices currently available as add-ons will next be built into the standard laser printers.

High-Performance Group 3 Fax: Many enhancements have been added to Group 3 fax since the initial recommendations were adopted in 1980. New enhancements being tested by manufacturers and circuit providers will allow Group 3 fax to do many of the things on the PSTN that Group 4 now does only on digital networks. Already, ECM with MMR compression is a standardized option, providing faster error-free fax copies on PSTN calls. Anticipated additional features are higher speeds and higher resolutions of 300 and 400 lines/in. Communicating at 300 lines/in. in Group 3 mode between laser printer fax arrangements is now being done and its use should expand rapidly. The 300 and 400 lines/in. resolutions match those of Group 4. Even 600 lines/in. may become important after the 64 kb/s ISDN interface is available. Work is under way on a simplified Group 3 mixed mode for use with computers that should reach standardization soon.

Higher modem speeds for Group 3 up to 28.8 kb/s will soon be available, doubling the 14.4 kb/s transmission rate of the V.17 modem now being used. In the United States, the EIA/TIA modem group, TR-30.1, tested suitable high-speed modem schemes. CCITT Study Group XVII now calls the modem V.$_{fast}$, but it will be assigned a number when the standard is issued. A probe technique may be used to check the communication channel quality quickly and select the modem speed. A channel that fails to meet the minimum quality requirements is dropped automatically and the call is redialed. Channel equalization may require sending a training signal in both directions at the same time. Fax data rates higher than 14.4 kb/s are unlikely to be approved by the CCITT before 1994.

Also under consideration are other factors that limit the number of pages that can be sent per minute including optimization of the protocol by shortening the initial handshake time from 15 s and other delays. Other improvements are appending the post-message commands to the fax message transmission, and using the 2.4 kb/s signaling rate for binary coded commands and responses. The 3- to 5-s time between pages becomes significant when page transmission times can be much less than 10 s per page. On channels where the error rate is very low, the protocol could provide switching to a mode of transmitting multiple pages before acknowledging receipt.

Group 3 on ISDN at 64 kb/s: A 64 kb/s interface for operation of Group 3 fax on the new ISDN is in the process of becoming a standard (using one of the B channels). Error correction is based on the selective repeat option, now a part of T.30. Full-duplex operation is proposed to speed up the error-correction process. The fax call is set up in the ISDN circuit-switched mode for DTE-to-DTE communication per CCITT Recommendation T.90 using the session elements of its procedure rules of paragraphs 2.2.1, 2.2.2., and 2.2.4 with the HDLC IE code of Group 4 facsimile class 1. The error-correction method is the one used for Group 3 fax Recommendation T.4, Annex A, transmitting documents as pages and partial pages with a frame size of 256 octets. With full-duplex operation in the 64 kb/s mode, page transmission continues without waiting for a response to the previous page. For calling a normal Group 3 fax connected to the PSTN, the ISDN 3.1-kHz audio bearer capability interface fallback is operated in the same manner as voice is handled. Half-duplex error correction is then used. Another optional capability of accessing the ISDN, known as "Group 3 Unrestricted Digital Information (UDI)," was also approved. This option allows communication between Group 3 fax machines and Group 4 Class 1 fax machines by utilizing Group 4 protocols.

Group 3 Fax Integrated into Other Products: Most data modems made today are CCITT V.22, a 2.4 kb/s full-duplex modem. The lowest cost fax modem today is V.27$_{ter}$ 4.8 kb/s half-duplex. Recently, an American modem chip manufacturer found a no-cost way to make a small change that would allow the V.24 chip to be used for the transmitting function of V.27$_{ter}$ in addition to V.24 operation. Nearly all modem chips being designed today have fax modem functions, and fax capability will find its way into communication products such as PCs in the same way in which digital clocks found their way into all kinds of appliances. In 1980, a fax modem required 10 LSI chips and 150 discrete components. Today, the same function can be found on one chip. In a few years, fax design should improve to further reduce the chip count per machine and thus the manufacturing costs. The same chip may contain T.30 protocol, T.4 image compression, scanner interface, and printer interface. This is especially good news for PC users. Addition of fax capability to a new computer should be quite inexpensive and doesn't even require a plug-in slot. Some manufacturers are already offering PCs with fax built in. The fax engine will also make it possible to lower the cost of fax machines significantly. It might be the boost needed for the home fax market to take off.

Small Group 3 Fax: When manufacturers started selling the smaller A5 and A6 fax they expected it might open up a new home fax market. They were looking for something to pick up the slack when the demand for standard page size business fax units tapered off with a maturing market. Since their introduction in Japan in about 1987, interest in Europe or North America has been slight. Although these small fax machines might find some niche in the market, none is evident yet.

14.2 THE FUTURE OF GROUP 4 FAX

Although plans called for Group 4 fax to be operating by 1984 on PSTN, it is not yet available. There is a good possibility that Group 4 will be limited to digital data channels and PSTN operation will never be offered. The future for extensive use of this standard is unclear. Digital fax for networking, store-and-forward, and image databases is in the offing and Group 4 might fill this slot. Development of a viable mixed mode with teletex under the OSI protocol is unlikely to be of much importance in the foreseeable future, but computer mixed mode is probable. Group 4 will have very little impact on Group 3.

14.3 OTHER FUTURE PROSPECTS FOR FAX

Now that Group 3 fax has finally been recognized as essential to business communication, what next? Will Group 3 fax keep pace with newer technology, or fall behind and be replaced? Visionaries of the future foresee computers that will use radio waves and become miniaturized to the size of a pen. This ultra-portable device would send and receive faxes, store and retrieve computer files, recognize handwriting, and respond to voice commands.

In the more immediate future, what may we expect? Changes are occurring so rapidly that any predicted advances are likely to be in effect by the time you read this statement. With that in mind, the following items are in the works or are proposed for the coming years:

Integrated Fax Equipment: The layout of the business office may change when most PCs are equipped to handle the faxing, either on LANs or as stand alone devices. Several functions, including fax, will be integrated into one multitasking unit. As these become standard home equipment, more workers will have the option of conducting their affairs away from the office—what the media refers to as "telecommuting."

The Home Market for Facsimile: In England in mid-1991, British Telecom (BT) tested a new service designed for the home fax user. Using a 900 number, a customer can call for an updated fax report from the BT database on the "Around the World" yacht race. A two- or three-page report is then faxed. During the trial, there is no 900 charge and only the standard telephone rate applies. The standard 900 rate of 33 or 45 p/minute will probably be charged when the service is expanded. This could be a start for fax access to many databases.

Facsimile Newspaper to the Home: At one time, more than a half-dozen morning papers in the United States were experimenting with afternoon summaries of the news, which they faxed to subscribers wanting a sneak preview of the next day's news. Most of these ventures were discontinued when the publishers found that readers were unwilling to pay premium prices for condensed stories, and were content to wait for the complete morning edition. Among the ones who stopped the fax editions were *The News-Sentinel* of Knoxville, Tennessee, the *Minneapolis Star Tribune,* and the *Chicago Tribune*. A few newspapers press on, sending to areas where its daily product isn't available. Japanese and Caribbean cruise ships regularly receive the *New York Times* facsimile edition of six to eight pages. The military personnel engaged in the 1991 war in the Persian Gulf were kept informed of events back home by fax newspapers. The *Hartford Courant* finds a limited but loyal audience for its fax sheet, especially at local businesses. "We use it as an early-warning notification about news of the company or of the opposition," says a spokesman for Travelers Corporation, Hartford, Connecticut.

Telepublishing: Some innovative publishing companies are using fax board systems to distribute newsletters and other time-critical information to subscribers with fax machines or boards. Such emerging applications are fueling rapid growth in the PC-fax board market.

2-D Bar Code Fax: Fax may find a new use for sending two-dimensional bar codes. The codes now in such widespread use have only one dimension, limiting the amount of information they can handle. The 2-D bars can pack several hundred characters into a square inch of space, containing as much as 10 times the normal amount of typewritten data that can be put on a letter-size page. It should be far simpler and more reliable than OCR scanning for reading received fax information into computer memory. Besides, there are only about 700 regular typewritten words per densely packed page. A small company could print lists of a shipment's contents along with its routing in bar code form and then fax it to its shippers and retailers where it could be scanned and stored in their computer files. The scanning of these codes, reading black-white spots, would be done in the same manner as facsimile messages are— starting at left top, sweeping across to right, row by row. No one can predict the market size or just how much fax will be a part of it at this point. It could be large considering the two billion dollar market for the linear bar codes today.

Much Higher Fax Speeds: Optical fiber to the home has been an economic reality for three years, with or without cable TV in the pipe. T-3 networking with business customer access at 45 Mb (equivalent to 672 voice channels) is starting. Optical broadband ISDN draft standards have been recommended by the CCITT and completed standards are expected in 1992. Fujitsu has demonstrated a 1.8 Gb/s (equivalent of 24,000 voice telephone circuits) optical fiber subscriber loop conforming to the CCITT draft standard. Bell Labs is experimenting with a device to transmit 350 billion light pulses a second in glass fiber in contrast to 2.5 billion pulses for the fastest commercial systems.

The summary for the foreseeable future for the different options follows:

Group 3 Fax: Group 3 fax has proven its ability to keep up with the rapid advances in technology and will continue its dominance for many years.

Group 4 Fax: Group 4 fax will continue to be used mainly by large corporations and it will still account for less than 1% of the fax machines used for some years to come.

Color Fax: The technology is now here, but production will be very slow until there is a proven business need that will pay for the higher cost fax machines. The situation is somewhat like the use of office copiers compared to color copiers.

In conclusion, fax will continue on the upswing far into the coming century.

Appendix 1
The Evolution of Facsimile

A.1 ELECTRICAL COMMUNICATION BEGINNINGS

Most people are surprised to learn that facsimile machines were in use before 1970. When they are told that the original fax network was in operation in the 1860s, not 1960, they are astonished!

The telegraph and facsimile were born at almost the same time and they had many things in common. Both sent pulses made by contact switching, interrupting current from a battery to convey information. Both received by marking on paper. Both connected sending and receiving units with a single wire, using ground to complete the circuit.

A1.1 The Morse Telegraph

Although Samuel F. B. Morse was known as a painter in his day, his enduring fame rests on being credited with invention of the telegraph. While returning from Europe aboard the packet ship *Sully,* in late 1832, he discussed electricity and magnetism with his fellow passengers and conceived the idea of an electric telegraph [1]. What resulted was a telegraph system with a recorder built around a picture frame from one of his canvasses. An electromagnet pulled down a pencil, marking dots and dashes onto a strip of moving paper driven by clock works. A weight on a cord over a pulley lifted the pencil between marks. For sending, a coded metal pattern key closed electrical contact springs to generate dots and dashes from a battery. Each letter of the alphabet had a different key to generate the desired code. Morse demonstrated his apparatus to Martin Van Buren, president of the United States in 1838, and was granted $30,000 for a telegraph line between Washington and Baltimore. On May 24, 1844, the resulting telegraph system sent the famous "What hath God wrought" message from the Supreme Court chambers in Washington, D.C., to the Baltimore & Ohio railroad station in Baltimore. This line was successful in public use and Morse offered his invention to the government. The offer was refused on recommendation of the postmaster-general who was "uncertain that the revenues could be made to equal the expenditures."

Development of the telegraph proceeded in spite of this setback. In 1861, the first transcontinental telegraph message was sent from California to Washington, D.C. By 1856, the telegraph operators had learned how to read relay clicks and didn't need the paper. The telegram services of Postal Telegraph and Western Union, dominant for record communication for many years, were replaced much later by Teletype, TWX, and Telex. Now, electronic mail from computer terminals often uses fax for fast delivery of messages.

Morse code was the shorthand that coded the alphabet efficiently by assigning the shortest codes to the letters used most often. This code concept was probably more important to communications development than the Morse telegraph equipment designs. Today, a similar concept codes Group 3 fax signals efficiently, with assignment of the shortest code words to the white (and black) spaces that occur most frequently. Although telegraph existed much earlier, the first Morse telegraph patent wasn't issued until 1848. The earlier systems didn't have the advantage of his telegraph code or the single-wire telegraph line.

A1.2 Early Fax

On November 27, 1843, a Scottish physicist named Alexander Bain obtained English Patent No. 9,745 for a recording telegraph (facsimile unit). Probably the inspiration for the first work on facsimile was the discovery that paper saturated with electrolytic solution discolored when electric current passed through it. Bain used a pendulum for both driving power and the clock for timing operations (see Figure A.1).

Bain devised a method to keep the sending and receiving pendulums in step at the start of each swing. At the sending end, electrical contact between stylus (K), a spring on the swinging pendulum arm, and metal printer's type (B) provided scanning. At the receiving end, a similar stylus on a swinging pendulum arm made marks on damp electrolytic paper. A battery (E) was connected in series with the transmitter stylus (K), a telegraph wire (LINE), the receiver stylus (K), and back to the battery (E) through earth ground (T). The transmitter stylus (K) wiped over the raised metal type (B), closing the circuit each time it touched the raised metal type face. As the receiver stylus wiped over damp electrolytic paper (A), current passing through it made marks corresponding to the pattern traced by the pendulum swing at the transmitter.

The printer's type and the recording sheet were in frames held up by cords. A clock-driven escapement mechanism (C) let out the cords to lower these frames one line height (scanning line) for each swing of the pendulum. The pendulum was kept in step by a synchronizing (sync) pulse for each swing to avoid skew of the recorded

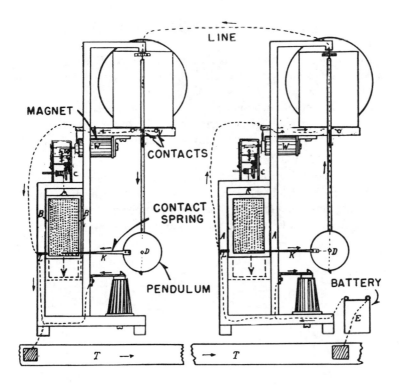

Figure A.1 Bain's recording telegraph.

fax image.[1] A latch magnet stopped the pendulum at the end of its swing until the sync pulse was received. It is believed that a working model was first constructed for the 1851 World's Fair in London when it was learned that a competing fax machine would be shown.

It is amazing that a fax machine could be made to work even before the invention of the telephone. To see just how difficult it was, consider the following major technical problems:

- *Driving power:* No electric motors existed. The power to move the scanning stylus of the early machines came from clock weights and gravity.

---

[1]This became known as stop-start synchronization. When the type was touched by the stylus at the transmitter (corresponding to black), marking started at the fax receiver. Marking continued until black was no longer sent from the fax transmitter. Any variation in the spot speed caused the marking to drift out of the proper position. To limit the error in recording spot position, the spot speed at the receiver is slightly faster than the fax transmitter. At the end of a line, the recording spot movement stops and waits for the fax transmitter to start the next line. The positional error is thus limited to the amount of drift between the spots in one line.

- *Scanning:* No photosensors existed. Cameras, which had just started to be used, took minutes to expose a picture.
- *Synchronization:* Rotating drums didn't stay in step. Even the stability of pendulum clocks was not accurate enough to send a whole page without intolerable skew of the received copy.
- Channels: The communication channel was a low-speed dc telegraph line with a single wire to ground. There were no amplifiers or repeating relays. Later, the pulses were repeated by very slow-operating relays, seriously limiting the facsimile transmission speed.

The second facsimile machine, constructed by English physicist Frederick Bakewell (1848 English Patent 12,352), was also shown at the 1851 fair in London. Bakewell's rotating drum and leadscrew design was probably constructed before Bain's pendulum design. While the Bain scanner used electrical contact between a stylus

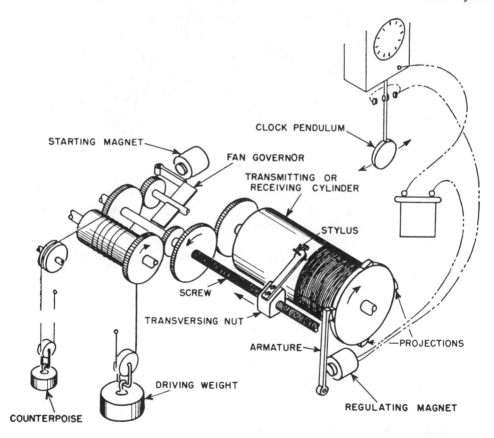

Figure A.2 Bakewell's rotating cylinder.

and a metal type face, Bakewell substituted a more convenient method by using insulating ink written on a metal surface. This system still wouldn't scan documents written on paper. At short distances, a low-voltage battery was adequate to provide the required current through the stylus for marking the chemically treated paper at the receiver. As the distance was increased, the higher voltage needed to produce the same marking current caused sparking to occur at the scanning stylus.

Bakewell's drum was rotated by gravity, with a driving weight and a cord wrapped a few turns around a drum. The drum rotated as the driving weight lowered, turning the transmitting or receiving cylinder through a gear train. Unless the transmitting and receiving cylinders were in exact step (in sync), the received image shape would be extremely distorted, making the system useless. The Bakewell design attempted to lock the cylinder rotation to a pendulum by correction with electromagnetic braking two to four times per drum revolution (see Figure A.2).

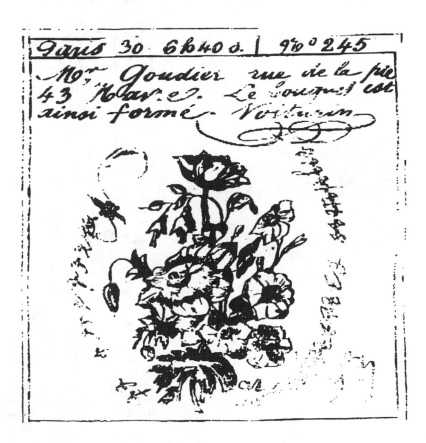

Figure A.3 Received copy—Pantelegraph, 1861.

Bakewell's method of keeping separate transmitting and receiving rotating drums in step was too crude to be useful. Acceptable results were achieved for the London fair by sending and receiving on the same cylinder, but this only sent the fax image from one side to the other. The rotating drum synchronizing problem was finally solved about 50 years later.

The first commercial facsimile service was inaugurated by Giovanni Caselli in 1865 using his Pantelegraph machine patented September 25, 1861. Figure A.3 is a reproduction of copy he received over a long-distance telegraph circuit that year.

The initial fax circuit between Lyon and Paris was later extended to several other French cities. The service was discontinued around 1870, about the time of the Franco-Prussian war. The Caselli design used a long pendulum (D) for driving power (see Figure A.4).

The pendulum swing was connected by rod (W) through a rocker arm (Y) to a transmitting stylus (V) and a receiving stylus. They swung back and forth in a 90-

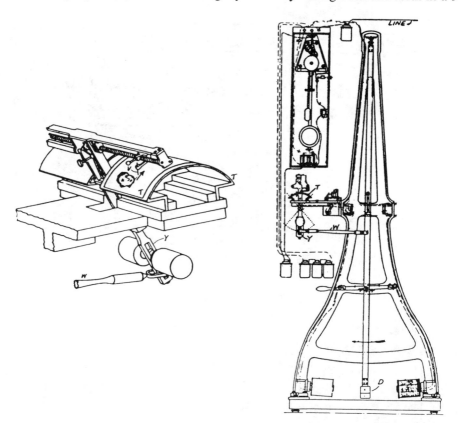

Figure A.4 First commercial fax—Casselli.

deg arc touching the outside of the sending and receiving drum segments (T). A leadscrew moved the styli one line per swing. It was remarkable that with the very limited technology available, the Casselli fax system could be developed and used commercially for about five years. As technology advanced, the pendulum design became obsolete.

A.2 FACSIMILE DEVELOPMENT PROBLEMS

Achieving satisfactory fax machine performance took many years, with contributions from thousands of people in fax and other communication arts. Progress was slow because improving performance in one problem area often revealed another problem previously hidden (see Figure A.5).

Notice that some of the five items used by Bain in the first fax unit continued to be used in later fax designs for 100 years. The pendulum gave way to a tuning fork frequency standard. The early attempts by D'Arlingcourt to couple the tuning

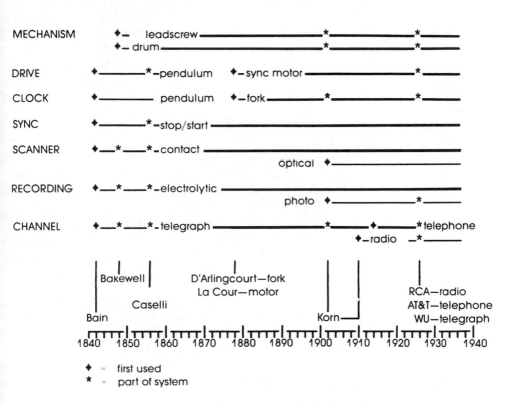

Figure A.5 Development of facsimile technology from 1840–1936.

fork tines mechanically to drive a rotating shaft (British Patent No. 1,920 in 1869) were not practical. Rotating drums became practical after La Cour made the first functional synchronous motor in 1878. The motor consisted of an electromagnetic coil next to the teeth of a gear. The gear was the motor rotor, which turned one tooth per pulse. To drive the motor, he added electrical contacts to the tines of a tuning fork, almost eliminating instability encountered by D'Arlingcourt (caused by changes in mechanical loading). Constant frequency pulses generated by a battery and the tuning fork contacts operated the motor in step with the tuning fork.

Tuning forks, the preferred method of synchronization used by analog fax machines for many years, start the scanning and recording spots at the same time, and the spot speeds are determined by independent frequency standards at both fax machines. Compare this with a clock that is set to the correct time and runs for days without needing to be reset. The accuracy requirements for facsimile are more stringent than a clock, however. For example, the total facsimile line length for an 8.5- $\times$ 11-in. page at 100 lines per inch scanning is $8.5 \times 11 \times 100 = 9350$ in. A clock stability of a minute a day (1 part in 1440) would give about 6.5 in. of skew[2] in the received copy, making it unacceptable. Accuracy of one second a day (1 part in 86,400) would cause a skew of more than one-tenth of an inch per page, and might be marginally acceptable, but a week or a month later the clock likely would be off at least three times this rate. Early fax machines reset their frequency standards often and in network operations, such as those for newsphotos, this was quite a problem. By the 1940s, the precision of tuning fork frequency standards (but not crystals) became good enough for most applications. Some analog fax machines such as newspaper publishing facsimiles and Group 2 facsimile still use this scheme. Electrolytic recording lasted into the 1960s.

A practical tuning fork and synchronous motor-driven fax system was later made by Arthur Korn of Germany. The Korn fax system heralded the use of optical scanning and photographic recording, still used in some fax systems today (see Figure A.6).

The transmitter lamp (23) is focused by a lens (22) into a small spot of light on the transparent original wrapped around a glass drum (4). Light passed through the original and the drum, was deflected downward by a mirror (29), and picked up by a selenium cell (2). The synchronous motor (18) turned the drum (4), which moved vertically 0.0127 in. (0.5 mm) per revolution.

In 1906 Korn's newsphoto facsimile equipment with optical scanning and photographic recording on film was put into regular service over telegraph circuits from Munich to Berlin. This was nine years before the telephone repeater was developed, making long-distance telephony practical. The Korn system later expanded to

---

[2]At the bottom of the fax recording page, a black dot that should be at the left edge of the paper would have drifted over by 6.5 in. Half-way down the page, the drift would be half as much.

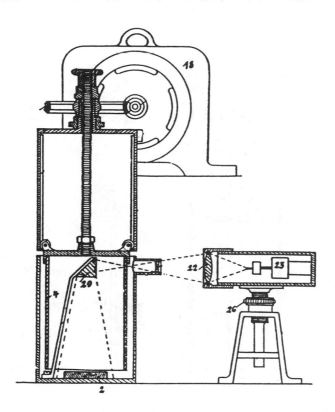

Figure A.6 Korn's optical scanning transmitter.

provide news picture service to London, Paris, and Monte Carlo (500 miles). Transmission time was 12 min per 5- × 8-in. page at a resolution of 51 lines/in. (2 lines/mm).

Korn's receiver was the first successful application of photography to facsimile. The picture rate was 300 pixels per second, later increased to 1000. The first design used a low-pressure gaseous discharge as the light source for recording. Relays were much too slow to turn on the lamp under control of the received fax signal. His spark gap modulator was marginal on speed. The vacuum tube would later make this type of light source the most popular one for fax recording, but the tube had not been invented. Korn then developed an electromagnetic light shutter or string galvanometer (71) (see Figure A.7). The shutter was a small piece of aluminum foil held by a loop of wire 77/78 in a magnetic field. A steady light source was focused onto the shutter. Light passing through when the received fax signal current caused the shutter to move out of the way was focused to record on photographic film.

The selenium photosensor, with its slow response speed, poor stability, and lack of uniformity in electrical characteristics, still limited performance of the fax

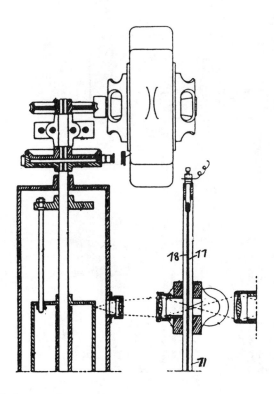

Figure A.7 Korn's telephoto receiver.

scanner. A gaseous-medium photoelectric cell patented in 1908 by two German scientists, Elster and Geitel, overcame these limitations; however, this cell would not pass the heavy currents needed in existing dc-loop facsimile equipment designs and could not be used for facsimile until the vacuum tube became available. Telegraph lines were suited for facsimile transmission inasmuch as they conveyed the on-off dc currents produced by the contact scanning or selenium photocells used by the fax machines.

A.3 LONG-DISTANCE TELEPHONE LINES IMPROVE FAX

The earliest fax machines used telegraph circuits to send fax because there were no telephone lines. Telegraph lines communicated with dc pulses and there was no low-frequency cutoff. Fax generated a pulse for each mark scanned, and the frequency could be very high compared with the hand-generated dots and dashes of the telegraph. Attenuation gradually increased with frequency, with no upper frequency demarcation point. The facsimile signal did not need to be modulated to pass from fax transmitter to fax receiver. The early telephones used a dc-loop with voice changing the resistance of a carbon granule transmitter button to generate the varying current needed for the earphone of the telephone receiver.

Up to this point, telephone lines could not communicate over the long distances that telegraph lines could. The addition of vacuum tube repeaters (amplifiers) to telephone lines was a major communication milestone. Shouting on long-distance calls was no longer required. More important though for facsimile was the possibility of sending much faster and farther. The transformers in the amplifier did not pass the varying dc, but the ac component caused by variation in dc current over the range of a few hundred hertz to about 3000 Hz passed through the amplifier. Facsimile could not be used on the new type of telephone channel until a modulator was invented to control the amplitude of a tone that would pass through the telephone channel. The first modulator for fax was probably a light chopper by Rosing, who applied for U.S. Patent No. 1,161,734 in 1911. A rotating disk with a ring of holes or teeth interrupted the light path in the scanner. This produced a constant frequency carrier tone, and its amplitude was controlled by the density of the page being scanned.

As the demand for telephone service increased, the older open-wire telephone lines were replaced by cables whose multiple pairs of wires handled more voice circuits. Cable telephone lines have high shunt-capacitance between the wires, causing the signal loss to increase rapidly with frequency, shortening the distance required between repeater amplifiers. Loading coils added in series with each wire converted the line into a low-pass filter, reducing transmission loss and improving the quality of voice transmission; however, these loading coils introduced most of the envelope-delay distortion. The combination of attenuation of higher frequencies by longer telephone lines and the effect of the amplifier blocking low frequencies from dc to a few hundred Hertz shaped the passband of a telephone channel into a U-shape curve that still exists today. Fax signals were then sent using double-sideband amplitude modulation of a carrier frequency of 1800 Hz since it was centered in the voice channel passband of about 300 to 3000 Hz. At higher speeds, envelope-delay distortion degraded the received picture quality causing smearing of line edges, ghosts, and other defects. The received facsimile picture quality was unacceptable in many cases. The slightly longer transit time over the telephone line for frequencies near the edge of the voice band caused envelope-delay distortion.

Later, 12 voice channels were sent over a single telephone channel. Frequency multiplexing systems using 4000-Hz bandpass filters to separated the channels. Although the channel upper frequency limit for a voice channel was about 3600 Hz, the overall end-to-end characteristics on telephone calls could only be relied on for a 3000-Hz upper frequency limit. The analog telephone switched network described above was known by various names as it evolved: POTS (Plain Old Telephone Service), long distance, DDD (Direct Distant Dialing), and today as PSTN (Public Switched Telephone Network) or GSTN (General Switched Telephone Network).

In this section, we discuss certain systems in detail. These systems show how differences in available technology affected the approach needed for development of the facsimile art, leading toward today's digital fax. Other significant fax systems were being developed at the same time.

In 1924, higher speed fax systems developed by Western Union, RCA, and AT&T were the next step in transmission of pictures (in the United States). The envelope-delay distortion problem and many other telephone line impairments were solved by AT&T when telephotography, its newspaper picture transmission service, was developed.

A transmitting and receiving telephoto system took a room full of equipment. The equipment sent 4.25- × 6.5-in. (108- × 165-mm) pictures. Resolution was 100 lines/in. with a drum speed of 100 rpm for sending at 1 in./min. The equipment was built like a lathe with a rotating drum and leadscrew. A dc shunt-wound motor drove the drum directly with a generator operating at 300 Hz, operating in a servo loop. The 300-Hz tuning fork was made of nickel-chromium steel for a small temperature-frequency coefficient. It was operated in an oven held to 50 ±0.1°C. The frequency was maintained to an accuracy of a few parts per million by manual adjustment when necessary. Vestigial sideband amplitude modulation was used with a carrier frequency of 2400 Hz.

Herbert Ives did much of the work on this program and is credited for the telephone line equalization used in telephotography. Envelope-delay distortion limits of no more than ±300 μs were needed for the telephone line between sending and receiving facsimile machines. Newly designed filters added propagation delay in the center of the voice band, making the delay more nearly constant and amplitude-versus-frequency filters corrected the frequency response over the range required for facsimile signals (1000 to 2600 Hz). Selection of lines for conditioning avoided those with electrical disturbances and distortions affecting the fax picture quality. Electrical disturbances include abrupt variations in line loss, envelope-delay distortion, noise, echo, and crosstalk. Each leg of a facsimile telephone circuit had separate filters to compensate for that particular section. Although the fax "private lines" were made from the regular telephone service lines, only a small percentage were conditioned for fax. Manual connection of these conditioned legs provided a "private line" point-to-point circuit or network where many newspapers received photos by fax at the same time. Before sending, a key switch on a simplexed dc control circuit set the other telephoto stations on the network to receiving mode. It also locked out the echo suppressors and the stepping of attenuation regulators. Facsimile was the only high-speed data transmission service at that time. The telephone line performance specifications set for facsimile were almost identical to those for data transmission over a voice channel adopted about 20 years later.

In the 1930s and 1940s newsphoto services such as Associated Press, Reuters, and UPI started to distribute pictures worldwide with private line networks and radiophoto. Each pixel with full gray-scale range, provided good copies of photographs. By contrast, office facsimile units have only black or white pels and cluster black pels to form dots of varying size similar to the screen dots in newspaper photographs. This produces a somewhat crude gray-scale representation at low resolution.

One of the Western Union fax developments resulted in a small-copy office fax unit called Deskfax. About 50,000 units were made to send telegrams between the customer office and the Western Union office. Their use was in offices where the volume of telegram business was not sufficient to have a send-receive teleprinter with a trained operator. This successful application disappeared with the demise of the telegram.

The AT&T telephoto system was later improved with the picture size increased to 11 × 17 in. (279 × 432 mm) and sold to Associated Press to initiate their Wirephoto™ service for newspapers. This system thus became the forerunner of today's private line newsphoto systems (Associated Press, United Press International, and Reuters).

In the fall of 1934, Associated Press contracted for a Wirephoto system from AT&T. The *New York Daily News* contributed $150,000 and several other large newspapers put up proportionate amounts. The *New York Times* was not told about the new venture even though the publisher, Adolph S. Ochs, was an AP director. Ochs, quite ill by then, was greatly concerned that the new service would put the Times Wide World Photos out of the photographic business. His son-in-law, Arthur Hays Sulzberger, wanted to outdo AP with a portable photofacsimile device that could be operated over regular voice telephone lines rather than the expensive AP system. Although Ochs didn't think it could be done, he gave Sulzberger permission to try.

Sulzberger contacted Austin G. Cooley who had worked on facsimile for 15 years and had developed a semiportable facsimile system. Cooley was given the job of trying to develop a fully portable unit for test. Fifty-nine work-intensive days later, he had one.

Before the new photofax equipment was ready, Sulzberger talked with the head of AT&T, Walter Gifford, and asked, "Does it make any difference to the telephone company if a telephone user talks English or French?"

Gifford said all conversation could be used if it was not profane.

"Then a telephone user can talk French or even Turkish, and that would be all right?"

Gifford nodded.

"How about Turkish or gibberish—that still all right?"

Gifford said, "Arthur, what are you getting at?"

"This: since it doesn't matter what language goes over a telephone, it should make no difference to you if we take a picture and transform its light values into sound values, send them over ordinary telephone lines, and then retranslate them into light values at the other end of the line."

Gifford thought awhile before his reply. "No, I don't think that would concern us at all."

An earlier report had assured Gifford that no picture transmission would work for more than 100 miles except on the expensive, specially selected and conditioned Wirephoto circuits set up by AT&T.

Thus it became permissible to send facsimile signals over the regular switched telephone network, providing the facsimile equipment was not connected electrically to telephone company equipment. Use was limited to newspaper and public services such as police.

The tests with Cooley's wirephoto equipment were successful. In 1935, Wide World Wire Photos (later called Times Facsimile Corporation) was formed, with Cooley running it, to build and operate facsimile equipments for the *New York Times*.

Experiments with Cooley's system were quietly going on in San Francisco at the time of the U.S. Navy dirigible *Macon* explosion off the California coast on February 12, 1935. World Wide photographers, present when the survivors were brought in to the harbor, took pictures and faxed them to New York. The first publication of any photographs transmitted by this method was carried by the *New York Times* in the account of the *Macon* disaster. The "W.W.W. Photo" credit line shocked telephone company executives and AP Wirephoto customers. They found it difficult to believe that good quality pictures could be sent over regular unconditioned long-distance telephone lines instead of the $3,000,000 special Wirephoto circuits. This meant that it cost no more to send a picture than to talk over the same telephone line.

Instead of being limited to a fixed picture network with sending access only at certain newspaper locations, pictures then were sent directly from the location of a news event to *Times* headquarters in New York. The photographer made a print of his picture for the facsimile operator. He then mounted it on a cylinder of a portable facsimile transmitter about the size of a small suitcase, a radical reduction in size from the room full of equipment required by Associated Press. He then placed a regular telephone call to the *Times* picture darkroom. Any telephone, including a coin-operated one, could be used. Where no ac power was available, a 6-V automobile battery served as the power source for the facsimile transmitter. An inductive coupling unit slipped over the telephone bell box, connecting the facsimile unit to the telephone line without a wired connection to it.

Long-distance telephone operators were a problem when sending fax pictures. They had been instructed to disconnect a circuit immediately when the customer was finished or when something went wrong with the call. Because the facsimile calls were longer than voice calls, they often monitored the call to see when it was done. When they heard the facsimile signal gibberish, the call was quickly disconnected. On pay phone calls, the fax operator had to convince the long-distance operator not to monitor and that he would pay even if it took half an hour.

Opening the plain old telephone system (POTS, now PSTN) to fax transmissions when overseas lines became available provided the channel necessary to access fax units anywhere in the world by merely making a telephone call. Without this access, Group 3 fax would still be a small, insignificant service.

At the start it was difficult to fabricate facsimile equipment because few of the parts needed were available. This was still the case in 1935 when Times Facsimile Corporation (TFC) began operations. Many of the mechanical, electromechanical, and electrical parts required were unique and were pushing the state-of-the-art for precision. Because there was no established source, the facsimile manufacturer had to design and make them or make arrangements with companies with the background and expertise to develop what was needed.

There was no motor that would fill the performance specifications TFC needed for its portable facsimile units. To achieve the rotational stiffness needed for high-quality recording, an 1800-Hz, 1800-rpm, 1/100-hp synchronous motor was designed and manufactured by TFC. The 50% efficiency was amazingly high. The gap between stator and rotor was only 0.001 in. Dies for the motor laminations were made in the TFC experimental machine shop. The stamping, heat treating, machining, assembly, and testing were also done in-house. Obtaining precision gears, bearings, and machining leadscrews with enough accuracy to prevent picture streaking was a serious problem. Even the optics for some of the facsimile systems required unique designs. Audio and power transformers, audio and power filters, solenoids, and other electromechanical components were designed and made at TFC.

Frequency standards with the long-term stability required for facsimile units did not exist. The tuning forks then used were low-frequency ones whose frequency was subject to atmospheric pressure variations and humidity changes. Crystals could be compensated to work over a limited temperature range and would require a closely regulated oven to achieve the five or less parts per million required. Even good crystals aged a few parts per million per month. With a crystal standard, the frequency would need resetting about six times a year to keep the older fax machines in step with those just manufactured. In addition, the necessary frequency divider circuits that changed the frequency from the megahertz range of "good" crystals to the audio frequency needed for driving fax motors were unreliable. For these reasons, tuning forks were used as the frequency standard for fax machines.

For the *New York Times* newsphoto equipment, an 1800-Hz tuning fork was developed by Garrett V. Dillenback. A nickel-chrome steel (similar to Invar™) tuning fork with a positive coefficient of frequency with temperature was silver soldered to a carbon steel tuning fork that had a negative coefficient of frequency with temperature. The laminated, bimetallic tuning fork was purchased (Riverbank Laboratories, Eisenhour patent) with a slightly negative temperature coefficient. The coefficient was tediously adjusted in steps by removing a small amount of steel from the thin carbon steel side with a surface grinder. Heat treating then removed the strains produced by grinding. After a check of frequency versus temperature, a smaller grinding step was taken, and the process repeated. This gave far better results than Invar steel tried by others.

During World War II, the Signal Corps needed transportable fax machines with a frequency standard that would remain stable for a year without resetting. Operation over a very wide temperature range was also necessary. A stable oven might have extended the performance to lower temperatures, but size restraints and warm-up time made this impractical. Hermetic sealing was required to prevent frequency variations due to pressure and humidity changes. Other problems were salt water corrosion and fungus problems caused by the tropics. Assemblies were made with the tuning fork and coils inside a hermetically-sealed cylinder. These designs required another compensation for the pressure variation inside the cylinder caused by temperature changes. Long-term frequency stability became a problem, probably caused by out-gassing from the driving-pickup coil assembly changing the operating conditions with time. Dillenback started to work on a new tuning fork oscillator design in a locked room. John Shonnard, an innovative TFC engineer, was assigned to help him, but every time he tried dropcloths were thrown over the work.

In frustration, Shonnard set up his own independent operation. He used a non-magnetic stainless steel case with the magnetically coupled drive and pickup coils mounted outside the case. The air was evacuated from the steel case before sealing it. This eliminated the air loading on the tuning fork tines and greatly increased the "Q," providing better frequency stability. The entire fork assembly, including coils, was placed in a larger hermetically sealed steel can to protect the coils from humidity and corrosive conditions. (See Figure A.8).

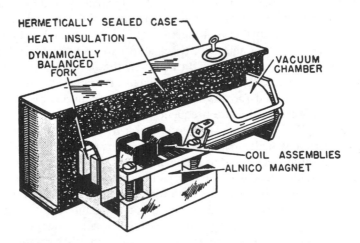

Figure A.8 Cutaway view of fork oscillator.

This design took care of both problems, and Shonnard was issued a patent. The processing of the tuning fork blanks went through painstaking development before long-term stability and other military requirements were met. Production tuning forks were individually aged and tested over a period of a month or more to make sure the tight specifications were met.

The tuning fork frequency standards had a very good performance record. During World War II, the Signal Corps had some problems with accuracy of a timer being made by Leeds & Northrup in Philadelphia. John Erhart, an engineer from the Facsimile Section of the Signal Corps Laboratories, was sent to investigate and took along one of the portable fax machines. He proceeded to plug in the fax machine and asked for once-per-second pulses from their frequency standard. The pattern recorded wandered back and forth like a sine wave, instead of tracing a straight line. When Erhart told them their frequency standard was not good, the president of the company was summoned. He told Erhart that their standard was developed over many years and took him down to the special basement room where the standard was held at closely regulated temperature and carefully shock-mounted to prevent any instability due to motions coupled through the earth. Who was he to question its accuracy based on a little fax machine? Erhart held his ground, however, and asked if they had a radio receiver. He tuned in WWV, the National Bureau of Standards, and recorded their once-per-second pulses. When a straight line was traced across the paper, the fax machine was shown to have orders of magnitude better accuracy.

When the picture service provided by the Associated Press expanded and improved, Sulzberger, publisher of the *Times*, sold Wide World Photos to AP, but kept the facsimile development and manufacturing facilities to build facsimile equipment for the U.S. government during World War II. He planned to dissolve TFC at the end of the war because the *Times* no longer needed its own telephoto equipment.

The U.S. military had become interested in this equipment and wanted a small-sized portable transceiver. The large Wirephoto receiver functions were squeezed into the small Wirephoto transmitter case. The unit could now send, receive positives on photographic paper, receive negatives on film, or receive on a direct recording paper. The fax machines were wired point-to-point with the discrete components soldered from pins on tube sockets to a tie point or ground. Each technician wired, debugged, and tested his assigned fax machine. The more experienced technicians had their own wiring layouts and tricks they had learned to make the finished unit meet performance specifications. It was difficult to prevent 1800 Hz from the power amplifier driving the synchronous motor from being picked up by the low-level, high-impedance amplifiers for the fax signal. The short connection between the phototube socket and the grid of the amplifier required a special metal cover. A shielded wire would not work at the two megohms impedance.

When one of the government engineers was testing a fax machine, he found a wire that was connected only at one end. Removal of the redundant wire resulted in an undesirable pattern in the recorded copy. When the wire was put back, the fax machine worked properly again. The technician had perfected a system of balancing out interference by introducing additional interference of opposite phase and magnitude. After testing by the Signal Corps, the FX-1B, a 22- × 12- × 10-in. militarized transceiver was designed and produced (see Figure A.9).

The FX-1B was one of the first pieces of equipment to pass successfully the rugged Signal Corps Laboratories environmental testing for military equipment. It was used during the invasion of Normandy to send photographs across the English Channel for directing artillery fire. In the China-Burma war theater, one of the FX-1Bs was jettisoned from an airplane. The case was severely damaged, but after replacement of a small casting by a TFC technician, it worked perfectly.

Another application of the FX-1B was sending up-to-date weather maps from Washington, D.C., for the service that ferried warplanes to Europe via Presque Isle, Maine; Gander, Newfoundland; Goose Bay, Labrador; and Reykjavik, Iceland. Only a very small portion of a weather chart could be sent at a time because of the 7- × 8.5-in. picture size. International standards for weather map fax transmission were established one day when this problem motivated two men to devise the solution. After struggling for months with the limitation, Air Force Sergeant Chuck Halbrooks added "modified" to an order for FX-1Bs and slipped it in with other papers awaiting signature. He then visited TFC and told Cooley he would soon receive this order.

Figure A.9 World War II facsimile receiver.

Halbrooks and Cooley quickly altered the design. The drum diameter was increased from 2.75 to 6 in., using 6-in. aluminum tubing, which was available without special order. This gave an 18.85-in. circumference for a usable copy width of 18 in. The drum length was increased to 12 in. The sending rate was increased by 50%. The 96 lines/in. leadscrew was retained. The new design worked very well and was standardized by the military, with orders eventually placed for more than 1000 units.

Halbrooks paid for his rash action by being transferred to duty in the Far East, but the Air Force had a much needed weather fax unit. The U.S. Air Force use of facsimile for weather map transmission during World War II had set the worldwide standards for weather facsimile. The CCITT had adopted somewhat different standards, but users abandoned them for those set at TFC. After the war, networks were set up for broadcast of facsimile weather charts over telephone lines and by HF radio.

Although production stopped on most military equipment at the end of World War II, the Army, Navy, Air Force, and the Weather Bureau needed many more Weatherfax units. Associated Press needed light-weight portable Wirephoto fax units similar to the FX-1B. In the next few years new facsimile equipments such as Weatherfax, Stenafax, Policefax, Pressfax, Messagefax, and many other types of specialized units were designed and manufactured. Faced with an expanding need for the TFC capabilities, Sulzberger abandoned his plan for closing down the facsimile operation, and kept it for another fourteen years until Litton Industries bought it and took over its operation. As the AP telephoto network developed, the large size of the AT&T design was found limiting. After a competing portable facsimile newsphoto system had been developed for the *New York Times,* arrangements were eventually made to procure portable units from the Times Facsimile Corporation. The facsimile receivers operated in a darkroom at the newspaper offices.

A facsimile edition of the *New York Times* was a journalistic milestone in 1956. A 10-page edition was sent from the *Times* offices in New York to San Francisco and distributed to the delegates at the Republican National Convention. Figure A.10 shows the transmitting room during the operation.

A special wideband 480-kHz channel provided by AT&T carried the facsimile signals for the one-week duration of the experiment. The *Times* was printed there from the full-page facsimile negatives. The quality of the paper was such that few delegates realized they were looking at a facsimile reproduction. The 200 lines/in. facsimile equipment, specially designed for the experiment, was the first fax that would send a full newspaper page at a time. Two full pages were mounted side by side on the same drum. In an earlier experiment in April 1945, the *Times* had published a 4-page edition for the United Nations conference at San Francisco using AP Wirephoto units to send a half page at a time with much lower resolution of 100 lines/in.

Based on this Pressfax equipment, a much higher resolution system was made for the *Wall Street Journal.* They built a new printing plant without typesetting capabilities in Riverside, California, near Los Angeles. A television channel from San

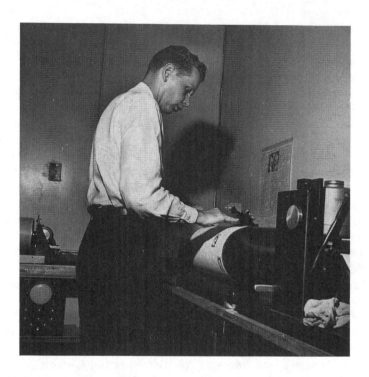

Figure A.10 First Pressfax newspaper.

Francisco connected the transmitter there to the receiver in Riverside. Functioning as replacements for typesetting, the Pressfax receivers produced full-page negatives so sharp (1000 lines/in.) that even their own technicians found it impossible to distinguish the papers printed in Riverside from those printed in San Francisco.

Today, newspapers and magazines are printed in plants that are thousands of miles away from the place where the pages are composed. High-speed, high-resolution facsimile units can send pages up to 22 × 28 in. (two full-sized newspaper pages) over wideband satellite or land lines. Both analog types and digital types of facsimile units are in use. Some units require a T-1 1.34-Mb or a T-2 6.34-Mb channel. Resolutions of 800 to 1000 lines/in. are commonly used, but 1800 lines/ in. and higher are available. The facsimile recording is made on a film negative or directly on a printing plate. The *Wall Street Journal, New York Times, USA Today,* and other newspapers send to many different printing plants via direct satellite broadcast. A satellite receiving station is located at each printing plant. *USA Today* covers the United States with 32 printing plants and has additional plants overseas. Color pages are sent by making three or four transmissions of the original color page using color separation filters.

Other office facsimile equipments were designed and manufactured in the United States, England, France, Germany, and Japan. At first, these were incompatible analog facsimile units that operated on different standards. Each manufacturer touted the advantages of its design and did not want compatibility because it would provide competition for its customers. Private telephone lines were used, because fax use of the regular switched telephone network was still limited to newspaper companies and certain government services. Most businesses either did not know facsimile existed or saw no use for it.

In the early 1960s, the Electronics Industry Association (EIA) established a technical committee TR-29 on facsimile equipment and systems. At its meetings the engineers were restricted by their companies from agreeing to a fixed set of specifications with normal tolerances because it would mean their designs would have to be changed. It took until October 1966 before EIA Standard RS-328, Message Facsimile Equipment for Operation on Switched Voice Facilities Using Data Communication Equipment, was published. This was the first U.S. "standard" on office type of fax. The following is quoted from RS-328:

> Each manufacturer has designed his facsimile equipment used for message communications to fit the requirements of his customers and the natural characteristics of the types of mechanisms employed when operating on a private line basis. These same equipments were initially used when operation of facsimile equipments on a regular telephone call basis became available. Operation between some of these equipments was not possible due to differences in the facsimile equipments. This Standard specifies machine characteristics which will ensure interoperation.

Using this standard, the received copy might be stretched from the original size or have parts near the edge of the page missing, but for the first time, diverse fax units could communicate. Each manufacturer stayed within the wide tolerances required to get the "standard," but didn't convert to the "recommended for eventual standard" items. Obviously, there was an acute need for a facsimile standard to a single set of performance specifications instead of a low grade of interoperability.

Compatibility improved as companies like Magnavox used the EIA-recommended fax equipment specifications on new equipment designs. Due to the marketing of the Magnavox units through Xerox, these standards were kept when Xerox started manufacture of their own units. Other companies such as Graphic Sciences and 3-M kept their own different standards even after the CCITT Group 1 facsimile standard was adopted.

A.4 CONNECTION TO THE PSTN

In early 1963, authorization was granted to send facsimile over the public switched telephone network (PSTN) using a facsimile coupling device with a special analog modem. Bell System Data Set 602A, connected between the fax machine and the PSTN, provided protection of the telephone system from noncompatible signals and dangerous voltages the customer might unwittingly send. The fax machine interface included 0- to 7-V dc analog baseband fax signals. The 602A converted the baseband fax signal into 1500- to 2500-Hz audio frequency shift tones sent over the telephone line (PSTN) to the receiving 602A and converted back to 0 to 7 V for the facsimile receiver. Although the Bell System modem worked quite well, it was not liked. Manufacturers had to change the fax machine design to bypass their own built-in modulator and provide a new interface to send fax over the PSTN instead of expensive private telephone lines.

Radio amateurs, called ham radio operators, had long used "phone patches" to connect occasional telephone calls to a foreign country. This unauthorized use of the AT&T lines had been tolerated, but, when a man named Carter who owned a small mobile radio communications operation, took on the giant AT&T to extend regular telephone calls through his mobile radio equipment, no one thought he had a chance. Connecting any "foreign equipment" to the telephone network had been vigorously and successfully defended by AT&T, but they lost this one and a whole new era of telecommunication began.

With the Carterphone decision in 1967, fax machines and other terminals could use the PSTN. Acoustic or inductive coupling connected the signals through a regular telephone handset. Electrical connection to the telephone network was not allowed. The fax manufacturers then used acoustic coupling, avoiding the Bell System analog modem, even though acoustic coupling had some problems with room noise and distortion caused by the carbon granules of the telephone transmitter. Bell System issued Technical Reference PUB 41803 in November 1968, Acoustic and Inductive Coupling for Data and Voice Transmission. Most fax machine manufacturers furnished acoustic couplers and abandoned the more expensive 602A.

Finally, in July 1969, the fax machine could electrically connect its signals to the PSTN, but only through a telephone-company-provided device that isolated and protected the telephone network. Bell System practices required use of a *data access arrangement* later known as *data coupler CBS*. The room noises and other distortions to the fax signal were eliminated, but the customer still had no direct access to the telephone wires. Modulating and demodulating functions were performed by the customer's equipment, but the Bell System retained responsibility for network protection, including network control signaling. The fax machine could originate a call (equivalent to lifting a telephone handset from its cradle), dial, and automatically answer a call (equivalent to lifting a telephone handset from its cradle in response to ringing) or terminate a call (equivalent to hanging up). The CBS controlled the maximum signal power that could be sent on the PSTN. It also provided network control signaling (telephone line isolation, a line-holding path for dc supervision, ring detection, customer's off-hook control, and a means for transmitting customer-originated dial pulses), surge and hazardous voltage protection, longitudinal imbalance protection, and remote test features.

In the automatic answer mode, the customer's fax machine provided the logic necessary to answer a call. The CBS coupler detected the incoming ringing signal, indicating this to the terminal on the ring indicator (RI) interface lead. To answer the call and to trip ringing, the customer's terminal turned ON the coupler off-hook (OH) lead. If not already turned ON, the customer's terminal then turned ON the data mode (DA) lead. After a 1- to 3-s interval to allow for proper registration of the call by automatic message accounting equipment at the central office, the transmission path (DT and DR) was cut through, the CCT interface lead turned ON, and data transmission began.

In June 1978, the Federal Communications Commission (FCC) issued Part 68 regulations for direct electrical connection of fax machines and other devices to the PSTN. Before connection is allowed, the equipment is tested for compliance with FCC Part 68 and assigned a registration number by the FCC. Part 68 requirements are about the same as the Bell System specifications for protection of the public telephone network. The ringing signal (between tip and ring) for an incoming call operates a relay or logic through an optical isolator to start the fax machine receiving protocol. Fax signals are coupled through a transformer that provides protective isolation of high voltages, but can pass dc currents of more than 100 mA through the winding connected to the telephone line. Customer-supplied electronic circuitry still could not be connected directly to the telephone line. At first, the only FCC approved couplers were in a self-contained box available from companies that manufactured CBS couplers for the telephone companies. Later, fax machine manufacturers designed their own equipment for meeting FCC regulations with the coupler inside the fax machine. For the first time, the fax machine connected directly to the telephone line by plugging into a standard RJ-11 telephone jack like a regular telephone.

When the laser became a reality, a laserphoto recorder was developed for AP. This fax machine did not require a darkroom and eventually replaced the fax recorders built by Times Facsimile Corporation. Today, out-of-town pictures printed in newspapers are sent by facsimile from almost any place in the world. Thousands of newspapers receive these pictures at the same time. Associated Press now uses a direct-broadcast satellite channel operating at 9.6 kb/s. Resolution is 170 lines/in. for an 8- × 10-in. picture, sent in 2 or 3 min. Eight bits are sent per pixel, for 256 gray-scale shades. A helium-neon laser spot is swept across the recording paper by a mirror galvanometer, exposing dry silver photographic paper. A thermal unit inside the fax machine fixes and develops the image.

Both Reuters and United Press International now have laser newsphoto recorders similar to the AP recorder. Probably some of the earlier design UPI electrostatic recorders are still in service. Each recorded pixel is first written with a full width charge corresponding to black over a rhombic-shaped area the height of the recording line. A single stylus mounted on a belt moves across the page to apply the recording charge pattern. If this pixel is black, nothing more is done. For half gray, the charge is neutralized over half the spot width or for white, over the entire spot. The lightest gray will be a bar that is 1/64th the width of the pixel. At normal viewing distances, it is difficult to tell the difference between the fax recording and a photographic print.

An electronic picture desk at some newspaper offices stores the pictures in memory as they are received from the newsphoto network. The editor can then view them on a CRT screen and select those desired. These pictures are edited electronically in the picture desk and only those selected need be printed for use in the newspaper.

A.5 GROUP 1 FACSIMILE

Standards for Group 1 made possible the consideration of more generalized business use of fax. Group 1 provided compatibility between fax units outside North America, but those in North America were different and could not communicate with Group 1 fax units. Most of the specifications were the same, except for the black and white frequencies, as shown in Table A.1.

The U.S. engineers thought that 2400-Hz black and 1500-Hz white worked better over their phone lines than the CCITT 2100-Hz black and 1300-Hz white of Group 1. The U.S. salespeople mistakenly called the U.S. fax Group 1. Although the Group 1 units generally worked better than the earlier office fax units, they were still unreliable 6 min/page analog units, which gave fuzzy copy and required much manual attention. Many units offered an optional mode that moved the original page through in 4 min instead of 6 min. This produced lower resolution in the paper feed direction for even lower copy quality. This option was thus a poor attempt to increase the transmission speed.

Table A.1
CCITT Group 1 and Group 2 Fax

	Group 1	AM.6M	Group2
Lines per minute	180	180	360
Modulation	FM	FM	VSB AM/PM[a]
Carrier frequency			2100 ± 10 Hz
White signal	1300 Hz	1500	Maximum carrier
Black signal	2100 Hz	2400	26 dB minimum lower

[a]VSB is vestigial sideband; PM is phase modulation.

The EIA TR-29 standards work was still not a team effort to develop a standard that all companies would follow, insofar as the fax engineer from each company defended its own company's fax machine designs. The fax machines were unable to communicate very well with those from another company, and none was compatible with European designs. European countries dominated the CCITT (and CCIR) and U.S. participation in international fax standardization was practically nonexistent. Both groups thought their designs were correct and the others were wrong. The U.S. fax machine manufacturers thought that the European PTTs had the attitude that if the United States doesn't play the game their way, it can't use their telephone circuits.

The U.S. fax machines still had differences that distorted the received copy shape or created operational problems between machines of different manufacturers. The TR-29 chair, Ken McConnell, requested that all U.S. fax machine companies participate in TR-29 in order to develop meaningful standards. Later, compatibility between these fax machines improved and some 6-min fax machines were even made to work with the CCITT Group 1 standard by throwing a switch. Finally, some U.S. fax companies went to the CCITT meetings as private companies because there was no channel set up to forward their ideas as a U.S. position.

A.6 GROUP 2 FACSIMILE

Users who had accepted the quality of Group 1 needed a faster system. Both Xerox and Graphic Sciences developed and marketed new fax units capable of 3 min/page instead of 6, or 2 min/page instead of 4 min. Xerox had a frequency modulation (FM) scheme and Graphic Sciences had an amplitude modulation (AM) scheme. The AM system had the capability to send gray scale while the FM system did not. Before CCITT Group 2 standards existed, the two competing 3 min/page systems were proposed to the CCITT. The CCITT agreed that comparison tests should be made to determine the better system. The U.K. Post Office did the evaluation by using black-white copy, testing many different lines, and switching between the two systems on each call. The AM system gave somewhat better results overall and was selected for Group 2. The 3-min fax equipment already in service was not compatible with the new CCITT standard. The new Group 2 standard, based on 3-min machine designs that had a customer performance record, was a definite improvement. Adoption of the standard by the CCITT and worldwide implementation opened the door to universal fax machines. It provided the impetus for pursuing a standard for digital fax. The teamwork between the TR-29, BFICC, and engineers from other countries was excellent and resulted in a good standard. Because the few digital fax machines operating on private standards were very complex and expensive, it was expected that Group 2 would be the dominant fax standard for many years.

The Japanese established efficient facsimile manufacturing facilities that, combined with low labor costs, allowed them to take over the design and manufacture of most facsimile equipment. CCITT standards opened up worldwide markets for the Japanese equipment. The much lower price of Group 2 fax units allowed them to compete favorably against the expensive private-standard digital facsimile units, which became available in 1974. Even after the Group 3 standards existed, the Group 2 price advantage remained for a few years. However, digital fax was showing its worth in higher speed and better quality fax copies for those customers who could afford expensive machines that worked only with others from the same manufacturer. The same engineering committees that successfully developed Group 2 fax machine standards set to work on Group 3 standards.

A.7 BACKGROUND OF DIGITAL FACSIMILE

The earliest digital fax units used the adaptive run-length coding algorithm patented by Donald Weber. This coding removes redundancy from the page being sent and thus shortens the transmission time. A digital code word represents the number of successive white picture elements along the scanning line before the next black pixel. The next code word represents the number of black pixels following the white run. Because the code words are usually much shorter than the number of pixels, it takes fewer bits to send the page. Single-line coding under this patent was used in Dacom's Rapifax 100. A three-line technique under the same patent is used for coding newspaper pages for fax transmission.

The digital modem for the Rapifax 100 was the first modern LSI high-speed modem to be used successfully on regular telephone lines (PSTN). The modem itself further reduced transmission time by coding 4 bits at a time, requiring only 1200 baud (changes per second of the signal state on the telephone line) to send 4800 b/s.

A.8 DEVELOPMENT OF THE GROUP 3 STANDARD

Standards for fax machines made in the United States were developed by the EIA. The following information from the TR-29 committee meeting minutes shows some of the contributions it made to the CCITT Group 3 facsimile recommendations:

January 1975: The CCITT planned for the Group 3 specification to be generated by French and English postal services and manufacturers. Primary concern for TR-29 was the generation of G3 subminute digital fax machine standards.

June 1975: A completely new scheme was proposed for G1, G2, and G3, involving binary signaling for handshaking between sending and receiving fax machines as opposed to the tonal technique currently under CCITT consideration.

August 1975: Planned binary signaling with the V.21 (or V.23) modem for facsimile handshake.

September 1975: It was agreed that the receiver should tell its option capabilities to the transmitter following the CED answer tone as proposed by Graphic Sciences.

October 1975: A Special Rapporteur's Group on T.4 recommended rates up to 9.6 kb/s for Group 3. Most of the Group 3 standard was developed between TR-29 and the British Post Office, with cooperation from England, France, Germany, Japan, and other countries [3].

September 1976: Some proposals by other groups "might be interpreted as requiring an external modem. EIA members plan to provide the V.27$_{ter}$ modulation system internal to the machines. To do otherwise would be difficult economically and technically in light of T.4 requirements."

During the generation of the Group 3 standard, many long day and evening sessions took place at the CCITT meetings in Geneva. Each country had its concerns and many proposals were made to add protective details to the standard. The chair of CCITT Study Group XIV was conscious of the wrangling that might occur. He used a slogan that was very successful in preventing undue complexity: "If in doubt, leave it out." The Germans wouldn't allow any modem to be connected to their lines unless it was furnished by the FTZ. The French wanted to limit equipment connected to their lines to fax machines made in France. One of the most important tasks in developing the Group 3 fax standards was selection of a coding scheme to reduce the number of uncoded bits per page from about two million to 400,000 or less, allowing faster transmission of fax pages. This process is called *redundancy reduction* or *source encoding*.

Concern was expressed in the CCITT about selecting a code that would not require royalty payments. The modified Huffman code was considered because it was a very efficient run-length code and had no active patent. Huffman coding requires a separate code word for each white or black run length encountered. The code words are assigned with the shortest length words for the run lengths that occur most often. The number of pels per scan line was 1728 using the CCD scanner chips then available. This meant 3456 code words because the run-length statistics are different for black runs and white runs. Bob Krallinger, then chair of TR-29, worked out a modified Huffman system that greatly reduced the number of code words by coding each run as two words. All run lengths up to 1728 were reduced to only 92 code words using the MH code tables. This system was much more easily implemented. To select good code tables, the probability of each run length needed to be determined. Eight test images were selected by the CCITT as representative of documents that might be sent for business use of fax. These were scanned 10 to 20 times with histograms made of each run length. The multiple scanning reduced the variation in run lengths on a given page as caused by page placement and skew. Even a small skew reduces some of the white run lengths between printed lines.

After the modified Huffman code was accepted, it became evident that most of the fax machine manufacturers planned to furnish their own private two-dimensional code to achieve faster transmission rates. Private codes were allowed on a nonstandard provision of T.30, but these codes worked only between machines from the same manufacturer. Each company claimed a superior code, but when comparison tests were run, they only varied a few percent in transmission time per page. A relative address code was advocated for a standard option by the Japanese. In January 1987, KDD agreed to furnish the read code patent free if accepted as a standard. Fortunately, international cooperation prevailed again. The code was studied by the British Post Office and Harry Robinson came up with the modified read code, which was adopted by the CCITT.

One of the sticking points in the Group 3 standard was incorporation of an escape code, NSF, allowing fax machines from the same manufacturer to operate with any private enhancement they desired as long as the feature did not interfere with communication with a standard Group 3 machine. The TR-29 fax committee argued that NSF was essential to prevent freezing of the standard and making it prematurely obsolete. After many arguments, NSF was finally put into the specification, allowing undocumented private codes. It has allowed the manufacturers to invest development money for improvements in the Group 3 standard. Some of the best NSF ideas were later incorporated into the Group 3 standard as a recognized option, allowing use between fax machines of different manufacture.

In 1980 the first Group 3 fax machines cost three or four times as much as Group 2 fax machines, but over the next few years the price differential between Groups 2 and 3 diminished rapidly. The Group 3 standard proved far superior and, finally, manufacture of the Group 2 machines slowed down and stopped. In 1980 the CCITT adopted a standard for teletex, designed as a high-speed, high-technology replacement for telex. Facsimile was not taken seriously by many because it was an "inefficient" way to send text, requiring 10 times as much data to be sent for the same message. Yet, teletex has been a dismal failure while Group 3 fax has been almost unbelievably successful. Table A.2 shows technical progress in facsimile and some other communication systems since the first fax unit was conceived. There are too many other developments and contributors to the facsimile art to mention them all.

Table A.2
Facsimile Technical Progress 1843–1988

1843	First facsimile, Bain—Pendulum Type
1844	Telegraph, Morse
1850	Rotating drum, Bakewell—England
1865	First commercial fax, Caselli
1876	Telephone, Bell

Table A.2 (cont'd)

1902	Optical scan, Dr. Korn—Germany
1906	News photo service, Dr. Korn—Munich to Berlin
1907	Vacuum tube (Audion), DeForrest
1915	Telephone repeaters—long distance
1917	Teletype—AT&T
	Photofax in US—AT&T, RCA, and WU
1924	Bell 3002 envelope delay specs—VSB
1926	RCA transatlantic newsphoto service by radio
1928	Photo recording without optics, Cooley
1934	Associated Press Photofax News Picture Service
1936	Drum and helix recorder—electrolytic paper, Dr. Hogan
1936	Drum and helix recorder—carbon paper, RCA—Artzt
1936	Dry direct recording paper, Western Union—Teledeltos
1936	*New York Times* manufactures fax, Times Facsimile—Cooley
1943	Signal Corps Fax FX-1B, Times Facsimile
1943	Timefax—direct recording dry paper
1945	TV—regular broadcast in USA
1948	Western Union Deskfax—40,000 units
1956	Acoustic coupling on PSTN lines in USA
1958	Stewart-Warner Datafax
1959	Telautograph Quickfax
1960	EIA Committee TR-29 starts standard for fax
1965	EIA issues fax standard RS-328
	Magnavox Telecopier—Xerox markets it
1965	first US large-production office fax
1967	"Carterphone" decision—direct connection to PSTN
1967	Xerox manufactures fax
1967	DEX 1—graphic sciences fax
1968	CCITT Group 1 fax recommendation
1968	Scanatron message fax
1969	Digital fax starts, DACOM—Weber run length code
1970	Xerox 400
1972	3M enters fax market—VRC 600
	Manufactured by MGCS (Matsushita)
1973	3M 603—VSI/MGCS KD-211
1974	RapiFax 100 digital fax—DACOM
1974	QWIP 1000—Exxon
1974	Xerox 410
1974	CCITT Group 1 fax recommendation
1975	Xerox 200
1975	100,000 fax units in USA
1976	QWIP 1200
1976	CCITT Group 2 recommendation
1976	CCITT Starts Group 3 fax standards
1977	3M 9600—"Near Group 3" digital fax
1978	Panafax UF-20 and UF-320 digital fax

1978	DEX 5100 "Near Group 3" digital fax
	Southern Pacific—DMS 2000 "Near Group 3" digital fax
1979	Manufactured by Hitachi
	Telautograph Omnifax "Near Group 3" digital fax
1979	Manufactured by OKI—Thermal Recording
1979	NEC 6200 "Near Group 3" digital fax
1980	CCITT Group 3 recommendation
1984	CCITT Group 4 recommendation
1988	Error-correction mode
1988	Small-format (A5 and A6) Group 3
1991	V.17 14.4 KB/S modem, Group 3
1991	MMR Coding with Error-correction mode, Group 3

A.9 RADIO FACSIMILE

In 1910, Korn obtained German Patent No. 233,288 for a rather primitive method for sending fax by radio. Contact scanning was proposed to short out part of the antenna coil of a radio transmitter, changing the amplitude and frequency of the radio signal. This was probably not a practical system. It was in 1922 that Korn successfully transmitted photographs by radio from Munich to Rome and from Rome to Bar Harbor, Maine.

In 1924 RCA demonstrated transatlantic radiophoto transmission from New York to London and back again. The system was offered commercially as a radiophoto service two years later, and expanded into key cities throughout the world. In 1927 the RCA radiophoto was not well known, as shown in this quote from a Minneapolis newspaper. Pictures showed Lindbergh being greeted by Myron T. Herrich, our ambassador to France, and a picture of "Lindy" proudly standing beside his little silver plane, *The Spirit of St. Louis,* with the following headline and story: "One Triumph of Science Is Used to Tell of Another. The transmission of pictures by radio, the most recent major triumph of science, was employed to rush these pictures to the U.S.A. from Paris. They were sent by airplane from Paris to London, then sent by radio to New York, then relayed westward over telephone wires!"

Radio broadcast to the home has been tried many times. Of the systems tried, some were technical successes, but none ever paid for its costs. AM radio stations tried sending fax broadcasts from midnight to 6 A.M. when the station normally closed for the night. The Rayphoto system built by inventor Austin G. Cooley in 1926 had a drum and leadscrew for feeding a stylus needle along the surface of a drum as it rotated. The recording was made on photographic paper with light from a spark at the stylus exposing the paper. The fax machine used a wind-up record player to drive the recording mechanism.

In the 1930s fax newspapers were broadcast by WLW in Cincinnati, Ohio. A pendulum recorder was used.

Charles Young at RCA Laboratories developed a carbon paper recorder for recording on white paper. A pretuned radio receiver was set to the channel and a clock turned the equipment on at the time of broadcast. Similar equipment was adapted for shipboard use and weather maps were broadcast to a number of ships during their transatlantic crossings.

In the 1940s the FCC established standards for facsimile radio broadcast on FM radio channels. An 8.5- × 11-in. page was sent in about 3.5 min. John V. L. Hogan's company Radio Inventions helped to establish the service. Recording was on a roll of wet electrolytic paper using a helix and blade mechanism. Newspapers involved in this program included *The New York Times* (WQXR-FM), *The Miami Herald* (WQAM-FM), *The Philadelphia Inquirer* (WFIL-FM), *The Atlanta Journal* (WSB), and the Columbia Broadcasting System. See Chapter 11 for information on Japanese home fax broadcasts.

In 1947, broadcast of full-size weather maps started at W2XIK (later KE2XER) owned by Times Facsimile Corporation. Permission was obtained from the FCC to broadcast current weather charts as they were received on a wire line weather network from the Weather Bureau in Suitland, Maryland. Broadcasts were made five days a week simultaneously on three HF radio channels. Subcarrier FM was used initially, but the system was later replaced by frequency shift of the radio-frequency carrier. Weather maps and weather satellite photos are still being broadcast today using similar standards. Reception of current weather maps and pictures is possible on PCs using a single-sideband radio receiver and an adapter card. The pictures can be viewed on the screen or printed out. At least two companies sell kits for receiving this data.

REFERENCES

[1]   "Morse 'picture frame' instrument," *Western Union Technical Rev.* Volume 19, No. 4, October 1965, p. 163.

[2]   Service Bulletins, "Fork oscillator," Times Facsimile Corporation, Vol. 5, No. 1, pp. 22–23.

[3]   TR-29 minutes, Denver meeting, August 1977.

Appendix 2
Update on CCITT Fax Standards

After the first printing of the second edition of this book, CCITT Study Group VIII, Terminal Equipment and Protocols for Telematic Services, met in Geneva between April 22 and 30, 1992 and completed the actions for many new features. These changes, plus an update of changes from the October 16–25, 1991 session, are covered in this chapter. Some changes will not be effective until after the Plenary Assembly in March 1993.

A2.1 CCITT RECOMMENDATIONS APPROVED AT THE OCTOBER 1991 STUDY GROUP VIII MEETING

The following recommendations were approved:

T.90—Characteristics and Protocols for Terminals for Telematic Services in ISDN (changes). T.90 outlines the procedures for Telematic Services usage over the ISDN.

T.410 series—Open Document Architecture (ODA) and Interchange Format— (Color addendum amendments). This covers color processes that could be used in Group 3 and Group 4 fax machines if Study Group VIII approves color fax in the future.

A2.2 CCITT RECOMMENDATIONS APPROVED AT THE APRIL 1992 STUDY GROUP VIII MEETING

In addition, the following fax-related new or revised recommendations were approved for Resolution 2 accelerated procedures. Accelerated procedures balloting takes about 6 more weeks before the recommendations are in effect.

T.4 Annex C—File Transfer Using Group 3 Fax Protocols. File Transfer is an optional Group 3 fax feature that permits transmission of any data file with or without of 7.8 1/mm (198.12/in) versus 200 dpi is a difference of .94%. At the November CCITT meeting in Tokyo it was decided that 100 by 200 dots per inch is equivalent to the standard Group 3 fax resolution of 8 by 3.85 lines per millimeter. (See Table 3.6.)

Annex A—Optional error correcting mode (Blue Book).

Annex B—Optional error limiting mode (Blue Book).

Annex C—File Transfer Using Group 3 Fax Protocols. File Transfer is an optional Group 3 fax feature that permits transmission of any data file with or without additional information concerning the file. The content of the data file may be of any type of coding. Because the files must be reliably transferred, the use of *Error Correction Mode* (T.4, Annex A) is mandatory. Any of four transfer modes may be used.

1. *Basic Transfer Mode (BTM)*—BTM provides the Group 3 user with a means to exchange files of any kind (e.g., binary files, word processor native format documents, bitmaps, etc.) without any additional information.
2. *Document Transfer Mode (DTM)*—DTM provides the Group 3 user with a means to exchange files of any kind with additional information regarding the file (e.g. file name, file type, file coding, etc.). On the receiving side, it can either be handled by automatic processing or read by the user.
3. *Binary File Transfer (BFT)*—BFT provides the Group 3 user with a means to exchange files of any kind with additional information included in a file description and automatically processed at the receiving side. (See Recommendation T.30 Annex B.) The BFT protocol is described in Recommendation T.434.
4. *Edifact Transfer (EDI)*—EDI provides the Group 3 user with a means to exchange Edifact files coded according to ISO/IEC 9735 [4] rules. To transfer Edifact files, there is no need for a file description.

Annex D—Optional Character Mode of Group 3. Character mode is an optional Group 3 feature that permits transmission of character-coded documents by means of the T.30 protocol. Because the files must be reliably transferred, the use of *Error Correction Mode* (T.4, Annex A) is mandatory. In addition, Appendix II—Repertoire of Box-Drawing Characters, has been added.

Annex E—Optional Mixed Mode 1 (MM1) for Group 3. MM1 allows pages containing both character-coded and facsimile-coded information to be transferred between compatible apparatus. The use of the standardized *Error Correction Mode* (T.4, Annex A) and T.30, Annex A is mandatory with MM1. The page is divided into slices horizontally across the page,each slice containing either facsimile—or character-coded information, but not both.

Annex F—Call Selection.

Annex G—Group 3, 64 kb/s opertion over the ISDN. (See T.30, Annex C.)

A2.2 T.30—PROCEDURES FOR DOCUMENT FACSIMILE TRANSMISSION IN THE GENERAL SWITCHED TELEPHONE NETWORK

Password, Subaddressing, and Selective Polling of Group 3

Password (PWD). This optional signal indicates that the following FIF information is a password for the polling mode. It may be used to provide additional security to the facsimile procedure. PWD is sent if bit 50 in DIS is set. Format: 1000 0011. The facsimile information field of the PWD signal shall consist of 20 numeric digits. The least significant bit of the least significant digit shall be the first bit transmitted.

Selective Polling (SEP). This optional signal indicates that the following FIF information is a subaddress for the polling mode. Format:1000 0101. It may be used to indicate that a specific document shall be polled at the called side. SEP is sent if bit 47 in DIS is set. The facsimile information field of the SEP signal shall consist of 20 numeric digits. The least significant bit of the least significant digit shall be the first bit transmitted.

Subaddress (SUB). This optional signal indicates that the following FIF information is a subaddress in the called subscribers domain. Format: X100 001. It may be used to provide additional routing information in the facsimile procedure. SUB is sent if bit 49 in DIS/DTC is set. The facsimile information field of the SUB signal shall consist of 20 numeric digits. The least significant bit to the least significant digit shall be the first bit transmitted.

Additional DIS/DTC Bit Assignments of Group 3. The bit assignments for DIS/DTC as shown in Table 3.6 have been extended to allow the many new optional Group 3 fax features to be invoked. If Group 3 fax machines do not have these options, communication will proceed in a method that both fax machines have available. (See Table 3.6.)

Annex A Procedure for Document Facsimile Transmission in the General Switched Telephone Network Incorporating Error Correction (Blue Book).

Annex B Binary File Transfer (BFT). See T.4 Annex C, T.434, and para. 3.12.

Annex C—Group 3, 64 kb/s operation over the ISDN. A new 64-kb/s option for Group 3 fax operation on the public digital networks, such as the ISDN, uses full duplex or half duplex communication. The protocol employs the *Error Correction Mode* standardized option of Group 3 fax and is considerably simplified compared with the protocols used by Group 4 fax. Sending or receiving fax documents from another G3–64 fax machine is at 64 kb/s using one of the ISDN B channels. For communicating with a standard Group 4 Class 1 fax machine on the PSTN, the ISDN 3.1 Bearer Service is requested and the internal fax modem is used.

A2.3 OTHER NEW OR MODIFIED CCITT RECOMMENDATIONS AFFECTING GROUP 3 FAX

T.50—International Reference Alphabet (revised)

T.51—Coded Character Sets for Telematic Services (revised)

T.52—Non-Latin Character Sets for Telematic Services (revised)

T.60—Terminal Equipment for Use in the Teletex Service (revised)

T.61—Character Repertoire and Coded Character Sets for the International Teletex Service (revised)

T.80—Common Components for Image Compression and Communication: Basic Principles (new)

T.81—Digital Compression and Coding of Continuous-tone Still Images (new)

T.82—Digital Compression and Coding of Bi-Level Still Images (new)

T.90—Characteristics and Protocols for Terminals for Telematic Services in ISDN (revised).

This document outlines the procedures for Telematic Services usage over the ISDN.

T.122—Multipoint Communications Service (MCUS) (new)

T.123—Audio Visual Protocol Stack for Terminals and MCUS (new)

T.124—Generic Conference Control Application for Audiovisual Conferencing and MCUS (new)

T.410 series—Open Document Architecture (ODA) and Interchange Format—(Color addendum amendments)

This document covers color processes that could be used in Group 3 and Group 4 fax machines if Study Group VIII approves color fax in the future.

T.412—Open Document Architecture (ODA) and Interchange Format—Document Structures (ODL and Streams addenda)

T.417—Open Document Architecture (ODA) and Interchange Format—Raster Graphics Content Architectures (amendment to support additional bitmapping)

T.431—Document Transfer and Manipulation (DTAM)—Services and Protocols— Introduction and General Principles (revised)

T.432—Document Transfer and Manipulation (DTAM)—Services and Protocols— Service Definition (revised)

T.433—Document Transfer and Manipulation (DTAM)—Services and Protocols— Protocol Specification (revised)

T.434—Binary File Transfer (BFT) Protocol for the Telematic Services (new)

This document contains the protocol and the technical description for BFT. See chapter 3, section 3.12. Annex C of T.4 provides the technical details for file transfer within the Group 3 environment. Annex B of T.30 provides the optional File Diagnostic Message, while Appendix VI to T.30 provides the procedures for BFT with examples of the protocol.

T.501—Document Application Profile MM for the Interchange of Formatted Mixed Mode Documents (revised)

T.503—Document Application Profile for the Interchange of Group 4 Facsimile Documents (new)

T.505—Processable Mode (new)

T.506—Document Application Profile PM-36 for the Interchange of Enhanced Mixed Content Documents in Processable and Formatted Forms (new)

T.510—General Overview of the T.510 Series (new)

T.521—Communication Application Profile BT/O for Document Bulk Transfer Based on the Session Service (revised, according to the rules defined in T.62bis)

T.522—Communication Application Profile BT1 for Document Bulk Transfer (revised)

T.563—Terminal Characteristics for Group 4 Facsimile Apparatus (revised)

T.565—Terminal Characteristics for the Telematic Transfer Within the Facsimile Group 4 and Teletex Service (new)

T.611—Programmable Communication Interface (PCI) APLI/COM for Facsimile Group 3, Facsimile Group 4, Teletex and Telex Service (new)

A.2.4 CCITT QUESTIONS FOR THE NEXT STUDY PERIOD

The following list is intended to direct the activity of Study Group VIII for the XIth Plenary Period of 1993 through 1996. These questions will be finalized at the next meeting in April 1993.

Title	*New*	*Old Question*
A APPLICOM	X	
B Syntax Videotext		14
C ODA		27
D Color	X	
E Group 3 Fax		18
F Facsimile Test Chart and Test Documents		
G Videotex Protocol		15

Glossary of Facsimile Terms

AM-PM-VSB — Vestigial sideband amplitude modulation-phase modulation such as used for CCITT Group 2 facsimile.

Analog Facsimile — That form of facsimile which uses *analog facsimile signals* between the *facsimile transmitter* and the *facsimile receiver*. Areas of the *original* with a density between black and white may be recorded as gray shadings.

Bandwidth Compression — A technique to reduce the bandwidth needed to transmit a given amount of facsimile information in a given time or to reduce the time needed to transmit a given amount of facsimile information in a given bandwidth.

Baud — The number of changes in signal state per second in a digital signal sent by a modem. A baud may contain four or more bits as in a CCITT V.29 modem.

Binary File Transfer — An option in Group 3 facsimile that allows transmission of binary files between computers using the high speed facsimile modems and Group 3 error correction protocol.

Bit — The contraction for *binary digit*, the smallest amount of information in a binary system, a 0 or 1 condition.

Basic Measurement Unit (BMU) — A resolution unit of 25.4/1200 mm (or 1/1200 in). [This is the lowest common denominator for 300 and 400 lines/in.]

Byte — A string of eight bits used as a basic unit in a digital computer for memory storage and data processing.

CCITT — Consultative Committee on International Telegraph and Telephone. An intergovernmental advisory organization of the International Telecommunication Union, which recommends worldwide communication standards including those for *facsimile*. See Groups 1, 2, 3, and 4.

Color Facsimile System — A *facsimile* system that produces the *recorded copy* in more than one color. Typically, a full color image is produced by sending images for three primary colors.

Compatibility — Matching *facsimile transmitter* and *facsimile receiver* characteristics that permit the receiving of acceptable facsimile copy.

Compression Ratio — In *digital facsimile*, the ratio of the total bits used to represent the *original* to the total number of encoded bits.

Continuous Tone Image (Analog Gray Scale Image) — An image in which each resolvable element may be represented by one of a continuous range of tones.

Contouring — Density step lines in *recorded copy* resulting from quantization of an original image that has observable gray shadings between adjacent quantization intervals.

Cover Sheet — An optional page with addressing information, faxed before the first document page. It usually contains names of the sender, addressee, subject, comments, call-back phone number, and number of pages sent.

Digital Facsimile — That form of *facsimile* in which densities of the *original* are sampled and quantized as a digital signal for processing, transmission, or storage.

Direct Recording — That type of *recording facsimile* in which a visible *recorded copy* is produced without subsequent processing.

Document — A set of one or more pages which can be transmitted as a unit.

Electrolytic Recording — Recording with signal-controlled current through an electrolyte in the recording paper, depositing metallic ions to produce a mark.

Electronic Shading — An electronic method of compensating for variations in sensitivity of individual sensors of a sensor array or variation in illumination of copy being scanned. This may be done by correcting the analog signal from each sensor sample under control of stored digital information.

Electrosensitive Recording — Recording with an electrical signal which passes directly into the *record medium*.

Electrostatic Recording — *Recording* by means of a signal controlled electrostatic field. (Note: A toner is required to make the image visible.)

End-of-Line (EOL) — In *Group 3 digital facsimile* systems, a sequence of digital symbols introduced at the end of a scanning line to establish synchronization of decoding and for error detection.

Facsimile — The process by which a document is scanned, converted into the electrical signals, transmitted, and recorded or displayed as a copy of the *original*.

Facsimile Copy — A *recorded copy* of an *original* produced by a *facsimile recorder*.

Facsimile Receiver — The apparatus employed to translate *picture signals* from the communications channel into a *facsimile copy* of the *original*.

Facsimile Recorder — That part of the *facsimile receiver* which performs the final conversion of electrical *picture signals* to an image of the *original* on the *record medium*.

Facsimile Signal — See *Picture Signal*.

Facsimile Test Chart — A document used for evaluating the performance of a *facsimile* system.

Facsimile Transmitter — The apparatus employed to translate the *original* into *picture signals* suitable for delivery to the communication system.

Fax — An abbreviation for *facsimile*.

Fingerprint Facsimile — *Facsimile* equipment used to transmit fingerprint cards. (Note: Existing systems send 8×8-inch cards at 192 lines per inch.)

Ghost — In *analog facsimile*, a spurious image resulting from echo, envelope delay distortion, or multipath reception.

Group 1 — *Analog facsimile* equipment per CCITT Recommendation T.2. It sends an A4 or 8 1/2 $\times$ 11-inch page in 6 minutes over a voice grade telephone line using frequency modulation with 1300 Hz corresponding to white and 2100 Hz to black of the *original*. (Note: Because North American 6-minute equipment uses 1500 Hz white and 2400 Hz black, it is not compatible with *Group 1 equipment*.)

Group 2 — *Analog facsimile* equipment per CCITT Recommendation T.3. It sends an A4 or 8 1/2 $\times$ 11-inch page in 3 minutes over a voice grade telephone line using 2100-Hz AM-PM-VSB.

Group 3 — *Digital facsimile* equipment per CCITT Recommendation T.4. It sends an A4 or 8 1/2 $\times$ 11-inch page typically in one-half minute over a voice grade telephone line.

Group 4 — *Digital facsimile* equipment per CCITT Recommendations T.5 and T.6, which uses Public Data Networks and their procedures for essentially error-free reception. It may also be used on the Public Switched Telephone Network with an appropriate modulation process.

Halftone Image — An image that has been converted from a continuous tone image into a two-tone image while retaining the appearance of a continuous tone image.

Handshaking — An exchange of signals (called "control procedures") between the *facsimile transmitter* and *facsimile receiver* to verify that facsimile transmission can proceed, to determine which specifications will be used, and to verify reception of the documents sent.

HDLC — High level data link control. A synchronous protocol, with bit-oriented frames, for transferring data and control information over the data communication link.

Horizontal Resolution — The number of *picture elements* per inch (or millimeter) in the direction of *scanning* or *recording*.

Jitter (in Facsimile) — Irregular error in the position of the *recorded spot* along the recorded line. (Note: This is noticeable on the recording of a vertical line.)

K Factor (in Modified Read Coding for Group 3 Facsimile) — The number of facsimile scanning lines in a set used for coding. At the most, $K - 1$ lines are coded two-dimensionally to limit the disturbed area in the event of transmission errors. In CCITT Group 3, $K = 2$ for 3.85 lines/mm and $K = 4$ for 7.7 lines/mm. In Group 4, $K = \infty$.

Lines per Inch (or Millimeter) — The number of scanning or recording lines per unit length measured perpendicular to the direction of scanning.

Line-to-Line Correlation — The correlation of image information from scanning line to scanning line. Useful for two-dimensional coding, e.g., *modified read*.

Maximum Keying Frequency — The frequency equal to one-half the number of *picture elements* per second.

Mobile Facsimile — *Facsimile* equipment used in vehicles.

Modified Huffman (MH) Coding — A one-dimensional run length digital scheme of coding white and black runs, where the shortest length code words represent the most probable run lengths. MH is used by Group 3 facsimile.

Modified Read (MR) Coding — A two-dimensional optional digital coding scheme for Group 3 facsimile. (Note: MR provides an improved transmission speed over *modified Huffman* coding.)

Modified Modified Read (MMR) Coding — A two-dimensional coding scheme for Group 4 facsimile. (Note: MMR provides improved transmission speed over *modified read coding*.)

Newsphoto Facsimile — *Facsimile* equipment used to transmit photographs for newspaper or magazine publishing.

Original — A page which is transmitted by *facsimile*.

Pel — A *picture element* that contains only black-white information (no gray shading). See *Pixel*.

Photographic Recording — Recording by the exposure of a photosensitive surface to a signal-controlled light beam or spot. See *Electrophotographic Recording*.

Picture Element — The smallest area of the *original* sampled and represented by an electrical signal. See *Pel* and *Pixel*.

Picture Signal — A signal resulting from the *scanning* process or an electronically generated equivalent.

Pixel — A *picture element* that has more than two levels of gray scale information. See *Pel*.

Pixel Interpolation — Generation of additional unscanned *pixels* by logical comparison of nearby scanned pixels to simulate increased resolution. Interpolation may be one- or two-dimensional.

Quantizing Levels — In a *digital facsimile* system, the number of different gray steps representing a *continuous tone* image. See *Contouring*.

Record Medium — The physical medium on which the *facsimile recorder* forms an image of the *original*.

Record Sheet — The medium used to produce the *recorded copy*. The *record medium* and the *record sheet* may be identical.

Recorded Copy — A hard copy of the *original* produced by facsimile.

Recording — The process of converting the *picture signal* in a *facsimile receiver* to an image on the *record medium*. See *Direct Recording, Electrolytic Recording, Electrosensitive Recording, Electrostatic Recording, Ink Jet Recording, Magnetic Recording, Photographic Recording, Thermal Recording, and Xerographic Recording.*

Recording Spot — The image area corresponding to a *picture element* formed at the *record medium* by the *facsimile recorder*.

Redundancy Reduction — Coding for elimination of redundant information in the *picture signal* to reduce the amount of information needed for transmission or storage. (Note: The amount of *redundancy reduction* will vary with the information content of the *original*.) See *Compression Ratio*.

Resolution — A measure of capability to delineate picture detail.

Scale Factor — Ratio of m/n, where m = vertical offset, and n = horizontal offset.

Scanner — That part of the *facsimile transmitter* which systematically translates the *densities* of the *original* into a signal waveform.

Scanning — The process of successively analyzing the *densities* of the *original* according to a predetermined pattern.

Scanning Direction — Normal direction is from left to right and top to bottom of the *original*, as when reading a page of print.

Scanning Line Length — See *Total Line Length*.

Scanning Spot — The area on the *original* viewed instantaneously by the photo-sensor of the *scanner*.

Skew — (1.) The deviation of the *recorded copy* from rectangularity due to asynchronism between *scanner* and *recorder*. (2.) Angular misalignment of the *original* from the paper feed direction. (3.) Deviation of the angle of the *scanning line* or *recording line* from perpendicular to the paper path.

SMU — Scaled Measurement Unit. Basic measurement unit (BMU) × scale factor.

Soft Copy — That form of *facsimile* which displays the received image on a cathode ray tube or similar screen.

Subject Copy — See *Original*.

Synchronizing — The maintenance of the proper position of the *recording spot* while it is writing to produce an undistorted *recorded copy* of the *original*.

Thermal Recording — That type of *recording* which is produced principally by signal-controlled thermal action. (Notes: Direct *thermal recording* involves direct imaging on the *record medium*. *Thermal transfer* recording involves heat from a thermal print head transferring marking from a carbon ribbon or overlay sheet to another sheet, forming the *recorded copy*. Some recorders produce full color recordings by successively overwriting different colors in the same area.)

TLL—Total Line Length — The TLL is equal to the *spot speed* divided by the *scanning line frequency*. In *digital facsimile*, the TLL is equal to the *pels* per scan line divided by the number per millimeter.

Transmission Time — The time for sending a single page (i.e., elapsed time between the start of *picture signals* and the detection of *end-of-message signal* by the facsimile receiver).

Xerographic Recording — Recording by action of a light spot on an electrically charged photo-conductive insulating surface where the latent image is subsequently developed with a toner.

Bibliography

Albert, Arthur Lemuel, *Electrical Communication*, Second Edition, New York: John Wiley & Sons, 1940, pp. 3–6.

Bell, Trudy, "Technical Challenges to a Decentralized Phone System," *IEEE Spectrum*, September 1990, pp. 33–34.

Berger, Meyer, "The Story of the *New York Times*," New York: Simon and Shuster, 1951, pp. 408–413.

Bodson, Dennis, "The Federal Telecommunication Standards Program," *IEEE Communications Magazine*, Volume 23, No.1, January 1985, pp. 56–62.

CCITT Study Group VIII Contribution D134, "Explanation of the Use of the DTAM and ODA Recommendations for Facsimile Group 4," PTT Netherlands, Study Group VIII meeting, 5–14 October 1990, Geneva, Switzerland.

Cern, Dorthy M., "The United States Organization for the CCITT," *IEEE Communications Magazine*, Volume 23, No.1, January 1985, pp. 38–41.

Cohen, E.J., and William B. Wilkens, "The IEEE Role in Telecommunications Standards," *IEEE Communications Magazine*, Volume 23, No. 1, January 1985, pp. 31–32.

Costigan, Daniel M., *Electronic Delivery of Documents and Graphics*, New York: Van Nostrand Reinhold, 1978, pp.1–21.

———, *Fax: The Principles and Practice of Facsimile Communication*, Philadelphia: Chilton Book, 1971, pp.1–11.

———, "Standards in Europe," *International Electrotechnical Commission*, Volume XXIV, January 1991.

Fitzgerald, Karen, "Global Standards," *IEEE Spectrum*, June 1990, p. 45.

Hummel, Eckart, "The CCITT," *IEEE Communications Magazine*, Volume 23, No. 1, January 1985, pp. 9–11.

Jones, Charles R., *Facsimile*, New York: Murray Hill Books, 1949, pp. 1–23.

Kretchmer, Ken, *Commumnication Standards Review*, Volume 1, No. 1, January 1990.

Kretchmer, Ken, "Communications Standards: A Progress Report," *Telecommumications Magazine*, pp. 22–24.

Lohse, Edward, "The Role of the ISO in Telecommunications and Information Systems Standardization," *IEEE Communications Magazine*, Volume 23, No. 1, January 1985, p. 19.

Reynolds, F.W., "A New Telephotograph System," *Electrical Engineering*, September 1936, pp. 996–1007.

Ranger, Richard H., "Transmission and Reception of Photoradiograms," Institute of Radio Engineers, New York, June 3, 1925.

Selvaggi, Phillip S., "The Development of Standards in the DoD," *IEEE Communications Magazine,* Volume 23, No.1, January 1985, pp. 43–54.

Service Bulletins, Times Facsimile Corporation, "History of Facsimile," Volume 4, No. 1 and Volume 6, No. 10.

Sherr, Sava I., "Communications Standards and the IEC," *IEEE Communications Magazine,* Volume 23, No. 1, January 1985, pp. 25–27.

Tarjanne, Pekka J., "Open Frameworks for Telecommunications in the 1990's: Access to Networks and Markets," *Telecommunications Magazine,* April 1990, pp. 22–48.

"Facsimile Edition Hailed as Journalistic Milestone," *Times Talk,* Volime 10, No. 1, September 1956, pp. 1–4.

Urban, Stephen J., "Review of Standards for Electronic Imaging for Facsimile Systems," *Journal of Electronic Imaging,* Volume 1(1), January 1992, pp. 5–21.

Weinstein, Stephen B., "Broadband Communications," *IEEE Spectrum,* Volume 26, No. 1, January 1989, p. 43.

INDEX

Figures

---

*See errata sheets for corrected figures

Tables

The Artech House Telecommunications Library

Vinton G. Cerf, Series Editor